Women Philosophers in Nineteenth-Century Britain

Women Philosophers in Nineteenth-Century Britain

ALISON STONE

Great Clarendon Street, Oxford, OX2 6DP,
United Kingdom

Oxford University Press is a department of the University of Oxford.
It furthers the University's objective of excellence in research, scholarship,
and education by publishing worldwide. Oxford is a registered trade mark of
Oxford University Press in the UK and in certain other countries

© Alison Stone 2023

The moral rights of the author have been asserted

First Edition published in 2023

Impression: 1

All rights reserved. No part of this publication may be reproduced, stored in
a retrieval system, or transmitted, in any form or by any means, without the
prior permission in writing of Oxford University Press, or as expressly permitted
by law, by licence or under terms agreed with the appropriate reprographics
rights organization. Enquiries concerning reproduction outside the scope of the
above should be sent to the Rights Department, Oxford University Press, at the
address above

You must not circulate this work in any other form
and you must impose this same condition on any acquirer

Published in the United States of America by Oxford University Press
198 Madison Avenue, New York, NY 10016, United States of America

British Library Cataloguing in Publication Data
Data available

Library of Congress Control Number: 2022941806

ISBN 978–0–19–287471–9

DOI: 10.1093/oso/9780192874719.001.0001

Printed and bound in the UK by
Clays Ltd, Elcograf S.p.A.

Links to third party websites are provided by Oxford in good faith and
for information only. Oxford disclaims any responsibility for the materials
contained in any third party website referenced in this work.

Contents

Acknowledgements	vii
Timeline	ix
Abbreviations	xiii
Introduction	1
I.1 What This Book Is About	1
I.2 Approach and Methodology	6
I.3 Chapter Outline	13
I.4 The Social and Historical Context of these Women Philosophers	16
1. Women's Constrained Philosophical Participation	21
1.1 Introduction	21
1.2 Constraints, Print Culture, and Generalist Philosophy	22
1.3 Women's Participation Strategies	32
1.4 Anonymity and Signature in Nineteenth-Century British Writing	37
1.5 How Nineteenth-Century Women Became Forgotten	42
1.6 Two Case Studies: Cobbe and Blavatsky	46
1.7 Methodological Recommendations	54
2. Naturalism	56
2.1 Introduction	56
2.2 Shepherd, Causation, and Anti-Naturalism	58
2.3 Martineau's Earlier Philosophy: Moralist Necessarianism	66
2.4 Martineau's Naturalism in *Letters on the Laws of Man's Nature and Development*	73
2.5 Cobbe's Anti-Naturalist Moral Theory	81
2.6 Welby, Meaning, and Anti-Naturalism	88
2.7 The Trajectory of the Debate about Naturalism	97
3. Philosophy of Mind	98
3.1 Introduction	98
3.2 Lovelace and the Thinking Machine	101
3.3 Interlude: Carpenter	111
3.4 Cobbe on Thinking Brain versus Conscious Self	114
3.5 Naden and Hylo-Idealism	117
3.6 Blavatsky and Besant: Explaining the Mind	125
3.7 The Dialectical Emergence of these Accounts of the Mind	131

4. The Meaning of Evolution — 133
   4.1 Introduction — 133
   4.2 Wedgwood: Reconciling Evolution with Christianity — 136
   4.3 Cobbe on the Moral Dangers of Darwinism — 143
   4.4 Buckley Against Cobbe — 148
   4.5 Buckley's Moral and Religious Evolutionism — 153
   4.6 Wedgwood's Later Reassessment — 158

5. Religion and Morality — 164
   5.1 Introduction — 164
   5.2 Martineau and the Exterior Point of View — 167
   5.3 Eliot: Literature and the Expansion of Sympathy — 171
   5.4 Cobbe's Case Against Atheism — 179
   5.5 The Lee–Cobbe Debate — 181
   5.6 The Besant–Cobbe Debate — 187
   5.7 Evaluation and Comparison — 191

6. Progress in History — 196
   6.1 Introduction — 196
   6.2 Martineau and *Eastern Life* — 199
   6.3 Cobbe on the World Religious Progression — 205
   6.4 Wedgwood and *The Moral Ideal* — 209
   6.5 Blavatsky and Spiritual Evolution — 216
   6.6 Comparisons and Colonialism — 224

   Conclusion — 231

Bibliography — 233
Index — 257

Acknowledgements

I am grateful to many people who have helped me to write this book. The thoughtful, detailed, and constructive comments from the anonymous readers enabled me to make many improvements, and I have greatly appreciated the efficiency and enthusiasm of Peter Momtchiloff at Oxford University Press. Many people have helped and motivated me to think about nineteenth-century women philosophers, and they include Peter Adamson, Charlotte Alderwick, Michael Beaney, Carol Bensick, Sally Blackburn-Daniels, Deborah Boyle, Sue Brown, Sophia Connell, Anna Ezekiel, Patrick Fessenbecker, Kristin Gjesdal, Susan Hamilton, Kali Israel, Christia Mercer, Lydia Moland, Dalia Nassar, Stamatoula Panagakou, Anne Pollok, Trevor Pearce, Dorothy Rogers, Lisa Shapiro, Clare Stainthorp, Emily Thomas, and Giulia Valpione. Rachel Cooper and Sarah Hutton invited me to present parts of my work-in-progress, and I am grateful to those who asked me helpful questions on these occasions. I thank Haley Brennan for her excellent interview questions about these women philosophers on the ENN New Voices in the History of Philosophy podcast.

The Department of Politics, Philosophy and Religion at Lancaster University has supported me with sabbatical leave that expedited work on this book. The Content Team at Lancaster University Library, and especially Deborah Simpson-Davis, deserve my thanks for dealing with endless requests for help obtaining rare items. I am also grateful for help acquiring digitized correspondence from Lucy Lead, Michael Ruddy, and Randeep Atwal at the V&A Wedgwood Collection, Kolter Campbell at Northwestern University Archival and Manuscript Collections, Oliver House at the Bodleian Library, Kate O'Donnell at Somerville College Library, and Paul White at the Darwin Correspondence Project.

I thank the Principal and Fellows of Somerville College, Oxford, for permission to refer to the list of books given to the college by Mrs Pattison; The Charles Deering McCormick Library of Special Collections and University Archives, Northwestern University, for granting digital access to the Garnett Family Papers; the Cadbury Research Library, University of Birmingham, for permission to quote from the Martineau Papers; the V&A Wedgwood Collection, for permission to quote from the Wedgwood Mosley collection; and Johns Hopkins University Press, for permission to reproduce here parts of my article 'Later Nineteenth-Century Women Philosophers on the Mind and its Place in the World' which first appeared in *Journal of the History of Philosophy*, Volume 60, Issue 1, January 2022, pages 97–120 (Copyright © 2022 *Journal of the History of Philosophy, Inc.*). In addition, part of my article 'Martineau, Cobbe, and

Teleological Progressivism' from the *British Journal for the History of Philosophy*, Volume 29, Issue 6, pages 1099–123 (copyright © BSHP) is reprinted by permission of Taylor & Francis Ltd, http://www.tandfonline.com, on behalf of BSHP. Extracts from the correspondence of Ada Lovelace are reproduced by permission of Paper Lion Ltd and the Estate of Ada Lovelace.

Finally, I thank John Varty for his care, interest, and support.

Timeline

1799	Hannah More, *Strictures on the Modern System of Female Education*
1800	Elizabeth Hamilton (anonymous), *Memoirs of Modern Philosophers*
1801	Elizabeth Hamilton, *Letters on Education*
1807	Act for the Abolition of the Slave Trade
1818	Mary Shelley (anonymous), *Frankenstein*
1822	Charles Babbage designs a small working model of the difference engine. Harriet Martineau (as 'Discipulus'), 'Female Writers on Practical Divinity', *Monthly Repository*
1824	Mary Shepherd (anonymous), *Essay upon the Relation of Cause and Effect*
1825	Frances Wright founds the experimental community Nashoba in the U.S.A. Anna Doyle Wheeler (anonymous) and William Thompson, *Appeal of One Half the Human Race*; Anna Barbauld, *The Works of Anna Letitia Barbauld with a Memoir by Lucy Aikin*
1827	Mary Shepherd, *Essays on the Perception of an External Universe*
1831	Mary Prince, *The History of Mary Prince, A West Indian Slave, Related by Herself*
1832	The Representation of the People Act (or Great Reform Act) extends the franchise to around 20 per cent of adult men while formally excluding women from the franchise for the first time. Anna Jameson, *Characteristics of Women: Moral, Poetical, and Historical*
1832–4	Harriet Martineau, *Illustrations of Political Economy*
1833	The Slavery Abolition Act makes slavery illegal in most of the British Empire
1833–6	Various authors, *Bridgewater Treatises*, defend the compatibility of religion and science
1834	The New Poor Law standardizes arrangements for poor relief and establishes the workhouse system. Mary Somerville, *On the Connexion of the Physical Sciences*
1836	Harriet Martineau, *Miscellanies*
1837	Harriet Martineau, *Society in America*
1838	Harriet Martineau, *How to Observe Morals and Manners*
1839	Sarah Lewis (anonymous), *Woman's Mission*
1840	William Whewell, *The Philosophy of the Inductive Sciences*
1841	Caroline Frances Cornwallis (as 'A. Pariah'), *Philosophical Theories and Philosophical Experience*

1842	William Engledue defends materialism to the London Phrenological Association. William Benjamin Carpenter, *Principles of Human Physiology*, first edition
1843	Ada Lovelace (as 'A. A. L.'), 'Sketch of the Analytical Engine', *Scientific Memoirs*
1844	Harriet Martineau appears to be cured of illness by mesmerism. Harriet Martineau, 'Letters on Mesmerism', *The Athenaeum*
1845–6	George Henry Lewes, *Biographical History of Philosophy*, first edition
1845–52	The Great Famine rages in Ireland. George Eliot (anonymous), trans., David Friedrich Strauss, *The Life of Jesus, Critically Examined*
1847	The Factory Act limits the working hours of women and children in factories
1848	Harriet Martineau, *Eastern Life: Present and Past*
1848–64	Anna Jameson, *Sacred and Legendary Art*, multiple volumes
1851	George Holyoake coins the word 'secularism'. Harriet Martineau and Henry George Atkinson, *Letters on the Laws of Man's Nature and Development*; Harriet Taylor Mill (anonymous), 'The Enfranchisement of Women', *Westminster Review*
1851–3	George Eliot (anonymously) co-edits the *Westminster Review*
1853	Harriet Martineau, ed. and trans., *The Positive Philosophy of Auguste Comte*
1854	Mary Carpenter opens the Red Lodge Reformatory School for girls in Bristol, funded by Annabella Byron. Marian Evans (George Eliot), trans., Feuerbach, *The Essence of Christianity*
1855	William Benjamin Carpenter, *Principles of Human Physiology*, fifth edition; Frances Power Cobbe (anonymous), *An Essay on Intuitive Morals* Vol. 1
1856	George Eliot (anonymous), 'The Natural History of German Life', *Westminster Review*
1857	Obscene Publications Act
1857–8	Defeat of the Indian Rebellion against the East India Company
1859	Charles Darwin, *The Origin of Species*; John Stuart Mill, *On Liberty*; Karl Marx, 'Preface to a Contribution to the Critique of Political Economy'; Samuel Smiles, *Self-Help*
1859–60	Sarah Parker Remond tours the UK arguing against slavery
1860	George Eliot, *The Mill on the Floss*; various authors, *Essays and Reviews*, on contentious theological topics
1860–1	Julia Wedgwood (anonymous), 'The Boundaries of Science: A Dialogue', *Macmillan's Magazine*
1861	John Stuart Mill, 'Utilitarianism', *Fraser's Magazine*
1863	Frances Power Cobbe, 'The Rights of Man and the Claims of Brutes', *Fraser's Magazine*

1864	First Contagious Diseases Act, extended in 1866 and 1869
1866	Charles Bradlaugh founds the National Secular Society
1867	The Second Reform Act further widens the suffrage for men
1868	The University of London begins to admit women. John Tyndall, 'Scientific Materialism', address to the Mathematical and Physical Section of the British Association
1869	James Knowles founds the Metaphysical Society, where Huxley coins the word 'agnostic'; Girton College opens in Cambridge. John Stuart Mill, *The Subjection of Women*; Josephine Butler, ed., *Woman's Work and Woman's Culture*, including chapters from Cobbe and Wedgwood
1870	The Elementary Education Act establishes the beginnings of universal primary education; the Married Women's Property Act, extended in 1882, allows married women some property rights. Frances Power Cobbe, 'Unconscious Cerebration', *Macmillan's Magazine*
1871	Charles Darwin, *The Descent of Man*; Frances Power Cobbe, 'Darwinism in Morals', *Theological Review*; Arabella Buckley (as 'A. B.'), 'Darwinism and Religion', *Macmillan's Magazine*
1872	George Eliot, *Middlemarch*
1874	The East India Company is dissolved; the Factory Act raises the minimum working age, further limits the working hours of women and children and reduces the maximum working week; Besant joins the National Secular Society and begins to co-edit its journal the *National Reformer*. John Tyndall, 'Belfast Address' to the British Association for the Advancement of Science; Annie Besant, 'The True Basis of Morality'
1875	Helena Petrovna Blavatsky co-founds the Theosophical Society in New York; Frances Power Cobbe founds the Victoria Street Society, later the National Anti-Vivisection Society
1876	The Cruelty to Animals Act introduces a licensing system for vivisection; Alexander Bain founds *Mind*, the UK's first dedicated philosophy journal
1877	Annie Besant and Charles Bradlaugh stand trial for publishing literature on birth control. Harriet Martineau, *Autobiography*; Helena Petrovna Blavatsky, *Isis Unveiled*; Frances Power Cobbe, 'Magnanimous Atheism', *Theological Review*
1878	The Matrimonial Causes Act gives women of violent husbands the right to a separation, following Cobbe's article, 'Wife-Torture in England', *Contemporary Review*
1879	Helena Petrovna Blavatsky founds and edits *The Theosophist*; Somerville College opens in Oxford
1879	Arabella Buckley (as 'A. B.'), 'The Soul, and the Theory of Evolution', *University Magazine*

1880	Foundation of the Aristotelian Society, with Shadworth Hodgson as the first President
1881	Cobbe founds *The Zoophilist*; Vernon Lee, *Belcaro: Being Sundry Essays on Aesthetical Questions*
1882	Foundation of the Society for Psychical Research with Henry Sidgwick as first President
1883–8	Annie Besant edits *Our Corner*
1883	Vernon Lee, 'The Responsibilities of Unbelief', *Contemporary Review*; Frances Power Cobbe, 'Agnostic Morality', *Contemporary Review*; Constance Naden (as 'Constance Arden'), 'The Brain Theory of Mind and Matter', *Journal of Science*
1884	The Third Reform Act widens the suffrage still further for men; the Coulomb controversy about Blavatsky erupts. Frances Power Cobbe, 'A Faithless World', *Contemporary Review*; Constance Naden (as 'C. N.'), 'Hylo-Idealism: The Creed of the Coming Day', *Our Corner*
1885	The Society for Psychical Research issues the Hodgson report on Blavatsky; Annie Besant joins the Fabian Society. Annie Besant, 'A World Without God: A Reply to Miss Frances Power Cobbe'
1886	Repeal of the Contagious Diseases Acts; Vernon Lee, *Baldwin: Being Dialogues on Views and Aspirations*
1887	Blavatsky founds and co-edits *Lucifer*
1888	The *Proceedings of the Aristotelian Society* commence publication. Blavatsky, *The Secret Doctrine*; Wedgwood, *The Moral Ideal*; Mrs Humphry Ward, *Robert Elsmere*
1889	Besant joins the Theosophical Society and begins to co-edit *Lucifer*. Mrs Humphry Ward et al. (anonymous), 'An Appeal against Female Suffrage', *The Nineteenth Century*; Besant, 'Why I Became a Theosophist'
1890	Constance Naden, *Induction and Deduction*
1891	Constance Naden, *Further Reliques*
1893	Besant moves to India. Victoria Welby, 'Meaning and Metaphor', *The Monist*
1894	Vernon Lee, *Althea: A Second Book of Dialogues on Aspirations and Duties*; Cobbe, *Life of Frances Power Cobbe*
1896	Victoria Welby, 'Sense, Meaning, and Significance', *Mind*; Lee, 'Art and Life', *Contemporary Review*
1898	Cobbe founds the British Union for the Abolition of Vivisection

Abbreviations

The following abbreviations are used for repeatedly cited works by women philosophers discussed in this book. (Works by other authors, and works that are not repeatedly cited, are quoted using the author–date system.)

Mary Shepherd

EPEU	*Essays on the Perception of an External Universe* (1827). London: Hatchard.
ERCE	*An Essay upon the Relation of Cause and Effect* (1824). London: Hookham.

Harriet Martineau

EAT	Essays on the Art of Thinking (1829). In *Miscellanies* (2 vols, Boston: Hilliard, Gray and Co., 1836), vol. 1, 57–121.
EL	*Eastern Life: Present and Past* (1948). New illustrated one-volume edn. London: Moxon, 1875.
EPT	Essays on the Pursuit of Truth (1829). In *Miscellanies*, vol. 2, 174–95.
HMA	*Autobiography* (1877), 3 vols, reprint edn of the first two vols. London: Virago, 1983; and vol. 3 with memorials by Maria Weston Chapman, London: Smith, Elder & Co., 1877.
HMCL	*Collected Letters*, 5 vols, ed. Deborah Logan. London: Pickering & Chatto, 2007.
HMLFW	*Harriet Martineau's Letters to Fanny Wedgwood*, ed. Elisabeth Sanders Arbuckle. Stanford, CA: Stanford University Press, 1983.
IPE	*Illustrations of Political Economy* (1832–4), 19 vols. Boston: Bowles.
LLM	(with Henry George Atkinson) *Letters on the Laws of Man's Nature and Development* (1851). London: Chapman.
PP	(trans. and ed.) *The Positive Philosophy of Auguste Comte* (1853), 2 vols. London: Chapman.
SA	*Society in America* (1837), 3 vols. London: Saunders & Otley.

Ada Lovelace

AEN	*Ada: The Enchantress of Numbers*, ed. Betty Toole. Revised, abridged edn. Mill Valley, CA: Strawberry Press, 1992.
SAE	(Trans. and commentary) Sketch of the Analytical Engine invented by Charles Babbage, Esq. by L. F. Menabrea (1843). *Scientific Memoirs* 3: 666–731.

George Eliot

AB	*Adam Bede* (1859). New York: Open Road Integrated Media, 2015.
GEL	*The George Eliot Letters*, 9 vols, ed. Gordon Haight. New Haven, CT: Yale University Press, 1954–78.
MF	*The Mill on the Floss* (1860). New York: Open Road Integrated Media, 2016.
NHGL	The Natural History of German Life (1856). *Westminster Review* 66: 51–79.
PWR	Prospectus of the Westminster and Foreign Quarterly Review (1852). In *Selected Essays, Poems and Other Writings*, ed. A. S. Byatt and Nicholas Warren (Harmondsworth: Penguin, 1990), 4–8.

Frances Power Cobbe

AM	Agnostic Morality (1883). *Contemporary Review* 43: 783–94.
BS	The Brahmo Samaj (1866). *Fraser's Magazine* 74: 199–211.
CP	*The Cities of the Past* (1864). London: Trübner.
DM	*Darwinism in Morals, and Other Essays* (1872). London: Williams & Norgate.
DW	*The Duties of Women* (1881). Boston: Ellis.
ESS	*Studies New and Old of Ethical and Social Subjects* (1865). London: Trübner.
FW	A Faithless World (1884). *Contemporary Review* 46: 795–810.
HHR	*The Hopes of the Human Race, Hereafter and Here* (1874). London: Williams & Norgate.
IM	*An Essay on Intuitive Morals. Part I: Theory of Morals* (1855). London: Longman, Brown, Green & Longmans.
LFPC	*Life of Frances Power Cobbe, by Herself* (1894), 2 vols. London: Bentley.
MA	Magnanimous Atheism (1877). In *The Peak in Darien* (London: Williams & Norgate, 1882), 11–76.
MR	*The Modern Rack: Papers on Vivisection* (1889). London: Swan Sonnenschein.
SS	*The Scientific Spirit of the Age* (1888). London: Smith & Elder.

Helena Petrovna Blavatsky

IU	*Isis Unveiled: A Master-Key to the Mysteries of Ancient and Modern Science and Theology* (1877), 2 vols. New York: Bouton.
LHL	To Dr Lewins, and the Hylo-Idealists at Large (1888). *Lucifer* 1: 508–12.
MI	Modern Idealism, Worse than Materialism (1896). *The Theosophist* 18: 9–12.
SD	*The Secret Doctrine: The Synthesis of Science, Religion, and Philosophy* (1888), 2 vols. London: Theosophical Publishing.

Julia Wedgwood

BS	The Boundaries of Science (1860–1), Parts 1 and 2. *Macmillan's Magazine* 2: 134–8 and 4: 237–47.

MI	*The Moral Ideal: A Historic Study* (1888). London: Trübner.
NCT	*Nineteenth-Century Teachers* (1909). London: Hodder & Stoughton.

Victoria Welby

ELL	*Echoes of Larger Life: A Selection from the Early Correspondence of Lady Welby* (1929), ed. Nina Cust. London: Jonathan Cape.
GS	*Grains of Sense* (1897). London: Dent.
MM	Meaning and Metaphor (1893). *The Monist* 3: 510–25.
SMI	Sense, Meaning and Interpretation (1896), Parts 1 and 2. *Mind* 5: 24–37 and 186–202.
SU	*Signifying and Understanding: Reading the Works of Victoria Welby and the Signific Movement* (2009), ed. Susan Petrilli. Berlin: De Gruyter.

Arabella Buckley

DR	Darwinism and Religion (1871). *Macmillan's Magazine* 24: 45–51.
MT	*Moral Teachings of Science* (1891). New York: Appleton, 1892.
STE	The Soul, and the Theory of Evolution (1879). *University Magazine* 3: 1–10.

Annie Besant

ABA	*An Autobiography* (1893). London: T. Fisher Unwin.
AC	*Auguste Comte: His Philosophy, His Religion, and His Sociology* (1885). London: C. Watts.
AS	*Autobiographical Sketches* (1885). London: Freethought.
MPA	*My Path to Atheism* (1885). London: Freethought.
TBM	*The True Basis of Morality* (1874). London: Freethought, 1882.
WT	*Why I Became a Theosophist* (1890). New York: 'The Path' Office.
WWG	*A World Without God* (1885). London: Freethought.

Vernon Lee

B	*Baldwin: Being Dialogues on Views and Aspirations* (1886). Boston: Roberts Brothers.
Bel	*Belcaro: Being Essays on Sundry Aesthetical Questions* (1881). London: Satchell & Co.
SLVL	*Selected Letters of Vernon Lee, 1856–1935*, Vol. I, 1865–1884, ed. Amanda Gagel (London: Routledge, 2017), and Vol. II, 1885–1889, ed. Sophie Geoffroy and Amanda Gagel (London: Routledge, 2020).

Constance Naden

BT	The Brain Theory of Mind and Matter (1883). In *Induction and Deduction* (London: Bickers & Son, 1890), 155–66.
FR	*Further Reliques*. London: Bickers & Son, 1891.
HI	Hylo-Idealism: The Creed of the Coming Day (1884). In *Induction and Deduction*, 167–76.
ID	*Induction and Deduction*. London: Bickers & Son, 1890.
MP	On Mental Physiology and its Place in Philosophy (1889–90). *Proceedings of the Aristotelian Society* 1: 81–2.

Letters are cited giving sender and recipient (using initials for the women listed here), date, then page in the published edition.

Digital And Physical Archives

DCP	Darwin Correspondence Project, http://darwinproject.ac.uk. Cited *DCP* followed by letters by sender and recipient, date, and catalogue number.
DLB	Archive of the Noel, Byron and Lovelace Families. Bodleian Archives & Manuscripts, University of Oxford. Cited *DLB* (Dep. Lovelace Byron) by shelfmark number, followed by letters by sender and recipient and date.
Gale Historical Newspapers	https://www.gale.com/intl/primary-sources/historical-newspapers.
GFP	Garnett Family Papers (MS 164), Northwestern University, Archival and Manuscript Collections. Cited *GFP* followed by letters by sender and recipient and date.
Hathitrust digital library	https://www.hathitrust.org.
HM	Martineau Papers, Cadbury Research Library, University of Birmingham. Cited *HM* followed by letters by sender and recipient, date, and catalogue number.
VWF	Lady Victoria Welby fonds (F0443), York University Libraries, Clara Thomas Archives and Special Collections, https://digital.library.yorku.ca/yul-f0443/victoria-welby-fonds. Accessed 18 March 2022. Cited *VWF* followed by letters by sender and recipient and date.
WCP	The Alfred Russel Wallace Correspondence Project. https://wallaceletters.myspecies.info/content/epsilon. Cited *WCP* followed by letters by sender and recipient, date, and catalogue number.
W/M	Wedgwood Mosley Collection, V&A Wedgwood Collection, Barlaston, Stoke-on-Trent. Cited *W/M* followed by letters by sender and recipient, date and catalogue number.

Introduction

I.1 What This Book Is About

Many women wrote on philosophy in nineteenth-century Britain. Their writings cover the whole range of philosophical topics: knowledge, reality, science, evolution, morality, religion, the mind, history, aesthetics, and social and political issues. In this book I aim to bring to readers' attention some of these women, their key ideas, and the interrelations and conversations between them.

The book contributes to the recovery of women in the history of Western philosophy. So far historians of women philosophers have largely focused on the early modern period, *c.*1600–1800. So many important early modern women have been recovered—Elisabeth of Bohemia, Margaret Cavendish, Anne Conway, and Catharine Trotter Cockburn, to name just a few—that our whole story of early modern philosophy has been transformed. It is also widely recognized that twentieth-century women contributed greatly both to continental philosophy—as with Edith Stein, Simone de Beauvoir, and Hannah Arendt—and to analytic philosophy, as with G. E. M. Anscombe, Iris Murdoch, Philippa Foot, and Mary Midgley.

There has been much less recovery of women in nineteenth-century philosophy.[1] This is partly because the nineteenth century overall is rather overlooked by historians of philosophy. When attention is paid to the period, it is usually to 'the great *Continental* systems of thought' (Mander 2014: 1), not English-speaking or British philosophy.[2] Regarding Britain there are a few exceptions: John Stuart Mill, above all, followed by Henry Sidgwick and Thomas Hill Green. But the rule to which these are the exceptions remains: most histories of philosophy in Britain are liable to peter out around 1800 and resume after 1900. Thus, women philosophers in nineteenth-century Britain have been doubly hidden from view—first as women, second as members of a place and period that is already neglected. Many contemporary professional philosophers

---

[1] Histories of nineteenth-century philosophy regularly include few or no women—see e.g. Mander (2014), Wood and Hahn (2011), Stone (2011), Moyar (2012), and Stedman Jones and Claeys (2013). To be fair, Stedman Jones and Claeys include Lucy Delap's chapter 'The Woman Question and the Origins of Feminism'; Wood and Hahn include Christine Blaettler's 'Social Dissatisfaction and Social Change'; and Mander includes Barbara Caine's 'British Feminist Thought'. But this gives the misleading impression that women only thought and spoke about feminism.

[2] However, nineteenth-century *women* in continental European philosophy are neglected, although on German-speaking women, see Gjesdal and Nassar (2022).

would be hard pressed to name any nineteenth-century British philosophical women except perhaps George Eliot.[3]

One might assume that if people today are unaware of nineteenth-century British women philosophers (George Eliot aside), this must be because hardly any women were doing philosophy in Britain then, perhaps because patriarchy was then at its height. After all, it was the era when 'separate spheres' ideology prevailed, according to which women's proper sphere was the family and only the family. Institutions of higher education and most professions were closed to women for most of the century. Surely, one might think, it must have been virtually impossible for women to philosophize in these conditions.[4]

Plausible as these assumptions seem, they are false. Despite the patriarchal constraints, many women participated in philosophical discussion in nineteenth-century Britain. Some of them wrote straightforwardly philosophical prose works, while others used literature and various other forms of writing as their philosophical vehicles.[5] Here are twelve of these women, whose ideas will be discussed in this book:

Mary Shepherd's (1777–1847) publications included two highly regarded books, one on causation—*An Essay upon the Relation of Cause and Effect* (1824)—and the other on the reality of the external world—*Essays on the Perception of an External Universe, and other Subjects Connected with the Doctrine of Causation* (1827). Shepherd put forward a systematic metaphysics and theory of knowledge, advancing detailed criticisms of Hume and Berkeley amongst others.

Harriet Martineau (1802–1876) was a 'nineteenth-century intellectual powerhouse', the best-known British female intellectual in the first half of the century.[6] Her huge output spanned political economy, fiction, life-writing, sociology, history, religion, and philosophy, including *Letters on the Laws of Man's Nature and Development* (1851), an epistolary exchange with the 'phreno-mesmerist' Henry George Atkinson in which Martineau professed her commitments to atheism,

---

[3] On nineteenth-century American women philosophers, see the ground-breaking work of Dorothy Rogers (2005, 2021), and Rogers and Dykeman (2004, 2012).

[4] For instance, Collini (1993) assumes this. In his *Public Moralists, 1850–1930* the only women covered are Eliot and Mrs Humphry Ward (Mary Augusta Ward, though she published using her husband's name). It is a surprising account of 'public moralists' that omits Harriet Martineau, Frances Power Cobbe, Annie Besant, Josephine Butler, Florence Nightingale, and Octavia Hill (founder of social work and social housing). But, Collini says, *he* is not excluding women; the *Victorians* did, and the fact that Eliot wrote as 'George Eliot', Ward as 'Mrs Humphry' says it all (1991: 3). Actually these names reflect the contested character of anonymous, pseudonymous, initialled and signed authorship in the period (see Chapter 1). Moreover, other women besides Eliot and Ward were famous 'public moralists' using their own female names, as with Martineau, Cobbe, and Besant. The latter, for instance, was a celebrated public speaker routinely filling lecture halls all over the country. So it *is* Collini who omits women. I will explore in Chapter 1 how nineteenth-century philosophical women became forgotten over time, resulting in accounts like Collini's. Also, for an excellent recent corrective to Collini, see Dabby (2017).

[5] I am taking 'Britain' to coincide with the present-day United Kingdom plus Ireland, because the latter was then incorporated into Britain under the 1801 Act of Union.

[6] Quoting *Harriet Martineau and the Birth of Disciplines: Nineteenth-Century Intellectual Powerhouse* (Sanders and Weiner 2017).

materialism, scientific naturalism, and hard determinism. Through her condensed translation of Comte's *Course of Positive Philosophy* (1853), Martineau also fundamentally shaped the development of positivism in Britain.

Ada Lovelace (1815–1852) is hailed today as a pioneer of computer programming, based on her work with Charles Babbage on the 'analytical engine'—never built, but the prototype of a computer. Lovelace's reflections from the 1840s on the nature and possibility of artificial intelligence remain influential today. Her unpublished work contains many other interesting suggestions, ideas, and sketches for philosophical inquiries.

George Eliot (1819–1880) scarcely needs any introduction as a novelist, perhaps the greatest nineteenth-century British novelist. But her intellectual life also had a strong philosophical component, reflected in her novels and expressed in her many journal essays, her co-editing of the *Westminster Review* in the early 1850s, her letters, and her translations of David Friedrich Strauss, Ludwig Feuerbach, and Baruch Spinoza.[7] By translating the former two in the 1840s and 1850s, Eliot spearheaded the importation from Germany of 'Higher Criticism', the school of biblical interpretation that filtered out historical from mythic elements in the Bible. Other topics that Eliot addressed included sympathy, morality, historical progress, and the purpose of literature.

Frances Power Cobbe (1822–1904) was another nineteenth-century intellectual powerhouse, extremely well known and highly regarded, a prolific writer and periodical contributor, and a leading feminist and campaigner for animal welfare. All her public and political activity had a philosophical basis. Her first book, the two-volume *Essay on Intuitive Morals* (1855–7), set out her moral theory. This provided the framework within which, writing right up until her death, she addressed a great range of topics: atheism, the mind and unconscious thought, moral epistemology, aesthetics, history, evolution, and many more. She and Eliot were probably the most influential intellectual women in later-century Britain.

Helena Petrovna Blavatsky (1831–1891) has for her part been described as 'one of the most influential women of all time' (Godwin 2013: 15), because she created the first 'alternative religion': theosophy. Blavatsky herself considered theosophy to be a philosophical as much as a religious system. Her magnum opus was the two-volume, 1500-page *The Secret Doctrine* (1888), the most comprehensive statement of her vast system, in which she synthesized many world belief systems and esoteric traditions into an account of the universe as a whole, its spiritual evolution, and humanity's place within it.[8]

---

[7] Completed in 1856, the Spinoza translation remained unpublished in Eliot's lifetime; a recent edition is edited by Clare Carlisle (2019).

[8] Blavatsky was from Russia, but she belongs in this book because she based herself in England in her last years when *The Secret Doctrine* came out. It was also in Britain that Blavatsky established the journal *Lucifer*, one of her central vehicles for disseminating theosophical thought. Likewise, although

Frances Julia Wedgwood's (1833–1913) philosophical work spanned the 1860s to 1900s and was marked by careful, balanced consideration of opposing views. Her interests ranged over the metaphysical, religious, and ethical implications of Darwin's theory of evolution; arguments for women's rights and suffrage; biblical criticism; a large-scale account of the development of 'the moral ideal' across world civilizations; and Judaism's central contribution to European civilization. Her guiding principle was that we progress by developing conflicting ideas to the full before reintegrating them into higher syntheses.

Victoria Welby (1837–1912) moved on from her initial concern with scriptural interpretation to formulate a general theory of meaning and significance, called *significs*, from the 1880s onwards. She argued that scientific knowledge is embedded in acts of interpretation which radiate out to varying levels, the broadest of which give us access to the ultimate significance of the universe. Amongst Welby's other views, she argued that metaphor is essential to language. Her work links nineteenth-century religious and metaphysical preoccupations to the linguistic turn at the close of the century.

Arabella Buckley (1840–1929) is remembered mostly for her very widely read popular science books of the 1880s and 1890s. These had a philosophical dimension, maintaining that evolutionary theory supports a cooperative morality and not the 'survival of the fittest'. Buckley laid the groundwork for this view in essays of the 1870s arguing that Darwinian evolution is compatible with Christianity and morality, and that our evolutionary heritage inclines us to serve the social good unselfishly.

Annie Besant (1847–1933), like Martineau and Cobbe, was incredibly prolific, wide-ranging, and socially engaged. In the early 1870s she was a theist and follower of Cobbe, then in the mid-1870s Besant became a militant secularist who advocated utilitarianism and positivism and, from the mid-1880s, Fabian socialism. In 1889 she dramatically converted to theosophy, becoming one of the movement's leaders and moving to India in 1893, where the Theosophical Society, co-founded by Blavatsky in 1875, by then had its international headquarters. Thereafter Besant grew increasingly immersed in the struggle for Indian independence. Across the many phases of her intellectual life (one biographer speaks of the 'nine lives of Annie Besant'; Nethercot 1960, 1963), philosophical considerations were a constant presence.

Vernon Lee (1856–1935) is best known for her many writings on aesthetics, including *Belcaro* (1881) and the multi-part essay 'Art and Life' (1896). Although she was associated with the aestheticist movement, Lee criticized it, arguing that beauty and goodness necessarily went together. She also wrote on ethical, religious,

---

Vernon Lee grew up in mainland Europe, she published in British journals and was part of the British intellectual scene. Because of these cases I have framed this book in terms of 'Women Philosophers in Britain' rather than 'British Women Philosophers'.

and political topics, including vivisection, evolution, atheism, and utilitarianism. She experimented with forms that straddled the boundary between philosophy and literature, inventing what she called 'a sort of art-philosophy' (*Bel* 9).[9]

Constance Naden (1858–1889), writing in the 1880s, defended induction in science, atheism, and the metaphysical system she called 'hylo-idealism', on which we can know only our own ideas and nothing outside them, yet these ideas are merely the products of our brains reacting to physical stimuli. Before her untimely death she was moving in a different direction, towards an ethical synthesis of rationalism and utilitarianism.

This is a mere handful of all the women who philosophized in the period.[10] Thus Eileen O'Neill's insight concerning women in philosophy holds good for the nineteenth century as for other periods: whenever and wherever we look in history, women were there, doing philosophy (O'Neill 1998). It is the historical narratives from which women's work has gone missing. In O'Neill's metaphor, women wrote in 'disappearing ink'.

However, with earlier historical periods up to and including the early modern, historians are often forced to piece together women's philosophical thought from a paucity of surviving material. The nineteenth century is different. Its print culture was so extensive that large bodies of writing by women philosophers remain in libraries and, now, digital archives. Once I began to research women's philosophy in nineteenth-century Britain, I quickly realized there was a treasure trove of forgotten material here. It was like wandering into an unexplored mine full of riches while everyone around me was determined to keep eking out what they could from depleted mines marked 'Hegel', 'Kierkegaard', 'Nietzsche', 'Marx', and so on.

It might be replied that the mere existence of this forgotten material does not show that it has any philosophical value. Perhaps it has been deservedly forgotten. But the only way to ascertain whether it deserves to be remembered is to investigate it. In any case, we should be cautious about assuming that established canons simply track the merits of different authors' work. Scholars researching other places and periods of philosophy have consistently found good work by women and other

---

[9] Throughout I refer to Lee and Eliot by their pseudonyms, because this was how they opted to be known as writers.

[10] For instance, others I will not be discussing include Harriet Taylor Mill, author of 'The Enfranchisement of Women' (1851), and Anna Doyle Wheeler, co-author with William Thompson of the *Appeal of One Half the Human Race* (1825). For they wrote primarily on political philosophy, which is not one of the topics I am covering. This is because I want to show that women wrote right across the spectrum of philosophical topics, not only on social and political matters. Another omission is Frances Wright, who though most known for political philosophy also wrote on epistemology and ancient philosophy, but whose work largely post-dates her 1824 move to the USA and thus belongs more to the American philosophical conversation (for some of Wright's work, see Rogers and Dykeman 2012). Two less well-known figures that I have also regretfully omitted are Caroline Frances Cornwallis (e.g. Cornwallis 1841) and Anna Jameson (e.g. Jameson 1832 and [1848–64] 1892). The list of omissions could be extended almost indefinitely. Unfortunately one cannot write a book like this without making difficult choices about whom and whom not to include.

underrepresented groups that could have been included in the canon but was not. It was omitted, then, not on the basis of a neutral assessment of merit but due to a complex of factors including gender biases. I hope to show in this book that the same goes for women philosophers in nineteenth-century Britain.

I.2 Approach and Methodology

Given the large body of available philosophical writing by women, the challenge was to organize a portion of the material into a manageable account while covering enough ground to show readers the range, variety, and vitality of women's philosophical thought in the period. For the latter reason I rejected the option of focusing on just two or three women. Another option was to cover six or seven women with a chapter on each, following the model of Broad's excellent book on early modern women (Broad 2003). I decided against this because I thought it would make each woman's thought look more self-contained than it was, obscuring the ongoing conversations in which these women were taking part—crucially including conversations with other women. Illuminating these conversations is central to this book, so let me say more about it.

Sarah Hutton has shown that, to restore women to the history of philosophy, we need to situate their views in the intellectual landscapes of their times, moving beyond 'big names' and populating the entire fields of debate to which women belonged (2019: 688–90). These landscapes, though, were populated and partly shaped by the views of other women who have also become invisible to us. To recover a given woman's philosophical position, then, we ideally need to situate it in relation to other positions taken at the time not only by men but also by other women—which means recovering those other women too. They need not only be women that the author overtly discussed, but may be women whose positions helped to define the intellectual terrain in which she operated.

Here we may draw on Lisa Shapiro's proposal for viewing the history of philosophy as a series of conversations.[11] Reflecting on several strategies for including women in the history of philosophy, she observes:

> It is tempting to solve the problem [of women's omission from the history of philosophy] by sticking to the story one has been telling all along – the one that takes as its key figures a set of male philosophers – and to introduce some female characters along the way. (2004: 222)

For instance, one adds Elisabeth as a correspondent of Descartes, or Cockburn as a defender of Locke—or, regarding nineteenth-century Britain, Martineau as an

---

[11] Hutton likewise argues for a 'conversational' model of philosophy (see Hutton 2015: sec. 5).

interpreter of Comte, or Cobbe as a critic of Darwin. The advantage of this strategy is that it builds on already familiar narratives. But the disadvantage, Shapiro argues, is that since the narrative is already familiar, it is not clear what the women really add, especially as they are confined to supporting roles (223). Shapiro's preferred alternative is the conversational strategy, which she illustrates using the continuous conversation among early modern women philosophers on the topic of women's education. These philosophers built on and criticized one another, sometimes explicitly, sometimes more implicitly. But does focusing on conversations amongst women confine them to a ghetto of 'women's philosophy'? Not necessarily, Shapiro replies. Tracing women's conversations can instead enlarge our understanding of what issues were discussed in a given period and of the range of possible answers and approaches to these issues. This, Shapiro says, provides a stronger case for including women—because doing so expands and enriches our whole account of the philosophical past.

From this perspective, I aim to reconstruct the conversations and intellectual filiations amongst nineteenth-century women philosophers. In doing so, we can distinguish three sorts of filiations: (1) explicit conversations, agreements, and disagreements; (2) fuzzy cases where women seem to be responding to one another, and biographical and historical evidence suggests so (e.g. from correspondence, networks, and social circles), but they do not overtly mention one another by name in published work; (3) comparisons *we* can make between women's views, identifying how they defined their positions against competing alternatives that other women had partly shaped. Moreover, these three are not sharply demarcated.

Consider the following multi-faceted cases of filiations. First, regarding the mind: Martineau embraced a materialist view of mind in 1851, whereas Cobbe defended a form of dualism in 1870, explicitly aligning herself with the 'mental physiologist' William Benjamin Carpenter, who in the 1850s had positioned his dualism against Martineau's materialism. Then, in the 1880s, Naden defended materialism against the family of dualisms to which Cobbe's and Carpenter's theories belonged, without mentioning Cobbe by name. Later in the 1880s Blavatsky criticized Naden's materialism—explicitly—in a way that fed into Blavatsky's case for theosophy. Then Besant took up Blavatsky's arguments, again referencing Blavatsky explicitly.

Second, consider religion and morality: by 1850, the originally devout Martineau had embraced atheism; Cobbe criticized Martineau at length and explicitly in 1877, on the grounds that atheism undermines morality.[12] In 1883 Lee criticized Cobbe, defending morally responsible 'unbelief', again without

---

[12] On the overlapping terms *atheism*, *agnosticism*, *secularism*, and *freethought*, see Chapter 2, Sec. 2.4, and Chapter 5. Coining the label 'agnosticism' in 1869, Thomas Henry Huxley sought to demarcate it from atheism, as George Holyoake had previously attempted to do with 'secularism' in 1851, and George Henry Lewes with 'dogmatic' versus 'suspensive' atheism also in 1851 (where both Holyoake and Lewes were responding to Martineau's version of atheism). Each attempt merely added to a spectrum of views that was already too crowded and muddled to admit of any stable demarcations.

overtly mentioning Cobbe's name despite their friendship. Cobbe immediately penned a reply to Lee (explicitly). Lee's counter-reply eventually appeared in print in 1886. Meanwhile, Besant defended secular morality against Cobbe (explicitly); Cobbe retaliated (without naming Besant); and Besant came back with an even fiercer (explicit) critique of Cobbe's position. In sum, the filiations were sometimes direct, sometimes indirect; sometimes explicit, sometimes tacit; sometimes negative and critical, sometimes sympathetic and approving.

Why did women often leave the filiations tacit and indirect? This was because of several features of the patriarchal context, which I will explain further in Chapter 1.[13] In essence, the most accepted and respected authorities were men. In this setting women could most effectively insert themselves into a debate, and garner epistemic credibility, by invoking male authorities and situating themselves with explicit reference to men, while leaving their interlocutions with other women understated or unmentioned. We should remember here that nineteenth-century citation practices were very different from ours today. It was not normal practice to spell out and footnote all one's references. Frequently people would allude, quote from memory, or assume that their readers would know whom or what they were talking about. This was compounded by the fact that anonymous publication, and publishing under pseudonyms or initials, were standard in British periodicals for much of the century, and were not particularly unusual for books either, especially ones by female authors. Finally, authors, both men and women, sometimes hesitated to reference or mention women because it was thought to be degrading: to the referenced author, by exposing them as a woman who was inappropriately publishing intellectual work; and to the referencing author, by putting them in the wrong sort of 'feminine' intellectual company.

To take up O'Neill's disappearing ink metaphor again, then, nineteenth-century women *themselves* tended deliberately to reach for the disappearing ink when publishing their work. For example, Buckley happily told her friend Richard Garnett, after a trip to meet various Cambridge academics, that 'many of the present scientific men and women... had read my books' but then quickly added 'Do not repeat these details, many people would misconstrue my mentioning them': her influence had to remain invisible or she would incur criticism (*GFP*, AB to Garnett, 28 Aug. 1904). The unfortunate result of women's deliberate cultivation of invisibility is that when we search back through periodicals and books women's names are usually not there on the pages, making it hard to trace women's work and influence. Indeed, even historians of women in philosophy often focus on the relations of their selected women to male interlocutors and influences. For instance, it is highlighted that Shepherd knew Babbage but not Martineau (McRobert n.d.); Lee's relations to Walter Pater are explored but not to

---

[13] See also the helpful discussion of this issue by Bergès (2015).

Ward, Cobbe, or Welby;[14] Welby's correspondence with Peirce is scrutinized carefully (as in Hardwick 1978) but not that with Wedgwood, Ward, Lee, or Mary Everest Boole;[15] Wedgwood's letters with Darwin are highlighted but not those she exchanged with her mentor and role model Martineau.[16] Thus a common strategy is to elevate a given woman by relating her to well-known men. This is understandable. The men's names still carry more ingrained authority, the records of their contributions and impact are more visible and traceable, and women themselves selectively referenced men to amplify their own contested credibility. Women's practice of rarely mentioning one another has constrained us to reconstruct each woman's thought in isolation from the others—restoring their contributions one woman at a time, as it were.[17]

This is the pattern I aim to rectify, although, as we can see, reconstructing interwomen filiations requires some reading between the lines. But how to read between the lines? I adopt three methods.

First, I use *biographical and historical scholarship* and *autobiographical works* to reconstruct women's lives and relationships, their intellectual circles and lineages, and the communities of discourse and inquiry they belonged to. We should remember that their networks were relatively narrow because of class, cultural, and educational constraints, so that these women frequently moved in overlapping and adjoining circles. Some of them, like Martineau, Cobbe, Blavatsky, and Besant, were major public figures, making it prima facie plausible that others knew of their views even when no personal links existed. On these intellectual and discursive networks there is fortunately much excellent scholarship on which I have gratefully drawn, from history, history of science, English literature, history of political thought, studies of print culture, and other cognate fields.[18] Sometimes

---

[14] See Maxwell and Pulham (2006); Laurel Brake, in her chapter in this volume, does bring Ward in, but as background to Lee's relations with Pater. Or see Towheed (2006) on Lee on hereditary conscience—Towheed makes no mention of Cobbe, even though Lee's defence of hereditary conscience in *Baldwin* (1886) was primarily directed against Cobbe, as we'll see in Chapter 5 (Cobbe being a steadfast opponent of the idea of hereditary conscience).

[15] Even Petrilli's invaluable reconstruction of Welby's thought and conversations in *Signifying and Understanding* (*SU*) largely foregrounds her male interlocutors, except for Boole and Ella Stout. On Boole's wide-ranging projects developing the logical innovations of her late husband and exploring their metaphysical underpinnings, see Valente (2010).

[16] The invaluable online edition of Darwin's letters at https://darwinproject.ac.uk/ (Darwin Correspondence Project 2009) meticulously documents his correspondence with Wedgwood, Cobbe, and Buckley; but the focus is on their relations to Darwin, not each other.

[17] For example, Miranda Seymour suggests that Lovelace was the only 'female contender' for the authorship of the controversial 1844 work *Vestiges of the Natural History of Creation*, actually by Robert Chambers (Seymour 2018: 311)—but Martineau was at least as prominent a contender as Lovelace.

[18] This scholarship is not always recent. Vera Wheatley remarked in 1957: 'It is scarcely possible to read any book relating to the nineteenth century without finding in its index...the name of Harriet Martineau' (1957: 11). Today it can be quite difficult to find general books on nineteenth-century thought that *do* discuss Martineau; we seem to have gone backward. On the other hand, reading earlier literature one has to endure some dismayingly sexist remarks, like R. K. Webb describing Martineau's *Letters on the Laws of Man's Nature and Development* as 'fourth- or fifth-rate philosophising' (1960: 21)

all that remains is to draw out the philosophical significance of the material and join up the dots concerning women's philosophical filiations.

Second, I look at *correspondence*. Happily much of this is now collected, catalogued, and available, often in print or through libraries and archives. In some cases—for instance with Eliot, Martineau, Lee, and Welby—highly scholarly, published versions of some or all of their correspondence exist, on which I have again gratefully drawn. Correspondence may say more about travel itineraries, the weather, and health complaints than philosophy, but—crucially—it can tell us which women knew one another, which other women they knew of and were interested in, and which writings of other women they were reading and were exercised by. In the absence of citations, letters fill in some of the inter-women background lying behind published work that exclusively references men. Letters, after all, counted as part of the 'private' sphere in which women could appropriately talk about one another, whereas published work was part of the 'public' world in which women were supposed to be neither heard nor seen.

This is not to say that correspondence is useful only for exposing hidden links amongst women. Letters often served as a form of philosophical writing in their own right, as I will explain in Chapter 1. Many women used their extensive correspondence to exchange and explore philosophical ideas, and I will draw on letters for insight into their ideas as well as for evidence about inter-women conversations.

My third way of unearthing those conversations is to compare the *philosophical content of women's published writings*: for example, identifying formulations of questions or positions that closely resemble ones that other women used; tracing where phrases and concepts from one woman's work reappear in another's; spotting where a woman is tackling an issue in a way that looks framed by another woman's approach. I take all these to be prima facie evidence of intellectual engagement, especially when we are unlikely to find more 'visible' ink for the reasons I've outlined.

It is worth mentioning here that most of the published work by the twelve women featured in this book is readily available online. I am greatly indebted to all those who have catalogued the immense body of nineteenth-century printed material, de-anonymizing it and identifying many authors and pseudonyms, indexing and digitizing content, and so making it available for philosophical analysis. This process remains incomplete, but it is considerably further along than it was twenty or thirty years ago.

However, one might ask, why confine our attention to women's intellectual relations with other women? After all, nineteenth-century women referred to men

---

and Diana Postlethwaite saying that Martineau is 'the least intellectually gifted thinker' among the group of Victorian authors studied, and that her *Letters* 'often seem close to the lunatic fringe, light years away from the logical rigors of John Stuart Mill' (1984: 142).

more readily than other women; men sometimes formed interconnecting nodes between women, as with Carpenter in my earlier example regarding philosophy of mind; and men were often pivotal to the intellectual networks and landscapes to which women belonged. Moreover, archives contain much forgotten work by men that did not make it into the canon. Perhaps this work too deserves reappraisal; why prioritize women?

Certainly, some important and influential male philosophers in nineteenth-century Britain are neglected today: Herbert Spencer, George Henry Lewes, and Thomas Henry Huxley, to mention three. Yet, under-studied as these male figures are, their philosophical ideas have not been ignored as comprehensively as those of their female counterparts. For example, one can readily find abundant discussion of Huxley's agnosticism;[19] there are substantial accounts of the philosophies of Spencer, Huxley, and others;[20] and men's ideas are more often covered in general studies of the period, such as Mander (2020) or Moyar (2012). Another important gender difference is that *some* British men (albeit not many) entered the canon—Mill, Green, and Sidgwick above all; but no women did, not even once-massive public presences like Martineau and Cobbe. Women were excluded from the canon more systematically than men, which makes the need to recover women more pressing.

Even so, it may be objected that focusing on women's filiations with one another creates a misleading picture. For women did not engage only with one another; they had male interlocutors as well, and were intervening into fields of discussion which men did much to shape. Necessarily, then, some of these male figures will come into this book—Babbage, Carpenter, Huxley, Lewes; also Charles Darwin, Augustus De Morgan, William Rathbone Greg, Max Müller, Joseph Priestley, and John Tyndall—to give a non-exhaustive sample. Yet as this lengthy list indicates, the danger quickly grows that men's voices will crowd women's out, and women be reduced again to supporting cast members. The danger arises both because male intellectuals were more numerous and because nineteenth-century women selectively foregrounded their relations with men in their published work. To counteract this problem, I foreground women's intellectual relations with one another. I do so, too, in order to avoid reinforcing the assumption that men need to serve as reference points for making sense of women's ideas—for, after all, people very rarely make the same assumption the other way around.[21] I hope to

---

[19] On some of this literature, see Chapter 2, Sec. 2.4.
[20] For example, on Spencer, see Francis (2007), La Vergata (1995), and Taylor (2007); and on Huxley, see Blinderman and Joyce (1998), Byun (2017), and Lyons (1999).
[21] For example, in a brief account of Cobbe's publishing career, Linda Hughes (2009) notes its striking parallels with that of Matthew Arnold—along with the irony that few scholars would ever make sense of Arnold's career by comparing it with Cobbe's. On the wider pattern of treating historical women philosophers as 'handmaidens' to their better-established male counterparts, see Witt (2006: 342–3).

shift our orientation more deeply, although hopefully while retaining enough sense of the male interlocutors as not to distort the historical record.

I have said that these women philosophers deserve recovery, but the question of evaluation is somewhat complex. As Mary Ellen Waithe puts it, the problem with assessing historical women's philosophizing by asking 'does it advance the discussion?' is that advancement 'may be attributed as much to the capacity of those who hear the arguments to engage in them as to the quality of the arguments that are offered' (1987: vol. 3: xxxviii). In other words, evaluating the work of canonical authors is relatively straightforward because it has already undergone many reconstructions, criticisms, defences, and so on. We read Hegel today, for instance, against the backdrop of a large body of interpretation, historical contextualization, and rational reconstruction of his work. We come equipped to hear and engage with his claims. But we come to authors who were omitted from the canon with no such backdrop. Their arguments and perspectives are therefore more liable to be judged weak or implausible at first sight, and get quickly dismissed, because these authors have to fend entirely for themselves, so to speak, without an army of prior interpreters at their back. So we need to exercise some caution when evaluating the work of these women. Mostly, therefore, I will concentrate on presenting these women's ideas and reasonings clearly, in the hope that the interest, originality, depth, and other positive qualities of their work will speak for themselves. Evaluation cannot be completely avoided, though, because sometimes we need to identify tensions so as to reconstruct the further steps an author took to resolve them, or to pinpoint problems so as to understand why the author subsequently changed their mind or why others favoured alternative views. Accordingly I will offer some evaluation, though generally I try to balance criticisms with positives—for there *are* many positives of these women's philosophies, and I hope to help readers to see them.

Waithe's cautionary remark about 'advancing the discussion' bears particularly on one dimension of nineteenth-century British intellectual life: religion. 'The nineteenth century was a period of unparalleled religious vitality' in Britain, in Alasdair Crockett's words (1998: 3). He attributes this vitality to the unprecedented levels of religious dissent—encompassing up to a third of all Christians—with the Church of England becoming more intensive in response. The resulting 'period of remarkable growth in religious fervour, innovation and adherence' (6) meant that whether someone was, for example, an Anglican, a Dissenter, an atheist, a spiritualist, they could not avoid engaging with religion. As we will see, religious concerns were central to women's discussions of every issue covered in this book. Yet many contemporary philosophers are secularists. As such, the distinctive concerns of nineteenth-century British philosophers can be hard for readers today to access—which may partly explain the neglect of this period. Still, we need to open our minds and not dismiss people's claims out of hand because they have religious aspects, otherwise we will not get far with the philosophy of this place and period.

Two final aspects of my interpretive approach deserve comment. I shall use some broad labels such as 'materialist', 'dualist', 'determinist', 'compatibilist', and 'naturalist'. For instance, regarding philosophy of mind, I will characterize Cobbe as a dualist, Naden as a materialist, and Blavatsky and Besant as panpsychists. Some readers may find these labels too broad-brush to be useful. But while labels do not, in themselves, elucidate the specifics of anyone's position, they help to map the overall relations amongst people's positions and highlight people's respective places in the intellectual landscape. Labels, though not exhaustive, can be indicative, and indicators are useful when dealing with unfamiliar authors. For we come to these women's writings without the tacit understanding of where they stand on the philosophical spectrum that we already have for canonical figures like Descartes, Hegel, Wittgenstein, and so on.

Finally, as I have mentioned, I shall cover a large number of women, the better to convey the wealth and variety of women's philosophizing in this period. But one cannot cover a wide range without some sacrifice of fine detail. There will inevitably be occasions when readers are left with questions about aspects of the figures, ideas, and arguments under discussion. I hope this may motivate readers to delve further into these women philosophers for themselves.

I.3 Chapter Outline

Because of my desire to explore filiations amongst women, I have organized this book thematically. In each chapter I take a particular topic and reconstruct and compare the views on it of a subset of my twelve women, where their views emerged in sequential response to and reaction against one another, explicitly or implicitly or both. The themes and chapters are as follows—after Chapter 1, 'Women's Constrained Philosophical Participation', which enlarges on the cultural and historical context and on my analytical framework.

Chapter 2, 'Naturalism'. By 'naturalism' I mean the view that reality in its entirety can be understood through the methods of empirical science, a contested view right across the century. I begin in the 1820s with Shepherd's account of causation, which I argue is anti-naturalist. For Shepherd the causal principle is known by reason, is the precondition and not the result of scientific inquiry, and is bound up with God's existence as intelligent first cause. Slightly later in the 1820s, Martineau combined a belief in complete causal determinism and an inductive account of causation with faith in God as first cause and moral legislator. These views were an unstable mixture of naturalist and anti-naturalist elements. The naturalist leanings won out, and by the 1850s Martineau was giving as strong and uncompromising a statement of naturalism as we find anywhere in nineteenth-century thought. In the 1850s Cobbe opposed this kind of naturalism on the grounds that it could not adequately account for moral requirements, and in the

1880s to 1890s Welby argued that it could not account for meaning and significance. The chapter shows how women contributed to the whole shape of British philosophy in the period, from the early modern issues of causation and induction that concerned Shepherd and the younger Martineau, through to problems about naturalism and normativity, up to the linguistic turn as the century ended.

Chapter 3, 'Philosophy of Mind'. I begin in the 1840s with Lovelace. She was conflicted over machine intelligence and, connected with this, she was torn between materialism and dualism about the mind. On the materialist side, she was inspired by Martineau and a controversial group of materialist scientists around the journal *The Zoist*. On the dualist side, she was an interlocutor of Carpenter, who went on to give a dualist account of the relation between will, consciousness, and brain in the 1850s. In turn, Cobbe used Carpenter's work to defend her own distinction between the self and the brain. I then turn to the strong form of materialism that Naden put forward as part of 'hylo-idealism' in the 1880s. Hylo-idealism linked back to the earlier group around *The Zoist*, whose ideas Robert Lewins took up when formulating 'hylo-*zoism*', the view that Naden then adopted, developed, and renamed hylo-idealism. The name hylo-'idealism' notwithstanding, the position in fact turned upon a materialist account of mind. In turn again, Blavatsky's criticisms of hylo-idealism fed into her case for theosophy, specifically for her theosophical form of panpsychism. Blavatsky argued that materialist accounts of the mind, including hylo-idealist ones, could not explain the subjective quality of mental phenomena; the same consideration helped to motivate Besant to turn to theosophy.

Chapter 4, 'The Meaning of Evolution'. It is well known that in 1859 Darwin's *Origin of Species* occasioned intense debate about how far evolution was compatible with Christian belief. Less well known is that women made important interventions into this debate. Wedgwood argued in 'The Boundaries of Science' (1860–1) that evolutionary and religious perspectives could be reconciled when each abided by the limits proper to its field of inquiry. In the 1860s Cobbe agreed, but she changed her mind when Darwin brought out *The Descent of Man* in 1871. Cobbe now argued that treating our moral responses as inherited products of evolution, as Darwin did in *Descent*, undermines morality and religion alike. Simultaneously, Buckley began to develop her contrary view that the evolutionary process has given us cooperative and sympathetic instincts that support morality. She also argued, like Wedgwood, that evolutionary theory is compatible with God's existence and with our having immortal souls, although Buckley made sense of the soul in a unique way. In short, women divided over whether evolutionary theory was compatible with religion and morality, just as they divided over naturalism and materialism.

Chapter 5, 'Religion and Morality'. Cobbe's critique of Darwin was informed by her stance in *Intuitive Morals* that morality necessarily requires Christianity. For Cobbe, morality is a system of moral laws, laws presuppose a legislator, and absolutely binding laws presuppose a divine legislator; moreover, we cannot be motivated by moral imperatives unless we believe in immortality and moral progress in the afterlife. However, in Martineau's *Autobiography*, written in 1855, she argued that morality could and should be extricated from, and stand independently of, both religious faith and belief in immortality. A different route to a post-religious morality was simultaneously taken by Eliot, for whom morality depends on sympathy and sympathy can be expanded and cultivated by artistic literature. Cobbe criticized Martineau and Eliot in the 1870s, but two new women thereupon came to atheism's defence—Lee, advocating a sober, mournful, and responsible atheism in the 1880s, and the more forthright Besant who, pre-theosophy, was a passionate secularist. In the 1870s Besant argued against Cobbe that morality would gain by being set on a true scientific foundation rather than a false religious one. Cobbe expanded her defence of Christianity to say that it forms our entire horizon of meaning and value, and Besant then objected to that thesis too.

Chapter 6, 'Progress in History'. Most Victorians believed in what Martineau and Eliot called the 'Law of Progress': that all of history has been progressing towards a goal that is being reached in modern Europe, passing through stages embodied in successive world civilizations. Beyond that, women differed on the detail. For Martineau in the 1840s, the historical progression has moved from the religious philosophy of ancient Egypt through Judaism to Christianity; necessarily, the next stage is for the West to secularize. Cobbe, unsurprisingly, opposed this in the 1860s, giving a rival account of the world religious progression that culminates *in* Christianity, not beyond it. She relocated the start of the series in India, followed by Persia, Judaism, and then Christianity. In *The Moral Ideal* (1888), Wedgwood likewise traced a global progression in ethical thought that began in India and ended in modern Europe. Wedgwood, I will suggest, was synthesizing Martineau's and Cobbe's views by suggesting that the necessary next stage must be to reconcile the Christian aspiration towards an ideal with the scientific acceptance of natural reality. The direction of progress became more ambiguous in Blavatsky's *Secret Doctrine*, also from 1888. For her, we can only reach the next stage in the world's necessary spiritual evolution by recovering ancient wisdom. This is best preserved in the religious traditions of India. In retrospect, the ambiguity of Blavatsky's conception of progress exposes related ambiguities in the other women's theories, while overall the chapter shows that women made original contributions to nineteenth-century philosophy of history. Their theories were Eurocentric—albeit somewhat ambiguously so, especially in Blavatsky's case—but examining these Eurocentric theories remains worthwhile, for by examining the intellectual frameworks that have shaped our social world, we can better understand why it contains the global and racial inequalities that it does.

This outline makes apparent that some women will appear in this book more often than others, Martineau and Cobbe most of all. This is deliberate: Cobbe and Martineau were central to the period's intellectual life, engaging in virtually every debate and being very well known for doing so. Moreover, because they were so well known, many other women engaged with them—even if their publications do not make the fact explicit—so that Martineau's and Cobbe's writings serve as nodes interconnecting multiple women. Conversely, two figures who have received more attention already—Shepherd and Eliot—will play lesser roles here. I have prioritized figures who have not yet undergone significant philosophical recovery, as with Martineau, Cobbe, and Wedgwood, or, with Blavatsky and Besant, who have been discussed in religious studies but hardly ever by philosophers.

The thematic framework means that I cannot always look at women's writings in their order of publication. I do so as far as possible; but this has its limits, because inevitably women did not all address themes in the same order. I hope that the threads connecting individuals' ideas across themes and chapters are clear all the same. To help keep these threads in view, I will sometimes briefly fill in a given author's intellectual development over time, to contextualize the particular writings and ideas being discussed.

I.4 The Social and Historical Context of these Women Philosophers

The women who appear in this book were not representative of the full spectrum of social identities of their time. No less than five of them were of the aristocracy: Shepherd, Lovelace, Cobbe, Blavatsky, and Welby. Lee was also of semi-aristocratic descent and her family was very wealthy, as was Wedgwood's—the Wedgwood–Darwin family dynasty was very much part of the establishment. So was Buckley's family; her father was a Church minister and her brother became a baronet. Naden inherited considerable wealth, Martineau's family were wealthy manufacturers, and despite straitened circumstances Besant's background was upper-middle class, with a baronet among her relatives. Eliot was solidly middle class, her father being the land agent for the local aristocratic family. The sad fact is that because of the patriarchal constraints on women's intellectual participation in this period, women needed corresponding class and economic advantages to get around the constraints.[22] After all, before universal schooling began to be introduced with the 1870 Education Act, it was very difficult for working-class and less well-off women even to acquire an education. The culture of working-class autodidacticism was 'an overwhelmingly male territory' (Rose 2001: 18). As Rose documents, until 1870 women made up only about 5 per cent of the writers

---

[22] Of course, class limited many men's intellectual participation too, but less so than for women. For example, Alexander Bain was born to a weaving family but went on to establish the journal *Mind* and briefly held the Regius Chair of Logic at the University of Aberdeen.

of working-class memoirs which are our main source of knowledge about autodidacticism; and women are 15 per cent of those born after 1870. Even so there are fascinating cases, like Mary Smith, a working-class reader of Scottish philosophy, American transcendentalism, and German idealism who wrote on politics and campaigned for women's rights.[23]

Another limitation is that all twelve women discussed here were white. The black and ethnic minority population is estimated to have been small in nineteenth-century Britain—although population size is not decisive in itself: the working class vastly outnumbered the aristocracy but the latter had infinitely more say in philosophical debates.[24] What made it hard for black and ethnic minority women to contribute to philosophical discussion was that these women were largely poor and working class—not to mention the racial prejudices with which they had to contend.[25] Nevertheless, some black women influenced philosophical thought.[26] Mary Prince's 1831 slave narrative *The History of Mary Prince* drew white Britons' attention to the horrors of slavery, and Prince recognized the epistemic role of lived experience and emotions (Prince 1831: 23; see also Larrabee 2006). Also notable is Sarah Parker Remond, a black American woman who gave a speaking tour in Britain from 1859 to 1860 and stayed in the country until she moved to Italy in 1866. A 'brilliant orator', Remond pressed the case for abolition based on 'clear elucidation of just principles' (Fryer 1984: 435). Remond influenced Cobbe, and Martineau knew her as well.[27] Later in the century, Catherine Impey (herself white) edited the anti-racist journal *Anti-Caste* (1888–95), which was often critical of the British Empire.[28] Impey was eager for *Anti-Caste* to

---

[23] See Rose (2001: 45–6), Smith's autobiography (Smith 1892), and, on working-class nineteenth-century women's autobiographies more broadly, Boos (2017; part of ch. 8 is on Smith).

[24] In the late eighteenth century at least ten thousand black people lived in Britain (Myers 1996: 35). After slavery was abolished, the black British population is estimated to have either declined or remained largely constant right through the nineteenth century. As for British Asians, Rozina Visram estimates that 'From about the middle of the nineteenth century to...1914, several hundred Asians lived in Britain' (2002: 44). For context, the overall population was around 10.5 million in 1801, rising to 32 million by 1901. In 1891 there were around one hundred thousand Jewish people and almost two hundred thousand people who had been born in mainland Europe (Cook 2005: 108).

[25] The obstacles were so great, Dabydeen and Edwards maintain, that 'apart from Mary Prince's book, which is...a transcript of an oral narrative, Mary Seacole's autobiography is the only other book in English by a black woman in Britain published in the nineteenth century' (1991: 165; and see Seacole [1857] 2005). However, we should be cautious here, because as Bressey remarks, 'An assumed absence of black people in British archives has led to...their absence and exclusion from narratives of British history' (2010: 289). For example, take Ellen Craft. She and her husband William escaped from slavery, emigrated to Britain, gained an education (assisted by Martineau), and wrote a narrative of their escape, which although told only from William's perspective was actually co-authored by Ellen (see Craft 1860).

[26] On black people and presence in Victorian culture more widely, see Gerzina (2003); and, regarding Indians, Visram (1986).

[27] For more on Remond, see Salenius (2016).

[28] On Impey and *Anti-Caste*, see Bressey (2010, 2012, 2013), and Holton (2001). Impey was succeeded as *Anti-Caste*'s editor by Celestine Edwards, the first black (male) journal editor in Britain. He edited first *Lux* (1892–4), then *Anti-Caste* (1893–4), then *Fraternity* (1893–4); he died in 1894. See Fryer (1984: 277–9).

feature the voices of black men and women, though in the end those voices were drawn primarily from the USA.[29] For instance, Impey organized Ida B. Wells's 1893 tour of England and Scotland, in which Wells publicized her critical analysis of lynching.

Race, racism, and imperialism were on the philosophical agenda, then, and several of the women discussed in this book were keenly concerned with these issues. Cobbe and Martineau were abolitionists. Martineau made herself very unpopular on this account and faced death threats when touring the USA in the 1830s. She diagnosed American society as resting on a fundamental contradiction between its egalitarian principles and its practice of slavery (*SA* 2: 312). However, like many nineteenth-century British abolitionists, Martineau and Cobbe broadly supported the British Empire, seeing it as advancing anti-slavery and other progressive causes internationally.[30] Others such as Besant were more robustly critical of colonialism, which Besant argued was fundamentally a system of economic exploitation.[31] Blavatsky, for her part, revalued Eastern religion and philosophy in a way that complicated the standard Victorian picture of European progress and advancement. Theosophy thereby entered into a complicated relationship with the movement for Indian national independence (see Lubelsky 2012). I will discuss these issues in Chapter 6.

Hopefully what I have said so far has indicated that nineteenth-century Britain was, at least, not the insular place that negative stereotypes about narrow-minded and repressed Victorians might suggest. It was more of an open and cosmopolitan culture than we might assume, and this is mirrored in ways that our twelve women *were* diverse. Blavatsky was from Russia and had travelled around much of the world, living for years in India, Egypt, the USA, and possibly Tibet; Besant had Irish ancestry, and later moved to India and became a pivotal figure in the Indian National Congress; Cobbe was from Ireland, albeit from its Anglo-Irish ruling class; Martineau was descended from French Huguenot immigrants; Shepherd was Scottish; Lee was born in France, grew up moving between various mainland European countries, and spent most of her adulthood in Italy, while regularly visiting Britain and remaining active in British intellectual life. Welby had toured North and South America, Europe, Morocco, and the Middle East with her

---

[29] As Bressey says, 'Despite Impey's intention to support a diverse range of contributions, opinion pieces or original essays from black authors were rarely produced' (2012: 407).
[30] On this frequent mix of abolitionism and imperialism at the time, see Ferguson (1992), Midgley (1992, 1998), and on later-century entanglements of feminism and imperialism, Burton (1994). On Martineau on the British Empire, see Logan (2004, 2010); and on her abolitionism, see Wilson (2019). It is worth noting that Butler campaigned for the *Abolition* of the Contagious Diseases Acts, trading on the moral force of abolitionism, like Cobbe when campaigning for the *abolition* of vivisection.
[31] For some of Besant's anti-imperialist pamphlets, see Saville (1970: sec. III) and, on India specifically, Besant (1914 and 1916a). Another female critic of imperialism was Lovelace's daughter Anne Blunt, whose contributions have been overshadowed by or silently incorporated into those of her husband Wilfred Scawen Blunt (e.g. in Claeys 2010). However, on Blunt in her own right, see Melman (1992: ch. 12) and McCracken Lacy (2017).

mother when young;[32] while Martineau, Cobbe, and Naden toured the Near East, with Naden going to India as well.

In sexual and marital terms, Martineau, Cobbe, Wedgwood, Naden, and Lee never married, while Buckley married only at 44 and Eliot at 60, dying just a few months later (she married John Cross; she had previously, and scandalously, lived for twenty-five years with the already-married George Henry Lewes). Blavatsky and Besant both had marriages that broke down quickly and afterwards they lived as single women. Cobbe lived for thirty years with the female sculptor, Mary Lloyd; and Lee, whose gender presentation was ambiguous, had several long-term relationships with women, particularly Kit Anstruther-Thomson. In short, few of these women led conventional family lives by the standards of their times.

By now it is probably apparent that this book is weighted more towards the Victorian (c.1837–1901) than the Romantic era (c.1790–1837). This is partly because, as the century went on and print culture expanded more and more, increasing numbers of women began to publish philosophical work. There are simply more Victorian-era women philosophers available to look at. In addition, the formative decades for Romantic-era women's philosophizing were actually the 1770s to 1790s, thus predating the nineteenth century. For instance, although Anna Barbauld and Mary Hays continued publishing into the 1800s, their intellectual and publishing careers began in the 1770s and 1790s, respectively. Likewise with Joanna Baillie, a major figure in Romantic aesthetics but whose central philosophical statement, the 'Introductory Discourse' to her *Plays on the Passions*, dates from 1798 (see Baillie 1798). As these dates indicate, moreover—and as is anyway by now well established—Romanticism overlapped with the preceding Enlightenment era (c.1715–89) and was more Enlightenment's extension and radicalization than its rejection. In other words, Romantic-era women's philosophy often has more in common with the eighteenth than the nineteenth century.

Nonetheless I describe this book as being about 'nineteenth-century' rather than 'Victorian' women's philosophy. This is not only because I cover pre-Victorian work by Shepherd and Martineau, and because some ideas that technically fall within the Victorian period are still manifestly Romantic, such as Lovelace's reflections on poetic and imaginative science of the early 1840s.[33] Crucially, also, it was around 1800 that several developments occurred that shaped the entire coming century. Britain's distinctive periodical culture then began to emerge, marked by the founding of the *Edinburgh Review* in 1802; this was the culture in which nineteenth-century women's philosophizing took place. Central features of this culture such as anonymous authorship were established at the same time.

The year 1800 was also when certain core ideas about separate spheres and woman's mission were articulated. Those ideas precipitated out of the preceding

---

[32] At just 15, Welby brought out a book about her American travels (Welby 1852).
[33] On this aspect of Lovelace's views, see also Forbes-Macphail (2013: 149).

decade of contestation over women's rights, in which Enlightenment radicals like Mary Wollstonecraft and Mary Hays were opposed by conservatives spearheaded by the evangelical moralist Hannah More. There were moderate voices too, such as that of the Scottish philosopher Elizabeth Hamilton, as in her 1800 novel *Memoirs of Modern Philosophers* and her 1801 *Letters on Education*.[34] But More's ideas were most decisive for women's position in the coming century.

More argued that women had a special and vital moral mission (see More 1799). She therefore in fact wanted women's education to cultivate their rational capacities, to that extent agreeing with Wollstonecraft. For More, though, women's mission should be performed in the 'private' sphere—albeit that for More this was not simply the home but extended into charity and philanthropy. More was thus, as Anne Stott puts it, the 'first Victorian' (2003). Her thought embodied a tension that would run right through the century: if women had so much to offer morally, surely they should be able to participate publicly and contribute right across social life? Indeed, More herself thought so to an extent.

The ambivalent idea of women's moral mission did a great deal to shape the form and content of women's philosophical participation. For example, in debates about morality and religion, all the women discussed here defended morality. What they differed over was *how* morality was best defended: with or without religious support, on a Christian or a scientific basis, that of utilitarianism or evolution, or perhaps based on literature instead. But pushing science, literature, art, or anything else *against* morality was not a route that these women took. For the idea of women's moral vocation gave them a passport to participate in public debate and speak with authority on value-facing matters.[35] Given this constraint it was important that women used their voices to advocate, not undermine, morality. Otherwise they pulled the rug from beneath their own feet.

This returns us to the patriarchal constraints under which nineteenth-century philosophical women operated. The question then is how, given those constraints, women—even elite women—could be part of the world of debate and argue with men and one another at all. The short answer is that nineteenth-century Britain had a vibrant print culture, which sustained a particular kind of philosophy that was generalist rather than specialist. This print culture has been studied extensively by literary and historical scholars, but its bearings on the character of philosophy in the period, and on women's opportunities for doing philosophy, have not yet been fully appreciated. This is the topic of Chapter 1.

---

[34] On the *Memoirs*, see Boyle (2021c); on Hamilton's educational philosophy, see Gokcekus (2019).
[35] For further discussion of this, see Mermin (1993).

1
Women's Constrained Philosophical Participation

1.1 Introduction

The ideology of 'separate spheres'—that men and women belong respectively in the public and private realms—was notoriously popular in nineteenth-century Britain.[1] As enshrined in law, this ideology meant that women were legally incorporated under first their fathers then, on marriage, their husbands, only counting as independent rights-bearing persons if they remained unmarried or were widowed. The same ideology justified the exclusion of women from universities. One might assume that this patriarchal setting must have prevented women from doing philosophy. Yet in fact many women were philosophically active and made important contributions to the philosophical debates and agendas of the time.

How did women achieve this, given the patriarchal setting? The answer is that 'separate spheres' ideology never perfectly matched the complex and diverse realities of women's and men's lives. The reality outstripped the ideal; indeed, as Amanda Vickery has argued, 'the broadcasting of the language of separate spheres [was] a conservative response to an unprecedented *expansion* in the opportunities, ambitions and experience of late Georgian and Victorian women' (1993: 400).[2] In Sec. 1.2, I look at an expansive force that was crucial in enabling women to philosophize: Britain's vibrant print culture. This was vital to women's philosophical participation because for most of the century philosophical discussion was generalist rather than specialist, carried on in a generalist milieu sustained across books, periodicals, and other print media. Of course book and periodical culture was not devoid of patriarchal constraints, but women found ways of working within and against them, which I detail in Sec. 1.3. Furthermore, women availed

---

[1] An infamous example is from Tennyson's *The Princess*: 'Man for the field and woman for the hearth / Man for the sword and for the needle she / Man with the head and woman with the heart / Man to command and woman to obey / All else confusion' (1847: 116).

[2] Vickery is one of several historians to argue that 'separate spheres' never completely defined the reality of nineteenth-century women's lives; see also e.g. Davidson (1998), Peterson (1989), and Steinbach (2012). The fact that many women wrote philosophy in this period attests to the gap between ideology and reality. I still speak of separate spheres, though, because the ideology was powerful; as Vickery herself clarifies, she 'does not argue that the vocabulary of public and private spheres had no currency in nineteenth-century society' (1993: 400).

themselves of conventions around anonymity, pseudonymity, and publication with initials in a period when signed authorship was only gradually becoming the norm. I examine this in Sec. 1.4.

So women participated in the generalist philosophical culture, albeit under constraints. How, then, did their contributions become forgotten? Having been present in nineteenth-century philosophy's *history*, how did women become left out of its *historiography*? In Sec. 1.5, I identify some reasons, highlighting the professionalization and specialization of philosophy from the mid-1870s onwards,[3] which interacted to unfortunate effect with women's earlier participation strategies. The very type of philosophy women had been doing before—generalist and wide-ranging; committed on moral, political, and religious questions; writerly; often popular and accessible—now fell foul of an emerging expectation that the philosopher should be an expert, detached, analytically precise specialist. In Sec. 1.6, I look at two case studies of these dynamics at work: Frances Power Cobbe's rise and fall from high repute in her time to near-total invisibility today; and the joint roles of the Coulomb affair and Hodgson report in pushing Helena Blavatsky's spiritual philosophy outside academic respectability. More positively, in Sec. 1.7, I offer some recommendations for how to recover nineteenth-century women philosophers and undo the lingering exclusions from which they have suffered.

1.2 Constraints, Print Culture, and Generalist Philosophy

Let me begin with some constraints, for although 'separate spheres' was imperfectly realized, it still underpinned serious restrictions on women's intellectual lives. For much of the century women were excluded from higher and university education. Women campaigned long and hard to be allowed to study at university.[4] The beginning was Bedford College, founded in 1849; then the University of London began to admit women in 1868 and allowed them to graduate from 1878. Girton College, Cambridge, opened in 1869 and Somerville College, Oxford, in 1879. But women remained at an educational disadvantage, with girls receiving much more limited formal education than boys. Girls were usually educated at home, by family members, tutors, or governesses, rather than sent to school. There were exceptions: Harriet Martineau was educated for periods alongside her siblings at progressive schools in Norwich and Bristol, and George Eliot was sent to boarding

---

[3] Eileen O'Neill claims that the nineteenth century was 'the pivotal era of disappearance' for women's philosophy because this was when the discipline was 'purified' (2005: 186–7). In Britain, however, the 'purification' only happened at the end of the century. O'Neill is right to highlight purification; but this took place in Britain later than she maintains.

[4] What kind of education women should be allowed to have was itself a matter of philosophical debate. Emily Davies, with Cobbe, led the charge for women to study the same university curricula as men, against advocates of different or special education for women, who included Sidgwick and Butler (see Caine 1993 and Davies 1866).

school because of her mother's ill-health. Occasionally girls received an excellent home education, as Ada Lovelace did, receiving guidance from the scientific polymath Mary Somerville as well as tuition in advanced mathematics from Augustus De Morgan, one of the country's leading logicians.[5] Unfortunately most women fared worse than Martineau, Eliot, and Lovelace.

The justification for excluding women from formal and higher education came from separate spheres ideology. Because women's supposed role was to care for family at home, they did not need advanced education. Their reproductive physiology was regarded as draining, reducing their capacity for 'brain-work'. Women who indulged in brain-work were sometimes thought to be over-taxing their systems and making themselves ill. When Constance Naden died from complications arising from ovarian cysts, Herbert Spencer, despite praising her intellect, took her untimely death to show that she had over-developed it at 'a physiological cost which the feminine organization will not bear without injury more or less profound'.[6]

The same ideology underpinned women's formal exclusion from most professions, though again women began to penetrate some of them later in the century. A significant milestone was the 1876 Medical Act permitting women to become licensed medical practitioners. Once women's higher education was established, some women began to proceed to academic posts, with the classicist Annie Rogers becoming the first female tutor at Oxford in 1879. But it was slow progress, hard won. Right across the century, women remained barred from many intellectual and cultural spaces, organizations, and learned societies. For instance, the Metaphysical Society, founded in 1869 by James Knowles and a key forum for philosophical discussion, was men-only. The capstone on all these exclusions was women's lack of the right to vote or hold parliamentary office.[7]

How did women manage to do philosophy despite these barriers? One factor was that even when their formal education was limited, they often undertook stringent courses of self-education. Wedgwood taught herself Latin, Greek, French, Italian, and German; Eliot learnt French, German, Italian, Latin, Greek, Spanish, and Hebrew.[8] Languages were a strong point for many women, because fluency of written expression and proficiency in at least some languages besides English were conventional expectations for women of the middle-to-upper class. In addition, these women often had access to the well-stocked libraries of their own families, their relatives, or other local families. Women

---

[5] Lovelace's mother Annabella Byron directed her daughter's education with a firm hand, emphasizing the sciences to combat the passionate, Romantic inheritance that she feared Lovelace would inherit from her father. On Lovelace's education, see Hollings et al. (2017).

[6] Spencer to Robert Lewins, 10 June 1890, in Duncan (1911: 296).

[7] However, for ways in which women's exclusion from political debates and arenas was less total than we might assume, see Richardson (2013).

[8] Both Wedgwood and Eliot had some school education to start from, as I noted above regarding Eliot. Wedgwood spent time at a school run by Rachel Martineau, Harriet's sister.

sometimes started their own societies or branches of societies to pool knowledge: for instance, Caroline Cornwallis formed the 'A. B. C. Society' to collaborate on her series *Small Books on Great Subjects*, several of which were philosophical.[9] Women argued for their right to be part of learned associations,[10] undertake higher education, and participate in public debate; they insisted on their own intellectual ability and powers to reason. Crucially, women made all these arguments not only orally but also in print, taking advantage of the enormously rich publishing and literary culture.

This brings us to print culture, which was, I believe, the single most central factor enabling women to philosophize. The scale of nineteenth-century British print culture has only been rediscovered by scholars in the last thirty years, and its study is a flourishing academic field in its own right.[11] However, contemporary philosophers have not yet fully appreciated its significance, or the possibilities it opened up, for nineteenth-century women philosophers. So I will now sketch this culture before explaining how women used it to do philosophy in a public setting.

In nineteenth-century Britain, industrial developments such as steam-powered printing presses and rail distribution networks propelled an exponential growth in the quantity of printed material that was produced and consumed. This in turn produced such an increase in literacy that, by 1900, 97 per cent of British men and women were literate. The numbers of books being published rose steadily from around three thousand new titles a year in 1840 to seven thousand in 1900 (some of these titles having very large print runs). By 1900 fiction had leapt up to comprise the lion's share of titles, displacing religion, which had furnished the biggest percentage of all titles in the early 1800s (Eliot n.d.).[12] But fiction grew as a proportion of reading matter against a background where non-fiction writing was likewise gaining in popularity. Mirroring these trends, worries about 'obscenity' escalated, leading to the 1857 Obscene Publications Act—a piece of legislation of which Annie Besant fell foul in 1877 when she and her secularist ally Charles Bradlaugh published a new edition of Charles Knowlton's 1832 pamphlet *The Fruits of Philosophy*, dealing with birth-control.[13] Besant and Bradlaugh were arrested and stood trial, and though they were ultimately let off on a technicality the case led to Besant losing custody of her daughter. The trial testified to growing

---

[9] See Cornwallis to David Power, 14 January 1844, in Cornwallis (1864: 255–6).
[10] Moreover, women were not always entirely excluded. For example, women could be audience members at conferences of the British Association for the Advancement of Science, founded in 1831; see Higgitt and Withers (2008).
[11] See e.g. *Victorian Periodicals Review* and *BRANCH: Britain, Representation and Nineteenth-Century History*; The Victorian Web (n.d.); King et al. (2016), and Shattock (2017), and with particular reference to women, Easley et al. (2019) and Onslow (2000).
[12] This shows how acutely George Eliot grasped the direction of cultural travel when she conceived literature as stepping in to fill the moral role formerly performed by religion; see Chapter 5.
[13] On the trial and the philosophical issues at stake in it, see Peart and Levy (2005, 2008) and Richards (2020: ch. 8).

fears about the potentially 'immoral' consequences of an exponentially growing print culture.

Books were only one branch of this culture. Periodicals were equally if not more influential, because they were cheaper than books and so reached larger audiences. At least 125,000 journals, magazines, and newspapers came and went over the century (VanArsdel 2010). Some journals were dedicated to fiction, some combined fiction and non-fiction, and some were non-fiction only. The first journals were quarterly: the *Edinburgh Review* (founded 1802), *Quarterly Review* (founded 1809) and *Westminster Review* (founded 1824) were the big three (see Tables 1.1 and 1.2). Intellectually heavyweight, they spanned the political spectrum from liberal (*Edinburgh*) through conservative (*Quarterly*) to radical (*Westminster*).[14] These quarterlies were at first definitive for the nature of the periodical, but gradually they were displaced by cheaper but still intellectually heavyweight 'monthly magazines', such as *Macmillan's* and *Cornhill* (Hughes 2012).

From the 1870s onwards, the range of journals mushroomed. This marked a major intellectual shift. Initially, journal culture had been fairly unified, the 'common intellectual context' of the era (Young 1985: 125). But as titles and readerships proliferated, periodicals became more diverse. Specialist academic journals appeared, such as *Mind* in 1876 and the *Proceedings of the Aristotelian Society* in 1888, Britain's first specialist philosophy journals. New trade publications appeared; so did journals on hobbies, the arts, local areas, law, the military, history, transport, sports; cultural reviews; journals aimed at women, students, workers; political journals (e.g. anti-vivisection, temperance, feminist, and socialist journals); and religious and spiritual journals (e.g. theosophical journals, of which over sixty were appearing, internationally, by the 1900s). Thus, an ever-growing range of less mainstream, 'fringe' periodicals flourished, attached to particular cultures and networks. One was *Our Corner* (1883–8), the left-leaning cultural review that Besant edited; two others were the theosophy journals *The Theosophist* (1879–) and *Lucifer* (1887–97), both founded by Blavatsky, who was their main editor initially.[15] As this indicates, the proliferation of periodical types created new openings for women, not only as contributors but also as editors, where editorial opportunities had previously been limited. In 1837 Martineau had been invited to edit a proposed new journal on 'philosophical principles, abstract and applied, of sociology' but on the terrible advice of her brother James she declined the opportunity.[16] Although Eliot co-edited the

---

[14] Mill famously described the *Westminster Review* as the 'representative of the "Philosophic Radicals"' ([1873] 1981: 208).

[15] On *Lucifer*, see Ferguson (2020). Mabel Collins at first co-edited *Lucifer* but it was a very asymmetrical partnership and Collins was soon pushed out, and Besant pulled in.

[16] See *HMA* 2: 109–11, and Hoecker-Drysdale (1992: 70–1).

Table 1.1 Some significant journals that are relevant to this book

Journal	Established	Orientation	Estimated circulation	Frequency
Edinburgh Review	1802	Liberal	13,500 by 1818; 7,000 by 1860	Quarterly
Monthly Repository	1806	Radical, Unitarian	Max. 1,250	Monthly
Quarterly Review	1809	Conservative	8,000 by 1860	Quarterly
Blackwood's Magazine	1817	Conservative	7,500 by 1868	Monthly
Westminster Review	1824	Radical	4,000 by 1860	Quarterly
Fraser's Magazine	1830	Progressive/liberal	8,000 by 1860	Monthly
Saturday Review	1855	Conservative	20,000 by 1870	Weekly
Macmillan's Magazine	1859	Liberal	20,000 by 1860	Monthly
Cornhill Magazine	1860	Liberal, cultural-literary	100,000 in 1860, falling to 10,000–20,000	Monthly
Fortnightly Review	1865	Liberal, secular	3,000 by 1865	Fortnightly, then monthly from 1867
Englishwoman's Review	1866	Feminist	1,000	Monthly
Contemporary Review	1866	Broad Church	4,000 by 1870	Monthly
Nature	1869	Scientific	5,000 by 1870	Weekly
Mind	1876	Philosophical	unknown	Quarterly
The Nineteenth Century	1877	Secular	20,000 in 1877	Monthly
The Theosophist	1879	Theosophical	800 by 1880	Monthly
The Zoophilist	1881	Anti-vivisection	unknown	Monthly
Our Corner	1883	Secularist, cultural	500	Monthly
Lucifer	1887	Theosophical	unknown	Monthly

Source: Compiled from Brake and Demoor (2009), Cox (2005), Ellegård (1971), Morrison (2008), Hamilton (2015), Hanbery MacKay (2009), Levine (1990), Schroeder (2012), Sutherland (1986), and Tucker et al. (2020).

Table 1.2 Indicative list of journals in which women discussed in this book published

Shepherd	*Fraser's*
Martineau	*Monthly Repository, The Athenaeum, Westminster Review, Leader, Edinburgh Review, Daily News* (leader writer), *Cornhill*
Lovelace	*Scientific Memoirs*
Eliot	*Westminster Review* (inc. as co-editor), *Pall Mall Gazette, Leader, Blackwood's, Fraser's, Saturday Review, Fortnightly Review*
Cobbe	*Quarterly Review, Fraser's, Macmillan's, Leader, Cornhill, Theological Review, Fortnightly Review, Contemporary Review, Modern Review, The Zoophilist* (inc. as editor), *The Echo* (as leader writer)
Blavatsky	*The Theosophist* (inc. as editor), *Lucifer* (inc. as co-editor), *Light, Le Lotus, The Spiritualist*
Wedgwood	*Macmillan's, Westminster Review, Spectator, Contemporary Review, Cornhill, British Quarterly Review, National Review*
Welby	*Mind, Monist, Fortnightly Review, Church Quarterly Review, Journal of the Anthropological Institute*
Buckley	*Macmillan's, University Magazine*
Besant	*National Reformer* (inc. as co-editor), *Our Corner* (inc. as editor), *The Link* (inc. as co-editor), *Lucifer* (inc. as co-editor)
Lee	*Fraser's, New Quarterly Magazine, Contemporary Review, Fortnightly Review, Cornhill*
Naden	*Our Corner, Journal of Science, Knowledge, Agnostic Annual, Proceedings of the Aristotelian Society*

Note: I exclude any post-1900 publication outlets.

Westminster Review with John Chapman in the early 1850s, she (unlike Chapman) did so anonymously.[17]

By 1900, then, Britain had a far more diverse and pluralistic journal culture than in 1800. Mainstream general journals like the *Contemporary Review* and *Nineteenth Century* retained a big influence, but against an increasingly variegated surrounding landscape. The culture was becoming more fragmented, with members of specific groupings beginning to talk primarily to one another rather than to the culture at large. This had its positive side. The earlier culture rested on the masculine, upper-class voice of reasoned authority, the 'man of reason'. To that extent the fragmentation of print culture was a democratic development, giving voice to different identities. Yet women had been able to speak in the earlier voice of the 'man of reason', even if anonymously or pseudonymously (like Eliot), while

---

[17] On Eliot's role at the *Westminster*, see, inter alia, Gray (2000) and Haight (1969). A few of the other women who edited journals in the period were: Christian Isobel Johnstone, *Tait's Edinburgh Magazine* (1834–46); Eliza Cook, *Eliza Cook's Journal* (1849–54; Cook, exceptionally, was also working class); Bessie Rayner Parkes, *English Woman's Journal* (1858–64); and Jessie Boucherett, *Englishwoman's Review* (1866–70).

the new specialist venues and cultures brought their own forms of exclusion. Indeed, in this chapter I will argue that academic specialization took sexist exclusion to a new level. The story was not one of unidirectional progress.

Periodicals and books existed in symbiotic relation, for much of the content of journals was book reviews. But this was not the book review as we now know it. Nineteenth-century book reviews were often essay-reviews—long articles of ten thousand-plus words responding to a book with the reviewing author's own take on the issue.[18] An example is Cobbe's 'Darwinism in Morals', a twelve-thousand-word critique of the supposedly disastrous moral consequences of Darwin's evolutionary account of the moral sentiments. In short, the essay/review boundary was porous. This porous form was established initially by the *Edinburgh Review*, which simultaneously created 'a new figure in print culture: the professional critic' (Ferris 2012)—a figure that Martineau, Eliot, Cobbe, Julia Wedgwood, and Vernon Lee made their own.

Written forms were permeable in other ways too. Some books were translations, such as Eliot's translation of Feuerbach and Martineau's of Comte. Some essays were translations, as with Lovelace's translation of Menabrea's essay on the analytical engine; Lovelace's translation came with her extensive commentary, including her philosophical reflections on artificial intelligence (as we now call it). Similarly, Martineau's 'free and condensed' Comte translation was framed by her Preface envisioning the beneficial moral effects of positivism and giving it a distinctly British-empiricist spin as the 'philosophy of fact' (*HMA* 3: 323).[19] Thus 'original' analysis and argument, and 'secondary' translation and reviewing and commentary, blurred together.

Two final forms of writing that deserve mention are pamphlets and letters. Pamphlets or 'tracts' were essays or talks published as free-standing works, often for campaigning and persuasive purposes, as with Besant's secularist pamphlets and later her theosophical and anti-imperialist ones. These essays were often published by the same presses that brought out socialist, feminist, or anti-establishment journals.

As for letters, the typical middle-to-upper-class European woman of the time maintained a very extensive correspondence, not only with friends and family on personal matters, but frequently discussing substantial intellectual topics. Letters could therefore be a form of philosophical writing in their own right. Victoria Welby used them for this purpose to perfection. She exchanged hundreds of letters discussing meaning, language, and other philosophical topics with—amongst others—Bergson, Besant, Mary Everest Boole, Lee, Max Müller, Charles Peirce, Bertrand Russell, Spencer, John Tyndall, Mrs Humphry Ward, and Wedgwood

---

[18] Furthermore, there was a gradual shift from the pre-Victorian 'review-like essay' to the Victorian-era 'essay-like review' (Shattock 1989: 104–24; Robinson 2000: 168–9).

[19] On Martineau's version of positivism in the Preface, see Hoecker-Drysdale (2001).

(see Petrilli 2015: 77). Welby used correspondence to develop and test out her theory of meaning and expand it to accommodate the insights of others. Welby was not unique in using letters philosophically. Because letters counted as 'private', they were seen as an appropriate medium for women, and have been an important vehicle for women's philosophizing over the centuries (see Hannan 2016). Nineteenth-century women took advantage of correspondence to maintain intellectual networks and sometimes prolong conversations begun at the dinner parties that were a mainstay of bourgeois social life in this period. For although women's supposed domestic role obstructed them from being part of learned associations and societies, the same role ruled women *in* to these informal social gatherings based in homes, thereby giving them access to intellectual conversations after all.[20] The home, then, was in fact not unequivocally 'private' but could be a hub of debate; similarly, neither were letters entirely private. They were not infrequently read by and circulated amongst groups of people of varying sizes, and were often written in the knowledge that they might be widely shared and enter the public domain. Their ambiguous status is registered in Martineau's anxious insistence that her correspondents should destroy her letters. As Deborah Logan (2007) argues, Martineau was so adamant about the sanctity of her private letters *because* she was aware that they were always liable to become public—not least because she used letters as the basis or format of her *Letters on Mesmerism*, 'Letter to the Deaf', *Letters from Ireland*, and *Letters on the Laws of Man's Nature and Development*.

We have surveyed the main written forms that women used. The reader might be thinking: very well, but what has all this to do with philosophy? The answer is that for most of the nineteenth century periodicals, books, literature, and letters were where philosophical debate happened. That debate had a distinctive character compared to what came later: it was *generalist*. Philosophy of mind is a case in point. Before *Mind*, the Aristotelian Society (founded in 1880),[21] and other specialist venues were created, the broader periodical culture and republic of letters was the site for philosophical discussion of mind and psychology, often called 'mental science' or 'mental philosophy'. For instance, the periodicals amply discussed phrenology; this included some vehement criticism of Martineau's pro-phrenology stance in *Letters on the Laws of Man's Nature and Development* (1851). In this generalist setting the mind was addressed along with religious concerns around the soul and free will, on the one hand, and scientific discoveries

---

[20] As Leonore Davidoff showed, 'with the decline of public places of amusement for respectable families, dinner became the apogee of the social day' (1973: 47). Hence the proliferation of advice manuals for hosting and attending dinner parties, most famously Mrs Beeton's *Household Management* (Beeton 1861: ch. 40). From Beeton's and other such manuals, we learn that these parties might involve up to twenty people at a time, and that convention prescribed that husbands and wives must be invited together, so that women were generally present (see Jameson 1987 and Meir 2005).

[21] Incidentally, the Aristotelian Society explicitly included women.

about the brain and nervous system, on the other. Thus the mind was tackled not as a stand-alone topic but in connection with questions spanning metaphysics, epistemology, ethics, and religion. Accordingly, scholars from several 'disciplines' debated one another: theologians, moralists, literary critics, and physiologists, who were not yet demarcated from psychologists. One did not need to be a philosopher to discuss the mind—or to be an academic or have a degree at all.[22]

In short, women could participate in philosophical debates because the kind of philosophy that print culture sustained was generalist. However, one might ask: since women were barred from many learned societies and associations, were there no comparable barriers to women publishing in books, journals, pamphlets, and so on? Yes and no. Authors were generally expected to be men, and there was no shortage of people who believed women had no place in print. Yet some women—for instance Martineau, Eliot, and Cobbe—made their way to the heart of book and journal culture. The inroads these three made into the republic of letters show that women could get around expectations about male authorship. Let's consider these three women in turn.

Martineau laid the seeds of her subsequent reputation with many anonymous and pseudonymous articles in the Unitarian journal the *Monthly Repository* in the 1820s, before being catapulted to fame by her *Illustrations of Political Economy* of 1832–4. Her views and presence were now coveted by politicians, writers, and intellectuals of all stripes. In 1843 Elizabeth Barrett Browning called her 'the profoundest woman thinker in England', a widely shared assessment.[23] Martineau took advantage of her celebrity to write books in many forms and genres alongside a steady stream of agenda-setting journal articles, particularly in the *Westminster Review* and then the *Edinburgh Review*. By invitation, she wrote the widely read two-volume *History of the Thirty Years' Peace, 1816–1846* (1849–51) and was a leader writer for the *Daily News* from 1852 to 1866 (a liberal newspaper founded by Dickens in 1846). Her 1,642 leaders covered 'an astonishing range of subjects':[24] nursing, the Crimean War, the American Civil War, Ireland, British rule in India, 'juvenile delinquency', women's rights, and education, to mention just a few.

Eliot, as anonymous co-editor of the *Westminster Review* in the early 1850s, was a core member of the intellectual circle which centred around her co-editor, the radical publisher John Chapman, and which included Martineau, Mill, and Spencer (see Ashton 2006). Through her editorial role and her many *Westminster Review* articles, Eliot influenced informed liberal and radical thinking to a degree

---

[22] As Webb says, 'early Victorian culture was resolutely amateur' (1960: 245). And not only early Victorian: Brian Harrison notes an 1871 *Fortnightly Review* issue featuring Mill on Berkeley, Huxley on 'administrative nihilism', Henry Fawcett on British politics, Walter Pater on Michelangelo, fiction by Anthony Trollope, and Andrieu Jules on the Paris Commune (Harrison 1973).

[23] Browning to Hugh Stuart Boyd, 6 September 1843, in Kelley and Hudson (1984–91): vol. 7: 317.

[24] As Hoecker-Drysdale puts it (1992: 133–4).

that probably no other woman besides Martineau had previously achieved. Eliot co-authored the journal's influential editorial 'Prospectus' of 1852, which not only shaped the *Review*'s subsequent direction but also, by formulating the 'Law of Progress', crystallized what became the prevailing Victorian view of history, on which society is gradually and inexorably progressing towards greater civilization and prosperity.

> The fundamental principle of the work [the *Westminster Review*] will be the recognition of the Law of Progress:... attempts at reform... should be directed and animated by an advancing ideal, [so] the Editors will maintain a steady comparison of the actual with the possible, as the most powerful stimulus to improvement. (*PWR* 4)

The same 'Law of Progress' informed the panoramic vision most fully realized in Eliot's *Middlemarch* on which society is an evolving organic whole, individuals are its members, and their actions the incremental steps by which the whole advances along its way.

Cobbe's first book, the anonymous *Essay on Intuitive Morals* (1855–7), was followed by *Broken Lights: An Inquiry into the Present Condition and Future Prospects of Religious Faith* (1864). The latter, coming hot on the heels of powerful journal articles on welfare reform, animal rights, and feminism, cemented Cobbe's name; *Intuitive Morals* was now reissued with Cobbe's signature. Like Martineau a generation before, Cobbe ran with the publishing opportunities that now opened to her. She published dozens of articles in, amongst others, *Fraser's*, *Macmillan's*, the *Theological Review*, *Contemporary Review*, and *Cornhill*—that is, most of the leading later-century periodicals. She combined this with regular newspaper contributions, from 1868 to 1875 serving as leader writer for the London daily *Echo*. This allowed her to reach an even wider public than Martineau, for the *Echo*'s circulation soon reached one hundred thousand, whereas the ever-struggling *Daily News* had only ever managed around five thousand.

Martineau, Eliot, and Cobbe all adeptly used print media to philosophize. To be sure, not all their written output was philosophy: Eliot of course excelled at fiction, and both Cobbe and Martineau wrote a substantial amount of popular journalism. Indeed the last two have been celebrated as pioneering female 'journalists', trail-blazers opening the profession to women.[25] But they were not 'journalists' in the modern sense. Today, journalists write in newspapers and magazines whereas academics publish in specialist journals. In the nineteenth century this divide did

---

[25] Speaking to the Institute of Journalists in 1894, Catherine Drew praised three 'exceptional women,...[who] contributed to the best leading journals of the day able reviews of scientific, philosophical and literary books'—the three being Martineau, Cobbe, and Caroline Norton (Anonymous 1894: 31). For further discussion, see Hamilton (2012).

not yet exist. Newspapers and journals shaded into one another and, because the culture was generalist, to write a journal article *was* to make an academic contribution. Thus many of Martineau's and Cobbe's journal articles—and books—were philosophical, as were some of Eliot's many anonymous journal articles.

This point applies beyond these three women. Many other writers of the time, including such men as George Henry Lewes and Richard Holt Hutton, are likewise retrospectively classed as 'journalists', even though much of their work is philosophical and seamlessly crosses the divide between shorter, popular, more immediate response-pieces and longer, more in-depth and rigorously argued essays. They were 'journalists' only in that they published widely in the periodicals, this being the normal meaning of 'journalist' for most of the nineteenth century[26]—as Matthew Rubery remarks, 'By no means have literature and journalism always been thought of as distinct entities. The separation of the two discourses into the conceptual categories with which we are accustomed today transpired during the 19th century' (2010: 295). The separation began to emerge when Matthew Arnold condemned the emerging form, 'new journalism', as mere ephemeral, unreflective news reporting, contrasting it with the older thoughtful kind of periodical writing (Arnold 1887), which has since come to be called 'higher journalism'.[27] As Brake and Demoor put it, then, 'In Victorian Britain amateurs in higher journalism filled the space occupied today by academic intellectuals' (2009: 148). Yet unintentionally their comment shows the limitations of the category 'higher journalism'—it inevitably suggests that however 'high' someone's journalism may rise, ultimately it remains only journalism, 'amateur' and dilettanteish, not serious academic work. This categorization is therefore part of why figures like Lewes and Hutton—as well as Martineau and Cobbe—have been omitted from the history of philosophy.

To go back to the publishing careers of Martineau, Eliot, and Cobbe, one might press the question, *how* did they make such inroads into journal and book culture if it was expected that the 'man of reason' should literally be a man? These three women used several strategies to circumvent this expectation, strategies that other women employed too. Let us look at these strategies.

1.3 Women's Participation Strategies

(1) *'Popularization'*. In the obituary Martineau wrote for herself when she mistakenly expected to die soon, she renounced any claim to originality. '[S]he could

---

[26] See 'journalist, n.' *Oxford English Dictionary*, December 2021.
[27] One finds the epithet 'higher journalist' applied to Lewes and Hutton (e.g. by Tjoa 1978: Preface and 1), amongst others including Cobbe (e.g. by Hughes 2009). On the history of the category of 'higher journalism', see Walker (2018). The Victorians themselves regarded Hutton as an important theological thinker and literary critic (see Fulton 2016); I touch on his views on the mind briefly in Chapter 3 (and see also Stone 2022b: ch. 5).

popularize, while she could neither discover nor invent' (*HMA* 2: 572–3). Her *Illustrations* had made political economy accessible to the mass of people, and that was her forte, or so she claimed. Cobbe too described her first book, *Intuitive Morals*, as a popularization of Kant (*IM* x), although it actually set out Cobbe's own moral theory in which Kantianism was only one strand. 'Popularization' was a screen that women used; behind it, they covertly did original theorizing, while escaping the censure this might bring down on them were it openly proclaimed. For women were often thought to be incapable of having original creative thoughts. The period was heir to the Romantic ideology on which only men could produce and originate while women could merely reproduce and copy.[28] Popularizing the ideas of 'great men' was therefore deemed appropriate for female authors.[29] Even at the end of the century, Wedgwood still presented her collection of review-essays, *Nineteenth-Century Teachers* (1909), not as showing her own wide-ranging intellect at work but as handing down the wisdom of eminent men—only two of these essays being on women (namely Eliot and Martineau).[30]

(2) *Translating and educating*. 'Popularizing' men's ideas shaded into translating, editing, and commenting on them, all deemed suitably 'reproductive' enterprises for women. Martineau translated Comte; Eliot translated Strauss, Feuerbach, and Spinoza; Cobbe edited the multi-volume edition of the works of the American transcendentalist theologian Theodore Parker. Yet these were more significant enterprises than the notion of 'reproduction' captures. Martineau's translation of Comte was crucial for bringing positivism into Britain (see Wilson 2019); Eliot's Strauss and Feuerbach translations were important not only for disseminating German religious criticism but also for transmitting German thought into Britain more broadly (Ashton 1980);[31] and Cobbe's editorial work too furthered engagement with American philosophy. Translation thus widened the ambit of British intellectual life, while remaining relatively acceptable for women. Reciprocally, popularizing could be seen as translating complex ideas into the language of the people. And both popularization and translation shaded into education, deemed appropriate for women given their social role of providing care and education to the young. Martineau styled herself an educator of the people and Arabella Buckley portrayed herself as educating children about

---

[28] The classic critical analysis of this ideology is by Battersby (1989). That said, Romanticism was more multifaceted than this, and some women Romantics were influential in their time, such as Joanna Baillie, Felicia Hemans, and Mary Robinson (see e.g. Wilson and Haefner 1994). Their achievements co-existed in some tension with the association of genius with maleness, as when Byron remarked of Baillie in 1817: '"the composition of a tragedy requires *testicles*" [according to Voltaire]. If this be true, lord knows what Joanna Baillie does – I suppose she borrows them' (Byron 1976: 203).

[29] For further discussion with reference to Martineau, see David (1987: part one).

[30] 'The Moral Influence of George Eliot' [1881] (*NCT* 225–41), and 'Invalids' [1878] (*NCT* 347–53). The latter is on Martineau's memoir of illness *Life in the Sick-Room*, which Wedgwood considered Martineau's best work.

[31] Anna Jameson and Sarah Austin were also important in the transmission of German thought; see Johns (2014) and Johnston (1997).

contemporary science, although in private she said that her work was only 'elementary in [the] sense that I explain as I go' (*GFP*, AB to Garnett, 27 June 1886).

(3) *'Writing'*. Martineau, Eliot, and Cobbe were all celebrated as 'writers', a catch-all term applied to nearly all intellectual women of the time. The label worked partly because many women wrote fiction as well as non-fiction: besides her didactic political economy tales, Martineau wrote the novel *Deerbrook* (1839); Wedgwood wrote two novels before abandoning literature; Ward came to fame with the best-selling novel of ideas *Robert Elsmere* (1888); Naden published poems as well as philosophy. Admittedly, authoring rather than reading literature was still somewhat questionable, hence the male pseudonyms used by among others Currer, Ellis, and Acton Bell—that is, Charlotte, Emily, and Anne Brontë. But literature remained more open to women than philosophy, so it was easier to expand the category 'writer' to incorporate women who wrote philosophy than to expand the category 'philosopher' to admit women.

(4) *Women's moral authority*. Another strategy that women used drew on the idea of women's special moral vocation. Hannah More was the key source of this idea, which received another influential statement from the Rousseauian Sarah Lewis (anonymously) in *Woman's Mission* (1839). For Lewis, women have a special vocation for the moral regeneration and education of others. But women can only properly discharge this vocation within the home, otherwise the exigencies of public life will degrade women's qualities and their regenerative potential will be ruined. Thus Lewis invoked women's moral superiority to justify confining them to the home.

However, some women turned these ideas around to say that given women's moral superiority they must speak and write in the public sphere, imparting their moral wisdom to society at large.[32] Thus Martineau, Eliot, and Cobbe ardently defended morality. Martineau's first published essays of 1822–3, signed 'Discipulus', were on the conservative Hannah More, the radical Enlightenment philosopher Anna Letitia Barbauld, and the case for women's education. By placing herself under the sign of More *and* Barbauld, Martineau tacitly signalled what she was doing: speaking publicly for progressive causes (like Barbauld) based on her moral authority as a woman (like More).[33] Eliot, too, aimed to defend morality by retrieving its truly secular basis, hidden within the religious

---

[32] Thus, as I remarked in the Introduction, ideas of 'woman's mission' could be used *for* women as well as against them; see also Colley (2009: ch. 6, esp. 262–72) and Vickery (1993: 400–1).

[33] Specifically, in 'Female Writers on Practical Divinity' Martineau argued that More and Barbauld shared a heartfelt commitment to moral principle, which showed that religion is at root moral rather than doctrinal. In 'Female Education' Martineau reprised arguments in its favour made by Wollstonecraft without mentioning the latter's name; in 1820s England, Wollstonecraft was *persona non grata* due to her support for the French Revolution and her notorious personal life. Martineau went along with the consensus that Wollstonecraft had let her ideas down by being an excessively passionate character (HM to Georgina Cavendish, 16 and 21 October 1833, *HMCL* 1: 220–1, 228). In her *Autobiography*, Martineau reiterated that Wollstonecraft was not 'a safe example, nor... a successful champion of Woman and her rights' (*HMA* 1: 303; in full, see 1: 301–3).

framework that had now become indefensible. And Cobbe defended morality against the threats that she thought it faced (*contra* Eliot) from secularism, atheism, and agnosticism—and indeed from Darwinism, utilitarianism, science, and a host of other dangers.

Martineau, Eliot, and Cobbe exemplify a tendency for virtually all nineteenth-century philosophical women to defend morality. The position taken by Nietzsche, of being a critic of morality, was not readily available to women. If women undermined morality, they took away one of the main grounds on which they could intervene in public debates, as upholders of moral standards. For whereas women's epistemic authority remained doubtful and contested, their *moral* authority was widely accepted because of separate spheres ideology. Moral authority could be used as a platform to broader cognitive authority, but women could access that latter authority only as moralists and not as immoralists, amoralists, or anti-moralists. Severe penalties could fall on women deemed to be undermining public morals, as Besant found when she was tried for publishing the birth-control pamphlet, despite her insistence that she was acting in the service of morality.[34]

(5) *Social and political reform*. A related strategy was to philosophize in connection with political campaigns and movements for social reform—for instance, arguing against slavery or vivisection, for birth control or women's rights, for the repeal of the Contagious Diseases Acts or welfare reform. This strategy, again, ultimately drew on the appeal to women's moral vocation and the idea that society needed the benefit of women's moral wisdom.

Arguing against slavery could provide an entry-point into philosophical debates for black women, as we see with Sarah Parker Remond. Originally from Massachusetts, Remond toured England and Ireland in 1859 arguing for abolition. She refuted the view that black Americans were not yet ready for freedom because they were either too uncivilized, or too brutalized by their enslavement, or both. In an 1862 paper that was informed by her 1859 speeches, Remond maintained:

> [T]he process of degradation upon this deeply injured race has been slow and constant, but effective. The real capacities of the negro race have never been thoroughly tested; and until they are placed in a position to be influenced by the civilizing influences which surround freedom, it is really unjust to apply to them the same test, or to expect them to attain the same standard of excellence, as if a fair opportunity had been given to develop their faculties. ([1862] 1942: 218)

Remond was drawing on the republican tradition in political thought, specifically the idea that relations of domination and their 'dreadful and despotic influence'

---

[34] Besant spoke in her own defence: see Manvell (1976) and, for a more critical discussion, Janssen (2017).

produce vices of character (see Loewenberg and Bogin 1976: 248). If we make it a condition of a person having liberty that they already possess the character traits of a free person, then we will trap them in perpetual unfreedom. People need social and political liberty first if they are ever to achieve the virtues of freedom of character. Only once black Americans were free from domination, therefore, would they be able to reach their potential.

However, Remond crucially added, domination produces even worse vices in the dominating class: 'With all the demoralizing influences by which they are surrounded, they [the slaves] still retain far more of that which is humanizing than their masters' ([1862] 1942: 218). This point enabled Remond to claim that when she spoke as a 'representative' of enslaved Americans she did so with greater humanity and moral authority than slave-owners and their spokespeople (Loewenberg and Bogin 1976: 242).[35] Indeed, she said, she advocated abolition based on the 'broad, comprehensive, and intelligible principle of that mutual love and charity which ought to exist amongst fellow-beings' (245), and which had existed amongst the early Christians but which many supposed Christians today utterly failed to practise (Moynagh and Forestell 2011: 46). True Christian virtues were incompatible with the 'system of slavery and the immorality it engenders' (47). Remond was laying claim to the moral and spiritual authority that qualified her to speak and do so in public. This brings us to the next strategy.

(6) *Religious and spiritual authority.* This strategy was to philosophize about religious and spiritual questions from a standpoint of committed belief. Blavatsky conceived theosophy to be at once spiritual *and* philosophical. Cobbe's reputation was cemented by *Broken Lights*, in which she defended Theism, her rationally reconstructed, humane, and optimistic version of Christianity. Even Martineau, who became infamous for atheism, started off very devout, only gradually parting from Unitarian Christianity over twenty years. Across these women's differences, the overall strategy was to philosophize from *within* an outlook that was either religious (Theosophical, Unitarian, Theist, etc.) or post- or anti-religious (secularist, agnostic, atheist, etc.). This strategy made sense because women's moral vocation was usually taken to be spiritual at the same time, sincere morality and religious piety being assumed to form a piece. This assumption that morality and religion were inextricable became disputed later in the century, and some women—including Martineau, Eliot, Lee, Naden, and Besant (in her secularist phase)—insisted that morality needed to be extricated from religious distortions. But they still made this case in a setting where, as women, they were accorded special authority on the religion–morality nexus.

(7) *Diverse sectors of print culture.* As we have seen, late in the century periodicals, printing presses, and publishing companies became increasingly

---

[35] I rely on detailed press reports of Remond's talks in Dublin (Loewenberg and Bogin 1976: 238–49) and Warrington in Lancashire (Moynagh and Forestell 2011: 46–7).

diverse—culturally, politically, and in respect of religion and belief. Martineau, Eliot, and Cobbe rose to prominence within mainstream book and periodical culture, but some later-century figures like Besant made their names within left-of-field secularist and socialist circles. For example, besides editing *Our Corner*, Besant co-edited the secularist *National Reformer* from 1874 to 1885 and then founded and co-edited the short-lived socialist weekly *The Link* in 1888. Its mission statement came from Victor Hugo: 'I will speak for the dumb. I will speak of the small to the great and the feeble to the strong... I will speak for all the despairing silent ones.' This was a far cry from the claim of the mainstream journals to speak with the voice of respectable, reasonable, reputable authority. Reflecting this diversification of journal culture, Cobbe transitioned from the mainstream press into the new more radical terrain, once her uncompromising anti-vivisectionism had estranged her from many established journals. She now began to publish in anti-vivisection journals like the two she founded, *The Zoophilist* (1881–96) and *The Abolitionist* (1899–1949).

(8) Women's final strategy was to take advantage of conventions around *anonymous and pseudonymous publication*. This issue is sufficiently complex that it deserves its own section, which comes next.

To recapitulate so far, nineteenth-century women faced various formal barriers and exclusions from intellectual life, but the vibrancy and diversity of print culture worked in their favour. This enabled women to be part of philosophical debates, because those debates took place in the generalist setting that book and periodical culture sustained. To be sure, patriarchal expectations obtained in print culture too, but women developed strategies to get around them. The overall result is that women were constrained participants in philosophical debate: they took part, but did so using particular strategies that both reflected and subversively reappropriated aspects of separate spheres ideology.

1.4 Anonymity and Signature in Nineteenth-Century British Writing

A hallmark of nineteenth-century British prose writing is that much of it was published anonymously. This, too, was both enabling and constraining for women.

The convention for all types of publication to bear the author's signature only came in within Britain over the course of the eighteenth and nineteenth centuries. Between 1750 and 1850, over 80 per cent of fiction was published anonymously or pseudonymously: Jane Austen's first two novels, respectively 'by a lady' and 'by the author of *Sense and Sensibility*', are just two well-known examples. Although signatures were more common by the nineteenth century, anonymity remained unexceptional—*Frankenstein*, for example, came out anonymously in 1818. Likewise it was not unusual for non-fiction books to be anonymous: viz.

Locke's *Two Treatises*, Hume's *Treatise*, Paine's *Common Sense*, Wollstonecraft's *Vindication of the Rights of Men*. As these examples show, anonymity gave authors the protection to express controversial religious and political views, and it protected women from the charge that they should not be writing or publishing at all. However, by 1800, most non-fiction books appeared signed, to advertise the author's authority and credibility. A female name, though, was liable to undercut the author's authority. Thus women who published philosophical books remained disproportionately likely, right through the nineteenth century, to remain anonymous, use pseudonyms, or use their initials instead of given names.

Non-fiction journal articles, in any case, were standardly anonymous right through to the 1860s and beyond (unlike fiction in journals, which was usually signed). The principle of anonymity was established, as with many features of nineteenth-century British periodicals, by the *Edinburgh Review*, all of whose contributions remained anonymous right up to 1912. The editors of the first volume of the Wellesley Index to Victorian Periodicals estimated that until 1870, 97 per cent of articles were anonymous.[36] Change came through *Macmillan's*, the *Fortnightly* and *Contemporary Reviews*, and then *The Nineteenth Century*, 'pioneers in... the theory and practice of personalized criticism' (Brake and Demoor 2009: 19). The theory was that the author's signature vouched for their unique standpoint and critical acumen. Signature began to replace anonymity in journal essays and anonymity gradually came to look old-fashioned. All of this confirms Foucault's ([1969] 1998) point that the 'author function' is a contingent social construction and not a necessary condition of writing. Of course there were real living individuals holding the pens; but we do not necessarily have to group, read, and classify essays in terms of their authors. In the earlier nineteenth century the authority of journal articles derived not from the author's individual identity, but from the common identity of the respectable, reliable, authoritative 'man of letters', of which the editor's name stood as a pledge.[37]

How did this bear on women? All twelve of the women discussed in this book published at least some work anonymously, often their earliest work, for example:

Their first books, for instance Mary Shepherd's *Essay upon the Relation of Cause and Effect*, Martineau's *Devotional Exercises* ('by a Lady'), Cobbe's *Intuitive Morals*, Welby's *Links and Clues* (by 'Vita')—although Shepherd, Martineau,

---

[36] We are all indebted to the huge work of those involved in the Wellesley Index to Victorian Periodicals and its successor the Curran Index for providing an index to many authors and pseudonyms; for an introduction and starting point, see Wellesley Index (2006–21). Without their efforts many of women's periodical contributions would have been lost and projects like this book would scarcely be possible.

[37] Ironically, while ample scholarship exists on Kierkegaard's complex 'authorship' and on the early German Romantic idea of *Symphilosophie* (collaborative philosophizing), celebrating these radical experiments with authorship, lack of signature was in the same period absolutely mainstream and accepted in British philosophy, yet this fact has attracted virtually no philosophical analysis or attention.

and Cobbe all published their subsequent books signed once their reputations were established, and Welby went over to using 'V. Welby'.

Their earliest articles: Martineau's 1820s essays in the *Monthly Repository* were either signed 'Discipulus' or 'V' or were unsigned; Lovelace's translation and commentary on the analytical engine was initialled 'A. A. L.' (for 'Augusta Ada Lovelace'); Eliot's Strauss translation and her many contributions to the *Westminster Review* and *Leader* were unsigned, although this reflected these journals' policies (Martineau's *Westminster* and *Edinburgh Review* contributions of the 1850s and 1860s were likewise unsigned); Wedgwood's earliest articles, in *Macmillan's*, were unsigned, and so were her many contributions to the *Spectator*; and some of Besant's early pamphlets of the 1870s—for example on euthanasia, the existence of God, and rationalism—were anonymous, or even 'by the wife of a beneficed clergyman' in the ironic case of her 1873 pamphlet arguing against the divinity of Jesus Christ.

A contrasting case is Blavatsky's numerous unsigned contributions to *Lucifer* in the late 1880s. This is different because her name was on the cover as co-editor (at first alongside that of Mabel Collins, who was effectively her assistant). Any unsigned material was presumptively by Blavatsky. Whereas Blavatsky could advertise her editorial role in the 1880s, Eliot could not when she co-edited the *Westminster Review* in the 1850s: back then, a woman's name could not guarantee the editorial authority that stood in place of signatures on contributions. Once signed contributions became the norm, it became correspondingly more acceptable for women to serve as named editors, because the full burden of authority no longer rested on the editor's shoulders anyway.

The rise of signature presented women with a dilemma. Cobbe embraced signature, with almost all her work after *Intuitive Morals* appearing signed; she gladly assumed the mantle of a moral and religious authority. Most of Martineau's work after the *Illustrations* had made her famous was signed, as were Wedgwood's many essays in the *Contemporary Review* from the 1870s onwards, for by then she ranked as a reputable authority and guide. Less well-established women held on to what degree of anonymity they could. Buckley initialled her 1870s journal articles 'A. B.'—whereas she published her popular science books signed, a female name being perfectly legitimate on books cast as popularizing the discoveries of male scientists. Naden usually signed her philosophical essays 'C. N.' or 'C. A.' (short for her pseudonym 'Constance Arden'), although after she died, her fellow hylo-idealists issued her *Induction and Deduction*, *Further Reliques*, and *Complete Poetical Works* under her name. Blavatsky, for all her notoriety, still ideally preferred 'H. P. B.' or (as on the cover of *Lucifer*) 'H. P. Blavatsky', and Lee of course used 'Vernon Lee' almost without exception.[38] Welby used 'V. Welby', except for 'Meaning and Metaphor' which was signed with her full name.

---

[38] Otherwise 'V. Paget', e.g. in Paget (1883).

Until recently it has been assumed that anonymous or pseudonymous publication by women is undesirable, reflecting a patriarchal climate in which women dare not speak out in their authentic voices. But lately scholars have revisited and qualified this assessment, because the vast majority of men's journal output at the time was anonymous too, and because anonymity versus signature was anyway contentious and unsettled.[39] On the one hand, anonymity presupposed that the author was a reliable member of the community of like-minded men of letters. On the other hand, anonymity offered protection, allowing authors to speak more freely than they otherwise could in times when accusations of religious heterodoxy or excessive radicalism could close doors and destroy reputations. Anonymity meant that anyone could write critical reviews of works by big names—a cat could look at a king. Others objected to anonymity precisely *because* it permitted nobodies to criticize somebodies; they demanded that authors have the courage to put their names to their opinions. This overlooked the fact that some groups, such as women, had to pay a higher price for doing so. As Alexis Easley (2004) observes, then, anonymity, pseudonymity, and initials enabled women to intervene in debates free from the adverse judgements they could otherwise face as women. This protective factor is why many women held on to aspects of anonymity right through the century. Eliot held to the masculine pseudonym she had adopted in the later 1850s even after her real identity was known.[40] Likewise, Lee held on to her pseudonym and indeed called herself Vernon privately as well as publicly.

The issue of signature versus anonymity is a microcosm of women's constrained philosophical participation. Women could participate, and anonymity facilitated this—but by enabling women to conceal their femininity. Even when it was common knowledge that an author was a woman, as with Blavatsky, it remained wise to assume a neutral persona when writing (i.e. 'H. P. B.' or 'H. P. Blavatsky'). Epistemic authority remained presumptively masculine, even when everyone knew that the one taking up the authoritative voice was a woman.

Anonymity and its variations affected how readily women's interventions could be taken up, responded to, and remembered by others. As I mentioned in the Introduction, in the nineteenth century one did not usually spell out, footnote, or document all one's references to other writers, which were often left vague, allusive, or imprecise. This was for numerous reasons. As we can see from the fact that anonymity was normal, for much of this period claims, ideas, and writings were regarded not so much as the property of individual authors who must be given credit, but more as belonging to a common stock upon which everyone could draw. Because intellectual writing was not yet professionalized, the demands that all intellectual debts be scrupulously acknowledged and all claims

---

[39] Amongst those reappraising anonymity more positively, see Buurma (2007), Drew (2017), Easley (2004), and Onslow (2000).

[40] On the complexities of Eliot's names, see Gatens (2008).

rigorously verified were not yet in force. References could also be left unstated because readers and authors were assumed to belong to the same community of like-minded 'men of letters'; it could be taken for granted that one's readership knew whom one was referring to. Finally, the paucity of references flowed directly from the predominance of anonymity, for one could hardly reference an author by name when their work was published anonymously in the first place. The convention instead was to say, for example, 'A writer in the *Edinburgh Review* (no. 1)' or 'the author of "article X"' or 'the writer known as "A. B."'.

The sparing use of notes and references had different effects for women and men. Consider Thomas Henry Huxley's essay 'Mr. Darwin's Critics' (1871) defending Darwin against Alfred Russel Wallace and G. J. Mivart but saying nothing of Cobbe, a striking omission because Wallace, Mivart, *and* Cobbe were the three authors whose reviews of *Descent of Man* Darwin had invited.[41] Thus sometimes an author went unnamed because they were 'one of us' ('we all know who we are'), sometimes because they were *not* one of us and it would degrade the present author to mention them openly. Additionally, men and women were sometimes concerned that naming women authors as women would degrade them by exposing them to criticism on account of their gender. For instance, Darwin asked Charles Lyell how best to reference information he had been given by Buckley, who was Lyell's secretary at the time: 'I presume I may quote Miss Buckley about the roosting in trees...as "from information received through Sir C. Lyell". If you think I ought to name Miss B., please tell me, otherwise I will quote as above' (Darwin to Lyell, 25 March 1865, DCP-LETT-4794). We see the same chivalry on display when Anna Jameson disagreed about a point of Shakespeare interpretation with 'One critic, a lady-critic too, whose name I will be so merciful as to suppress' (1832: vol. 1: 57)—although Jameson said this (about Charlotte Lennox) in a signed work that revealed Jameson to be a 'lady-critic' herself! To give a third example, in *The Subjection of Women* Mill stated that: 'Two women, since political economy has been made a science, have known enough of it to write usefully on the subject: of how many of the innumerable men who have written on it during the same time, is it possible with truth to say more?' (1869: 130). That he does not name the two—Jane Marcet and Harriet Martineau—is presumably out of chivalry, since after all he is praising their level of knowledge.

To compound the situation, women themselves could gain some of the authority of which they were short by referencing men and not other women. For example, Buckley read Edith Thompson's *History of England* (1872) when working on her own history book, saying to her correspondent Richard Garnett:

---

[41] One of the pieces by Mivart that Huxley discusses had appeared anonymously, so he discussed it without naming the author, though he suspected it was by Mivart (Huxley to Darwin, 28 September 1871, DCP-LETT-7973). Huxley's silence on Cobbe was perhaps affected by their recent falling-out. They had been friends in the late 1860s, but after heated correspondence in 1870 over vivisection—which Huxley firmly supported—Cobbe severed ties with him (see Mitchell 2004: 202).

'I should like you to glance at Edith Thompson's book. Mine may be called more elementary... but it has all the information in it that hers has' (AB to Garnett, 27 June 1888, *GFP*). Yet Buckley's *High School History of England* (1891) contains no mention of or reference to Thompson.[42] To give another instance, Welby directed her published critiques of empiricism against Huxley, even though she had referred to Martineau in earlier unpublished writing on the topic and had criticized Besant on the same score in their correspondence.[43] In a pattern we will encounter regularly in this book, women engaged with one another in letters and unpublished writing, but swapped in male names and reference-points in their published work.

This practice was understandable and made sense for individual women, but over time its effects were damaging. Because women were not referenced, their work became quickly forgotten in a way that was not so true for men. For instance, the lack of references meant that Shepherd's work rapidly disappeared from view after she died, so that Cobbe, arguing in the 1850s that the causal principle is known a priori, seems to have been unaware of Shepherd's 1820s arguments to the same effect. Cobbe instead drew on Whewell, who had been influenced by Shepherd, but who had not referenced her. A lack of references quickly leads to a lack of historical memory.

1.5 How Nineteenth-Century Women Became Forgotten

Women took part in philosophical debates, but the playing field was not level, and unfortunately the very strategies that women developed in order to play on this uneven ground came to work against them. First, by pitching themselves as popularizers, educators, or commentators, women inadvertently paved the way for later generations to conclude that their work did not merit canonization because it was merely 'secondary' and derivative. Second, while anonymity and pseudonymity allowed women to partake of the collective authority of 'men of letters', this left in place the assumption that epistemic authority resided with men. Third, by publishing anonymously or pseudonymously, and by selectively referencing men rather than other women, women made it harder for subsequent generations to appreciate and trace their philosophical influence.

But the most decisive factor in these women's omission from the historiography of philosophy, I believe, was the professionalization of philosophy which took place from the 1870s onwards.[44] This was part of a wider sea change in British intellectual life as a whole, in which the academic disciplines established

---

[42] On Thompson, see Capern (2008).   [43] For details, see Chapter 2, Sec. 2.6.
[44] Gardner (2013) also highlights how our image of professional philosophy has become so narrow as to exclude much of women's historical philosophizing, and Logan argues that the 'strict codification of academic disciplines' has led to the 'virtual disappearance of Martineau and her works' (2004b: 46).

themselves, with their specialist journals, societies, and venues, from the 1870s and 1880s onwards. For example, *Mind* was founded in 1876 and *Brain: A Journal of Neurology* in 1878. Subsequently, the British Psychological Society was founded in 1901 and the *British Journal of Psychology* in 1904. After that point contributions to *Mind* on psychology diminished considerably (Hatfield 2010: 536)—philosophy and psychology had separated. This change in philosophy publishing—from generalist to specialist journals—went along with a change in the nature of the subject: whereas before mind-and-brain had been a common topic amongst physiologists, philosophers, and others, now the field was dividing. Across multiple domains, people were abandoning the earlier assumption that 'Minds of the first rank are generalizers; of the second, specializers' (Eastern Hermit 1878: 268).[45] Instead, people came to think that, to make real headway on a topic, one must break it down into components that can be thoroughly investigated using specialist methods proper to each of them. For this was thought to be how the sciences had achieved their results. The new attitude is encapsulated in George Stout's 1896 book *Analytic Psychology*:

> The time is rapidly approaching when no one will think of writing a book on Psychology in general, any more than of writing a book on Mathematics in general. The subject may be approached from the point of view of Physiology, of Mental Pathology, of Ethnology, and of Psycho-physical Experiment. Each of these methods has its own data, and its own distinct and independent ways of collecting and estimating evidence. (1896: vol. 1: ix)[46]

Furthermore, these intellectual developments correlated with institutional changes. More people were going to university, so the academic profession expanded; gaining a good degree became the de facto qualification for entering that profession; and academics became more focused on the particular subjects they were passing on to the next generation. And as specialist periodicals and forums were formed, being a credible party to specific discussions became increasingly dependent on publishing in the right venues, in the ways approved by members of the profession, and on being part of their community—which came, more and more, to mean holding an academic job in the relevant subject. Here we need to bear in mind that a 'profession' is not simply an occupation. As sociologists have shown, a 'profession' is a mode of *controlling* who can practise an occupation, how they enter it (e.g. by gaining qualifications and credentials, belonging to associations, publishing in suitable journals), what they must do

---

[45] This 1878 statement was itself a last-ditch defence of the older outlook against the rising specialist tide.
[46] Having said this, Stout proceeded to do older-style general philosophy-cum-psychology of mind. But he stressed that this was now only part, not the whole, of the subject; and that it could not substitute for detailed disciplinary inquiries but only organize and frame them (1896: x).

(e.g. teach philosophy), and what traits they must have (e.g. neutral detachment). 'Professional projects are strategies of occupational closure', as Anne Witz puts it, 'which seek to establish a monopoly over the provision of skills and competencies' (1992: 61). On the one hand, members of each profession are horizontally demarcated from one another—philosophers from physiologists, neurologists, natural historians, theologians, and so on—thus, professionalization and specialization go together. On the other hand, members of the professions are vertically separated from and ranked above all those who belong to no profession and concomitantly are non-specialists. So whereas there had been long been certain people employed as philosophers—for example, as Chair of Logic and Metaphysics at the University of Edinburgh, in the case of William Hamilton—for most of the century one did not have to hold such positions to participate credibly in philosophical debates. Having an academic job now took on new significance, and began to become a qualification for philosophizing, in the context of this change in which an occupation became an exclusive profession.

Through these developments, the all-round critic began to give way to a new persona, the professional specialist or expert. In the case of philosophical specialists, J. B. Schneewind has spoken of the 'new breed of philosopher' who 'saw philosophy as an academic discipline dealing with problems defined and transmitted by a group of experts who were the best available judges of proposed solutions' (1977: 6). He regards Alexander Bain, along with Thomas Hill Green and Henry Sidgwick, as exemplars. Having said this, the changes in question happened gradually, and so—taking philosophers in particular—the newer 'specialists' were still very much generalists compared to professional philosophers today. They typically taught right across the subject, made many big claims, and their interests remained wide—as with the fascination of many late nineteenth-century philosophers such as Sidgwick with parapsychology and psychical research. Even so, these were specialists compared to members of earlier generations such as Martineau, whose work spanned history, politics, economics, philosophy, and many other fields besides.

How did these developments bear on women? Because women's higher education was confined to a few institutions, there was room for only a very few women to enter the fledgling philosophy profession. A handful did, like E. E. Constance Jones, who became Lecturer in Moral Sciences at Girton in 1884, but this remained rare. Thus, given the historical legacy and partly continuing reality of women's exclusion from universities, the barriers to women participating in the new culture of professional philosophy were high. Admittedly, these barriers did not go up overnight. The newer specialist culture overlapped with the older generalist one, so that one could remain outside the academy, like Welby, and still be taken seriously within it. But this became increasingly difficult as processes of specialization built up their own momentum.

The rise of specialist philosophy created particular difficulties for women because it interacted with the earlier constraints under which they had operated. To establish philosophy's disciplinary credentials, and carve out their new identity as philosophical experts, practitioners had to distinguish their work from the earlier, generalist public culture. They distinguished their work from popular and public philosophy, endeavouring to be neutral and detached as opposed to being partisan or sectarian. They simultaneously sought to separate their work from that coming out of unorthodox milieux like theosophy, anti-vivisection, socialism, or feminism. The participatory strategies women had been using thus began to count against them. Claiming to popularize; navigating in the generalist periodical culture; claiming moral and religious authority; arguing for social and political reforms—such things showed that, whatever these women had been writing, it was not philosophy as we now know it. The image of the professional philosopher was built upon a contrast with such earlier figures as the critic, the writer, the reformer, the guardian of religion-and-morality, the public educator—all figures within which women had found ways to do philosophy.

These dynamics bore adversely on some male philosophers too. Take George Henry Lewes, mentioned earlier. Lewes's work was philosophical but wide-ranging and multi-disciplinary (to speak anachronistically); he had partisan links, having co-edited *The Leader*, a 'radical and pervasively political paper' (Brake 2021); and he was very much the cultural critic, at consummate ease in the generalist periodical culture. As I noted earlier, Lewes has become omitted from the history of philosophy under the assumption that he was merely a 'higher journalist'. Or consider Robert Lewins, Naden's mentor and fellow hylo-idealist who is even more forgotten than Naden herself. As a former army surgeon, Lewins was clearly an 'amateur' philosopher, and a partisan one: he proselytized for hylo-idealism and atheism in a militant campaigning style that was a far cry from considered academic detachment. Lewes and Lewins 'fitted' the emerging profession no better than Cobbe or Martineau.

So the professionalization and purification of the discipline did not lead to the exclusion of women alone. Many men were also excluded. However, *some* men's work made it into the emerging discipline, whereas none of women's did. We can get a sense of what was ruled 'in' from a list of books donated to Somerville College in 1884 which were selected, from the library of the late Oxford humanist Mark Pattison, by the Aristotle scholar Ingram Bywater. Bywater picked these books out for donation to Somerville library because he saw them as defining a canon and as models for students to emulate. The list covers a wide range of areas, but the philosophy selections are books by Bain, Bentham, Lotze, and Longinus; the logics of Hegel, Bain, and Mill; Aristotle's *De Anima* and the whole of Plato; and the complete works of Hooker, Berkeley, Shaftesbury, Voltaire, Tocqueville, Emerson, and Whewell. Very few works by women are on the list anywhere; these are Jane Austen's novels, an anthology 'The Female Poets', *The Renaissance of Art in*

France by E. F. S. Pattison,[47] Sarah Austin's writings on Germany, and the letters of Mmes de Sévigné and de Sablé—where, although de Sablé's letters are philosophical (see Conley 2000), in the list she is clearly placed as a letter-writer. In sum, women appear on this list as 'writers' of several kinds, not philosophers.[48]

It is hardly surprising that none of the canonized philosophers were women. Virtually all professional philosophers were men, so they sought to cement their profession with reference to (selected) male models and predecessors. But then subsequent entrants to the profession had to establish their credentials, in turn, by locating themselves with respect to the accepted figures, not the excluded ones. Once this process was repeated over several generations, the women discussed in this book were almost wholly eclipsed.

I now want to substantiate these claims about professionalization and make them more concrete with two case studies. They make for rather depressing reading; but sometimes we need to remember bad things as well as good ones.

1.6 Two Case Studies: Cobbe and Blavatsky

Cobbe's rise and fall. From the 1860s to 1880s, Cobbe's standing was extremely high. Her friends and interlocutors were an assemblage of the intellectual elite, both women—Mary Somerville, feminists such as Josephine Butler, as well as Besant, Lee, Ward and Wedgwood—and men—Darwin, Mill, Spencer, Lyell, Tyndall, Francis Galton, Tennyson, Wilkie Collins, and many others. Such was Cobbe's reputation in 1882 that when the scientist Richard Owen complained about her anti-vivisectionism, her defender Charles Adams queried whether Owen knew 'anything at all of the position Miss Cobbe holds in Intellect and Thought' (Mitchell 2004: 284). Yet now Cobbe is virtually unknown. How did this come about?

After the mid-1870s, Cobbe's thought went in one direction and the mainstream of science and philosophy in another. A key part of this change was that vivisection became a normal part of British science and medicine. Until the mid-1870s Cobbe led the campaign for vivisection to be regulated and performed only under anaesthetics, without cruelty, and when strictly necessary to find out important truths. She changed her mind when the campaign resulted in the 1876 Cruelty to Animals Act, which she considered watered down to uselessness.

---

[47] Pattison's wife, E. F. S. Pattison, later known as Emilia Dilke, was an eminent art historian who had previously written on philosophical aesthetics (Dilke 1869, 1873).

[48] Pattison Gift Book, October 1884, Somerville College, Oxford. The list illustrates a pattern that Judith Johnston has noted: although nineteenth-century women 'were enormously productive and highly successful, as translators, biographers, historians, philosophers, critics and editors', nonetheless their fiction writing 'has been...privileged over [their] non-fiction' (1997: 17).

Despairing of the prospects for effective regulation, she decided that vivisection was wrong absolutely and must be abolished. This drove her into a protracted struggle against much of the scientific and medical establishment, leading her to break from many of her former interlocutors, including Darwin, Tyndall, Carpenter, and Galton.

Cobbe was pilloried and ridiculed in parts of the press. Allegedly the sensible, rational, male establishment accepted the need for animal experimentation; ill-informed women headed by Cobbe were obstructing progress. The issue went beyond vivisection and concerned the broader trend towards professionalization, which Cobbe recognized to be underway. In her 1881 essay 'The Medical Profession and its Morality'—which tellingly, and unusually for Cobbe, was anonymous—she argued that doctors were monopolizing professional control of medicine out of base self-interest dressed up as expertise.[49] The issue of vivisection was also entangled with the rise of specialization in philosophy. To return to philosophy of mind again, the conviction was growing (as we saw regarding Stout) that the mind must be investigated through specialist methods, including those of experimental physiology. Two of the key figures pushing to make psychology an empirical science were James Ward (see, especially, Ward 1886) and Michael Foster, who established the Physiological Laboratory of the University of Cambridge in the 1870s. Foster spearheaded a transformation of physiology, importing new experimental methods from mainland Europe (see Boddice 2011: 216). Animal experimentation was at the centre of these methods. Consequently Foster was one of the people—along with Darwin and Huxley—who opposed the initial bill for regulating vivisection that Cobbe drafted and that her allies presented to parliament in 1875.[50] Thus, because the rise of specialist philosophy was bound up with an aspiration to greater scientificity, it was indirectly implicated in the increasing normalization of animal experimentation. Cobbe saw professionalization, specialization, and reliance on vivisection as intertwined, and opposed them all.[51]

An infamous moment in the struggle between Cobbe and her adversaries took place at an 1892 church congress during a tense debate over vivisection. An anonymous reporter in the *Times* paraphrased Cobbe's adversary Victor Horsley as follows:

---

[49] Cobbe criticized doctors for enforcing the Contagious Diseases Acts, practising vivisection, advocating compulsory vaccination, and pathologizing women's bodies. The essay drew replies from Carpenter, Elizabeth Blackwell (the first woman to practise medicine in Britain), and 'two members of the profession'. See Cobbe (1881) and the subsequent July 1881 issue of the *Modern Review*.
[50] Foster contributed to the *Handbook for the Physiological Laboratory* (Burdon-Sanderson et al. 1873), in which various scientists described animal experiments they had carried out and how to perform them. The *Handbook* became hugely controversial and was a particular target of Cobbe's ire. Indeed, a major spur to the 1876 regulatory legislation was concern about the practices described in the book; see Atalić and Fatović-Ferenčić (2009).
[51] For Cobbe's critique of the rise of what we now call 'scientism', see SS 3–36.

Those who considered themselves to be fit to judge upon the question might be divided into three classes [Horsley said] – (1) those who knew well the sciences of physiology, pathology, practical medicine, and surgery; (2) those who were ignorant of these sciences; (3) those who knew something, but who deliberately falsified the facts. To the first class belonged the whole body of the honourable members of the medical profession. To the second and third classes belonged the anti-vivisectionists.... [Horsley] described Miss Cobbe's book on the subject as one of the rankest *impostures* that had for many years defaced English literature.... [According to Horsley] Miss Cobbe had *deliberately and fraudulently misrepresented* the actual facts [of many experiments].

(Anonymous 1892a: 6; my emphases)

Cobbe was opposing vivisection within the terms of the older culture, as a critic and thinker with all-round moral authority; the new specialist culture was rendering that standpoint obsolete. Now only 'honourable members of the medical profession' were qualified to speak about scientific, medical, and physiological practice; those outside the profession were necessarily ignorant—or, worse, they were fraudulent impostors.

The Nine Circles of the Hell of the Innocent, the book against which Horsley inveighed, was actually written by Cobbe's research assistant G. M. Rhodes. Unfortunately for Cobbe, Rhodes had misrepresented some of the experiments detailed in the book. Cobbe had no choice but to apologize (Mitchell 2004: 338–40). This was one of several similar incidents that caused Cobbe to lose her authority in many eyes and go from being respected to being somewhat disreputable.[52] By the time that Cobbe died in 1904, she had come to stand for sentimental and partisan anti-vivisectionism, a far cry from what professional philosophers aspired to be: neutral, detached, specialized, and rational.

Blavatsky, the Coulomb Affair, and the Hodgson Report. Before she created theosophy, Blavatsky had been active in spiritualism. Women were heavily represented in spiritualism generally, with many mediums being female. This was because spiritualism offered women a unique route to epistemic authority, as Alex Owen (1989) has shown.[53] When in trances, possessed by spirits, or channelling spirit communications, women could utter statements and show levels of insight that would otherwise meet with disapproval and scepticism but were deemed more acceptable when women were merely the messengers. Spiritualism thus started from the assumptions that women are receptive, selfless, and only capable of reproducing the ideas of others—and on this basis legitimized women in uttering and enacting some decidedly risqué and transgressive claims and

---

[52] These incidents are chronicled in Williamson (2005).

[53] See also the classic account of the rise of spiritualism in the nineteenth century by Oppenheim (1985).

behaviours. As such, spiritualism was a subversive reappropriation of separate spheres ideology.[54]

Blavatsky took this strategy several steps further with theosophy and blended it with some of women's other strategies for intellectual participation. She claimed to have received much of her spiritual wisdom from Masters or Mahatmas in India and Tibet. In transmitting theosophical wisdom, she was merely passing on what these spiritually advanced beings had taught her, and indeed were directly spiritually dictating to her:

> [S]omeone positively *inspires me* – ... more than this: someone enters me. It is not I who talk and write: it is something within me, my higher and luminous Self, that thinks and writes for me. ... Someone comes and envelops me as a misty cloud and all at once pushes me out of myself, and then I am not 'I' any more – Helena Petrovna Blavatsky – but someone else.
> (HPB to V. de Zhelihovsky, June 1877, letter 83, in Blavatsky 2004)

This 'higher and luminous Self'—'H. P. B.' as Blavatsky's inner circle called her—had transcended the material, sexed body of Helena Petrovna Blavatsky.

Through her spiritual training, Blavatsky maintained, she had developed her powers to perform 'phenomena' such as making objects appear and disappear. Trivial in themselves, such displays revealed the soul's great powers, usually untapped because our souls are entangled with material desires and feelings. When other theosophists, specifically Alfred Percy Sinnett and Allan Home, wanted to communicate with the Mahatmas, Blavatsky began in 1880 to pass letters back and forth between Sinnett, Home, and the Mahatmas. This correspondence—the 'Mahatma Letters'—lasted until 1887, ran to 1,300 pages, and formed the basis of Sinnett's 1883 book *Esoteric Buddhism*, a key statement of theosophy which did much to arouse British interest in it.[55] The Mahatma letters were at the heart of the Coulomb controversy that erupted in late 1884. This controversy has been extensively discussed before, but it is relevant here because it bears on women's epistemic authority and the dynamics of how then-prominent intellectual women became left out of the history of philosophy.[56]

The couple Emma and Alexis Coulomb were former staff of the Theosophical Society headquarters in Adyar, India. They alleged that Blavatsky had been

---

[54] On Harriet Tubman's parallel version of the same strategy with respect to the African-American tradition of hoodoo, see Stewart (2020).

[55] The letters themselves were later published by Barker (1923).

[56] On the controversy, see Cranston (1992) and Lachman (2012); on esotericism as 'rejected knowledge', see Hanegraaff (2012); and on the gender, racial, and colonialist dimensions of the controversy, see Barton Scott (2009) and Dixon (2001). Those sympathetic to theosophy may be frustrated, especially given Harrison's (1997) criticisms of the Hodgson report, that I am raking over these matters again, but I find them telling about the processes by which women have been excluded from philosophy.

producing phenomena fraudulently using secret trapdoors, sliding panels, and similar devices. The Coulombs also published letters, allegedly from Blavatsky, in which she admitted to forging the Mahatma Letters (see Patterson 1884). Supposedly, then, the Letters were really authored by Blavatsky and the wisdom she put in the mouths of the Mahatmas was actually her own. One might think this is not exactly a big revelation. But the Coulombs' revelations threatened to *discredit* Blavatsky under the assumption that a woman speaking in her own voice, based on her own experience, reading, and insight, lacked epistemic authority—that the only possible authorities here could be the (male) Masters, so that if they were fictitious then only sham and deception remained. The very fact that the Coulombs' claims were a threat shows how pervasive those assumptions were, so much so that Blavatsky traded on them herself when claiming merely to channel the wisdom of her spiritual superiors. Her attempt to use these assumptions subversively, in the service of her own authority, seemed set to blow up in her face.

Into this already inflamed situation came the investigation of Blavatsky by the Society for Psychical Research (SPR), founded in 1882, whose first president was Henry Sidgwick. Modelling itself on the Royal Society, the SPR aimed to investigate paranormal and psychical phenomena using the scientific method: neutral, detached, impartial observation under controlled conditions, eliminating extraneous variables, and carefully comparing successive experimental results to reach a firmly grounded conclusion. Or in the SPR's 1883 mission statement, 'The aim of the Society will be to approach these various problems [of spiritualist, hypnotic, and psychical phenomena], without prejudice or prepossession of any kind, and in the same spirit of exact and unimpassioned inquiry which has enabled Science to solve so many problems' (SPR [1883] 2021). The aim was by no means to discredit all 'psy' phenomena, but rather to sort the wheat from the chaff and discern which phenomena were genuine. Early members numbered Richard Hodgson, Frederick Myers, the philosopher of music Edmund Gurney, the philosophical Irish author Jane Barlow,[57] the philologist Hensleigh Wedgwood (Julia Wedgwood's father), Sidgwick's wife Eleanor who later became principal of Newnham College Cambridge, Mary Everest Boole, and the future prime minister Arthur Balfour. It was a line-up of eminent figures and, although I have highlighted some women, the SPR was heavily male-dominated.[58] Moreover, its ideal dispassionate investigator was implicitly masculine, someone able to stand back from his emotions to face facts. The SPR investigated many mediums, around half of them female; effectively this treated the masculine scientific community as qualified to assess

---

[57] On Barlow, see Uckelman (2019).
[58] On the history of the SPR, see e.g. Haynes (1982). To be fair, most theosophists were male too, but Blavatsky's presiding role made a key difference. It was exceptional for a philosophical/religious movement to be female-headed (the other example was Christian Science, founded by Mary Baker Eddy). Consequently theosophy attracted many original women such as Besant, Anna Kingsford, Mabel Collins, Katherine Tingley, and Alice Bailey.

the truth or falsity of what mediums claimed. The battle, as between Cobbe and the medical–scientific establishment, was between male, expert, scientific authority and females whose utterances could not necessarily be trusted.[59] Like Cobbe with her critique of medical immorality, Blavatsky tried to turn the tables.[60] She savaged modern scientists in *Isis Unveiled* (1877), most of all Darwin and Huxley, for their crude materialism and empiricism. In contrast, Blavatsky maintained, *she* had the genuine, original wisdom of the ancients.

The SPR had already decided to investigate the Theosophical Society in 1884 and assigned the inquiry to Hodgson. When the Coulomb controversy broke, he took it into his remit. He went to Adyar, collected testimonials from many theosophists and their associates, examined the Society's premises, and subjected documents including the Mahatma Letters to calligraphic analysis. He concluded that Blavatsky *had* forged the letters. Based on his report, the SPR declared:

> This [the Letters] is not the only incidence of *fraud* in connection with... Blavatsky... For our own part, we regard her neither as the mouthpiece of hidden seers, nor as a mere vulgar adventuress; we think that she has achieved a title to permanent remembrance as one of the most accomplished, ingenious, and interesting *impostors* in history.   (1885: 207; my emphasis)

The language was remarkably like that in which Horsley condemned Cobbe's book a few years later: 'one of the rankest *impostures*... for many years... Miss Cobbe had deliberately and *fraudulently* misrepresented the actual facts' (my emphasis).[61]

Some debateable assumptions informed the Hodgson report. First, if the letters were in disguised or modified versions of Blavatsky's handwriting as Hodgson concluded, their content could still have been conveyed to her by the Mahatmas, communicating with her spiritually and using her body as their 'channel', akin to a medium.[62] If the letters drew on books Blavatsky had read and made points found in her other works, as Hodgson concluded as well, the Mahatmas could still have been using her as their tool, with the tool inevitably expressing their insights by way of her own background knowledge. Thus although Hodgson claimed that his investigation was neutral and unprejudiced (e.g. 1894: 133), he seems to have presupposed the impossibility of such spirit communication at the outset—or, more precisely, to have assumed that if the Mahatmas were involved then there

---

[59] See also Owen (1989: 230–1).

[60] 'One way to read the history of the Theosophical Society... [is] as a series of attempts to create a usable version of both eastern and feminine authority' (Dixon 2001: 19).

[61] 'Imposture' was a recurring theme; Lee described Blavatsky as 'the most arrant impostor from sheer love of imposture and excitement' (VL to Mary Robinson, 19 November 1884, *SLVL* 1: 594).

[62] As Blavatsky said: 'when a Master says "*I* wrote that letter", it means only that every word in it was dictated by him and impressed under his direct supervision. Generally they make their chela [organ], whether near or far away, write... by impressing upon his mind the ideas they wish impressed' (1888: 93).

must be physical evidence manifesting this (i.e. their own handwriting). That is, the Mahatmas must be physical beings operating on the normal laws of the physical world. But Blavatsky denied this, complaining that the SPR, like modern science generally, took for granted a materialist world view (1888: 93). Perhaps Hodgson would reply that if spiritual phenomena have no direct physical manifestation then there is no way of investigating them. But for Blavatsky this again assumes that the only possible investigative method is that of empirical science.[63]

Second, and most importantly for us, Hodgson continued to assume that if Blavatsky were writing in her own voice, as a Russian-born woman knowledgeable about esoteric traditions and world religions, then far from being an authority she was a fraud. However, perhaps Hodgson and the SPR would reply that there would be nothing fraudulent if Blavatsky simply and openly spoke in her own voice; the fraud was *her* claim to be channelling higher authorities. But as Blavatsky confessed in a letter of January 1886, 'Was it *fraud*, Certainly not... the only thing I can be reproached with... though I have not *deserved* it... *is* of having... used Master's name when I thought my authority would go for naught' (Blavatsky 1886). At this point Blavatsky came close to acknowledging explicitly that, given prevailing sexist assumptions, she could *not* simply speak in her own voice, and that she had found ways around the problem: using initials and semi-private letters; claiming to disseminate the wisdom of her superiors; and appealing to women's spiritual receptivity.[64] What Hodgson and the SPR were not acknowledging, then, was that in practice it was very difficult for women to speak in their own voices and still maintain any authority.

Racial and imperial politics were at stake in the discrediting of Blavatsky too. The Coulombs had published their letters in the *Madras Christian College Magazine*, a Christian missionary outlet that was eager to discredit Indian nationalism, therefore to discredit claims for the worth of India's native spiritual traditions, therefore to discredit Blavatsky's claims to that effect. And on the European side, if the Letters were really written by the Masters—allegedly two Tibetans, Kuthumi (or Koot Hoomi) and Morya—then by implication the ultimate wisdom resided with the 'Orientals', from whom Europeans needed to be educated as Blavatsky had been. The esteemed Orientalist and founder of comparative religion Max Müller found this patently absurd:

---

[63] Eleanor Sidgwick argued that the SPR should perform 'physical tests' to establish, by elimination, the cases where something was occurring that was impossible under the laws of nature (1885: 430–2). Hodgson took the Mahatma Letters to have failed this test. But for Blavatsky the problem remained that physical tests were not appropriate to spiritual phenomena and many genuine spiritual phenomena would be falsely judged to fail them.

[64] I do not mean that she deliberately and consciously adopted these solutions. I am sure that she genuinely believed in the Mahatmas, as when she claimed that 'someone' else inspired her to write—although notice that there, too, she immediately equated the 'someone' with her *own* 'higher Self'. Unconsciously, though, she had found a solution to the problem of women's lack of epistemic authority; but that solution was now being held against her.

We, the pretended authorities of the West, are told to go to the Brahmans and Lamaists of the Far Orient, and respectfully ask them to impart to us the alphabet of true science. (1893: 774)[65]

After all, for most Victorians it was axiomatic that Christian Europeans were more advanced than 'Orientals'. In this respect too, Hodgson's inquiry was less neutral than he maintained. By discrediting Blavatsky, professional men of science could avoid an embarrassing situation where, apparently, they had much to learn from Eastern outsiders.

The Coulomb affair and Hodgson report were not the peculiar and marginal episodes they might seem to be, and neither were Cobbe's skirmishes with her pro-vivisection opponents. Both dramatize the change in epistemic power relations towards the end of the century. New standards for authoritative, professional, scientific expertise were coming in, which conflicted with the forms of thinking and writing that women had developed in response to patriarchal constraints. Consequently both Cobbe and Blavatsky were accused of fraud and imposture: pretending to possess an authority and expertise for which they did not have the proper expert qualifications.[66]

Cobbe and Blavatsky were facing attack in the 1880s just as growing numbers of intellectual women were coming forward. Naden and Lee began publishing in this decade, Besant was by then a major public figure, and Wedgwood was publishing some of her best-known and most ambitious work. Women were entering universities: both Naden and Besant were university-educated, although Besant was judged too politically radical to be permitted to graduate. Women were writing more books and articles than ever, and editing periodicals more openly than ever before, with Besant editing or co-editing three journals in the 1880s alone. Perhaps the tightening of professional and disciplinary boundaries was a backlash against these developments. If one now had to be a qualified expert with the right credentials in order to speak, then that moved the goalposts to intellectual participation back out of most women's reach.

---

[65] Müller began: 'It is sometimes represented as the height of professorial conceit that scholars like myself, who have never been in India' should write on the topic; 'they are told that they have no right to speak' (1893: 767)—this was not Blavatsky's view, though she did regard lack of first-hand experience of India as a limitation. Evidently rattled, Müller made it clear who really had no right to speak: Blavatsky. She was 'excitable', 'hysterical', used 'barefaced tricks', 'thought that she could fly though she had no wings', had 'ceased to be truthful', 'misunderstood, distorted, caricatured' Buddhism... and so on (767ff.).

[66] The Hodgson report was not the end of criticism of Blavatsky. Within a book denouncing Blavatsky which was sponsored by the SPR and was prefaced by a note from Sidgwick on Blavatsky's 'imposture' (Cranston 1992: 298–9), William Coleman (1895) heavily criticized her for paraphrasing sources without acknowledgement. This is doubly ironic: as we've seen, spelling out all one's sources was not standard scholarly practice then; and referencing *women* was often seen as positively inappropriate. Blavatsky was being held to a different standard from her male contemporaries.

1.7 Methodological Recommendations

Nineteenth-century women's philosophy became forgotten in two stages. Earlier, women participated in philosophical debates albeit in a constrained way. Later, philosophy became a specialized profession and many earlier-century figures fell out of the newly narrowed discipline. This exclusion fell on many men as well as women,[67] but it landed especially heavily on women for a cluster of reasons. Owing to the legacy of women's historical exclusion from universities, nearly all of the emerging generation of professional philosophers were men, who remodelled the discipline in their own image. They remodelled it in contrast to the popular, public, generalist philosophy of the preceding century. But it was just this kind of philosophy that many women had been doing, because print and periodical culture had been open to them in a period when most other avenues were closed.

Fortunately, even this tale of exclusion yields a constructive side. By reversing the mechanisms by which women became excluded, we can generate some methodological rules for how to re-include them.

First, we should not demand from nineteenth-century women's work the level of disciplinary specialization characteristic of much twentieth-century philosophical work (by men and women alike). We should not, in looking for historical women philosophers in the nineteenth century, confine our attention to those who look like professional specialists *avant la lettre*.

Second, what should we positively look for? We should be open to women doing philosophy by arguing for social and political reforms, or for Christianity or spirituality or secularism; or doing philosophy in a generalist, wide-ranging style, or in public settings where philosophical argument and rhetorical persuasion converged. We should be mindful of the participation strategies that women used: they may have claimed to be mere popularizers or commentators; they may have taken partisan standpoints on religion and politics; they may have written anonymously or pseudonymously; they may have philosophized while reviewing work by others. They may have called themselves educators or reformers; others may have called them writers, journalists, or critics. And we should be open to women philosophizing within various written genres: didactic tales, travel-writing, life-writing, letters, novels, translations, dialogues, criticism. All these forms could be, and were, turned to philosophical purpose in the period.

---

[67] For instance, the case of Alfred Russel Wallace shows that there were men as well as women who suffered from being discredited in this period, in Wallace's case due to his belief in spiritualism. In late 1879 Buckley asked Darwin to secure a position for Wallace, in recognition of his scientific achievements, but though Darwin tried, he reported back to her: 'I grieve to say that Hooker [the President of the Scientific Society]... has convinced me that the plan is hopeless.—He says that Wallace gave deep offence by bringing on before the British Association *in opposition to the Committee* a discussion on Spiritualism' (Darwin to AB, 19 December 1879, *DCP*, DCP-LETT-12365).

Third, we can be open to these varied modes and genres of philosophizing but should not require them. After all, some nineteenth-century women's work, for example Shepherd's critical analyses of Hume's and Berkeley's arguments, come close to what we have come to expect of philosophy: detailed, careful, point-by-point critical examination of other people's arguments. Moreover, some women's work was recognized by the emerging community of specialists, as when Welby published in *Mind* and *The Monist* and Naden in the *Proceedings of the Aristotelian Society*. And some women wrote in conventional philosophical forms like the treatise and the essay, as Cobbe did. We should be open both to what adheres relatively well to our received conceptions of philosophy and what ranges further afield from it.

One might ask: are we then to count *anything* women wrote as philosophy? Anita Superson raises this problem apropos of Catherine Gardner's *Empowerment and Interconnectivity: Toward a Feminist History of Utilitarian Philosophy*. If Catharine Beecher's books on household management are to count as philosophy, Superson asks, what doesn't? Surely some criteria must govern what we are and are not to treat as philosophy (Superson 2013). Perhaps we could adopt Mary Ellen Waithe's criterion in her history of women in Western philosophy, which is that a woman counts as doing philosophy if her work corresponds to any existing philosophical theory, movement, doctrine, or debate (1987: vol. 4: xx). Yet one might object that on this criterion a woman's work can only count as philosophy if it can be put into sufficiently close relation to some existing part of the male canon.

The dilemma, then, is this. Women have had to philosophize under constraints, and so they have not always done philosophy in the same ways as their male contemporaries. Given this, any delimitation 'philosophy in this period was X' risks excluding women, some of whom were perforce doing something different. But without such delimitations, it is unclear what we are even trying to include women in, and on what grounds we are including them.

My imperfect solution in this book is to take a set of topics that, I hope, we can agree are philosophical: whether empirical science is the only possible source of knowledge on all matters; how to understand the relations between soul, mind, and brain; what evolutionary theory implies regarding religion and ethics; whether morality necessarily requires a religious foundation; and whether there has been progress across history. I take these to be philosophical questions simply because they are general and concern ultimate, wide-ranging, foundational matters. Of course many more concrete or applied matters are also philosophical—for instance, some of the heated nineteenth-century debate over vivisection was philosophical. But the topics I've chosen are not meant to be exhaustive, only—I hope—to be fairly uncontroversially philosophical. The task then is to look at what women said about these topics, whether in conventional or unconventional forms and places. In the hope that this says enough to vindicate my approach for now, let's proceed to our philosophical topics.

2
Naturalism

2.1 Introduction

In this chapter I reconstruct where Mary Shepherd, Harriet Martineau, Frances Power Cobbe, and Victoria Welby stood on a central fault-line in nineteenth-century British thought: naturalism versus anti-naturalism. By naturalism, I mean the philosophical stance that reality can be completely understood using the scientific method and that this method is empirical and inductive. The division between naturalism versus anti-naturalism was central to nineteenth-century British philosophy, as John Skorupski (1993) and Robert Stern (1998) have shown. Much less recognized is that women contributed significantly to shaping this division. Martineau was one of naturalism's best-known exponents in the period. She came to embrace naturalism wholeheartedly by 1850, and her thought will be central to this chapter. Her naturalist outlook contrasts, in one temporal direction, with that of Shepherd in the 1820s. Shepherd understood causation in a way that, in retrospect, we can identify as largely anti-naturalist. In the other temporal direction, Cobbe and Welby subsequently argued that naturalism could not adequately account for moral requirements (Cobbe, 1850s) or meaning and significance (Welby, 1880s–1890s).

These four were by no means the only women to engage with naturalism, but they indicate the spectrum of views that women, like men, took on the issue. It was unavoidable because of the rapid pace of scientific discovery and development in the period. To some intellectuals, such as Martineau, these developments showed that science could provide a comprehensive account of the world with no need for religion. Such assessments were highly controversial, though, with most people wanting to continue to combine science and religion. The debate over naturalism thus drew in all the intensity of whether science and religion could be reconciled, and if so along what lines.

A complication in considering women's views on naturalism is that the word was only acquiring its philosophical meaning in the period. Martineau was crucial to that acquisition. Opposing *supernaturalism*, she agreed with her interlocutor Henry George Atkinson that 'we require no supernatural causes when we can recognise adequate natural causes inherent in the constitution of nature' (*LLM* 7; see also 206, 216–22). As for the related concept of empirical science, a *science* for centuries had meant a systematically organized branch of knowledge, like the

German *Wissenschaft*. In the eighteenth century a *science* came to mean a branch of study which rises from observations to general laws, that is, is empirically based. We find this usage, for instance, in the radical Enlightenment philosopher Joseph Priestley, whom Shepherd repudiated but Martineau revered.[1] Then, over the nineteenth century, science became equated with *natural* science, eventually making once-popular expressions like 'mental science' obsolete.

So the word *naturalism* was not yet fully present; but it was taking shape, and so was the concept. That said, even today there remains little consensus on what philosophical naturalism consists in (see Papineau 2021). The view I find most useful is Finn Spicer's (2011), on which naturalism is a cluster concept and someone is more or less of a naturalist the more strands of the cluster they subscribe to and the more firmly they do so. The strands are: (1) rejection of 'first philosophy'; (2) rejection of a priori knowledge; (3) thinking that philosophy must be continuous with the empirical sciences; (4) a materialist view of mind; (5) denial of any non-natural or supernatural entities and agencies, such as God, the soul, or spirit; (6) thinking that moral knowledge either reduces to, or extends and is continuous with, empirical knowledge about facts obtaining in the natural world. In this light, we will see that by the 1850s Martineau endorsed all six strands. But what held them together, for her, was the conviction that empirical science gives us exhaustive knowledge of reality. So I shall use Spicer's cluster to disentangle the elements of naturalism, while also treating the view that empirical science can exhaustively account for reality as the unifying thread. Together the cluster and the thread allow us to map women's takes on naturalism in the period.

Did these women form their views in response to one another? Shepherd and Martineau became acquainted only in the 1830s after forming their opposed accounts of causation. Martineau disparaged Shepherd's account as divorced from empirical reality and devoid of practical use. As for Cobbe, she knew and rejected Martineau's naturalism as an account both of causation and morality. Cobbe's (negative) link with Martineau is partly indirect and goes by way of George Henry Lewes, who was intellectually close to Martineau in the 1850s when the two were both promulgating Comteian positivism. Cobbe's transcendentalist alternative to naturalism was also indirectly (and positively) influenced by Shepherd on causation, this time by way of William Whewell. As for Welby's anti-naturalism, this again linked back (negatively) to Martineau, both directly as well as indirectly through Thomas Henry Huxley, whom Welby criticized and who had been in the same circles around the *Westminster Review* as Martineau and Lewes back in the 1850s. These four women, then, were part of a continuous history of debate about naturalism. Their ideas interrelated, both critically and

---

[1] Priestley said, for example, that 'a small share of *natural science*... generally accompanies conceit and dogmatism', criticizing people who dismissed the results of 'experiments' out of hand on the basis of dogmatic theories (1777a: 162).

constructively, even when the relations were indirect; for they were making moves in an intellectual space that the other women's contributions had helped to delineate.

That we have to relate Cobbe to Martineau partly through Lewes, Cobbe to Shepherd through Whewell, Welby to Martineau partly through Huxley, and indeed Shepherd to Martineau partly through their different reactions to Priestley, exemplifies two features of the context on which I have already commented. First, because men's voices carried greater authority, women—like men—referred preferentially to men and not women. So we regularly have to piece together women's negative and positive relations to one another from behind their manifest references to men. Second, therefore, recovering women's philosophical views often requires recovering the views of their male contemporaries who, like Priestley, Whewell, Lewes, and Huxley, have regrettably been forgotten as well, albeit less so than the women. Restoring women's voices means filling in the broader fields of debate into which they were intervening.

Because naturalism is such a multifaceted and overarching issue, this chapter is long and covers a lot of terrain. To carve out a coherent narrative I will proceed chronologically, through Shepherd's analysis of causality in the 1820s (Sec. 2.2); Martineau's earlier mix of naturalism and anti-naturalism in the 1820s (Sec. 2.3); her full-blooded naturalism of the 1850s (Sec. 2.4); Cobbe's argument in the 1850s that naturalism cannot adequately account for moral requirements (Sec. 2.5); and Welby's argument in the 1880s–1890s that it cannot adequately account for meaning and significance (Sec. 2.6). Finally, I will briefly pull together how discussion of naturalism evolved over the century (Sec. 2.7).

2.2 Shepherd, Causation, and Anti-Naturalism

By her twenties, Shepherd was already drafting manuscripts 'exposing errors in the reasoning of Hume's atheistical treatises...' (Brandreth 1886: 28–9). Typically for her time, Shepherd took Hume to have argued that sensory impressions only ever give us successions but no 'hidden connections', making belief in causal necessity a mere habit without rational warrant. Shepherd disagreed on not only metaphysical but also religious grounds, because she thought—again typically of her era—that in denying the reality of causation Hume was undermining belief in the first cause, God. Her determination to refute Hume culminated in her (anonymous) 1824 *Essay upon the Relation of Cause and Effect*, which also advanced her positive theory of causation. She went on to use this theory to argue against external world scepticism in the (signed) *Essays Upon the Perception of an External Universe* of 1827. But I'll focus here on her theory of causation.

Happily, unlike much of the woman-authored philosophy discussed in this book, Shepherd's theory of causation has lately received attention and reconstruction and been interpreted in various ways.² However, it has been very largely isolated from the contributions of other women of the period. Thus, what I want to add is threefold. First, I argue that Shepherd's theory of causation is in the main anti-naturalist.³ Second, I put Shepherd into conversation with other women philosophers after her. Third, I thereby hope to show how the early modern issues of causation and induction that occupied Shepherd (and the earlier Martineau) evolved into Victorian-era concerns with the viability of naturalism as a total programme. So although I discuss Shepherd relatively briefly, she still plays an important role in my narrative. I intend her presence to illuminate how the more familiar early modern debates segued into the issues of science, value, and meaning which perturbed the Victorians.

Reason and causation. For Shepherd, '*reason*, not *fancy* and "custom", leads us to the knowledge, That every thing which begins to exist must have a Cause' (*ERCE* 27; some interpreters call this the 'causal principle', and so will I). For every object that begins to exist having not done so previously, something must explain this change. Objects cannot just pop in and out of existence at random or we would be in an unintelligible, chaotic world—objects 'cannot suddenly alter their nature; be "*non-existent*" this minute, and existent the next"' (38).⁴ Nor can an object cause its own beginning, for then it would have to exist already. The cause must therefore be some other object. For Shepherd, it is not by repeatedly observing things beginning to exist that we learn that other things always cause them to do so. Rather we know by reason that other things *must* be the cause. Thus 'we can know, through reason, that various metaphysical principles are *necessary* truths', as Deborah Boyle puts it (2021b).

In what sense do we know the causal principle by reason? Shepherd's key contention is that things cannot begin to exist just of themselves. She repeatedly says that it is a contradiction to think that things can so begin. Why is this contradictory? As she explains it, beginning or coming into existence is an action, an action is a quality, and a quality is necessarily a quality of some object, but *ex hypothesi* that object does not exist yet (*ERCE* 35). The contradiction in saying that a thing begins of itself, then, is that one is both denying that the object exists until it has begun and affirming that it already exists in order to perform the action of beginning itself. Or, as she puts it, 'existence, in order to be, must begin to be,

---

² See, inter alia, Atherton (1996), Bolton (2011, 2021), Boyle (2017, 2020, 2021a), Fantl (2016), Folescu (2021), Lolordo (2019), and McRobert (n.d.).

³ This might seem anachronistic given that the meaning of *naturalism* had not then stabilized. How could one be an anti-naturalist before there were any self-professed naturalists to oppose? My answer is that we may still class Shepherd as an anti-naturalist because her views do map (largely antithetically) onto the elements of the cluster *naturalism*; because those she criticized—Hume, Priestley, William Lawrence, Thomas Brown—were considerably more naturalist measured against the same cluster; and because the legacy of Shepherd's ideas was to become part of later-century anti-naturalism, as we will see.

⁴ On Shepherd's view that spontaneous alterations in the order of nature are impossible, see Fantl (2016).

and...beginning an action (the being that begins it *not supposed yet in existence*), involves a *contradiction in terms*' (35–6; my emphasis). Having established that an object cannot produce itself, we can infer that something else must produce it: 'objects which we know by our senses do begin their existences, and by our reason know they cannot begin it of themselves, must begin it by the operation of some other beings in existence' (43). So, for Shepherd, we know that objects cannot begin of themselves because it is self-contradictory to say that they can, and from there we can deduce that their causes must instead be other objects.[5]

Having made these points in relation to objects, Shepherd applies them to qualities too. For any new quality of an object that begins to exist, this again must have a cause other than that quality itself. To use one of her own examples, some wood put in a fire begins to burn (57). Here it is not quite right, according to Shepherd, to say that the wood's quality has *changed* from, say, dryness to combustion; rather, a *new* quality (combustion) has begun to exist (47). But 'objects, in relation to us, are nothing but masses of certain qualities' (46). If we list the wood's total qualities, that exhausts what it is. Shepherd subdivides these qualities into the qualities of an object in relation to us (the qualities we perceive it to have) and its qualities 'independent of our senses', which are its powers to affect other objects (46); from this perspective, the qualities we sense result from an object's powers to affect us (53). Since an object is the sum total of its qualities, when it acquires a new quality as the result of a causal action, it is a *new object* or *new nature* (47). '*Cause producing Effect*, therefore,...is a *new object* exhibiting *new qualities*; or, shortly, the formation of a new *mass of qualities*' (50). This is why, for Shepherd, the causation of new objects and of new qualities are in fact one and the same and what goes for one goes for the other.[6]

Shepherd is departing here from the more standard view that objects can change their qualities, as a result of causal interactions, while remaining the same underlying objects. What can be said for Shepherd's view? Consider the

---

[5] Several interpreters—Bolton (2021), Folescu (2021), and Paoletti (2011)—argue that all of Shepherd's arguments for the causal principle are question-begging. For Folescu, on her own terms Shepherd should have regarded the causal principle as foundational and intuitive rather than being provable by demonstration. Indeed, Shepherd later referred to the truth 'that no quality can begin its own existence' as a 'primeval truth' that is 'the key to every difficulty' (*EPEU* 138). Nonetheless, in the *Essay*, as Folescu admits, Shepherd explicitly and repeatedly says that the causal principle is known by reason. For Bolton, Shepherd's view is that we are naturally inclined to hold the causal principle which then allows us to pursue inquiries, make predictions, and build a coherent system of knowledge; viewed in this wider context, we have good reasons to hold the principle (2021). Reasonable as this coherentist line of defence is, Shepherd is at least *attempting* to make a non-question-begging argument for the causal principle. For two detailed reconstructions and defences of Shepherd's argument, see Landy (2020a) and Wilson (2022).

[6] Shepherd therefore says that in causal relations, the relata are not only qualities but also objects (46–7), which she calls 'new natures' insofar as they are effects (47). On at least one occasion she refers to these new natures as 'events'—'in the union of Fire and Wood, there exists immediately combustion as a new event in nature' (57). However, Landy argues that properly, for Shepherd: 'Events or occurrences are...*abstractions* from the more fundamental ontological category of objects and are not the proper relata of causal relations' (2020b: 2).

same example of burning wood as compared to non-burning wood. The former has a completely different set of qualities: not only does it emit heat and smoke, it smells different, has a different texture, colour, and so on. So total is the change that it is at least as plausible to consider the burning wood as a new object than as the same old object (wood) with different qualities (burning). Or consider a chemical interaction, as when iron rusts through contact with air and water—more technically, when the iron interacts with oxygen and hydrogen to produce hydrated iron oxide. It is not merely that the iron remains constant and has gained a new quality, rust; rather, some of what was iron has become a new substance, hydrated iron oxide. These sorts of phenomena motivate Shepherd's position.

Reason and like causes. Shepherd argues: 'That *reason* forces the mind to perceive, that *similar* causes must necessarily produce *similar effects*' (27). Shepherd's argument here relies on her idea of the crucial experiment (43), that is, a controlled experiment capable of establishing conclusively that objects of kind *a* suffice to produce objects of kind *b* by causal action. When we put wood in a fire and combustion occurs, then if nothing else has changed, we know through reason that putting the wood in the fire produced the combustion, because (from the causal principle) the combustion cannot have arisen on its own and 'there is nothing else to make a difference' (44). But by the same token we know that putting wood in a fire is *sufficient* on its own to produce combustion; after all, nothing else was involved. But since putting wood in a fire is sufficient to produce combustion, on any occasion when wood is put in a fire this will produce combustion (48) (assuming that no countervailing variables intervene, like the wood being soaked in water beforehand). Thus it is not from seeing repeated instances of wood placed in fire then burning that we generalize to a law that placing wood in fires causes it to burn. On the contrary, having seen this only once, we grasp that the same effect must invariably result from the same cause, other things being equal. As Shepherd puts it:

> One trial is enough, in such circumstances, as will bring the mind to the following reasoning. Here is a new quality, which appears to my senses: But it could not arise of itself; nor could any surrounding objects, but one (or more) affect it; therefore that one, (or more) have occasioned it, for there is nothing else to make a difference; and a *difference* could not '*begin of itself*'. (43–4)

> When an event happens under one set of circumstances, not under another in all respects the same, save ONE; *that one* is a *true cause*, and a *necessary* one.... This... is a *strict necessity*, and can enable the mind to predicate for the future as for the past. (66–7)

If an occasion arises when we put wood in a fire and no combustion occurs, then we know that something has changed. Perhaps one of the objects—the wood or the fire—has changed its qualities, that is, in fact we are dealing with different objects (soaked wood rather than dry wood). For, as we saw earlier, according to Shepherd qualities are really powers. Different qualities mean different causal powers mean different causal reactions.

Boyle (2021b) and Bolton (2010: 256) argue that Shepherd's appeal to the example of crucial experiments shows for her we can know some necessary truths on an a posteriori basis—specifically truths that objects of kind *a* necessarily produce objects of kind *b*. I interpret Shepherd differently. The key passage in question is this:

> ONE trial would be enough, under certain *known* circumstances. Why? Not from '*custom*', because there has been *one trial only*; but from *Reason*...for there is nothing else to make a difference, and a different quality could not '*begin its own existence*'. It is this sort of REASONING UPON EXPERIMENT,...which generates the notion of Power, and necessary Connexion; and gives birth to that maxim, '*a like Cause must produce a like Effect*'. (ERCE 44–5)

For Shepherd, by 'reasoning upon experiment' we grasp the necessary causal connections between objects of kinds *a* and *b*, leading us on to grasp the general principle that like causes necessarily produce like effects. We grasp that *a*s must produce *b*s because we have eliminated all other potential candidates for the production of *b* along with all interfering and confounding variables, which enables us to identify *a*'s causal powers in their own right. We grasp these powers by *applying* the general causal principle that 'every thing which begins to exist must have a cause' to the specific relation between objects that we observe in the experimental situation. Everything that begins must have a cause; *b* has begun to exist and must have a cause; all else having been eliminated from the scene, the only possible cause is *a*; therefore *a* suffices to produce *b*; therefore *a*s must always produce *b*s. For Shepherd, then, we know that *a*s must always produce *b*s by applying to experience the causal principle which we know by reason independent of experience. We make sense of the many causal relations in the world, and have ordered experience, by applying a priori principles to experience—'reasoning upon experiment'. Thus it is reason that supplies universality (*a*s always cause *b*s) and necessity (*a* necessarily causes *b*), while experience supplies the particulars.

To be sure, Shepherd does say that we elicit the further 'maxim' that like causes must always produce like effects. But for Shepherd this is not extrapolated from experience. On any given occasion when we learn that *a*s suffice to produce *b*s, it is experience—not repeated observations but crucial experiments—that supplies the details of what *a* and *b* consist in. The underlying principle that 'a like cause must produce a like effect', however, we grasp by reason, as Shepherd says: it is '*reason that forces the mind to perceive*' this principle (27). Experience tells us which kinds of objects cause which other kinds of objects, while reason again supplies the elements of universality and necessity—*all* like causes *must* produce like effects.

Synchronicity. Shepherd takes the prima facie surprising view that causes and effects are necessarily synchronous with one another. The more common view, she says, is that causes and effects are consecutive in time: 'They may also *seem* to follow one another, and *time* to elapse between the operation of the Cause, and the appearance of the Effect' (29). In fact, she objects, this is impossible. If there is a gap between cause and effect in time, then (i) when the cause is active the effect is not yet in existence, leaving nothing for the cause to act on; (ii) by the time that the effect comes into existence the cause is no longer there, so that we have returned to saying that the effect begins to exist of itself, which we know it cannot. While 'an object, in order to act as a Cause, must be in Being antecedently to such action; yet when it *acts as a Cause*, its *Effects* are *synchronous with that action*' (49). For instance, both wood and fire were already in existence but when put together, their conjunction produces combustion, and the conjunction and combustion are synchronous.

This creates a puzzle, however, for there are constant chains of causal actions in nature and Shepherd accepts that: 'A *chain of conjunctions of bodies*, of course, *occupies time*' (50). She gives the example of taking food causing nourishment:

Here the nature of nourishment, is a process which begins to act immediately that food is in conjunction with the stomach. 'That we are nourished'; is only the last result of a continuous chain of causes and effects, in formation from the first moment the food enters the stomach... [T]he effect of *nourishment*, being *subsequent* to, and at such a distance of time from, the original Cause, is only so, on account of its being the effect of a vast number of causes, of unions of objects in succession. (51–2; my emphasis)

But how can digestion take time if it is composed of a chain of causal actions in which *a* causes *b* causes *c* causes *d*, and so on, but where *a* and *b* are synchronous, *b* and *c* are synchronous, and so are *c* and *d*, and so on? David Landy argues that Shepherd's solution is that there are interstitial times between the causal combinations in these chains (Landy 2020b). Causal combinations can impart motion, and objects continue in motion until it brings them into their next causal interactions, where these motions occupy time (which fits with what Shepherd says about causation and motion in the *Essays*; see *EPEU* 370).[7]

---

[7] Another potential part of the solution might be that 'synchronous' need not always mean 'instantaneous'. It can also mean 'going on at the same rate and exactly together, as two sets of vibrations or the like' ('synchronous, adj.', *Oxford English Dictionary*). Perhaps, then, there can be cases in which *a* causes *b* continuously, so that *a* and *b* co-occur within an extended time-slice. For instance, when Shepherd says, 'the cause has not acted, *is not completed*, till the union has taken place, and the new nature is formed with all its qualities, in, and about it' (*ECRE* 50), this seems clearly to imply that at least some causal actions are not completed all at once but occupy duration. The problem, though, is that Shepherd often does pair 'synchronous' with 'instantaneous', for instance speaking of 'instant synchronous effects' (*ERCE* 97) and saying that an effect 'must instantly, and immediately, have all its peculiar qualities' (*ECRE* 50).

To return to naturalism. As I read Shepherd, on all six strands of the cluster she leans away from naturalism.

(1) *A priori reason*. We know the causal principle by reason and it precedes and structures our experience of an ordered, intelligible world. Observation and experiment identify which particular causal powers particular kinds of object possess (*ERCE* 139). But these inquiries are conducted on the presupposition of the *general* causal principle which we bring *to* experience (139–40). We do not derive this general principle from experience, for without it we could not make sense of any particular causal relations in the first place.[8]

(2) *'First philosophy'*. For Shepherd, as McRobert sums up, 'reason supplies... the true foundation for science, moral philosophy and belief in God' (n.d.: 177). In particular, Shepherd says of the sciences that

> all the conclusions its method of induction demonstrates, depend for their truth upon the implied proposition, 'That like cause must have like effect'; a *foundation* which [is] the only foundation for the truths of physical science, and...*gives validity* to the result of any experiment whatever. (*EPEU* 279; my emphasis)

(3) *Philosophy prior to empirical science*. The causal principle, known by reason, provides the indispensable basis for the natural sciences and for empirical investigation. Since philosophy makes the causal principle explicit and shows that we have rational grounds for believing in it, philosophy provides a grounding for empirical science.

(4) *Non-natural agencies*. For Shepherd, the defence of causation is integrally connected with the defence of God's existence as 'first' cause: 'To account for the facts we perceive, "there must needs be" one continuous existence, one uninterrupted essentially existing cause, one intelligent being' (*EPEU* 151). For we cannot

> imagine the existence of a series of dependent effects without a continuous being of which they are the qualities, and [to do so] is equal to the supposition of the possibility of every thing springing up as we see it, from an absolute blank and nonentity of existence. (391)

Just as there must be a cause of every particular object beginning to exist, equally there must be a cause of the entire causally interconnected set of objects. This entire order of causes and effects cannot just randomly pop into existence, nor can

---

[8] Again, if Folescu is right that the causal principle is really self-evident and intuitive for Shepherd, she would still remain a non-naturalist, because the principle would still precede and make possible observation and experiment rather than deriving from them.

it be the cause of itself for then it would have to exist already. So it must have a prior cause, namely God.

> Whatever variety and changes of beings there are, all changes must finally be pushed back to that essence who began not, and in whom all dependant beings originally resided, and were put forth as out goings of himself in all those varieties of attitudes which his wisdom and benevolence thought fit. (189)

The world is intelligible in virtue of conforming to the causal principle, and it has this intelligibility because of God's causal action in sustaining this entire order. As such God is an intelligent first cause, the 'universal mind' (390), whose 'eternal continuous capacity' subtends the ordered intelligibility of the world.

(5) *The mind.* Shepherd is a dualist for whom body and mind are 'essentially different' (155). The mind is the power of having sensations, and sensations are in themselves 'unextended' (386). In practice we never experience sensation without the body and brain, which both excite sensations of extension and form the system of causes necessary for sensations generally. Nevertheless, considering whether the mind can exist separate from the body: 'Abstractedly there seems no hindrance for such separate existence', because 'we know not whether in many other beings, sensations may not go on without brain' (156), being sustained on some alternative basis. And so we may rationally believe in posthumous existence, in which sentience would continue supported by some 'other cause equal to the brain, a finer body, an ethereal stimulus' (158).

(6) *Ethics.* Shepherd did not address ethics in any detail, but she inclined towards non-naturalism, as we can see from her criticisms of the physician William Lawrence. In the 'vitality debate' of the 1810s, he maintained that life was immanent in matter, not separately infused into it by divine action.[9] Amongst Shepherd's objections, she complained about the '*absurdity of moral treatment*, to a *material mind*' (*ERCE* 172). That is, we can only have a moral obligation to perfect ourselves if we have minds or souls not reducible to the brain and body, albeit closely bound up with the latter. We can then expect our souls to continue their course of 'moral amelioration' in the afterlife (*EPEU* 378).

Admittedly, there are more naturalist elements in Shepherd's thought as well. Because she sees philosophy as grounding empirical science and explaining why controlled experiments are crucial, she envisages continuity—mutual support— between philosophy and science. Her ontology is internally informed by science, since for her objects are constituted as members of kinds by their causal powers, which we identify and classify through scientific experimentation. And although she is a dualist, she stresses the close connection between mind and body. She

---

[9] On this debate, see Ruston (2005: ch. 1) and on Shepherd's take on it, Boyle (2021a).

maintains that sensation depends for its occurrence and content on the brain and nervous system, and holds that sensation will only be possible for us posthumously if we have some other 'finer' kind of body. Nonetheless, these are naturalist leanings within an outlook that is anti-naturalist overall—after all, on a cluster-based account one can be more or less of a naturalist or anti-naturalist. That Shepherd leans away from naturalism can be substantiated further by looking, in contrast, at Martineau's naturalism.

2.3 Martineau's Earlier Philosophy: Moralist Necessarianism

Martineau went on a long philosophical journey from the 1820s to the 1850s, most of it in full public view, for her 1832–4 *Illustrations of Political Economy* made her a celebrity whose every intellectual and political move was chronicled and debated in the periodical press. She began as a devout Christian and ended up an atheist, positivist, materialist, and hard determinist. Her journey has been narrated before,[10] but I want to bring out her *philosophical* evolution, from a position in the 1820s that was largely naturalist but still had substantial anti-naturalist strands, to full-blooded naturalism in the 1850s. Her abandonment of religion was a big part, but still only part, of this evolution.

In this section I reconstruct her earlier philosophical position.[11] It centred on belief in complete causal determinism, combined with an empirical and inductive account of causation quite opposed to Shepherd's account of causation, which Martineau went on to reject.

Martineau's earlier position was shaped by her background in Unitarianism, a form of Dissenting Christianity that went back to the Reformation but had assumed the particular shape that influenced Martineau with Priestley's work in the late eighteenth century. In *A General View of the Arguments for the Unity of God and Against the Divinity and Pre-Existence of Christ*, Priestley ([1788] 1812) argued that Jesus was an exceptionally good man and a moral exemplar, but entirely human. That said, Unitarianism's importance for nineteenth-century British culture lay not so much in theological doctrine as in its Enlightenment character, which, again, came largely from Priestley. Through his work, Unitarians came to hold that nature follows invariable laws laid down by God, so that by learning about nature's laws and workings we can better do God's will (Gleadle 1998: 11). Due to this religious vindication of scientific investigation and free rational inquiry, Unitarianism became 'a religion for intellectuals', as the

---

[10] See e.g. Boucher-Rivalain (2012), Hoecker-Drysdale (1992), Hunter (1995), Logan (2002), Pichanick (1980), Roberts (2002), Thomas (1985), Wheatley (1957), and Webb (1960).

[11] This has received very little attention. Even Martineau scholars tend to pass over this phase of her thought briefly or begin with the *Illustrations*.

translator and Germanist Susanna Winkworth remarked in 1856 (see Gleadle 1998: 10, 193). Consequently, even though Unitarianism always remained fairly small as a denomination,[12] it exerted a disproportionately great intellectual influence throughout the century. Just a few of those it influenced were William Benjamin Carpenter, Cobbe, Darwin, Charles Dickens, Elizabeth Gaskell, Ada Lovelace, John Stuart Mill, Constance Naden, Harriet Taylor, and Julia Wedgwood. Unitarianism was socially progressive, as we will see in Martineau's case. Following Priestley, she believed in human perfectibility and that everyone can improve themselves, at least given the right education and environmental circumstances.[13]

Martineau's early writings appeared in the *Monthly Repository*, a radical Unitarian journal.[14] Her very first essays on 'Female Writers on Practical Divinity', signed 'Discipulus', already evinced some of her key commitments: that the moral core of religion is more important than doctrine; that morality turns not on feeling but on reason, on acting consistently from principle; and hence that moral action is done from duty, not inclination (see also *EAT* 203, 209). Martineau published numerous subsequent essays in the *Repository* over the 1820s, later gathered into the signed collection *Miscellanies* (1836). Many of these essays were on theology and metaphysics, signed 'V', and from them we can identify the main elements of her early stance.

Epistemic virtues. She stressed the moral and intellectual virtues required for, and gained by, pursuing the truth and carrying out disinterested, impartial inquiry in a methodical way (*EAT* 67–77).

Necessarianism. Martineau's biggest influence was Priestley, for whom the world is an immense causal chain, each effect necessitated by all those preceding it, and all leading back to God as first cause. God is, moreover, an intelligent first cause who has ensured that the world is intelligible, composed of causal sequences that proceed invariably according to identifiable laws. For Priestley, human actions are determined like other events: actions are done from motives, and motives arise from causal chains (1777b: 26–56). Concomitantly, Priestley denied any mental substance separate from the body and identified the mind as merely the form of material chains of cause and effect within the brain.[15] He insisted, though, that he was a compatibilist: as long as we act from motives arising within our own brains along non-pathological routes, we are acting freely. Contrary to critics who thought his position left no room for moral responsibility, he insisted

---

[12] There were about fifty thousand Unitarians in Britain by 1851, according to Ruth Watts (1980: 274).
[13] It should be noted that Harriet's brother James Martineau completely reshaped Unitarianism in the latter half of the century. On his philosophy, see Waller (2014).
[14] From 1828 under W. J. Fox, the journal became 'an avant garde production... far ahead of its time, promulgating in the 1830s what only became current in the 1860s' (Armstrong 2021). Priestley was the journal's central reference point. Lewes, Taylor, and Mill published in the *Monthly Repository* in the 1830s; see Mineka (1944). (Indeed, Mill and Taylor met through Fox.)
[15] On Priestley's philosophy, see Wolfe and Wunderlich (2020).

that the 'doctrine of the *necessary influence of motives* upon the mind of man makes him the proper subject of discipline, reward and punishment, praise and blame' (86).

Martineau's enthusiasm for Priestley set her far apart from Shepherd, who opposed Priestley as vehemently as Hume. Her early manuscripts were directed against not only the 'atheistical' Hume but also '...the unitarian doctrine of the then new philosopher, Priestley' (Brandreth 1886: 29). Unfortunately, Shepherd's writing on Priestley is lost (Boyle 2018: 3). But we can infer that she objected to Priestley first, as she did to Hume, on the charge of atheism.[16] Denying the divinity of Jesus Christ placed the Unitarians so far outside Anglican orthodoxy that they were widely seen as atheists (Priestley's views being deemed so incendiary that he was called 'Gunpowder Joe'). Second, Priestley understood causation in terms of the transmission of material–energetic force. But, Shepherd says when objecting to Newton's account of attraction, '*Attraction* is a word fitted to keep the Deity forever out of view' (*EPEU* 367), because it construes the universe as full of movement all of itself without need of divine direction (362–71). Though she is discussing Newton, the point made here readily transfers to Priestley and thus indicates part of why Shepherd rejected his position. As she would have seen it, for Priestley, God instigates a material–energetic causal chain, and so he has been reduced to the prime force and is not really God, the supreme intelligence.[17] If, on the other hand, causal relations are universal and necessary and known by reason, then God is indeed a properly *intelligent* first cause (151–2), underpinning a rational and intelligible universe.

Unlike Shepherd, Martineau enthusiastically subscribed to Priestley's vision of 'eternal and immutable laws, working in every department of the universe, without any interference from any random will, human or divine' (*HMA* 1: 111). That said, Martineau was concerned lest complete causal determinism undermine responsible moral action. This was an especially pressing issue for her because she thought that moral action must be done from rational principle. So she argued that, on the necessarian view, what actions we take matters more than ever because every action is pregnant with countless consequences (1: 111–12). One might say that surely all our actions have consequences anyway. But for Martineau the consequences are further-reaching given universal determinism, because one can no longer imagine that whatever one does, others retain the free will to do whatever they may choose regardless. Instead, given universal determinism, what others become motivated to do depends on a causal chain that inescapably includes my own actions. Thus for the necessarian, one cannot escape or alleviate one's responsibility for one's own actions by leaving it to others to

---

[16] As McRobert suggests (n.d.: 55).
[17] Priestley insisted that God was an intelligent first cause, but this must have looked like trying to square the circle.

make the right choices; if I make the wrong choices, this will contribute, however minutely, to making others more likely to do wrong as well.[18]

What are the right choices? The recognition of how profoundly our actions affect others supplies Martineau with an answer: the right actions are the ones that have the most beneficial consequences for everyone, and consequences are beneficial if they increase overall well-being (*HMA* 1: 111–12). Perhaps surprisingly, though, Martineau repeatedly insisted that she was not a utilitarian.[19] But this, I believe, can be explained as follows. She thought that to act effectively and produce beneficial consequences, we must obey the laws regulating the natural and social world; we should not vainly try to act against these laws, which will only be self-defeating and result in thwarted intentions, unsatisfied desires, and unhappiness ([1831] 1836a: 276–9). There are, she stated, 'a few grand principles, which, if generally understood, would gradually remove all the obstructions, and remedy the distresses and equalize the lot of the population' (*IPE* 1: ix). Thus, for Martineau, the individual should not try to calculate the best consequences on his or her own, but should instead follow these 'grand principles' or general rules for action, which are supplied by the invariant laws that regulate natural and social life. Plausibly, then, she rejected utilitarianism because she equated it with act-utilitarianism (so that there is a case for saying that, despite herself, she was a kind of rule-utilitarian).

Associationism. Martineau upheld David Hartley's associationist view of mind (*HMA* 1: 104; *LLM* 118–19; see also *HMCL* 1: 18ff.).[20] Like other associationists, Martineau rejected innate ideas and held that our chains of associated ideas are built up contingently depending on our experiences. As such, we can potentially improve our thinking and establish sounder associative chains, especially if education establishes virtuous habits of thinking early in our lives. Because nothing is innate, everyone is equally capable of learning to think well, so long as education reaches them early enough (*EAT* 122). Thus, Martineau's associationism went along with a belief in human perfectibility—in the realistic possibility of a 'general improvement of the intellectual constitution' (93)—and thus in the importance of education. We improve our thinking by observing multiple cases of succession and learning to eliminate extraneous and adventitious variables (101): for example, ascertaining whether *b* always follows *a* other things being equal or whether *b* only follows *a* when *c* is present. In this way we learn

---

[18] Martineau put the argument more caustically: 'The indolent dreamers whom I happen to know are those who find an excuse for their idleness in the doctrine of free-will, which certainly leaves but scanty encouragement to exertion of any sort' (*HMA* 1: 112).

[19] HM to Henry Crabb Robinson, 8 January 1841, *HMCL* 2: 76; HM to Henry Reeve, 21 February 1859, *HMCL* 4: 155.

[20] Conversely Shepherd critiqued associationism at length: '*an association of ideas* will never prove any other existence than that of *an association of ideas*, but...*reason* has power to deduce the knowledge of an *universe*, existing independently both of ideas and their associations' (*EPEU* 270).

which sequences are really invariant; we learn to generalize judiciously and carefully, not in undue haste.[21]

An inductive account of causation was central to Martineau's outlook. She maintained that we only ever observe successions, no hidden mechanisms or 'secret connexions'. This denial that we can know of any real 'necessary connections' may seem an odd fit with her necessarianism. But in fact they went together, for Martineau thought that 'secret connexions' were unnecessary for science and that invariant natural laws could exist and be known without them (*EAT* 78; *EPT* 175, 241–2). From enough observations of succession, and by eliminating extraneous variables, we can reliably generalize that bs always succeed as and that, invariably, 'certain antecedents have certain consequences' (*EAT* 78). From there we may generalize to 'the uniformity of causation' as a whole (*EPT* 175). This, for Martineau, exhausted causation: a causal relation is an invariant, law-governed succession (175–6).

An inductive defence of induction was another piece of Martineau's picture. We must 'follow the inductive method in all researches', she stated (*EAT* 73). Thus, biting the bullet, she argued not only that we are justified, having repeatedly observed successions of a by b, in generalizing to an invariant law that bs follow as and as precede bs. We are also justified, having done this repeatedly, in generalizing to the conclusion that the inductive method is reliable because we have found it so thus far. Having ascertained that to date 'the familiar operation of ascertained causes is perpetual and uniform, we are obliged...to ground our expectations on our experience of the latter' (*EPT* 192).

Martineau noted that she differed from the 'Scotch school'—Thomas Reid et al.—because they granted more role to intuitions. She did not mention Shepherd amongst this school,[22] and seemingly did not know Shepherd's work when writing her 1820s *Monthly Repository* essays. Martineau and Shepherd became acquainted in London in the 1830s. Shepherd then asked to read some of Martineau's *Monthly Repository* articles and Martineau had them posted to her: 'It *can* do no harm' (HM to W. J. Fox, 18 June 1833, *HMCL* 1: 201). As that remark hinted, any enthusiasm on Shepherd's part was not reciprocated:

> How different were those parties [i.e. ones Martineau enjoyed] from the express 'blue' [blue-stocking] assemblies of such pedants as Lady Mary Shepherd! She went about accompanied by the fame given her by Mr. Tierney, when he said that there was not another head in England which could encounter her on the subject of Cause and Effect...; and it did indeed appear that she was, in relation to the

---

[21] Martineau's views recall those of Elizabeth Hamilton, who likewise combined associationism with a belief in perfectibility and hence in the importance of education; see Gokcekus (2019) and Hamilton (1801). Martineau knew Hamilton's work (HM to Philip Pearsall Carpenter, 12 December 1854, *HMCL* 3: 337).

[22] On Shepherd as part of Scottish philosophy, see Boyle (2017).

subtlest metaphysical topics, what Mrs. Somerville was to mathematical astronomy. The difference was, – and a bottomless chasm separated the two, – that Mrs. Somerville was occupied with real science, – with the knowable; whereas, Lady Mary Shepherd never dreamed of looking out first for a sound point of view, and therefore wasted her fine analytical powers on things unknowable or purely imagined. (*HMA* 1: 370–1)

Martineau branded Shepherd a 'pedant' who lacked sound judgement about what is real and knowable. This was not, as Lolordo claims, because Martineau was 'not...a fan of philosophy' (2020: 4). Rather, as we can see, Martineau disagreed philosophically with Shepherd's account of causation.

Martineau did not stop to spell out the nature of the disagreement, but we can. Both women oppose Hume, whom they construe as holding that belief in causation is irrational and unwarranted;[23] both defend causation against him partly in order to defend belief in God as first cause. For Shepherd, we have rational warrant for believing in necessary causal connections, grounded in God; for Martineau we have rational warrant for believing in invariant laws, deriving from God. There the similarities end. For Shepherd the causal principle is known by reason prior to experience, whereas for Martineau it is from the experience of regular successions that we generalize to belief in causation—she says, 'have we any belief in the connexion of cause and effect antecedent to experiment? I doubt it' (*EPT* 174–5). Thus, for Martineau, causal relations just *are* regular successions, whereas for Shepherd real causation only takes place when one object necessarily produces another, which involves causal powers, while for Martineau there is no warrant or need for believing in any such powers. In sum, Shepherd met Hume with a metaphysical account of causation; for Martineau this was unnecessary and went illegitimately beyond observation, and Hume could be met instead with an inductive account of causation as law-governed succession. For Shepherd, conversely, all induction depends on the causal principle and the principle that like causes produce like effects, and without these rational presuppositions no inductions can be made in the first place (*EPEU* 279–80).

For Martineau, a further merit of her view of causation was its practical consequences. Indeed, it directly engendered her project in the *Illustrations of Political Economy*. Presupposing our perfectibility and the importance of education, the project was to educate the public in the laws of political economy and so enable people to act in accordance with economic laws (*EAT* 281; *IPE* 1: ix). For there *are* invariant laws of social and economic life, just as there are of nature, according to Martineau; invariant laws hold everywhere. For example, because it is an economic law that the division of labour increases productivity, working

---

[23] Martineau based her view of Hume on his *Dialogues*, which she branded a work of 'deception' (*EAT* 84).

people's well-being will ultimately increase if they adjust to rather than resist this division. Again, because labour is the source of value, labouring is more productive when done freely; thus, slave labour is economically unproductive. Moreover, slavery violates liberal principles of free trade: free trade means that labour contracts must be entered into freely, making slavery absolutely wrong.[24] Each *Illustration* takes one economic law and shows how people's lives go better if they follow it. Thus, invariant laws provide us with rules for action: if we follow them then we can act effectively, 'influencing general happiness' (*IPE* 1: x). And because we ought to do what increases happiness, these rules of action are moral imperatives, and political economy is part of 'moral science' (1: xiii).[25]

To return to naturalism, the earlier Martineau already leaned in that direction. She rejected innate ideas and a priori knowledge: 'I... have no belief in Pure Reason, as put forth by Kant' (HM to William Furness, 28 November 1836, *HMCL* 1: 321). She saw our minds as part of nature, operating on the laws governing the association of ideas, laws that we can identify on an inductive basis. The right method of inquiry into both nature and mind is inductive and starts from observation (*EAT* 73, 193). Laws reign everywhere; everything is determined. Hence the right actions are those that align with these laws of natural and social life, about which we can learn inductively.

But there were anti-naturalist elements too. Martineau continued to believe in God, immortal souls and the afterlife, spurning the 'Hydra-headed monster of Atheism' ([1830c] 1836c: 238). Admittedly, she denied that we can *know* about God, the soul, or the afterlife, since we cannot observe them (*EAT* 72). Nonetheless, we must believe in God, as first cause and the origin of the causal chain ([1832] 1836b: 99), and as the foundation of our moral obligations (*EAT* 113). And we must believe in the soul and the afterlife because this gives purpose to our moral strivings, as our souls will continue to develop towards perfection after our bodies die (120–1). Bound up with these religious beliefs, Martineau emphasized that moral action is done from principle and duty, and that we must act responsibly and cultivate intellectual and practical virtues.

Shepherd's account of causation, I suggested, was largely anti-naturalist, albeit with some naturalist aspects. Conversely, Martineau's early position was largely naturalist but with some anti-naturalist strands. She combined them by holding that we ought to act in accordance with nature's invariant laws, which descend from God as first cause, making him the ultimate source of our moral obligations. Her early view can be called *moralist necessarianism*. It was an unstable combination. Despite Martineau's best efforts, the determinism pulled against the stress

---

[24] On the division of labour and slavery, see, respectively, Martineau's second and fourth tales 'The Hill and the Valley' and 'Demerara'.

[25] Thus Martineau insisted that the *Illustrations* was a 'work of Morals' (HM to Brougham, Wednesday November 1832, *HMCL* 1: 167) and that she wrote it as a 'Moralist' (HM to William Tait, 1 May 1834, *HMCL* 1: 244).

on responsible moral agency, while the inductivism pulled against the belief in God, the soul, and immortality by entailing that they were unknowable. Martineau's earlier stance, I believe, is interesting not despite but because of these instabilities, for it shows how, despite her valiant effort to hold her religious and naturalist commitments together, they intrinsically pulled in opposite directions. The dilemma this created for Martineau was one with which many other nineteenth-century thinkers wrestled.

In Martineau's case something had to give, and over the next two decades her naturalist side won out. But first came her travels around North America in the 1830s. In her resulting book *Society in America*, she recast religion as the belief in an *im*personal first cause, speaking positively about atheism:

> Religion is, in its widest sense, 'the tendency of human nature to the infinite'... It is in this widest sense that some speculative atheists have been religious men... though unable to personify their conception of the Infinite. (SA 3: 224–5)

Martineau's God was becoming more and more of a theoretical abstraction.

Soon afterwards Martineau became so ill from an abdominal tumour that she retired from public life to Tynemouth, where she remained housebound from 1839 to 1844. She made a miraculous recovery and promptly embarked on a 'grand tour' of Egypt and the Near East. These travels dealt the final blow to her already attenuated faith and she abandoned Christianity.[26] This left her ready to embrace a thoroughgoing naturalism, as she did, dramatically, with the 1851 *Letters on the Laws of Man's Nature and Development*.

2.4 Martineau's Naturalism in *Letters on the Laws of Man's Nature and Development*

Martineau seemed to have been cured of her illness by mesmerism: specifically by the 'phreno-mesmerist' interventions and guidance of Spencer T. Hall, assisted by the formidable practitioner Mrs Montagu Wynyard, Martineau's maid Jane Arrowsmith, and with advice from fellow phreno-mesmerist Henry George Atkinson. Mesmerism was a huge craze in 1840s Britain (see Winter 1998). In 'phreno-mesmerism' it was combined with phrenology, the practice of inferring people's psychological traits from the shapes of their skulls. Phreno-mesmerists stimulated parts of a mesmerized person's head to activate the traits and energies thought to correspond to that region of the brain. Martineau's remarkable

---

[26] Martineau's Eastern travels yielded *Eastern Life* of 1848. I defer to Chapter 6 consideration of its complex case for secularism, since this is bound up with the overarching metanarrative of the development of civilization which she sets forth in that book.

recovery understandably convinced her that phreno-mesmerism worked.[27] Seeking to understand the theory behind the practice, in 1847 she initiated an in-depth correspondence with Atkinson, much of which she published as the *Letters*.

This text has been described as 'one of the strangest works to carry the name of a reputable writer' (Webb 1960: 293). This is because Martineau, a famous and highly regarded public intellectual, solicits and laps up ingratiatingly the views of the younger, less well-known, and verbose Atkinson. But the form of *Letters* was strategic. Martineau coaxes Atkinson into expanding on a naturalist world view and explanatory programme of the sort to which she had already independently gravitated. She admitted as much in her *Autobiography*, saying that by 1847 she had already 'come by the views which I have absurdly supposed to derive, in some necromantic way, from Mr. Atkinson ... [and] my passage from theology to a more effectual philosophy was, in its early stages, entirely independent of Mr. Atkinson's influence' (*HMA* 1: 280-1). 'Mr Atkinson is not the author of my opinions', she added (HM to Mr Bogue, Winter 1851, *HMCL* 3: 184).

Yet this was not how Martineau depicted things in *Letters*. Instead, she presented her own latest standpoint mainly through Atkinson's words, presumably thereby hoping to deflect criticism.[28] For, at this time, being accused of 'materialism' could destroy one's intellectual reputation and career (see Winter 1997). The epistolary form allowed Martineau to try to protect herself by posing as merely disseminating a man's ideas.

The defensive strategy failed—not least because Martineau repeatedly corrected Atkinson when he lapsed into talk of immaterial forces, God, or spirit, exposing herself as the more consistent naturalist of the pair (e.g. *LLM* 157, 164). Criticism of *Letters* was ferocious: a slew of hostile reviews came out; several friends broke with her in horror; and once her brother James Martineau joined the chorus of unfavourable reviewers the siblings were forever estranged (see Martineau 1851). One can see why Eliot called *Letters* the 'boldest [book] ... in the English language' (GE to Charles Bray, 4 October 1851, *GEL* I: 364).

The book's perceived atheism was at the heart of the controversy, closely followed by its materialism (see e.g. Froude 1851). But Martineau complained that her critics had fastened on the 'merely collateral' part of the book and missed its 'essential part, – its philosophical Method', that is, the scientific method of observation and induction (*HMA* 1: 217-18). In fact, *naturalism* was the book's unifying thread, from which all its other aspects followed, including its particular form of atheism and its materialist approach to the mind. Let us look at

---

[27] After her death it emerged that her symptoms had been temporarily relieved because her tumour had expanded beyond her pelvic cavity, which happened to coincide with the mesmeric treatment; see Ryall (2000).

[28] As Hoecker-Drysdale argues (1995: 158-60).

Martineau's naturalist position in this book, focusing on letters contributed by Martineau (rather than Atkinson) unless otherwise indicated.

Scientific method. Science is the source of all knowledge, and science begins with observations and rises from these to theory; Martineau pledges her allegiance to Bacon (*LLM* vii–x, 1–4). Observations must be made by a 'truly impartial inquirer' (11), with all religious preconceptions set aside, along with any endeavour to fit facts to pre-existing doctrines (11–15). From observations we rise to grasp the laws governing them. This is the highest level of generality to which we can ascend—'all we know is, that every thing occurs and proceeds by immutable laws' (28). The phrase '*all* we know' is key: 'We know nothing beyond law, do we?' Martineau asks Atkinson: 'And when you speak of God as the origin of all things, what is it that you mean? Do we know anything of origin?' (164). No, she went on, we do not: we must reject

> the baseless notion of a single, conscious Being, outside of Nature, – himself unaccounted for, and not himself accounting for Nature! – How far happier... how much wiser to admit – that we know nothing whatever about the matter! (218)

Atheism. Understandably, Martineau was widely taken to be denying that there is a first cause, and this was explosive. For Diana Postlethwaite, 'Martineau was the first... brazenly and unequivocally to assert that God was dead' (1984: 146). But did she? Martineau reassured her interlocutors again and again that she was not an atheist.[29] However, when doing so she consistently distinguished between *popular* and *philosophical* atheism. The former was a bogeyman conjured up by religionists; the latter was the view with which she sympathized (*HMA* 1: 188–9). On the philosophical atheist view, we cannot avoid postulating or supposing a first cause, since the rational mind must seek an explanation for why there is anything at all. But we cannot know anything about such a cause (in Kantian terms, we could say, it is a regulative principle only). Because we cannot know about any such cause, we have no grounds to 'personify' it (i.e. to identify it with a divine person). For instance, amongst Martineau's many similar statements to this effect, she wrote to Atkinson in 1847:

> As to what my present views are, they are just these. I feel a most reverential sense of something wholly beyond our apprehension. Here we are, in the universe! This is all we know; and... we must feel that there is something above and beyond us. If that something were God... he would consider those of us the noblest who must have evidence in order to [have] belief; – who can wait to learn, rather than rush into supposition. (*HMA* 1: 290)

---

[29] See e.g. Martineau to Charlotte Bronte, Winter 1851, *HMCL*: 184; HM to F. J. Furnivall, 5 October 1851, *HMCL* 3: 211; HM to Charles Kingsley, 27 June 1851, *HMCL* 3: 236; HM to Richard Monckton Milnes, 20 April 1855, *HMCL* 3: 357–8; HM to Patrick Bronte, 13 November 1857, *HMCL* 4: 51.

We must feel that there is something beyond us, a first cause (*HMA* 3: 291), yet we may not personify it or claim to know about it. Consequently: 'There is no theory of a God, of an author of Nature, of an origin of the universe, which is not utterly repugnant to my faculties' (*LLM* 217).

Was Martineau positively denying that God exists—atheism—or only saying that we cannot know whether he exists—agnosticism? Recent scholars often class her as an agnostic. But the word *agnosticism* was not coined until 1869, by Huxley. For him, it meant 'suspense of judgement on all questions, intellectual and moral, on which we have not adequate data for a positive opinion'.[30] In one of his subsequent clarifications, he said:

> I invented the word 'Agnostic' to denote people who, like myself, confess themselves to be hopelessly ignorant concerning a variety of matters, about which metaphysicians and theologians, both orthodox and heterodox, dogmatise with utmost confidence.[31]

Huxley was seeking to differentiate his position from both (dogmatic) theism and (dogmatic) atheism, while maintaining that the only positive knowledge that we can have comes from observation and induction from observations. On the last point, his position is identical to Martineau's of thirty years before.

Indeed, she too in 1851 sought to differentiate her position from dogmatic atheism by distinguishing between popular (i.e. dogmatic) and philosophical atheism. But she still spoke of philosophical *atheism*, not a philosophical suspension of belief. This was because, for Martineau, we cannot know anything about God since his existence is beyond the scope of empirical inquiry, which is the only route to knowledge; *but* we therefore have no grounds for believing that he exists at all. This kind of stance is sometimes called *negative atheism*,[32] a label that I believe accurately captures Martineau's position, in which agnosticism and atheism converged. They often converged in this way in nineteenth-century Britain, with emphasis placed on our lack of grounds for positive belief rather than our lack of grounds for either belief or disbelief.[33]

---

[30] Actually this is Richard Holt Hutton's (anonymous) description of Huxley's views (Hutton 1870b: 136). Hutton was the first person to use the word 'agnostic' in print (again anonymously in Hutton 1869: 642). But Hutton was taking up Huxley's use of the word at the Metaphysical Society, founded in 1869. Huxley himself used the word in print for the first time only in 1879, apropos of Hume (Huxley 1879).

[31] This letter of Huxley's to Charles Watts (a secularist who fell out with Bradlaugh and Besant over the birth-control pamphlet) was printed in the *Agnostic Annual* in 1884; see Huxley et al. ([1884] 2021). Literature on Huxley and agnosticism is extensive; see e.g. Dockrill (1971), Lightman (1987), and Lyons (2012).

[32] Whereas positive atheism is the view that we *can* know that God does not exist (see Bullivant 2016).

[33] Lewes (anonymously) criticized Martineau on the grounds that 'Dogmatic Atheism, or the unequivocal denial of a God' could not be warranted empirically, but only 'Suspensive Atheism, or

Materialism. Fertile as the scientific method is, Martineau laments, it has not been fully extended to the human mind (*LLM* 13–14, 25–8). 'Metaphysicians' (such as Swedenborg) have obstructed inquiry by adopting 'the unphilosophical notion of an ulterior Spirit or Soul which uses the brain as its "instrument"' (92–3) and which is known through introspection or a special spiritual sense. Until recently we lacked a method for explaining our cognitive powers on a material basis, and so had to fall back on these ideas of spirit, just as people used to explain lightning and rainbows as creations of the gods (27). Fortunately, we now can observe the workings and causal–energetic interchanges amongst the brain, nervous system, body, and environment, and can start to map out how these produce our cognitive powers. This is how to learn about the mind: by studying it as part of nature using the same methods of observation and induction that have proven reliable and effective elsewhere. 'All the conditions of man and mental peculiarities are now traced to physical causes and conditions, exhibiting clear determining laws' (6). We do not yet know all the laws governing how 'Thought and Feeling [are] results of the brain', but we have learnt enough to be confident that empirical science will provide a full explanation in time (26).[34]

Martineau's confident denial of the soul may seem to jar with her professed admission of the limits of what we can know. Huxley, for example, would later take the contrary view that one cannot be committed to empirical investigation *and* to materialism, because the latter is a dogmatic overarching thesis of the sort that a commitment to empiricism rules out (1888: 239–40). For Martineau, though, it is the materialist programme that humbly confines itself to what can be known through observation and induction. 'Spiritualism', conversely, makes claims about spiritual agencies that we cannot possibly know, which deters us from studying the brain empirically and so inhibits the growth of knowledge.[35]

Determinism. In the *Letters*, Martineau now embraces hard determinism. Atkinson describes human beings as 'puppets': 'I am as completely the result of my nature, and impelled to do what I do, as the needle to point to the north, or the puppet to move according as the string is pulled' (*LLM* 132). Martineau had long been a determinist, following Priestley, for whom all actions issue from motives

---

the state of absolute non-affirmation', neither affirming *nor* denying God's existence—i.e. effectively, agnosticism (Lewes 1851: 202). In contrast, the self-professed secularist George Holyoake, a big Martineau fan, held that because her position was based on an admission of non-knowledge it was not best described as atheism anyway but as 'secularism' (Holyoake 1851a, 1851b, and see my discussion of Holyoake in Chapter 5). Here Holyoake coined the term 'secularism', doing so with reference to Martineau, so that the word bears the trace of her once-massive presence.

[34] Martineau later reiterated the need for a scientific approach to the mind, first studying the facts of the brain and nervous system and then seeing how they support our mental powers (HM to Henry Reeve, 23 February 1868, *HMCL* 5: 208).

[35] Another aspect of *Letters*, then, is the denial that any spiritual powers or agencies are involved in mesmerism; all mental powers and effects 'science is tracing to their origin, or abiding place, in the brain' (*LLM* 123). Incidentally, Martineau did explicitly call herself a materialist: 'My opinions [on the mind] are... "Materialistic"' (HM to G. Babb, 17 January 1871, *HMCL* 5: 283).

and all motives issue necessarily from chains of prior causes. But in *Letters*, rather than talking of determining psychological forces such as motives, she stresses the determining '*physical* causes and conditions' of the brain and body and the exterior environmental influences on them (6; my emphasis). She repudiates the view that 'mind [is] entirely independent of body, and ha[s] some unintelligible nature of its own, called free will, – not subject to law... though a man has no more power to determine his own will than he has wings to fly' (6). If free will *did* exist it would be 'a self-determining power, independent of laws, in the human will' (*HMA* 1: 111). But 'these popular notions are mere delusion' (*LLM* 6). There is no free will, then; the belief in it is mere delusion, a hangover from earlier eras when we lacked a scientific explanation for our thoughts and feelings.

Why does Martineau not retain her earlier compatibilist view of freedom? She does not spell her reasoning out, but part of the answer surely lies in her experiences with mesmerism. On Priestley's compatibilist view, with which Martineau previously agreed, an action is free if it is done from the agent's own motives, whatever the causal chain producing these motives. But Martineau's apparent mesmeric cure must have led her to see our motives and other thoughts and feelings as being constantly shaped by the outside world (and see *LLM* 41–6). This does not strictly contradict Priestley. Yet what is now salient to Martineau is that even actions that issue from an agent's own motives still ultimately issue from the external influences upon those motives. In all cases, the ultimate reality is simply that people's actions are determined by outer forces.

Laws of action. Perhaps surprisingly, Martineau continues to insist that action must be done from duty and principle, from 'obedience to Nature's laws' (283). This is partly a legacy of her earlier outlook, and partly because she continues to see the world as regulated by unvarying laws. Since these laws obtain, she thinks, we can only act in ways that will reliably produce beneficial consequences by following these laws. Rational principle, not sentiment, must accordingly remain our guide to action (282–5).

This ongoing emphasis on action from principle may seem to conflict with the hard determinism that Martineau has now adopted, but to her mind they are consistent. For her, the only effective moral principles are ones expressing the invariant laws regulating the universe. But these laws include the ones that regulate the causal workings of our minds as material entities and their interactions with the outer environment. In this way, Martineau's belief in complete causal determinism and her emphasis on principles as the basis of morality go together, united by the concept of invariant laws. Yet one might ask why following laws of nature should necessarily be beneficial, rather than, say, leading to a war of all against all. Martineau is more optimistic, because she believes that if one rises to a grasp of universal laws then one transcends selfishness, by becoming able to act impartially, from principles that have consequences for everyone, including oneself as merely one amongst others:

[W]e feel a contentment in our own lot which must be sound because it is derived from no special administration of our affairs, but from the impartial and necessary operations of Nature, – contented as we are with our share of the good and the evil of human life [and] raising and disciplining ourselves for no end of selfish pleasure or ransom... (*LLM* 285)

Martineau's naturalism in the Letters. Putting all the preceding together, Martineau is now a naturalist along every strand of the cluster. She despairs of 'the hopelessness of the metaphysical point of view' (*HMA* 2: 217), instead putting science at the head of inquiry—so, affirming (1) no first philosophy and (2) no a priori knowledge. Instead, (3) philosophy must restate and clarify the results of empirical science and debunk outdated metaphysical residues—that is, philosophy must be continuous with the sciences. She (4) takes a materialist view of the mind, (5) denies God, the soul, and any spiritual agencies, and (6) derives moral knowledge about how to act from laws of nature that are known inductively.

Martineau's thoroughgoing naturalism is interesting on several counts. It not only shows that women contributed to the formulation and development of naturalism in the period. We can also see how she has reached her new outlook by retaining some elements of her earlier moralist necessarianism (e.g. the idea of invariant laws) and rejecting others (e.g. the belief that these laws are laid down by God). Notably, one element that she retains is her optimism and commitment to a morality of principle. This makes Martineau's naturalism interestingly different from the more pessimistic forms of naturalism espoused by some of her contemporaries such as Schopenhauer. For him, all of nature manifests the endless, insatiable striving of the will, so that the world is inescapably full of conflict and suffering (Schopenhauer [1844] 1966). For Martineau, in contrast, following nature's laws allows us to improve the world for everyone; naturalism and social progress go hand in hand.

Turn to positivism. Martineau now gravitated to Comte. One of his central theses was that all societies obey the 'law of the three stages': theological, metaphysical, positive. In the theological stage, people explain events by divine legislation; in the metaphysical stage, events are explained by abstract causes, forces, and powers; and in the 'positive' stage, events are explained scientifically (i.e. by observation and induction to general laws) and our knowledge of these laws is organized into a system of the sciences. Not surprisingly, this appealed greatly to Martineau when she read about it in George Henry Lewes's *Biographical History of Philosophy* (1845–6). She then read Comte's *Cours de Philosophie Positive* (1830–42): his systematization of present scientific knowledge, including the historical and social-scientific knowledge from which the law of the three stages was itself inductively derived.

Committed as she always was to educating the public, Martineau became eager to disseminate Comte's system. She translated his *Cours*, in the process condensing it from six volumes into two. In her Preface, she envisaged positivism providing the public with a new and secure ground of belief and action, their previous religious moorings having fallen away:

> We are living in a remarkable time, when the conflict of opinions renders a firm foundation of knowledge indispensable,... to our intellectual, moral and social progress.... The supreme dread of every one... is that men should be adrift for want of an anchorage for their convictions.... [A] multitude... are alienated for ever from the kind of faith which sufficed for all in an organic period which has passed away, while no one has presented to them... any ground of conviction as firm and clear as that which sufficed for their fathers in our day. The moral dangers of such a state of fluctuation... are fearful in the extreme... When this exposition of Positive Philosophy unfolds itself in order before their eyes, they will, I am persuaded, find there... an immovable basis for their intellectual and moral convictions. (*PP* 1: iv–vi)

She excised Comte's Religion of Humanity, his proposed humanist successor to Christianity. Comte thought that although Christianity was no longer intellectually credible, the sentiments of social solidarity which religion fostered were vital, and a way to preserve them was needed. Martineau disagreed, and her Preface shows why.[36] For her, we must act *not* primarily from feelings but from firm and consistent principles—'immovably based' convictions. People act rightly (i.e. beneficially for the general happiness) when they obey the laws of nature and society. It is 'a firm foundation of knowledge', not warm sentiments about Humanity, that provides a sound basis for action and fosters social cohesion.

Martineau's turn to positivism enabled her to reject religion more emphatically than ever. For she took from positivism that the highest level of generality we can reach is that of the branches of science dealing with each region of laws of nature. We need not attempt to derive this total set of laws from any first cause; the only 'explanation' of these laws that we need is just their assemblage and organization in a system. The highest level of explanation is the system of sciences, which displaces theology and metaphysics.

She explained this in a later letter to Henry Reeve. Two different meanings of law tend to be confused, she says here. One is law as decree, which applies in government, and presupposes a human or divine will to issue the decree: it 'admits

---

[36] She may also have rejected Comte's Religion of Humanity because it was bound up with his regressive views of women. For Comte, women were to serve as objects of men's devotion in the family, fostering the social sentiments men were then to transpose into the outer public world. Cobbe (1869) and Blavatsky (*IU* 75–83) criticized Comteian views of women; while, on the Religion of Humanity, Eliot vacillated, Besant embraced it, and the Fabian socialist Beatrice Webb was drawn to it; see Pickering (2017).

the consideration of a *Cause*, – the Supreme Will...being the assumed Cause' (HM to Henry Reeve, 7 August 1868, *CLHM* 5: 228). The other is law as

> *the General Fact*, to wh[ich] special facts may be referred, by wh[ich] facts from a wide range of observations are classified, – that reference and classification constituting *Explanation* in its philosophical sense...No question of the ... *cause* of the phenomena, enters into the inquiry at all.

The domain here is nature, and no agency decreeing laws of nature need be presupposed. These laws need not be derived or traced back to a cause at all, only stated in systematic order. The critics only think there must be a God to lay down the laws of nature because they have confused the two meanings of law. Thus Martineau now thought that we do not even need to postulate a first cause; the rational mind can manage just fine without it.

I have argued in this section that by the 1850s Martineau moved over to full-blooded naturalism. But one key part of her earlier moralist necessarianism survived into her later thought: the direct derivation of moral principles from natural laws. This gave her naturalism its marked optimistic and progressive flavour. Yet it also compromised the consistency of her position. For when she recommended that people *should* act according to natural laws, she presupposed that it was possible for people, out of ignorance of these laws, to act in ways that go against them and produce harmful and self-destructive consequences. But then it seems that social laws, at least, cannot be invariant after all, otherwise we would not be able to act contrary to them. It appears that we *are* free to follow these laws or not, despite Martineau's claim that these 'laws...cannot be broken by human will' (*HMA* 1: 111).

Furthermore, Martineau's position was not altogether free of the same confusion between two senses of law that she diagnosed to Reeve, for she took laws of nature not merely to state facts but also to legislate for human action. This confusion was a residue of her earlier combination of naturalist and anti-naturalist ideas. But perhaps it also pointed to a broader problem with the naturalist standpoint she had developed. Perhaps that standpoint could not in itself do justice to morality or yield the moral prescriptions Martineau wanted to draw from it, and Martineau could only generate those prescriptions by surreptitiously retaining residual aspects of her earlier religious stance. This was Cobbe's assessment, and it helped to motivate her to defend an explicitly religious account of morality.

2.5 Cobbe's Anti-Naturalist Moral Theory

Cobbe admired Martineau as a role model of a woman intellectual making a living and shaping public debate by writing and publishing under her own name. Cobbe also admired Martineau's moralism. To her regret they never met in person; Cobbe tried to arrange it, but Martineau was by then too unwell (*LFPC* 2: 203-4). However, Cobbe profoundly disagreed with Martineau's naturalism, atheism, and empiricism, which, Cobbe thought, could not sustain a morality of principle as Martineau believed them to do. Cobbe dealt with this at length in 'Magnanimous Atheism' in 1877. But the grounds of the disagreement were laid long before—in Cobbe's *Intuitive Morals* of 1855-7, where she argued that naturalism cannot provide a sound basis for morality.

Cobbe makes this case in volume 1, chapter 2, 'Where the moral law is found'— namely, the law is 'found', or known, by a priori reason and not by induction from empirical facts. Cobbe maintains that 'experimentalism' cannot account for moral knowledge, and specifically that it cannot account for the universal and necessary character of fundamental moral truths and requirements. For her, this failure exactly parallels experimentalism's inability to account for the universality and necessity of certain principles that regulate our knowledge of nature, centrally causality.

Here Cobbe agrees with William Whewell that the causal principle regulates all our empirical knowledge and is known a priori as a precondition, not a result, of empirical inquiry. Whewell in turn had been influenced in this view by Shepherd. Whewell and Shepherd knew one another in Cambridge and London in the 1820s; he called her an 'unanswerable logician'; he inquired after further unpublished work of Shepherd's after her death; and he used one of her works as a textbook in university teaching at Cambridge (according to Brandreth 1886: 29, 118-19). Combining this evidence with the similarity between Whewell's a priori view of the causal principle and Shepherd's, we can conclude that Shepherd's *Essay* informed Whewell's view of causation. Cobbe does not refer to Shepherd directly and seems to have been unaware of her work.[37] All the same, a line of intellectual descent runs from Shepherd to Cobbe through Whewell. At least indirectly, therefore, Cobbe's case against naturalism builds on Shepherd's account of causation.[38]

Unlike Shepherd, though, Cobbe addresses causality not in its own right but only as a waystation towards her conclusion that experimentalism cannot account for the universality and necessity of basic moral principles. After all, *Intuitive Morals* is a treatise on ethical theory. Cobbe aims in it to create a new 'system of morals' which treats the 'law of right' as an end in itself transcending empirical

---

[37] Cobbe referred favourably to other Scottish philosophers, namely Dugald Stewart and Thomas Reid, saying that what these two saw as intuitive, Kant saw as a priori, and that she combines both (*IM* 48).

[38] We might wonder whether Cobbe might have learnt about Shepherd from Charles Lyell, to whom she became close, for, according to Brandreth, Lyell as well as Whewell called Shepherd an unanswerable logician (1886: 29). But even if Lyell recommended Shepherd to Cobbe, this would not have been in time to inform *Intuitive Morals*, since Cobbe only got to know Lyell in the 1860s (*LFPC* 2: 84).

nature (*IM* v–vi). To create this system Cobbe synthesizes Kantianism, theism, and intuitionism.

Volume 1, chapter 1 effects the synthesis of Kantianism and theism. Cobbe argues that the basic moral concept is duty and that duties are binding on all rational agents. Collectively these duties comprise the moral law. But a moral law presupposes a moral legislator, namely God. Only if the moral law is legislated to us by a higher, divine authority can we explain its binding, obligatory force.[39]

In making these arguments, Cobbe draws on the *Metaphysic of Ethics*, John Semple's 1836 translation of several works of Kant's: the *Groundwork*, part of the *Critique of Practical Reason*, and the *Metaphysics of Morals*. Cobbe also refers to Meiklejohn's 1855 translation of the first *Critique*; thus, Cobbe knows Kant's work quite well (in addition, she could read German). Here it is worth detouring for a moment to consider how well-known Kant's work was in nineteenth-century Britain. As I mentioned earlier, Martineau rejected Kant's a priorism in 1836; she also referred to Kant in the *Letters*, talking of 'his doctrine that space and time are not objective realities but conditions of human ideas' (*LLM* 162) and agreeing with Kant that time is the form of inner sense (163)—although she proceeded to look for a physiological basis of this form of experience. The cases of Cobbe and Martineau suggest that by mid-century Kant's work was reasonably well assimilated. As René Wellek showed in *Kant in England, 1793–1838* (1931), Kant's ideas were gradually imported and diffused over the early nineteenth century. Influential figures such as Coleridge and Thomas Carlyle played important roles in this diffusion.[40] As a result, interest in Kant grew, leading to Semple's and Meiklejohn's translations, which led in turn to a deepened engagement. This is reflected in the familiarity with Kant that we see in Martineau and Cobbe.[41]

To return to *Intuitive Morals*, in chapter 2 Cobbe brings in the intuitionist aspect of her approach. In nineteenth-century Britain, intuitionism and utilitarianism were the two main alternative approaches in metaethics. The two camps agreed on the substantial content of morality and that morality was a matter of knowledge, not feeling, but they offered different accounts of moral motivation and the nature of moral knowledge and facts. Generally for utilitarians, moral principles—such as 'pursue the greatest happiness of the greatest number'—were derived from empirical knowledge of what people actually desire (happiness) and from our observations of which courses of action augment or reduce people's happiness. Conversely, for intuitionists, basic moral principles were known immediately and were not derived from any other prior knowledge.

---

[39] For a more detailed account of Cobbe's ethical theory, see Stone (2022a).
[40] See Class (2012) on Coleridge's importation of Kant.
[41] More broadly, 'by 1860 the ideas of Kant were fairly well assimilated. It was possible to...find broadly reliable and reasonably engaged discussions of his views' (Mander 2011: 17).

Within this broad division, there were of course many differences between different intuitionists (as between different utilitarians). 'Intuition' itself was variously understood. In *Intuitive Morals*, Cobbe amalgamates a number of senses of 'intuition', claiming that intuition is not only the faculty by which we apprehend moral truths but also the same as both a priori reason and God-given conscience (*IM* 61-2). Why does Cobbe not simply say that we know moral truths a priori; what work does the appeal to intuition do? It enables her to make the link with religion, by saying that 'intuition...is God's tuition' (37). What we intuit (i.e. grasp a priori) is what God is showing to us through our use of reason. For when we use reason, we participate in the supersensory domain, which brings us closer to God. Cobbe also acknowledges a scholastic background to the concept of intuition:

> The schoolmen divided all knowledge into 'cognitio intuitiva' (that which we gain by immediate presentation of the real individual object) and 'cognitio abstractiva' (that which we gain and hold by the medium of a general term). (62)

Thus, intuitive knowledge is not derivative but 'fundamental' (62); it is immediate or direct—what we know by intuition we apprehend all at once, as a whole, rather than deriving it from a sum-total of parts; and in intuitive knowledge we directly apprehend reality itself. Specifically, for Cobbe, we apprehend the reality of the moral laws legislated by God, which transcend the empirical, natural world. For Cobbe, therefore, intuitive knowledge is not the immediate perception of moral properties in the world but is the rational grasp of moral requirements that obtain in the supersensible world.

With this background to Cobbe's overall standpoint in place, we can turn to her anti-naturalist arguments in chapter 2 of *Intuitive Morals*. Cobbe opens the chapter by categorizing the sciences into *exact sciences* (like mathematics and geometry), which rest on deductions from axiomatic necessary truths, that is, truths known a priori without any contribution from sensation; and *physical sciences*, which rest on inductions from experimental contingent truths that state observed facts. By induction, we rise to general truths like 'all vertebrate animals have red blood' (45). These general truths, like the particular observational truths from which they have been induced, remain contingently true in that the facts they refer to could conceivably have been otherwise. However, in all these contingent physical truths, whether general or particular, both sensation and intuition cooperate. That is, all have a priori (intuitive) as well as empirical components.

One a priori component that Cobbe highlights is the 'idea of causation': the axiom that every effect must have a cause (*IM* 48). Here she sets herself against Lewes, who had given an inductive account of the causal principle (*IM* 47, referring to Lewes 1845-6: vol. 3-4: 133). For Lewes, from many observations of specific correlations between *a*s and *b*s we infer that *a*s cause *b*s and, from many such cases of causal correlations over time, we infer to the higher-level general truth 'every effect has a cause'. 'Cause' here just means 'invariable succession'. Lewes argued this against Whewell, who held that we must already have the a priori idea of the causal principle to be able to identify any correlations as cases of causation in the first place, correlation not being itself sufficient for causation (Whewell 1840: vol. 1: 158–9). Cobbe sides with Whewell and argues against Lewes that no amount of observations can ever warrant the inference that *every a must* cause *b* or that *every* effect *must* have a cause. We can never get universality and necessity from the contingencies of sensation. Universality and necessity must have a different source and be supplied by the mind a priori (*IM* 47).

Lewes's view of causation is very similar to Martineau's, and this is no accident. The work by Lewes that Cobbe refers to is his extremely widely read *Biographical History of Philosophy*. The work went through many editions, but when Lewes wrote the first edition of 1845–6, which Cobbe discusses, he was a Comteian positivist and presented the entire history of philosophy as leading up to Comte. For Lewes, Comte concluded the centuries-long process in which philosophical speculation had been superseded by positive science. Lewes went on in the early 1850s to expound Comte's views (anonymously) in the weekly journal that he co-founded and co-edited from 1850 to 1854, the *Leader*.[42] Those articles went into his 1853 book *Comte's Philosophy of the Sciences*. Near its start he proclaimed that:

> In the *Positive* phase the mind, convinced of the futility of all inquiry into *causes* and *essences*, restricts itself to the observation and classification of phenomena, and to the discovery of the invariable *relations* of succession and similitude which things bear to each other: in a word, to the discovery of the *laws* of phenomena.
> (1853: 11)

Martineau had read Lewes's *Biographical History*, which galvanized her to read Comte. Because she then wanted to disseminate his views, she and Lewes found themselves competing to popularize Comte.[43] Thus Lewes and Martineau were at this point engaged in a common programme and, notwithstanding certain differences, they had similar philosophical orientations.[44] Moreover, they moved in the same radical liberal and secular circles around the *Westminster Review* and the

---

[42] On *The Leader*, see Brake (2021). Martineau and Eliot both contributed, Eliot very frequently, and all anonymously. Cobbe also contributed numerous unsigned pieces in 1867.

[43] 'In 1853, within weeks of each other, rival publishers released Martineau's *The Positive Philosophy of Auguste Comte* and Lewes's *Comte's Philosophy of the Sciences*. Both...contained abridgements of recent translations of Auguste Comte's *Course in Positive Philosophy*' (Rilett 2016). On Lewes's positivism, see also Barrat (2005).

[44] Regarding the differences, they particularly disagreed over psychology: for Lewes, positivism allowed for the science of mind to draw on introspection as well as physiology; doing so was necessary because pace 'Materialists' 'no amount of ingenuity will make an "impression" transmitted along a

Leader. Cobbe knew of this proximity between Martineau and Lewes, not least because it was pretty common knowledge. So although she directed her criticisms against Lewes, through him she was criticizing the whole family of positivist-leaning thinkers that included Martineau.[45]

There is a religious element to Cobbe's criticism of Lewes. For Cobbe, causation and religion are integrally linked, just as they were for Shepherd, Martineau, and almost everyone at the time. Cobbe remarks: 'Hume, by proving that the idea of causation could not be legitimately derived from experience, believed that he had undermined the throne of the Great First Cause' (*IM* 48). Thus (like Shepherd) Cobbe understands Hume to have argued that from observation we can only ever get correlation, the further idea of a necessary connection being a mere rationally unwarranted habit. And, Cobbe takes it (also like Shepherd), in debunking causation Hume at once undermined belief in God as first cause. In contrast Cobbe defends causality *and* God, together.

However, Cobbe's connection of causality with God is somewhat circuitous because she does not connect them on the grounds that God must be presupposed as first cause. Rather, for Cobbe, given that moral laws exist, God must be their legislator. God is not first cause of nature, but first legislator to moral agents. Cobbe calls this the 'moral argument' for God's existence (e.g. *IM* 11), and maintains: 'Kant has admirably proved that it must be on *moral* grounds that a true faith in God is alone to be obtained' (1857: 62).[46] This further leads Cobbe to qualify the scope of the causal principle. Every *phenomenon* must have a cause, but the causal principle does not apply to such noumenal realities as God or our immortal souls: 'No one believing either in an infinite or in finite spirits ever deemed them ruled by the same necessity of causation, or that the world of noumena is bound by the same chain as the world of sense' (*IM* 48). God and the soul are not physical, not part of nature, and so do not fall under the causal principle. Thus Cobbe espouses a 'two-world' metaphysics, dividing the non-material realm—of God, the soul, the moral law, and the afterlife—from material nature.

---

nerve...explain the nature of *perception*' (1853: 215). Martineau in contrast thought that the mind *did* have to be approached entirely as part of nature, physiologically, with no recourse to unscientific introspection, as she made clear in *Letters* (Eliot sided with Lewes; GE to Sara Hennell, 2 September 1852, *GEL* II: 54). Martineau and Lewes also disagreed over atheism, as noted above, and Lewes further criticized Martineau for neglecting the emotions and deifying law (Lewes 1851). Finally, in 1853, Lewes was already beginning to move away from Comte.

[45] Consequently, when Cobbe criticized Martineau later in 'Magnanimous Atheism', she criticized her along with other positivists, treating them as a group—in which she included Eliot, the middle term between Martineau and Lewes, and Martineau's close friend in the early 1850s.

[46] She refers in this connection to Kant's first *Critique*, in Meiklejohn's (1855) translation. The moral argument for God's existence became increasingly important over the century, as arguments from design lost their credibility. One of the most developed statements of the moral argument came from James Martineau (1888: esp. 17–18). His position was informed by his extensive conversations with Cobbe—their letters reveal 'his almost humble dependence on her judgment' (Mitchell 2004: 151) (the two were friends from the 1860s onwards).

But how then are God and causality connected? Cobbe maintains that we know that every event must have a cause 'by the *a priori* operation of the mind itself' (*IM* 61), and that 'we acquire necessary truths by the mind's own operation' (46). 'What truth soever is necessary and of universal extent "is derived by the mind from its own operation, and does not rest on observation or experiment"' (51).[47] For Cobbe, then, *we* impose the causal principle upon experience because the inherent operation of our minds requires us to think that every event must have a cause. Presumably Cobbe means that the mind must impose the causal principle upon sensation as the precondition of having intelligible experience, although she does not quite say so. In that case, Cobbe connects God and causality as follows: God is the supreme legislator in the moral domain and the source of 'musts' in the sense of moral requirements; the human mind is the legislator in the natural domain and the source of 'musts' in the sense of causal necessities. The mind stands in the same regulatory role vis-à-vis nature as God does to the soul; causality is the middle term in the former case, morality the middle term in the latter.

Probably most readers today will be sceptical of this two-world metaphysics. But seen in relation to Martineau's late letter to Reeve on 'General Facts', Cobbe's position at least has the advantage that it does not equivocate on 'law'. Instead, Cobbe distinguishes moral laws, as prescriptions legislated by God, from causal laws, as necessities that the mind imposes on experience to make it intelligible. Moreover, in neither case is 'law' a synonym for 'General Fact', for mere regularity is not law. Both senses of law are prescriptive, although in different ways.

Cobbe has dealt with causality as part of her classification of the sciences. With that classification in place, she argues that morality is an exact—pure a priori—science. Its basic axioms are a priori principles such as 'benevolence is right' and 'falsehood is wrong'. These are universal and necessary truths. Thus, really the axioms are 'benevolence *must always* be right' and 'falsehood *must always* be wrong'. 'Right' means obligatory and 'wrong' prohibited, so that these axiomatic truths specify obligations (*IM* 9). To be sure, determining how to apply these principles in reality is complicated. We cannot simply deduce the applications, for they involve empirical input. But neither can we generate practical principles purely inductively. We can ascertain empirically which kinds of actions produce the most happiness and unhappiness, but we cannot get from these empirical generalizations to the knowledge that it is right or wrong to produce happiness or unhappiness (*IM* 71–2). Instead, we must carry out a 'traduction' whereby we combine an a priori principle ('benevolence must always be right') with an empirical generalization ('caring for companion animals makes them happy') to yield a practical prescription ('it is right to show care to companion animals') (*IM*

---

[47] Cobbe is partially quoting from Semple's introduction to his Kant translation (Semple 1836: xxv).

76); the now-archaic 'traduction' referred to a middle form of syllogistic reasoning that was neither inductive nor deductive.[48]

Cobbe's central argument regarding morality has the same structure as her argument regarding causality: we cannot get binding normative requirements out of empirical generalizations, just as we cannot get necessary causal relations out of empirical regularities. In the moral case, empirical generalizations can only ever give us contingent truths ('*b*s make *a*s happy') but not universally necessary moral requirements ('benevolence is right') or practical prescriptions ('it is right to do *b* to *a*'). In short, we cannot derive normativity from natural facts.

Cobbe, then, is an anti-naturalist along all six strands of the cluster. She (1) upholds 'first philosophy': philosophy theorizes the basic principles underlying the various sciences, as she does in *Intuitive Morals*; (2) affirms that there is an a priori component in all of our knowledge; (3) divides the pure a priori from the physical sciences, making philosophy and empirical science discontinuous; (4) is a dualist for whom the immortal soul is separable from the mortal body (as we will see in Chapter 3); (5) affirms the existence of God, the soul, the moral law, and the afterlife; (6) treats moral knowledge as a branch of pure a priori knowledge, discontinuous from the empirical sciences. Compared to the later Martineau, Cobbe was at the opposite end of the naturalist/anti-naturalist spectrum. The two agreed that morality was a matter of duty and principle; but the philosophical standpoints on which they based this were poles apart.

2.6 Welby, Meaning, and Anti-Naturalism

Although Welby was born in 1837, it was only after 1870 that she undertook an intensive programme of self-education and developed her philosophy. She did so partly by corresponding with many other intellectuals: sending them drafts of her work, soliciting their feedback, and hosting intellectual gatherings, making herself 'a centre for the transmission of ideas' (Thayer 1968: 306). The first outcome was her work of scriptural interpretation *Links and Clues* (1881), which already embodied Welby's distinctive approach to meaning. Over the 1880s she became convinced that meaning and interpretation were just as relevant to science as they were to scripture. She addressed the relation between science and meaning repeatedly, effectively critiquing naturalism in the process. We see this in, amongst others, her unpublished essay 'Law of the Three Stages' (1886) and her published articles 'Meaning and Metaphor' in the *Monist* (1893)[49] and 'Sense, Meaning and Interpretation' in *Mind* (1896). I will focus on these in reconstructing Welby's anti-naturalism.

---

[48] See 'traduction, n.', *Oxford English Dictionary*.
[49] *The Monist*, founded in 1890, was the first American specialist philosophy journal, closely followed by the *Philosophical Review* in 1892.

First let me note how these writings fit into the broader contours and character of Welby's thought. In the 1900s she further enlarged on and systematized her views of meaning and language, particularly in *What is Meaning?* (1903) and finally *Significs and Language* (1911). She also addressed the reality of time in *Mind* (1907, 1909). Throughout the intervening years, she produced many unpublished drafts and notes and kept up her very extensive correspondence (which, she said, had 'outgrown [her] power to deal with it'; *VWF*, VW to Mary Everest Boole, 1 December 1889). Her letters and writings covered mind, the self, nature, life, history, and evolution amongst many topics. Welby's strategy for doing philosophy was thus multifaceted. She published in the nascent milieu of professional philosophy (*Mind*, *The Monist*) while also using some of women's older participatory strategies—doing 'writerly' and religious philosophy in *Grains of Sense* and *Links and Clues*, and making use of salons and letters. Indeed, Welby used correspondence to an exceptional degree, repurposing this 'private' medium to her intellectual ends.[50] Scholars of Welby's correspondence have focused on her male interlocutors,[51] but there were many female ones too, including three women who figure in this book: Annie Besant, Vernon Lee, and Julia Wedgwood. Some of the connections with Besant will come in here.[52] Welby made no direct reference to Shepherd or Cobbe, though, and she referenced Martineau only briefly. All the same, that latter reference reveals a thread that links Welby's anti-naturalism (negatively) to Martineau, partly through Huxley.

In 'Law of the Three Stages' Welby takes issue with Comte's progression religion–metaphysics–positivism, under Martineau's translation as the 'Law of human progress' (*PP* 1: 1–2).[53] Welby restates this position thus:

> We ostentatiously abjure 'mythology' or 'metaphysics' and take refuge in the obviously or apparently useful. We insist on rigidly confining ourselves to plain and provable fact, ... we retreat to the 'recesses of hard dry logic' and the nucleus of ... 'matter of fact' and 'common-sense'. (*SU* 333)[54]

---

[50] Her daughter Nina Cust published selections from her 1879–91 and 1898–1911 letters as *Echoes of Larger Life* (*ELL*, 1929) and *Other Dimensions* (1931). A larger selection is in *Signifying and Understanding*, edited by Susan Petrilli (2009). Welby's letters with Peirce have been published in their own right (Hardwick 1978).

[51] However, see Pietarinen (2013) on the correspondence with Peirce of both Welby and the American logician, psychologist and pragmatist Christine Ladd-Franklin.

[52] Welby's letters with Wedgwood will come into Chapter 4. For a full list of Welby's correspondents, see *SU*, Appendix 3. Lee met and became friends with Welby in 1886 (*SLVL* 2: 181–2); thereafter they met frequently and discussed philosophy, and Lee described Welby as 'extremely metaphysical and mystical' (VL to Matilda Paget, 11 July 1887, *SLVL* II: 371–2).

[53] Eliot had simultaneously formulated the 'Law of Progress' (*PWR* 4), and was also enthusiastic about positivism, calling Martineau's Comte edition 'her great work' (GE to George Combe, 20 November 1853, *GEL* VIII: 88).

[54] In *SU* Petrilli titles the essay 'Threefold Laws', one of Welby's several alternative titles for it. I prefer 'Three Stages' because it shows the engagement with positivism. Indeed, Welby initially shared the essay with the arch-positivist Frederic Harrison, who urged her to submit it to *The Nineteenth Century* (see *ELL* 165–70).

Welby objects that what had seemed a promising approach to the human race, promising because it recognized that humanity is advancing and evolving dynamically and historically, has led only to a 'blank wall'. Instead she proposes three different stages of human thought: (i) morality/religion/philosophy, all of which assert absolutes—the stage of the 'primitive dogmatist' (336); (ii) experimental science; (iii) 'The vitally energetic, the spiritually generative,... waiting for us not before, but after, we have let patience have her perfect work' (337). Thus, *pace* Comte and Martineau, science is only the *second* stage, metaphysics having been amalgamated into the first with theology; and there is a new third stage, which goes beyond dogmatic religion *and* experimental science, encompassing them both in an ascending, dynamic, onward spiritual movement.

Welby objects to positivism, then, under the distinctly British-empiricist slant that Martineau gave it as the 'philosophy of fact' (*HMA* 3: 323). The 'philosophy of fact' was also championed by Huxley, of whom Welby proceeded to make several critiques, first in 'Truthfulness in Science and Religion' of 1888 (*SU* 197–207), then in 'Is There a Break in Mental Evolution?' of 1890 (*SU* 207–9),[55] then, above all, in 'Meaning and Metaphor' of 1893. In this essay her central contention is that

> [M]eaning – in the widest sense of the word – is the only value of whatever 'fact' presents itself to us.... Significance is the one value of all that consciousness brings, or that intelligence deals with; the one value of life itself. (*MM* 524)

Welby is explicitly opposing Huxley's claim that scientists must avoid treating metaphors and symbols as part of the facts. Huxley urged scientists to avoid the 'intellectual shadow-worship' of personifying such hypotheses as 'law, and force, and ether'; this was an outdated hangover from theology. A 'true scientific culture' must instead recognize that these hypotheses are merely symbols and not 'real existences' (Huxley 1886: 505–6). Laws, forces, and so on are merely symbols that we have devised as provisional ways of making sense of observed facts; they are not themselves part of the facts.

Huxley, and his scientific empiricism, was thus Welby's central foil in the early 1890s. But an indirect link with Martineau remained, because Huxley's empiricism had taken shape in a period when he was close to what Deborah Logan calls the '*Westminster Review*'s Comtist coterie' (Logan 2009). Having read Comte in the 1840s, Huxley (anonymously) reviewed the Comte works by both Martineau and Lewes for the *Westminster Review* in January 1854, at the height of the pair's competition to disseminate Comte, and when Chapman and Eliot had just commissioned Huxley as the *Westminster*'s science reviewer. Huxley favoured Martineau over both Comte himself—too verbose and long-winded—*and* Lewes.

---

[55] The former appeared in the *Church Quarterly Review*; the latter was presented at the British Association for the Advancement of Science.

He complained that Lewes tended, undesirably and inconsistently for a positivist, to smuggle in his favoured scientific 'speculations' as if they were facts (Huxley 1854: 254–5).[56] We see the legacy of Huxley's engagement with positivism when he went on to claim that 'law' and 'force' only name abstractions and not factual realities.

Admittedly, in the 1860s Huxley became highly critical of positivism. He denounced Comte's Religion of Humanity, his collectivism, his outdated scientific knowledge, and his futile attempt at a complete systematization of knowledge (see Huxley 1869). Above all, Huxley objected that positivism had fossilized from a method into a *credo*. The elements of lasting value in positivism were its empiricism and inductivism, for Huxley; but in the name of these very commitments, one should not adopt fixed systems of the sort into which positivism had degenerated. These criticisms notwithstanding, for a time in the 1850s the positivist circle that included Martineau had informed Huxley's commitment to empirical scientific method. As such, when Welby criticized Huxley, she was targeting a family of empiricist views to which Martineau had contributed. This is registered in the fact that Welby had directed her first anti-positivist critique against Comte and Martineau, though Welby changed her target instead to Huxley in her published work (exemplifying the wider pattern for women to reference men instead of women in their publications).

In short, Welby made her critique of naturalism-cum-positivism-cum-empiricism within a field of discussion that went back to Martineau's *Letters*. On the one hand, Welby's work looks ahead to the linguistic turn; on the other hand, it looks back to nineteenth-century debates on science and religion in which Martineau had been central. With this background in place, let us examine what Welby called her 'Critique of Plain Meaning' (*MM* 513).

Gathering facts presupposes a pursuit of significance. Scientists only ever investigate certain facts because they sense that these facts are of broader significance. They seek to 'resume the value of innumerable observed facts under formulae of significance like gravitation or natural selection' (*WM* 6). Even in making supposedly impartial observations we are gathering related facts and identifying patterns under which they fall. It is not quite that observation is invariably theory-laden, rather that it is always motivated by the search for the significance of facts. This is because the human mind inherently reaches for significance (*MM* 524): we are intelligent beings who read messages and look for links amongst the materials with which our senses present us (*SMI* 187). Because this is inherent in the mind, having grasped the significance of one set of facts, we then inevitably look for higher levels of significance that unite the significant groupings we have already grasped, and so on endlessly. The mind reaches ever higher. Or as Welby

---

[56] Eliot lamented the contrast between Huxley's 'contemptuous notice' of Lewes and his 'unmitigated praise of Miss Martineau' (GE to John Chapman, 17[?] December 1853, *GEL* II: 132).

wrote to Besant in 1890, 'my thought is a world-thought; its imagery necessarily rises from the planetary to the solar and then to the cosmical order' (*VWF*, VW to AB, 18 October 1891).

'Facts' presuppose language. Huxley believed in 'a body of terms which are direct expressions of "fact"' (*MM* 514). Conversely for Welby, any statement of the 'facts' in language already embodies meaning in a broader sense than Huxley allowed. Most basically, for Welby, language is meaningful in that it conveys 'thought', and 'thought' for Welby is the mental act of linking a manifold of things or elements together because we have the sense that they have a shared significance (*SU* 466). So: 'We may appeal to "hard, dry" facts; but we perforce put something out of ourselves, even into these. They become "facts" under the quickening touch of "mind"' (*MM* 514). This 'quickening touch' is not primarily intentional. Rather, the language we use unselfconsciously is a field of inherited connotations, metaphors, assumptions, and 'unconscious survivals'. For example, the word 'earth', even in a geology paper, carries meanings ranging from 'soil' to 'the home of humanity'; whenever we use the word all these links are in play in the background (515). Welby thus sees metaphor as inherent in language, because what language does is make connections amongst a manifold, and metaphor is a key way that it does so.

Linguistic ambiguities are best acknowledged. Scientists who insist that they deal in literal statements of plain fact ignore this complex, mobile play of meaning and metaphor in language. This leaves them its unwitting captives, at the mercy of the inherited connotations that they refuse to acknowledge. The result is untold confusion within science, a 'plague of misunderstanding which is fatally raging amongst us' (*GS* 136). For scientists make ambiguous statements without noticing it, and then project their own unexamined assumptions onto one another, assuming that others understand words in the same way that they do.

What we need, though, is not to eradicate or prune away these inherited webs of meaning—which is impossible if we are to speak and write meaningfully—but to reflect self-consciously on these webs and so be aware, when speaking about (say) the earth, *which* inherited meanings we want to carry forward. For example, Welby suggests, Darwin's title *Descent of Man* was 'a bull'—one of 'those devastating animals which overrun the fair fields of literature' and sow confusion everywhere. For his real aim was to document 'the Ascent of Man' (*GS* 99–100), that is, how humanity has *emerged from* lower animals rather than *regressed back* into their condition. He could have avoided much confusion and opprobrium by using the right word for his theory: *ascent* not *descent*.

Meanings can illuminate significance. The very idea of confining ourselves to bare facts presupposes inherited meanings congealed in the words 'fact', 'basis', 'ground', 'solid', and so on (as when we 'base' our theories on facts, form 'solidly grounded' generalizations, etc.). That is, not only are certain facts picked out *as* facts because they bear on a significant generalization, but also the word *fact* is embedded in complex chains of metaphors—specifically 'earth-bound' ones. The language is 'let us stick to solid ground', 'let's not fly into airy speculations', and so on. This restricts our thought, inhibiting our minds from following their natural inclination to rise to solar and cosmic levels and engage in the highest-level, most speculative acts of interpretation. Empiricism holds us back from seeking and finding significance. As this criticism of earth-bound metaphors conveys, Welby considers some inherited meanings more illuminating than others. Some of these inheritances may drag us down, as with earth-bound metaphors, but other inheritances, when recognized and followed out, can guide our thought upwards towards the real significance of things. But without attending to embedded linguistic chains, we cannot ascertain which chains are worth retaining and thinking with, and which are obstreperous 'bulls' and best set aside.

Sense, meaning, and significance. How does Welby understand these terms, which figure centrally in her anti-positivist argument? She elaborates in 'Sense, Meaning and Interpretation'.[57] Given the complexity of ingrained meaning, she contends, it is futile to try precisely to define and demarcate these terms; besides, precise definitions lose much of language's value—its depth, flexibility, ambiguity, and rich suggestiveness (*SMI* 1: 34–5). All these qualities can greatly illuminate matters of real significance, if we are open to them. Thus, although Welby warned about ambiguous and confusing 'bulls', for her we avoid ambiguity and confusion by acknowledging language's complexity rather than trying, quixotically, to eliminate it (2: 191).

Accordingly Welby approaches 'sense', 'meaning', and 'significance' by unfolding some of their many existing meanings. 'Significance' is something's importance, value, interest, and broadest-level placement in the whole scheme of things (1: 27). 'Sense' is the tacit awareness that there must be some significance to a phenomenon, and an implicit and instinctive judgement about where that significance lies (1: 26). 'Meaning' is the thought (about significance) that is conveyed in language by the sets of connections it makes, connections that are initially unconscious but can be brought into our awareness (1: 29).

Although Welby is part of the linguistic turn, she is very far from being a logical positivist. She rejects strict definitions and the attempt to isolate observation statements, and she finds some of the most significant statements in the religious and metaphysical domains that logical positivists find meaningless. Her views have some affinities with post-structuralism, because for her language is polysemous and pervaded by metaphor. However, Welby is a realist, for whom the polysemy and metaphoricity of language enable it to tap into the deepest strata of reality. If we can 'expand the area of really significant expression' (i.e. attend to ingrained meanings and pick out the worthwhile and illuminating ones) then we

---

[57] She did so too in *What is Meaning?* and other post-1900 writings but, given my nineteenth-century remit, I confine myself to her pre-1900 work.

can '*expand the present limits of valid speculation*' (1: 33, 31). Speculation is valid because significance is not merely a construction of our minds; significance is really out there in the world, and our minds reach towards it. By riding on the waves of language, as it were, we can reach deeper levels of real significance, so that 'our knowledge slowly grows to a fuller harmony with the Infinite Reality' (2: 197).

Idealism. We see that Welby was a kind of idealist, for whom reality exists at multiple levels from the most material to the most ideal.

> Mine is the ideal realism which absorbs and digests materialism and turns it into life-tissue. Part of the process is the transformation of the central concept from matter into motion, from the static which is secondary, episodial, incidental, contributory, into the dynamic which ... is original and originative, ... evolutionary and executive. Thus my ideal realism becomes the real idealism.
> (VW to Maclure 1888–90, *ELL* 232–3)

On this view, matter is derivative and secondary. It points beyond itself to the broader web of significance that overreaches it, 'the *true Fact*...which is beyond the skin-deep appearances of space and time, while including all they teach' (VW to Eliza Lynn Linton, 1886–8, *ELL* 175; my emphasis). Welby's idealism is 'real', then, because for her significance is really out there in the universe: significance is 'the true fact', more ultimate than any 'mere sense-impression'. But this is *ideal* realism because the significance that is really out there is not itself material; rather, it binds material things together and supplies the overarching horizon in which they are embedded.[58]

I approached Welby's 'critique of plain meaning' by pointing out that the field of discussion into which she was intervening had been shaped by Martineau's naturalism. This field was shaped by other women too, among them Besant, with whom Welby exchanged letters. This conversation did not make it into Welby's published work. But I want to look at it briefly, because it reveals more of the background of inter-women conversations in which Welby developed her ideas.

Welby wrote to Besant when the latter had recently converted to theosophy. There were affinities between Welby's idealism and theosophy, because the theosophists also thought that matter was derivative of higher spiritual levels of reality and that the universe was in continuous dynamic and spiritual evolution. Given these affinities, Welby took an interest in theosophy, and so she initiated the

---

[58] There are affinities with Hegel's absolute idealism. After Welby shared 'Three Stages' with Bradley, he responded (appreciatively): 'The philosopher with whom...you have conclusions most in common is Hegel' (Bradley to VW, 1886–8, *ELL* 167). She then read Hegel, but objected that he petrified the dynamic movement of thought into a closed system (VW to C. F. Keary, 1886–8, *ELL* 170).

conversation with Besant.[59] Yet Welby distinguished her philosophical outlook from theosophy on several grounds, putting forward her criticisms of theosophy to Besant.

Insofar as theosophy reaches for the highest levels of significance, Welby says, well and good. But really that pursuit of significance is best pursued scientifically, albeit by a science that acknowledges the speculative aspirations that drive it as well as its background in language. Science *can* acknowledge these; contra Besant, we need not renounce science to obtain significance. Thus, Welby explains, she is not criticizing science per se—she speaks to Besant of 'that science which you used to revere *as I do now*' (*VWF*, VW to AB, 18 October 1891; my emphasis). However, scientists are not well serving themselves by insisting on plain facts and literal statements. Instead they should re-embrace the quest for significance that actually animates their inquiries.

In any case, Welby continues, Besant is treating theosophy as if *it* simply stated plain facts, ignoring the metaphorical nature of theosophical terms like 'plane', 'monad', and so on. Whereas 'the first sign that you are really applying your unusual critical powers to the theories you now accept, will be... your unsparing analysis of its mode of figuration' (VW to Besant, 18 October 1891). As things stand, though, Besant is merely transposing onto theosophy the same narrow empiricist, positivist belief in facts that she had formerly held as a secularist (when Besant had indeed been heavily influenced by Comte, on whom she wrote a book in 1885, following in the footsteps of Martineau and Lewes; see *AC*). Thus, Welby says, Besant's current uncritical attitude to theosophy follows predictably from her previous outlook (*VWF*, VW to Besant, 24 September 1891). When Besant now says that theosophy provides an 'immutable basis' for knowledge and ethics, the same old restrictive earth-bound vocabulary is still in the driving seat (VW to Besant, 18 October 1891).

In this light we can appreciate why there was a degree of vagueness in Welby's claims about higher levels of significance. Whereas Besant's new mentor Helena Blavatsky developed an elaborate and systematic account of the deep-level spiritual structure of reality, Welby did not want to set up a rival account to that of the sciences. Spiritual reality must be reached through and beyond science, and—as she said in 'Three Stages'—*after*, not before, patient scientific investigation has had its perfect work. We cannot yet anticipate what this will yield.

---

[59] 'I have... followed your mental course... for some years', Welby explained to Besant when initiating the conversation (VW to Besant, 24 September 1891). Welby read Sinnett's *Esoteric Buddhism* (1883), Anna Kingsford and Edward Maitland's mystical work *The Perfect Way* (1882), issues of Blavatsky's journal *Lucifer*, and at least some of *The Secret Doctrine* (*VWF*, VW to Besant, 24 September 1891). Several clippings of news items about theosophy from around 1890 are in the Victoria Welby Fonds; see also Senate House Library (n.d.).

We can now resume where Welby stands on naturalism: namely, she is an anti-naturalist on all strands of the cluster.[60] (1) She believes in 'first philosophy': our mental inclination towards ultimate significance (i.e. metaphysics) always drives empirical inquiry. (2) Sense, meaning and significance necessarily precede and guide empirical inquiry, and although particular languages and their ingrained meanings are historically evolved, they all rest on a common drive towards significance—called 'mother-sense' or 'primal sense'—that underlies the human signifying capacity (Petrilli 2009: 142). (3) Philosophy as reflection on sense, meaning, and significance can assist and orientate empirical science, but it cannot be continuous with empirical science in the sense of following empirical methods. Rather, empirical inquiry is part of and depends on a bigger whole, the pursuit of significance, where philosophy's task is to reflect on that whole and make it intelligible. (4) The mind is irreducible to the brain, because subjective experience is irreducible to physical processes (*SU* 471).[61] Moreover, when we claim that the mind is the brain, we are already *interpreting* the brain and its significance, an interpretation formed by our minds as they make sense of the world: 'mind interprets (otherwise inscrutable) body by its power of perception, judgment, reflection, inference...' (472). (5) Reality has non-natural dimensions: the high levels of solar, cosmic, and divine significance that enfold the earth. For significance ultimately consists in patterns—webs of connections which are not as such material. The higher we rise up the levels of connections, the further we ascend above anything material. (6) Far from our knowledge of values deriving from our knowledge of facts, our prior sense of value impels us to seek, classify, and theorize facts in the first place.

Finally, in terms of naturalism's unifying thread—empirical science as the only possible source of knowledge—Welby is emphatic that science *cannot* be our sole source of knowledge, for it depends on language and the mind's interpretive activity. Science is encompassed in the same field of interpretation as metaphysics, which reaches towards highest-level significance, and in the same linguistic background out of which poetic literature arises. To be faithful to its own animating motivations, science needs to accept and work with, not against, the metaphysical and poetic impulses that are proximate to it.

---

[60] Welby did use the word *naturalism*. She objected to '"naturalism", which is the un-doing, the reversal, of Nature's upward, ascendant tendency – the un-becoming' (VW to Mrs Clifford, 1888–90, *ELL* 251).

[61] Welby's arguments here, in 'Mental Biology or Organic Thought' (1887), are similar to those of Besant and Blavatsky, which we'll examine in Chapter 3. Like them, Welby argues that we can only make sense of the mind–body relation on a panpsychist basis. 'All we know of matter is resistance. Now as Spirit is Ultimate Energy it implies resistance; that is, the idea of matter lies within that of "Spirit"' (VW to Linton, 1886–8, *ELL* 175).

2.7 The Trajectory of the Debate about Naturalism

My narrative in this chapter shows how far naturalism evolved and gained ground over the century, in part through Martineau's efforts. In 1800 hardly anyone saw science as exhausting our knowledge of reality. Empirical science took its place alongside other epistemic sources, whether they were characterized as faith, reason, or intuition; and in a variety of ways science and religion were taken to go together. One way was Priestley's view that by learning nature's laws one can better follow the divine plan. Shepherd offered another way; for her, reason justifies the basic principles of scientific investigation and confirms the core tenets of the Christian religion, so that scientific inquiry is embedded alongside reason and faith.

The early Martineau likewise combined scientific-empiricist and religious claims, but in an uneasy amalgam which ultimately gave way to her full-blooded naturalism in the 1851 *Letters*. This decisive statement showed the world what naturalism looked like, as Martineau exalted empirical scientific method as the only possible route to knowledge and consequently embraced materialism, hard determinism, and atheism, while denying any supernatural agencies or entities. As Martineau now saw it, there could be no more compromise between religion and science; the former had been holding the latter back, and now the latter must have its day.

Martineau's position in 1851 was highly controversial, but it presaged a naturalist current that became increasingly mainstream and acceptable as the century went on. We see this in Huxley's career, for example. Yet, though naturalism gained confidence over the period, it did not straightforwardly prevail. Rather, as naturalism came into its own, its limitations came into view too. Cobbe and Welby were amongst those who picked up on these limitations. For Cobbe, naturalism could not account for the universality and necessity of either causality or moral requirements. As we've seen, her arguments on this score came down indirectly from Shepherd, so that one legacy of Shepherd's ideas was to become part of the arsenal of anti-naturalism.

Nonetheless, naturalism forged ahead and it became increasingly common to present science as an exhaustive world view in its own right. For Welby, this only threw the limitations of naturalism into even sharper relief. She reminded empirical scientists that their inquiries depended on a background of meaning and significance which could not be accounted for within empirical science itself. For Welby, to appreciate that background we must adopt idealism and recognize the multiple spheres of significance rising from the earthly to the solar, cosmic, and divine. Thus, with every step forward that naturalism took, anti-naturalists were there to reply that religion and metaphysics were also needed for a complete comprehension of the world.

3
Philosophy of Mind

3.1 Introduction

In this chapter I examine the philosophies of mind of Ada Lovelace in the 1840s, Frances Power Cobbe in the 1860s–1870s, Constance Naden in the 1880s, and Helena Blavatsky and Annie Besant in the late 1880s. To map out their positions in general terms, we can say that Lovelace was torn between dualism and materialism, while Cobbe espoused a form of dualism, Naden a form of materialism, and Blavatsky and Besant a form of panpsychism. They elaborated these positions in unique ways. Lovelace addressed the mind in connection with artificial intelligence and mesmerism. Cobbe gave an account of unconscious thought, on the basis of which she differentiated the conscious soul from the unconsciously thinking brain. Naden's materialism was part of her distinctive metaphysical standpoint, 'hylo-idealism'. And Blavatsky and Besant identified an explanatory gap between objective brain processes and subjective experience, a gap, they argued, that only theosophical panpsychism could bridge.

In important respects the work of these women differs from contemporary philosophy of mind. These women addressed the mind not as a standalone topic but together with metaphysics, ethics, and religion, just like their male contemporaries. These discussions of mind took place in the generalist periodical culture, in which 'all levels of Victorian society actively discussed the mind's capabilities and what they might mean for individuals and society' (Torgersen 2017: 135). In this setting, mind was addressed together with religious concerns around the soul and free will, on the one hand, and scientific discoveries about the brain and nervous system, on the other. Physiologists were showing in unprecedented detail how mental powers depended on the brain, nervous system, and body. This threw up the question of how to reconcile this new physiological knowledge with Christianity—if it could be so reconciled at all. Given these wide-ranging concerns, these women did not write about the mind in the fine detail characteristic of twenty-first-century philosophy of mind. Consequently they often treated as synonyms concepts that look quite different to modern readers, as when Naden claims that the mind *depends* on, *is*, is a *function* of, and *correlates* with the brain. The distinctions amongst these claims paled into insignificance besides such overarching issues as whether the mind could survive the body's death and, if not, where that left personal immortality and Christianity.

These religious considerations raise the question of whether it is right to say that Lovelace was drawn towards materialism or that Naden was a materialist. For we might wonder whether the highly religious climate meant that no one could safely identify as a materialist. Certainly doing so was controversial, as we saw in Chapter 2 regarding the heated criticism of Harriet Martineau and Henry George Atkinson's *Letters on the Laws of Man's Nature and Development*. Martineau's standing was high enough that she could survive the controversy, but few others were equally well placed and being deemed a 'materialist' was liable to destroy one's career and reputation. Even so, people took the risk. A case in point is William Engledue, who openly championed 'Materialism' in his provocative opening address to the London Phrenological Association in 1842. He defined materialism as the view 'that organised matter is all that is requisite to produce the multitudinous manifestations of human and brute cerebration' (1843: 7). No 'spirit' or 'immaterial something' needed to be 'superadded to ... the brain', as it was by the 'supernaturalists' for whom 'man possesses a spirit superadded to, but not inherent in, the brain' (7). Engledue's statement was controversial but also influential, as we will see in this chapter. Moreover, even though many people worried that materialism undermined belief in the immortal soul, others such as Naden embraced materialism all the more eagerly *because* of its pro-secularist implications. From both sides, then, '"scientific" debates over mind, body and soul in the 1800s [were] inseparable from the religious debates concerning these matters – it is ... anachronistic to separate the two' (Reed 1998: 3).

As is already apparent, in describing these women's philosophies of mind I shall use the labels 'materialism', 'dualism', and 'panpsychism'. Although these headings are general, they provide a useful starting-point for mapping how these women's views were located both in the broader landscape of competing perspectives on the mind and in comparison to one another. As regards these comparisons, how far did these women adopt their views of the mind in response to one another? Lovelace was inspired by Harriet Martineau—though not her 1851 *Letters* but her earlier 'Letters on Mesmerism' of late 1844. Martineau's inspiration was one factor drawing Lovelace towards materialism, although she pulled back. When Cobbe criticized materialism, however, she set her sights not on Martineau—despite knowing Martineau's work, as we saw in Chapter 2—but rather on the German arch-materialist Ludwig Büchner. Meanwhile, on the positive side, Cobbe's account of mind owed much to the account of 'unconscious cerebration' of the most celebrated physiologist of the age, William Benjamin Carpenter. Carpenter in turn had known Lovelace and discussed the mind with her in the immediate wake of her work on the 'analytical engine' with Charles Babbage. Thus, a side-aim of this chapter is to document the continuity running from Lovelace's and Babbage's ideas on the analytical engine into later-century thinking about unconscious mind, or 'mental automatism' and 'latent thought' as it was often called.

So there is a partly explicit and partly implicit triangle amongst Martineau and Lovelace (positive, explicit), Cobbe and Martineau (negative, implicit), and Cobbe and Lovelace (positive, implicit). As for Naden, she criticized dualism but did not overtly target Cobbe.[1] Instead Naden opposed a family of dualist theories that she saw as making unacceptable compromises with religion, a family to which Cobbe's theory belonged.[2] In contrast to these mainstream dualist positions, Naden affiliated herself with the left-of-field secularist milieu that the earlier Besant did much to shape. Naden published in Besant's journal *Our Corner* and with the Freethought Publishing Company, the organ of the National Secular Society, which at the time was led by Charles Bradlaugh along with Besant. Finally, Blavatsky's and Besant's relations with the other women are more explicit. Blavatsky overtly criticized Naden's materialism, while Besant—having supported Naden, translated Büchner, and explicitly criticized Cobbe during her secularist phase—now just as explicitly positioned herself as Blavatsky's protégée having turned to theosophy in 1889. Besant was convinced by Blavatsky that materialism could not adequately explain subjective experience, and this helped to convince Besant in favour of theosophy. Overall, then, a complicated mix of types of filiation is in play.

Of course, these women were not only informed by one another. Lovelace was in conversation with Babbage, Carpenter, and the group of phreno-mesmerists that included William Engledue. Cobbe was greatly influenced by Carpenter and opposed Büchner. Naden was heavily influenced by Robert Lewins, whose views had roots in the phreno-mesmerist discussions of the 1840s. For their part, Blavatsky and Besant both drew on John Tyndall to make the case that an explanatory gap separated objective brain processes from subjective experiences. So these women were not theorizing the mind in a vacuum, but in conversation with male interlocutors. We need to remember these male interlocutors—Carpenter, Lewins, Tyndall—to make sense of the women's views.

The chapter is structured as follows: Sec. 3.2 is on Lovelace; Sec. 3.3 is on Carpenter, the key node connecting Lovelace to Cobbe; Sec. 3.4 is on Cobbe on

---

[1] Clare Stainthorp has commented to me: 'Naden...almost exclusively discusses male philosophers/writers rather than writings by women—because she wanted to be "taken seriously" and as engaging with "major" philosophical figures, while distancing herself from work deemed feminine and therefore perceived as a different class of philosophical thought' (personal communication).

[2] We see Naden repudiating 'orthodox dualism' in 'Animal Automatism', her 1882 review-essay on Thomas Henry Huxley's *Science and Culture, and Other Essays* (ID 193–202). She says that for Huxley: 'Though the brain is sense-creating, and therefore world-creating; though, "so far as we know, the change in the sensorium is the cause of the sensation," we are now gravely called upon to doubt the existence of matter', and that Huxley considers materialism no more credible than animism or pre-established harmony (196). Naden continues, 'Obviously we have not to join issue with Pre-established Harmony, or with orthodox Dualism, but with what may be denominated Absolute Agnosticism, and which, if logically carried out, would be as fatal to science as it is to philosophy' (197). In other words: Naden is defending materialism against Huxley's scepticism, without reverting to either pre-established harmony or animism, which latter she equates with 'orthodox dualism'.

'unconscious cerebration'; Sec. 3.5 is on Naden's 'hylo-idealism' and her theory of the mind; Sec. 3.6 is on Blavatsky and Besant and their criticism of materialism; and Sec. 3.7 brings out a dialectical dynamic in which each of these women's views of mind emerged in response to problems in the view preceding it.

3.2 Lovelace and the Thinking Machine

Ada Lovelace has come to be hailed as a visionary pioneer of computing. Sometimes she is even described as the first computer programmer because of her collaboration with Charles Babbage on the analytical engine, which was effectively a prototypical computer. But Lovelace is rarely seen as having said anything philosophical, although she described herself as 'a bit of a philosopher, and a very great speculator' and 'a *Poet*... an *Analyst* (& Metaphysician); for with me the two go together indissolubly' (AAL to Babbage, 16 February 1840, *AEN* 83; AAL to Babbage, 30 July 1843, *AEN* 157). When Lovelace *is* recognized to have made a philosophical contribution it is generally on artificial intelligence. Alan Turing was the first to recognize the significance of her thinking about this issue,[3] when he identified and sought to counter what he called 'Lady Lovelace's objection' to his imitation game argument.[4] While it is best to avoid anachronistically projecting later debates about artificial intelligence back onto Lovelace, she did consider whether a machine such as Babbage's analytical engine could think. She was torn on the issue, and this pertained to the mind because she and Babbage defined thought and mind in terms of each other, such that thinking is 'the operations of mind' and the operations of mind are thought (Babbage [1837] 1989: 31). Therefore, in equivocating on whether the engine could think, Lovelace was equivocating between materialist and dualist views of the mind.

To appreciate this we first need some background. Lovelace was born Ada Byron, the daughter of the poet Byron and Annabella Byron, though as the two were separated she never knew her father.[5] She first met Charles Babbage in 1833 when she and her mother attended one of his 'glorious soirées', as Martineau called them (*HMA* 1: 268). Babbage wowed his audiences with his small-scale

---

[3] See also the subsequent discussions of Lovelace as philosopher by Toole (1991) and of Lovelace on the mind by Green (2001, 2005).

[4] For Turing (1950), if a machine could perform sufficiently well at the imitation game, then we would have grounds to conclude that it can think. He took 'Lovelace's objection' to be that the machine cannot be intelligent because it cannot 'originate' the rules of the game. Others have argued that Lovelace's 'origination' provides a better, more demanding and accurate, criterion for artificial intelligence than the Turing test (Bringsjord et al. 2001). Others again defend the Turing test (Oppy and Dowe 2020). Here I suggest that in any case this is not unequivocally Lovelace's view.

[5] There is now an abundance of Lovelace biographies: Stein (1985), Woolley (1999), Essinger (2014), and Seymour (2018).

working model of the 'difference engine'.[6] The engine was so named because it automatically implemented a technique, the 'method of differences', for performing certain mathematical calculations. Babbage had initially designed this model back in 1822 and then sought funding to build a full version, but as the engineering proved more difficult and expensive than he had expected, a decade later the scale model remained all that existed. Annabella Byron marvelled at what she called the 'thinking machine', telling her friend William King in June 1833 that she and Ada 'both went to see the *thinking machine* (for such it seems) last Monday' (quoted in Stein 1985: 42). Lovelace proceeded to study the engine's operating principles and became Babbage's friend and regular visitor. After a hiatus in her studies from 1836 to 1839 while she bore three children, in 1840 she resumed her study of advanced mathematics, including differential calculus, with Augustus De Morgan. Amongst his many contributions in mathematics and logic,[7] De Morgan recognized that algebraic symbols could stand for all kinds of things, not only quantities. Algebra, he said, can be viewed 'either as a science of quantity, or as a language of symbols' (1837: 3) where: 'A symbol is any thing which can be placed before the mind as a representation of any other thing' (59). Accordingly he used his 1837 textbook, *The Elements of Algebra Preliminary to the Differential Calculus*, to teach students how to perform 'operations with pure symbols' (122). This would be important for Lovelace.

Meanwhile, in the later 1830s, Babbage had launched his plans for the 'analytical engine', which was to be much wider-ranging than the difference engine, able to calculate any function, and even carry out symbolic algebra. The new engine never got built either, investors being deterred by Babbage's previous failure to deliver on the difference engine. Nonetheless he tried to drum up financial backing, in part by lecturing on the engine in Italy. This inspired Luigi Menabrea to write an article in 1842 explaining the engine, which Lovelace translated into English in 1843 as part of the effort to drum up British funding for the machine by stressing how far it surpassed its now-failed predecessor the difference engine. Her translation appeared, signed 'A.A.L.', in *Scientific Memoirs*, a journal that shared continental European scientific research with Britons. Lovelace appended notes and a commentary more extensive than Menabrea's original piece.[8] She had many plans for further writings, but in the end the annotated 'Sketch of the Analytical Engine' was her only published work (besides

---

[6] Martineau also saw the engine in this period; she laments the silliness of 'a lady' who asked Babbage: 'If you put the question in wrong, will the answer come out right?' (*HMA* 1: 268). Shepherd, too, saw the difference engine; on how it informed her philosophical views, see McRobert (n.d.: 146–50).

[7] On De Morgan, who is probably second only to George Boole in his importance for nineteenth-century logic, see Allard (2014) and Gray (2014).

[8] It used to be assumed that Babbage must have been the 'real author' because Lovelace could not possibly have had the mathematical knowledge on display in the technical parts of the commentary. However, Hollings et al. (2017) have conclusively established that she did.

one book review of a novel). Otherwise we know her philosophical views from her extensive correspondence, a substantial amount of which Betty Toole has published as *Ada: The Enchantress of Numbers* (*AEN*).

Turning to Lovelace's view of mind in the 'Sketch', she explains that the engine can perform operations with symbols that stand for any subject matter, not only numbers: 'The Analytical Engine is an *embodying of the science of operations*' (*SAE* 694), where:

> [B]y the word *operation*, we mean *any process which alters the mutual relation of two or more things*... This is the most general definition, and would include all subjects in the universe. In abstract mathematics, of course operations alter those particular relations which are involved in the consideration of number and space... But the science of operations... is a science of itself, and has its own abstract truth and value; just as logic has its own particular truth and value, independently of the subjects to which we apply its reasonings and processes. (693)

That the analytical engine was not confined to numbers marked it out as (what we now call) a computer rather than merely a calculator. Hence this passage is often brought up to evidence Lovelace's visionary anticipation of a general science of computing. But seen in its context she is simply restating De Morgan's conception of a science of 'operations with pure symbols'. The twist, though, is her claim that the *engine* can perform these operations; they need not be done by a human being. Complex logical operations are not exclusive to the human mind.[9]

The fact that the analytical engine can perform calculations using symbols shows the unity of abstract mental processes with material processes:

> In enabling mechanism to combine together *general* symbols in successions of unlimited variety and extent, a uniting link is established between the operations of matter and the abstract mental processes of the *most abstract* branch of mathematical science. (*SAE* 697)

More specifically, the engine, as a material object moving through a chain of causes and effects, is thereby performing calculations; thus when calculations are performed generally this must also occur through material causal processes (e.g. in the brain); so, as calculations are just one instance of abstract mental processes, those processes generally must be accomplished through material

---

[9] In turn, De Morgan's subsequent formulations were surely influenced by Lovelace's account of the analytical engine: 'A calculus, or science of calculation,... has organized processes by which passage is made, or may be made, mechanically, from one result to another. *A calculus always contains something which it would be possible to do by machinery*' (De Morgan 1849: 92; my emphasis).

causal sequences (e.g. in the brain).[10] Abstract symbolic processes involve no transcendence of material nature but are transacted in and by material nature. Do these abstract symbolic and calculating processes constitute reasoning? Lovelace seemed to think so:

> We are not aware of its being on record that anything partaking in the nature of... the Analytical Engine has been hitherto proposed, or even thought of, as a practical possibility, any more than the idea of a *thinking* or of a *reasoning* *machine*. (697; my emphases)

That is: only with the analytical engine has it become practically possible to engineer a thinking or reasoning machine. Menabrea had stated to the contrary that 'the machine is not a thinking being, but simply an automaton which acts according to the laws imposed on it' (675). But Lovelace added a footnote to that statement: 'This must not be understood in too unqualified a manner' (675)—in other words, she disagreed and thought the machine could think.[11]

Lovelace was drawn, then, to the view that the most abstract powers of thought and reasoning are 'united' with material causal processes. She moved in circles where exactly that view was being discussed. In 1841 she questioned William Engledue's associate John Elliotson about whether 'electricity [is] the bond of union between the *mind & muscular action*' (Stein 1985: 132). Elliotson had been forced out of his medical position in 1838 over his support for mesmerism, and in 1843 he began co-editing the phreno-mesmerist journal *The Zoist*. These materialist views were contested, but were in the air that Lovelace was breathing.

However, in the 'Sketch' she then offered a reason why the machine's operations with symbols might not constitute thinking or reasoning after all:

> It is desirable to guard against the possibility of exaggerated ideas that might arise as to the powers of the Analytical Engine.... The Analytical Engine has no pretensions whatever to *originate* anything. It can do whatever we *know how to order it* to perform. It can *follow* analysis; but it has no power of *anticipating* any analytical relations or truths. (722)

---

[10] As Green (2001) remarks, these claims 'virtually commit her... to mechanistic materialism with respect to the mind'.
[11] Babbage was warier, saying that, in claims about machines 'thinking', 'think' is used merely analogically: 'In substituting mechanism for the performance of operations hitherto executed by intellectual labour...[t]he analogy between these acts and the operations of mind almost forced upon me the figurative employment of the same terms. For instance, the expression "the engine *knows*, etc." means [only] that...a certain change in its arrangement has taken place...' ([1837] 1989: 31). Contrast Lovelace, for whom: 'The engine is capable of feeling about to discover which of two or more possible contingencies has occurred' (*SAE* 675).

These statements have been commonly taken as either denying artificial intelligence or providing a demanding test for it, but they pertain to the nature of the mind as well. They seem to say that material processes are not enough for thought, which also requires free will.

To explain: for Lovelace, the engine can only perform operations under rules already given to it but not originate the rules governing its operations. It cannot decide for itself what principles to follow, only follow those someone else has chosen. And, she says, the engine cannot 'anticipate'. This relates to a draft essay she wrote in 1841 on the role of imagination in science (a recurring theme in her notes and letters).

> *What* is Imagination?... First: it is the *Combining* Faculty. Secondly: it *conceives* & brings into *mental* presence that which is far away, or invisible... Hence is it especially the *religious* faculty; the ground-work of *Faith*.... [It] is the *Discovering* Faculty, pre-eminently.... Mathematical Science shows what is.... But to use & apply that language we must be able to fully appreciate, to feel, to seize, the unseen, and the unconscious. (*AEN* 94)

Thus Lovelace saw imagination as crucial for grasping links between separate areas of inquiry, enabling us to form higher-level unifying theories in which 'The intellectual, the moral, the religious [are] all naturally bound up and interlinked together in one great and harmonious whole' (AAL to Andrew Crosse, 16 November 1844, *AEN* 215).

In saying that the engine cannot 'anticipate', then, plausibly she thought that the engine can perform complex calculations but not make imaginative leaps to connect hitherto separated subject-matters. 'Origination' relates to the free creation of new ideas and meaningful connections as well as to free choices about rules to guide action. In sum, the engine can perform only the mechanical part of thought, but thought *as a whole* extends beyond mechanical calculations to encompass broader processes of imagination, conception, combination, appreciation, and so on. Lovelace may have attributed these wider-ranging powers of thought to the soul conceived as distinct from the brain: the soul takes wing while the brain does mere mechanical foot-soldiering.[12]

Along these lines Lovelace pulled back from saying that all thinking consists of physical processes, perhaps partly on account of her religious beliefs.[13] The same

---

[12] Lovelace complained to Andrew Crosse about 'the scientific and so-called philosophers... [who] are but half prophets – if not absolutely false ones. They have read the great page simply with the physical eye, and with none of the spirit *within*' (AAL to Crosse, 16 November 1844, *AEN* 215).

[13] Lovelace thought that in calculating the laws of nature we are reading the book of God (*SAE* 696). Babbage took a similar view in his Ninth Bridgewater Treatise, his unofficial supplement to the eight commissioned volumes (Babbage 1838).

attraction to and recoil from materialism recurred in her subsequent thought, as I now want to explore.

In late 1843 Annabella Byron hired Carpenter to tutor Lovelace's children. Carpenter would later become Britain's most influential physiologist, his *Principles of Human Physiology* standard reading for medical students, going through numerous editions.[14] In 1843, though, he was rising but not yet established. At first he and Lovelace became very close. Historians have focused on their romantic attraction, but it was intellectual as well.[15] Carpenter told Lovelace, 'my great ambition is to devote my mature years to the prosecution of metaphysical study [.] ... I look to *you* for great help in it' (Carpenter to AAL, December 15 1843, *DLB* 169).[16] The particular subject they had been discussing was the mind and whether it was necessarily embodied. Lovelace had maintained that 'the form of *corporeity* must exist in all beings of limited function', that is, all finite minds. Carpenter was less sure: 'I should like to keep [this] in view for future discussion', in which, he continued, he expected 'to receive as well as to impart' knowledge.

Unfortunately their intimacy overstepped the bounds of propriety and they retreated into a more detached relationship over 1844–5, mainly discussing Carpenter's tutorial duties, before he left his position in mid-1845. Throughout this period (late 1843 to mid-1845) Carpenter shared his publications with Lovelace, including the second (1844) edition of his *Principles of Human Physiology*. Among the topics they discussed were Mill and De Morgan on logic, spontaneous generation, the *Vestiges of the Natural History of Creation*, and the indivisibility of the will.[17]

With the *Principles*, Carpenter distanced himself from his earlier work.[18] In 1837 he had envisaged making physiology a science akin to physics, treating human and animal physiology as one. Animals reason, are conscious, and perform voluntary actions, he maintained, lamenting the arrogance of those who see these powers as exclusively human, when really human powers differ from those of animals only in degree, not kind (Carpenter 1837: 23). Within this framework, Carpenter analysed voluntary actions, in animals and humans alike, as follows. All outer impressions received by the nerves are transmitted to the '*sensorium commune*', the centre where all nervous effects converge. Sometimes this produces sensations—mental phenomena of which we are conscious. Sometimes, however,

---

[14] On Carpenter's huge influence on nineteenth-century British medicine, see Lidwell-Durnin (2020).

[15] On Lovelace and Carpenter's relationship, see also Winter (1998), Woolley (1999: 285–99), and Seymour (2018: 285–8).

[16] All quotations from Lovelace's correspondence are reproduced with the permission of Paper Lion Ltd and the Estate of Ada Lovelace.

[17] See *DLB* 169, Carpenter to AAL, 17 July 1844, 23 October 1844, 19 November 1844, 25 November 1844, and 2 December 1844.

[18] On Carpenter's overall thought and intellectual development, see Delorme (2014) and Kosits (2018).

the nervous motions gathered into the common centre instead directly affect one another, producing 'purely instinctive and involuntary actions', also called '*excito-motor*' actions, with no sensation present (43). At other times, sensations are attended to (whereupon they become perceptions), and those perceptions sometimes prompt us to form volitions, mental acts that change the state of the sensorium, which then affects the nerves producing (voluntary) motion (27–9). On Carpenter's early view, then, mental processes including volition are part of physical processes and the mind is completely integrated into nature.

An 1840 review of his *Principles of General and Comparative Physiology* found the book far too heterodox to be recommended. The reviewer accused Carpenter of taking a deist view of the 'machine of nature' and endorsing 'the doctrines of materialism' by reducing the vital principle and the mind to causal interactions of matter (Anonymous 1840: 219, 228). Carpenter had to escape these charges to achieve professional success—that is, he had to distance himself from 'the doctrines of materialism' (see Winter 1997). He did this in the *Principles of Human Physiology* by starting to work out a different approach: human powers remain the further development of animal powers but there is also an essential difference. Humans can improve themselves through the use of *intelligent will* (Carpenter [1844] 1845: 67–8). We differ from animals not in our intrinsic reasoning abilities but our possession of immortal souls (68), which are the source of our will, and which we can use to gain voluntary control of and develop our powers. It is desirable to gain as much voluntary control over our own automatic processes as we can, the better to regulate and improve ourselves (see e.g. 190).

It is tempting to think that Carpenter reached this view partly under the influence of his conversations with Lovelace.[19] For these conversations took place just after she had written the 'Sketch' proposing that what the analytical engine lacks is precisely voluntary control over the principles regulating its own activities.[20] Perhaps Carpenter took up this insight, using it to inform the sharpened distinction between humans and animals that he was then attempting to draw. After all, he had told Lovelace that he hoped to profit from her insights concerning the mind and metaphysics.

Lovelace, however, was more interested in Carpenter's account of 'excito-motor' or 'automatic' action. Under his guidance, she told her mother, she was pursuing 'advancing studies on the Nervous System [which] show...that the

---

[19] He did not envisage their conversations to be one-way. As he explained to Lord Lovelace, he wanted the tutoring position partly for 'the advantage which the continual contact with a mind, so acute and vigorous as Lady Lovelace's, cannot fail to impress upon my own, in the pursuit of our common objects' (Carpenter to Lord Lovelace, 2 December 1843, *DLB* 169). He had a 'very high admiration for her intellectual powers, and a strong desire to aid in the development and training of them' (Carpenter to Lord Lovelace, 17 January 1844, *DLB* 169).

[20] She must have given Carpenter a copy, because she distributed the 'Sketch' as widely as she could (Stein 1985: 123; amongst philosophically minded women, the recipients included Joanna Baillie and Anna Jameson).

simply organic or reflex... portion of the Nervous System acts wholly independently of sensations & of the mental' (AAL to Annabella Byron, 10 October 1844, *AEN* 205). She brought this to bear on one topic in particular: mesmerism.

The craze for mesmerism was then at its peak. Lovelace had been interested for some time, hosting mesmeric demonstrations by Elliotson in the early 1840s (Gray 2018: 84; Seymour 2018: 248–9). Her interest was now rekindled by Martineau's apparent cure from illness by mesmerism in mid-1844. That 'cure' was a major public event, amply covered in the mainstream press and arousing the interest of the royal family.[21] Everyone was talking about it, Lovelace included: 'I have been thinking much about the Mesmerism in Miss Martineau's case' (AAL to Annabella Byron, 10 October 1844, *AEN* 205). Did the case prove that mesmerism worked—or that Martineau's magisterial judgement had failed? Opinions divided. For some scandalized Christians, mesmerism was a hair's-breadth away from black magic. For some proponents, mesmerism confirmed that spiritual agencies and forces existed. For other proponents, mesmerism was fully explicable on a material basis; this camp included Hall and Atkinson, the architects of Martineau's apparent mesmeric cure, the editors of *The Zoist*, and Martineau herself.[22] Finally there were 'philosophic sceptics' like Carpenter, who thought that mesmeric effects must actually have a mental or psychological explanation, as he insisted to Lovelace.[23]

Martineau's account of her cure, 'Letters on Mesmerism', came out in *The Athenaeum* in November and December 1844, reissued as a book in early 1845 that sold out in days. Lovelace excitedly read Martineau's letters. She requested her mother's permission to write to Martineau (Annabella Byron and Martineau were friends), saying that she wanted to 'draw her [Martineau's] powerful understanding to the subject, more *systematically & forcibly*, than perhaps would occur unless she is a little *suggested to*' (AAL to Annabella Byron, 10 October 1844, quoted in Stein 1985: 135–7). Having written, she told her mother, 'I hope [Martineau] & I shall enter on *mesmerical correspondence*' (AAL to Annabella Byron, 11 November 1844, *AEN* 210). She then wrote to her friend Woronzow Greig (Mary Somerville's son):

---

[21] For a brilliant account, see Winter (1995).

[22] Kaplan (1975) usefully distinguishes between mesmerism's scientific defenders, its spiritualist defenders, and its opponents. On Martineau's opposition to the spiritualist interpretation, see Martineau (HM to Miss Carpenter, 17 April 1866, *HMCL* 5: 137; HM to Henry Reeve, 3 December 1867, *HMCL* 5: 201). Martineau nonetheless fell out with Elliotson when the *Zoist* unfavourably reviewed her *Letters* (see Claggett 2010: 68).

[23] 'In dividing mankind into *believers* and *disbelievers in Mesmerism*, you have left out one class, in which I sh[ou]ld at present include myself – that of philosophic sceptics... Miss Martineau's Letters has made *not the least* impression on me... It wants... every requisite for a fair experiment' (Carpenter to AAL, 1 December 1844, *DLB* 169). 'I quite agree with you as to the *reality* of... phenomena of Mesmerism; but the question is, "Can they be produced without the knowledge of the subject that some effect is anticipated?"' (Carpenter to AAL, 2 December 1844, *DLB* 169; see also AAL to Annabella Byron, late 1844, *AEN* 205).

> I have my hopes, & very distinct ones too, of one day getting *cerebral* phenomena such that I can put them into mathematical equations; short a *law*, or *laws*, for the mutual actions of the molecules of the brain;... Have you heard about Miss Martineau & the Mesmerism? There *can* be *no* doubt of the facts, I am persuaded. I have seen her letters... All this bears on *my* subject – it does not appear to me that *cerebral* matter need to be more unmanageable to the mathematicians than *sidereal & planetary* matter & movements; if they would inspect it from the *right point of view*. I hope to bequeath to the generations a *Calculus* of the *Nervous System*. (AAL to Greig, 15 November 1844, *AEN* 214–15)

Lovelace's proposal for a 'calculus of the nervous system' is often noted. What is rarely noted is that she intended it as a response *to Martineau*, with whom she hoped to collaborate on the 'calculus'. Unfortunately Martineau was too busy to reply; she asked Anna Jameson, a mutual friend of hers and Annabella Byron's, to apologize to the latter: 'The only drawback [of my cure] is the lap fulls of letters.... [W]ill Lady Byron accept this, through you, as to themselves? We serve the sick first, – but a mountain of correspondence remains untouched' (HM to Anna Jameson, Wednesday October 1844, *HMCL* 2: 334).

So Lovelace had to pursue her thinking about mesmerism without Martineau. This interest flowed naturally from her work on the analytical engine: in both the engine and the mesmerized subject, automatic processing or operations occurred, without will, and maintained purely by material processes. From Carpenter, Lovelace knew that reflex actions could occur that bypassed consciousness: 'in certain cases effects on the simply *organic* system take place instead of on the *sensational*, or *mental* systems' (AAL to Annabella Byron, 10 October 1844, *AEN* 205). As she stated in this letter, she believed that this happened in at least some cases of mesmerism. Lovelace thus favoured a materialist account of mesmerism—as we can see from her letter to Greig, in which she aspired to explain mesmerism scientifically, demystifying it and leaving no room for any occult forces.

This view of mesmerism pulled Lovelace once more towards a materialist view of the mind. For she hoped to explain mesmerism as part of a complete explanation of the motions of the cerebrum and the nervous system, treating them as part of material nature, following intelligible laws and capable of being measured, quantified, and calculated. This was the same kind of materialist programme that Carpenter had espoused in the late 1830s, although Lovelace gave it a more mathematical flavour. She averted any religious doubts she may have had by maintaining that it was not an irreligious programme.[24] Rather, it went with a form of pantheism: 'God is one, and... all the works and the feelings He has called

---

[24] Nor was it for Carpenter, who was a devout Unitarian. However, because his early materialism led to his being misunderstood as an atheist, he had to devise a non-materialist stance.

into existence are ONE... There is too much tendency to making separate and independent bundles of both the physical and the moral facts of the universe. Whereas, all and everything is naturally related and interconnected' (AAL to Crosse, 16 November 1844, *AEN* 215–16).

Lovelace never brought her explanatory programme to fruition, but she pursued it some way, writing a review-essay (never published) responding to William Gregory's 1846 'abstract' of an 1845 work by the German natural philosopher Karl von Reichenbach which was gaining much attention in British scientific circles. Reichenbach claimed that mesmeric phenomena had led him to discover a new vital force, named 'Od' after the Norse god Odin.[25] In her review Lovelace judiciously concluded that detailed, systematic experimental investigation of so-called 'Reichenbach phenomena' was needed; their existence should not simply be taken on trust. But Reichenbach's merit was to 'open out new and infinite fields for investigation, ... indicating tracks for connecting together branches of natural science hitherto unlinked; for instance terrestrial magnetism and human physiology' (Lovelace, quoted in Gray 2018: 95). She spoke of 'daring indications of the time when some great atomic law may unite and harmonise all nature', alluding to the correlation that Michael Faraday had recently established between magnetism and light, which she took to suggest that both magnetism and light, and perhaps by extension all forces, manifested a single more fundamental force.[26] For Lovelace, then, the life-force manifest in human physiology was another form of the same force at work in magnetism and other non-animate natural phenomena. There was no *separate* life-force—as was often maintained by those who saw life as a special divine addition to matter. For these 'transcendentalists', life must be explained by a transcendental, non-natural vital force, whereas their adversaries the 'immanentists' maintained that life emerges naturally within matter through its intrinsic energy. For the latter group life was material; for the former it was non-material.[27] Transcendentalists generally saw the soul as a further addition to vital force, so that transcendentalism lined up with dualism and immanentism with materialism. Lovelace was favouring immanentism and seeing thought as merely another manifestation of the same force that is present in bodies as life, and in non-living objects as magnetic attraction, gravitational attraction, and so on.

But once more Lovelace pulled back. Expressing scepticism about the exaggerated claims of some mesmerists, she hinted that actually the psychological power of suggestion might lie at the heart of mesmeric phenomena: 'We could wish even

---

[25] See Gregory (1846); and, on Gregory, Kaufman (2008). Martineau was another enthusiast, urging Carlyle to read Reichenbach (HM to Thomas Carlyle, 5 March 1846, *HMCL* 3: 50).

[26] On all this, see Stein (1985: 151–3). Lovelace had previously written to Faraday hoping to collaborate with him too, but he was too unwell (see *AAL* 210–13).

[27] See Jacyna's (1983) classic reconstruction of this huge vector of nineteenth-century debate. *Transcendentalism/immanentism* was the terminology used at the time; see e.g. Lewins ([1873] 1894: 28, 42). Carpenter had previously defended immanentism (Carpenter 1837); Shepherd had opposed it (see Boyle 2021a); and Martineau went on to support it in the *Letters* (*LLM* 5–7).

the name Mesmerism to be dropped. We associate with it a disgusting tissue of human imposture & weakness' (Lovelace, quoted in Gray 2018: 94). Here she was leaning towards the more sceptical stance of Carpenter and, particularly, James Braid, who argued that suggestion was at the root of mesmerism and on whose work Carpenter built. Braid, like Lovelace, reviewed Reichenbach in translation and argued that Reichenbach had overlooked 'the important influence of the *mental* part of the process, which is in active operation with patients during such experiments' (1846: 5). In the version that Carpenter subsequently developed, suggestion involved the *will*, an immaterial agency (Carpenter 1852). Thus, in adopting this psychological account of mesmerism—and therefore, like Braid, reconceiving it as hypnotism—Carpenter reintroduced a clear distinction between the immaterial will and the material operations of the brain and body. Lovelace seems to have become convinced, since she never published her review of Reichenbach, dropped mesmerism, and professed more and more distance from it over the later 1840s.

Her inquiries were then cut short by her death from cancer at just 37. But contrary to some recent popular portrayals, Lovelace was not a lone genius. Rather, she was at the intersection of several conversations: about symbolic algebra, the difference and analytical engines, mesmerism, and the unity of natural forces. Those conversations included other women, notably Martineau. From Lovelace two threads lead on to the other women of this chapter: to Cobbe through Carpenter; and to Naden through Robert Lewins, who in the 1870s reinvigorated the immanentism and materialism of the 1840s. But, first, to Carpenter.

3.3 Interlude: Carpenter

Carpenter completed his move away from his early materialism with the account of mind presented in the 1855 fifth edition of his *Principles of Human Physiology* (in earlier editions he had only covered the mind cursorily, if at all). In 1855 Carpenter positioned himself against—of course—Martineau and Atkinson, who had given 'the latest and most thorough-going expression of this doctrine', 'materialism', on which

> *all* the operations of the Mind are but expressions or manifestations of material changes in the brain;... thus Man is but a *thinking machine*,... his fancied power of self-direction being altogether a delusion. (1855: 771; my emphasis)

In contrast, Carpenter now insisted that '*conscious volitional* agency... is the essential attribute of Personality', in God and humankind alike (786). From this perspective, he completely recast his earlier account of the physiology of mind as follows.

He distinguished between the *sensorium* and the *cerebrum*. Sense-impressions made on our nerves may, but often do not, reach the sensorium, which is the condition of consciousness: only when the sensorium receives and is activated by sensory impressions can one be conscious of them. However, many purely physical processes—such as breathing, the heart beating—occur automatically without reaching the sensorium; so do many 'ideo-motor' and 'cerebral' operations. The cerebrum is the organ that performs intellectual operations and regulates 'ideo-motor' activities such as playing the piano, swimming, and so on. But this 'organ of the intellectual operations is not itself endowed with consciousness' (536). The bulk of the intellectual processing that it performs occurs automatically without ever reaching awareness.

Carpenter further distinguished *volitional, voluntary,* and *automatic action*. We can initiate actions voluntarily and gain voluntary control over previously automatic cerebral and ideo-motor processes. An act is *volitional* if I decide to perform it and can do it only by maintaining continuous willed and attentive focus on it—say, when learning to play the piano, or to perform certain mathematical operations. Over time this instils habits, through which the activity enters my automatic repertoire, whereupon I can also perform it *voluntarily*: deciding to do it then leaving my system to get on with it automatically until I choose to stop. Carpenter encouraged people to gain increased voluntary control over their cerebral and ideo-motor processes, the better to regulate and order their thoughts and actions (625).

He then distinguished *soul* and *body*. Volition depends on consciousness: I cannot will to do anything unless I consciously frame the volition to do it. Consciousness depends on the sensorium: an 'active condition of the nervous matter of the sensorium...[is] the immediate antecedent of *all* consciousness' (542). However, consciousness does not reduce to but is rather in a 'correlation' with an active state of the sensorium. In itself, consciousness is immaterial and belongs to a distinct psychical agency (the soul). The soul has the power of will, that is, it can form volitions. When I choose to perform some operation, my will affects my nervous matter, which affects my cerebral processes, which may in turn affect my motor movements. The immaterial soul initiates these chains of physical effects through the 'metamorphosis of mind-force into nerve-force and *vice versa*' (543). In the converse direction, activation of the sensorium 'affects' consciousness (550). For Carpenter, then, the sensorium is the junction between mind and body.

Finally he introduced the concept of '*unconscious cerebration*'. Non-conscious cerebral operations, Carpenter maintained, do *not* constitute either unconscious reasoning (589, 643) or unconscious thought (1871: 211). Both are contradictions in terms, because reasoning and thought are necessarily conscious and require the cooperation of the immaterial soul. He therefore described non-conscious cerebral and ideo-motor operations as 'unconscious cerebration'.

The irony, though, is that the word 'cerebration' registers the materialist climate out of which Carpenter's account had emerged. For Engledue had introduced 'cerebration' in his infamous 1842 address. But for Engledue, cerebration was '*the function of the brain,* ... resulting from a peculiar combination of matter', and that was the end of it (1843: 7). In contrast, for Carpenter, automatic cerebration was only a part, and ideally a subordinate part, of the total person as a soul–body union. *Cerebration* had migrated into a respectable dualist register.

How far did this account of the mind reflect the influence of Carpenter's earlier exchanges with Lovelace? We might think not very far, because their views were quite different. As we saw earlier, mesmerism suggested to Lovelace that the body was caught up in a field of material force causing it to perform various actions, with or without consciousness, which was only a further expression of material force. Carpenter instead worked out a psychological explanation of mesmerism which left room for free will. On his view, the hypnotized person temporarily relinquishes their will and instead comes under the hypnotist's will. But in this respect, he said, the hypnotized patient is 'for the time being ... a mere *thinking automaton,* the whole course of whose ideas is determinable by suggestions operating from without' (1852: 147; and 1855: 798). The language of the 'thinking automaton' is reminiscent of the analytical engine—as is the phrase '*thinking machine*', to which Carpenter said that Martineau and Atkinson had reduced the mind (771). Even for 'Man in the state of normal activity', he added, 'insofar as the directing influence of the Will over the current of thought is suspended, the individual becomes a *thinking automaton*' (816; my emphasis). Thus, on the one hand there is will, which belongs to the soul or psyche; on the other hand are automatic operations and processes, in respect of which the person is merely a *thinking automaton.* To be consistent Carpenter should presumably have spoken of a 'cerebrating' automaton, but the substantial point remains. The cerebrum, like the analytical engine, performs intellectual operations automatically (i.e. without being conscious of doing so). Not being conscious, it can exercise no volition over its operations—recalling Lovelace's claim that the engine cannot 'originate'.

This language of 'thinking automata' suggests that Carpenter's discussions with Lovelace—in which 'thinking machines' and mesmerism were in play together—may have informed his conception of automatic cerebral processes as 'unconscious cerebration'. Certainly, others made this connection. For example, Richard Holt Hutton commented that on Carpenter's view 'under certain circumstances the brain works ... automatically, and ... this brain-work is no more identical with the work of the true self than the calculating machine by which Mr. Babbage performed abstruse calculations ... is identical with the true self' (Hutton 1870a: 1314).[28]

---

[28] And soon after, Hutton complained: 'It has struck me that a loose ... mode of speaking ... of the intellect generally as an automatic machine independent of consciousness, has grown up of late ... [on which] the brain, as distinct from the mind, is a sort of intellectual *weaving-machine* ...' (1874: 201; my emphasis)—another allusion to the analytical engine, as it was partially inspired by the Jacquard loom.

3.4 Cobbe on Thinking Brain versus Conscious Self

Carpenter's account of unconscious cerebration formed the starting point for Cobbe's philosophy of mind in her 1870 essay 'Unconscious Cerebration', which was complemented by her 1871 follow-up 'Dreams as Instances of Unconscious Cerebration'.[29] For Cobbe, as we know from Chapter 2, morality and religion were inextricable, and she theorized knowledge and reality in a way that cohered with these moral and religious commitments. She was drawn to Carpenter's work because he reconciled brain and soul in a way that was compatible with Christianity. She took up his work to argue that the thinking brain differs from the conscious self; that the conscious self is the soul; and that because the soul differs from the brain it can live on after the body and brain have died.

Cobbe singled out Ludwig Büchner to stand for the view that she opposed,[30] on which science shows that the brain performs all the functions of thought and memory, so that any appeal to an additional conscious self is unnecessary speculation. This threatened to rule out both moral responsibility and personal immortality. Cobbe conceded that the brain does indeed perform the intellectual functions that were previously attributed to a separate mind. But we can accept this and still hold that 'the conscious self is not identifiable with that matter which performs the function of Thought' (*DM* 307). That is, thought and the mind are functions of the brain[31] (like Lovelace and Babbage before her, Cobbe assumed that thought and mind are co-extensive). But the conscious self, which is the locus of responsibility and immortality, is something different.

This is where Cobbe brings in unconscious cerebration, though she argues, contra Carpenter, that unconscious cerebration is unconscious *thought*—so that, while retaining his word 'cerebration', she changes its meaning. She argues this by first documenting many examples of unconscious cerebration. For instance, unconscious cerebration is at work when people compose artworks automatically or when asleep (as with Coleridge's *Kubla Khan*), and when people spontaneously wake from sleep at a prearranged time, because their brains have been counting out the time unconsciously; unconscious cerebration is behind dreaming, which results from unconscious 'brain-work' operating on 'laws' distinct from the ones that regulate conscious life (*DM* 313); when people seem to see ghostly

---

[29] Carpenter and Cobbe knew one another, partly through his sister Mary, at whose Red Lodge reformatory school for destitute girls Cobbe worked in the late 1850s. The school was funded by Annabella Byron, whom Cobbe admired. I have discussed Cobbe's and William Benjamin Carpenter's relations a little further in Stone (2022b).
[30] She referred to his best-selling 1855 book *Kraft und Stoff*, of which Besant later produced a partial translation (*ABA* 262). Besant also showcased some of Büchner's work in *Our Corner*.
[31] 'Function' is, we can see, Cobbe's word; Naden would use it too, as did others such as Huxley, who stated that 'consciousness is a function of the brain' (1899: 135). The rise of this word reflects the fact that physiologists were analysing how bodily organs, including the brain, perform characteristic activities (i.e. functions) enabled by their physical structures.

apparitions, it is because memories on which their brains have unconsciously been dwelling have suddenly broken through into consciousness; and likewise, when people burst into inappropriate behaviour, it is because unconscious thought-processes have broken past their conscious powers of self-restraint.

From these and a profusion of other examples, Cobbe infers that the brain can unconsciously remember, understand, imagine, perform habitual activities, count time, and reason. On the last, Cobbe is firm: the brain can unconsciously reason, as on occasions when we give up a problem as insoluble and then find that our brains work out the solution for us later on, or during the night while we are asleep (*DM* 308–9). Can the brain unconsciously *think*? Cobbe answers yes, because 'it would be an unusual definition of the word "Thought" which would debar us from applying it to the above phenomena, or compel us to say that we can remember, fancy, and understand without "thinking" of the things remembered, fancied, or understood' (*DM* 330).

Cobbe's recognition of unconscious thought and the distinctive laws that regulate the construction of dreams may seem a startling anticipation of psychoanalysis,[32] especially when she remarks upon

> the small share occupied by the Moral Law in the dream world... We commit in dreams acts for which we should weep tears of blood were they real, and yet never feel the slightest remorse.... [T]he animal elements of our nature assert themselves – generally in the ratio of their unnatural suppression at other times – and abstinence is made up for by hungry Fancy spreading a glutton's feast. The *want* of sense of sin in such dreams is... the most natural and most healthful symptom about them. (*DM* 314–15)

The same points—that when we dream the moral censor is relaxed, and normally repressed impulses come to imaginary fulfilment—would later be central to Freud's theory of dreams.

But looking backwards in time rather than forwards, Cobbe's ideas came out of a pre-existing tradition of British thought about the unconscious, a tradition in which Carpenter was central;[33] and *his* views were informed by reflection on both mesmerism and the analytical engine. Cobbe differed from Carpenter above all in arguing that unconscious cerebration was thought. This issue was not solely one of terminology. In allowing that the brain can think, Cobbe came closer towards the sort of materialism that had been championed by Engledue, on which cerebration

---

[32] She analysed these laws further in 'Dreams as Instances of Unconscious Cerebration'. Here she argued that the dreaming brain converts memories, sentiments, and sensations into ideas following principles that are also at work in the cultural production of mythic symbols.

[33] On this tradition, see Bourne Taylor (2000) and Bourne Taylor and Shuttleworth (1998).

is all there is to thought and no 'supernatural' mental agencies, will, or soul need to be postulated at all.

Cobbe tried to avoid that conclusion, however. She argued:

> Is this instrument [the brain] *ourselves*? Are *we* quite inseparable from this machinery of our thoughts? If it never acted except by our volition and under our control, then, indeed, it might be somewhat difficult to conceive of our consciousness apart from it. But every night a different lesson is taught us... the dreaming brain-self is not the true self. (*DM* 361–2)

That is, Cobbe counts the existence of unconscious thought *against* the materialist view that the self is the brain. For it shows that there is a difference between unconscious thought—the cerebral operations automatically carried out by the brain—and the conscious self—the agent who can knowingly and voluntarily initiate and direct courses of thinking and acting (*DM* 332).

Cobbe is an anti-Cartesian insofar as she upholds the existence of unconscious thought, since for Descartes thought was necessarily conscious. But Cobbe is still a dualist, albeit a non-Cartesian one, because she attributes consciousness to a non-material self that she separates from the brain and body. She identifies this self with the immortal soul. Here she quotes Ecclesiastes 12:7: '"when the dust returns to the dust whence it was taken, the Spirit" – the Conscious Self of Man – "shall return to God who gave it"' (*DM* 334). By adding the clause about 'the Conscious Self', she signals her equation of self and soul.

Cobbe's position is interesting in several ways. She offers rich insights into many everyday mental phenomena and behaviours which she thinks are best explained on the assumption that unconscious thought occurs. Given all these phenomena, she rejects Cartesianism, and yet, partly on religious grounds, she wants to hold on to a non-material core of the person separate from the brain. She therefore identifies the soul as the bearer of consciousness and free will, and distinguishes it from the unconsciously and automatically thinking brain. All of this yields an original stance in the philosophy of mind.

However, there are problems with Cobbe's differentiation of conscious self from thinking brain. As she admits, it might be objected that, though the brain may be able to think without consciousness, this does not show that the self can be conscious without a brain (334). She replies that it at least shows that the relation between conscious self and thinking brain is variable and intermittent, hence that the two are separable, hence that it is at least possible that the former can persist without the latter (333). But the critic might respond that the relation is variable because only some thoughts rise to consciousness, though consciousness remains a function of the brain and cannot exist without it. Thus Cobbe's arguments are insufficient to show that the self can be conscious without a brain.

Moreover, her arguments seemed to entail on the contrary that consciousness *did* depend on the brain. So Richard Holt Hutton argued, pointing out that any conscious perception is composed of innumerable micro-perceptions that do not in themselves reach the level of awareness. Being unconscious, these micro-perceptions must in Cobbe's terms be automatic functions of the brain. But since the sum total of many such micro-perceptions makes up a conscious perception, that conscious perception must also be a function of the brain (Hutton 1870a: 1315).

Another overarching problem with Cobbe's position was that if the conscious self does not think, remember, or reason (etc.), because all these are functions of the brain, then vanishingly little work remains for the self to do. To be sure, for Cobbe, the self exercises volition and bears moral responsibility. But it is not clear how, in the absence of any intellectual powers, the self *can* exercise will, or how it can bear moral responsibility in the absence of memory. Perhaps it does this by using the brain as its organ, but this still seems to entail that in itself the self is entirely empty and impotent.

For these several reasons, Cobbe's critics—such as Hutton, 'E. V. N.' (1870), and Anonymous (1873)—believed that she had conceded too much to materialism, so much as to render the soul empty and consciousness a mere effect of the brain. These problems were more acute for Cobbe than Carpenter, because he denied that the brain on its own could think, whereas Cobbe affirmed that it could, thereby relocating yet another key capacity of the soul—thought—onto the side of the brain. This is why the issue of thought versus cerebration was substantial and not only terminological. The effect of these problems was that Cobbe's dualist critics judged her to be sailing unduly close to the materialist wind, while for materialists her arguments inadvertently confirmed that the soul was otiose, an unnecessary supernaturalist relic that had no explanatory work left to do.

3.5 Naden and Hylo-Idealism

The volatile climate of 1830s–1840s materialism, mesmerism, and immanentism that had swirled around Lovelace, Martineau, Engledue, and Carpenter was formative for the man who was Naden's key philosophical influence, Robert Lewins. Indeed, there were some conspicuous parallels between Lewins and Carpenter. Lewins followed in the footsteps of his father, a highly scholarly medical doctor, and gained a medical licence at Edinburgh in 1841, where Carpenter had graduated in 1839; also like Carpenter, Lewins authored a prize essay, and he seemed en route to an illustrious medical career (Moore 1987: 231).[34]

---

[34] Interestingly, Samuel Smiles, author of the Bible of Victorian self-improvement *Self-Help* (1859), was a medical apprentice to Lewins's father in the 1820s; see Smiles (1905: 28–35).

But then he swerved off course and joined the military in 1843, serving as an army surgeon overseas, before retiring in 1868 and immediately re-entering the British philosophical conversation with an unorthodox and polemical brand of atheism and materialism, 'hylo-zoism'.

Perhaps because the late 1830s and early 1840s had been his formative period, Lewins directly resumed the 1840s discussion about the unity of natural forces and the material basis of mind. In 'On the Identity of the Vital and the Cosmical Principle', he maintained that life 'results not from the introduction of any new element *special* to itself, but solely from a specific arrangement [of matter] under more complicated conditions than those in which is no life' (1869: 4). There is no special vital force; rather, '*vital force* ... and *physical force* ... are one and the same'. Nor is there any special mental force. On the contrary the 'force that gives us power to feel and to think [is] that which moves the world' (5), the connecting link, he suggested, being electricity, for there is an 'identity of electrical and nervous force'. Here he referred back to Faraday—where, we recall, the idea that electricity unites body and mind was one Lovelace countenanced back in the 1840s, likewise with reference to Faraday, although in both cases they were going beyond Faraday himself.[35]

Lewins was thus, as he went on to say in *Life and Mind*, an immanentist (Lewins [1873] 1894: 28, 42). The 'burning question of our age', he told Naden, 'is ... whether Hylo-zoism or its opposite be true? I have called it the question of Transcendentalism or Immanentism' (Lewins to Naden, 14 November 1878, in Lewins [1887] 2020: 85). Lewins's immanentism was an inheritance from the 1840s circles around *The Zoist*, as we see from his calling his standpoint hylo-zoism. Others saw the link too: 'Thalassoplektos', who edited the 1894 edition of *Life and Mind*, added an appendix quoting Engledue's 1843 address at length and spelling out Lewins's complete agreement with Engledue's materialism (Lewins [1873] 1894: 47–8).[36]

Having distilled his hylo-zoist outlook, Lewins marshalled a group of adherents. The whole group tirelessly expounded and propagandized the position from the 1870s to 1890s, authoring 'over twenty pamphlets and books and ... a barrage of articles, reviews, and letters to periodicals' (Smith 1978: 304). Their most articulate and cogent member was Naden, whom Lewins met in 1876.[37] By 1880 Lewins

---

[35] In 1846 Faraday gave a talk in which he suggested that matter might at its most basic level be force, but he stressed that this was merely provisional speculation and would quite likely prove to be false (see Faraday 1846). For further discussion of Faraday's views, see Utke (1994).

[36] The militant secularist W. Stewart Ross is the named editor of the 1894 edition, but 'Thalassoplektos' was actually the pseudonym of another secularist, M. C. McHugh (see Corbeil 2019), whereas Ross's usual pseudonym was 'Saladin'. Authorship aside, these 1894 additions confirm what a rallying-point Engledue's materialism still was.

[37] Naden has been chiefly remembered for her poetry, on which see, e.g. Alarabi (2012), Moore (1987), and Thain (2003). However, more recently, Thain (2011), Stainthorp (2017, 2019), and Huber (2022) have recovered Naden as a philosopher and scientist as well as poet. Stainthorp's work has been essential in driving the recovery of Naden.

had persuaded her to join the hylo-zoist fold.[38] Once on board, Naden made the case for the position clearly and directly, in marked contrast to Lewins's writing which was almost comically awash with learning, allusions and word-play. Naden also renamed the position 'hylo-idealism', which the group followed. One might wonder whether this name change was to avoid negative associations with *The Zoist*, but this seems unlikely, for Naden had no fear of taking bold and controversial positions. I will suggest shortly that the name change had more to do with her atheism.

Hylo-idealism never exhausted Naden's interests. She wrote on epistemology, metaphysics, history of philosophy, aesthetics, and ethics, and was moving away from hylo-idealism before her tragically early death. Nonetheless she was best known for her hylo-idealist writings and it is these on which I shall concentrate here,[39] especially two key essays: 'The Brain Theory of Mind and Matter; or Hylo-Idealism', signed 'Constance Arden', the lead article in the *Journal of Science* for March 1883;[40] and 'Hylo-Idealism: The Creed of the Coming Day', signed 'C. N.', which appeared in Besant's *Our Corner* in 1884. Hylo-idealism combines two key theses: on the one hand, idealism—all that I can know is my own ideas, so that 'man is the measure of all things', and each of us lives in our own self-generated mental world; on the other hand, *hyle*-ism, that is, materialism—the agency producing these ideas is the brain, responding to causal stimuli impinging on it. Given the latter, a materialist theory of mind is a core part of hylo-idealism.[41]

To start with the idealist side, Naden holds that 'man is the maker of his own Cosmos, and...all his perceptions – even those which seem to represent solid, extended, and external objects – have a merely subjective existence, bounded by...his sentient being' (*BT* 157). Naden takes it that we do not perceive objects directly but only indirectly, through representations or ideas of them. But then we cannot get beyond our ideas to access any objects with which to compare them. We therefore have no grounds to believe that our ideas in any way resemble that which lies beyond them, or that our ideas give us access to the things they represent. Naden argues that as this goes for all our ideas, each of us lives in our own world, and these worlds are our own individual visions.

But, Naden adds, the reason *why* we only see our own ideas and world-visions is because of how our brains work. Consider sight: when light acts on the normal

---

[38] The other hylo-idealists were E. Cobham Brewer (pen-named 'Julian'), Herbert Courtney, and George McCrie.
[39] Naden's hylo-idealism was discussed in the *Contemporary Review*, *Monist*, and *Journal of Mental Science*. Indeed 'hylo-idealism' became such a buzzword that Wilde gave his 1887 story 'The Canterville Ghost' the subtitle 'A Hylo-Idealistic Romance' (Wilde knew Naden's philosophy; see Thain 2011: 22–3).
[40] This journal had until 1891 been the *Quarterly Journal of Science*, founded in 1864, one of several periodicals popularizing the latest scientific research (see Lightman 2016).
[41] For another recent reading of Naden on which, her concerns to unite idealism and materialism notwithstanding, she is a materialist above all, see Huber (2022).

retina, one sees a whole range of colours, whereas a colour-blind person with different retinas sees a more limited range (*BT* 159). This exemplifies the general process whereby things affect our sense organs, which convey stimuli through our nervous systems to our brains, which in turn 'transmute identical stimuli, conveyed...by different channels, into results' (160), yielding a panorama of sights, smells, sounds, and so on. So 'the world-vision, to which alone the mind has access, is made *inside*, and not outside, the *cerebrum*' (158, 160; my emphasis). Thus Naden's idealism ultimately rests on her materialism, as we see when she says that: 'All ideas...are of course equally subjective, *since none can boast an origin higher than the human brain*' (165; my emphasis). We each live in worlds of our own making because these worlds are what our brains produce in processing stimuli from the matter around them. It is the dependence of thought on the brain, for Naden, that entails that we cannot know the world as it is independently of the brain and its mechanisms for converting stimuli into representations.

Naden maintains that we need not posit any spiritual or non-material forces, agencies, or qualities within matter to explain how it can operate creatively in generating mental representations. Matter contains inherent 'material energy': it is not imbued with any non-material animating principles, but matter is already energetic, its parts acting on one another of their own momentum (*FR* 125). Thus Naden, like Lewins, is an immanentist. Once certain energetic parts of matter enter sufficiently complex configurations, living organisms result, some of which evolve internal configurations sufficiently complex—containing spinal column, nervous system, cerebrum, and so on—that they have sensation. As Naden puts it, 'the human organism is a self-acting machine, differing from the lowest forms of life only in its greater complexity' (*ID* 194).

How exactly does Naden see the mind/brain relation? She states that ideas 'correlate' with and 'correspond' to bodily states (*FR* 124); the psychical 'depends' on the physical (*MP* 81); the brain's processes 'cause', 'generate', and 'produce' ideas (*FR* 124; *BT* 164); and 'perception, emotion and thought are simply the special sensations or functions of the...encephalon' (*FR* 195). Overarching these different formulations, Naden is adamant that physiological research has demonstrated that psychical life is completely dependent on physical life, in a way that demolishes dualism.

Naden was uncompromising in her rejection of dualism. In 'Hylo-Zoism versus Animism' of 1881 (*FR* 191–7), she opposed J. H. Barker's animism, equating animism with 'orthodox dualism' (*ID* 197). Barker had argued that human life and the mind cannot be explained as merely further-developed manifestations of animal life, nor can animal life be explained as manifesting a prior cosmic life (Barker 1881). For 'cosmic life' is merely metaphorical: matter, just as such, is not alive. The presence of life and mind in animals requires a separate active principle, the soul or *anima*. The same goes for human beings; in both human and animal cases, life arises from the union of soul and body. The human soul, however, is distinctive in that it is immortal, created by God, and will survive the body's death.

Contra Barker, Naden denies that there is any such soul or separate mental substance: 'To regard the intellect as an entity, separable from the myriad [physical] factors, which unite to produce and direct it, is...absurd' (*BT* 164). Ideas and mental functioning completely depend on the brain for their occurrence, so neither can possibly occur without a brain and body. Whereas for Barker invoking souls is necessary because we cannot explain how mental qualities arise on a purely physical basis, Naden disagrees. For her, we can explain this perfectly well on the basis that matter is already energetic and that sensation results once its energetic interconnections become sufficiently complex.

Consequently, for Naden, personal immortality is ruled out: the only part of us that is immortal and will endure after we die is the material-energetic life-processes and forces of which our bodies and minds are composed.[42] Naden also rejects Barker's argument that our exercises of free will show that the soul is different from the body (*FR* 194). For Naden, when I exercise free will in, say, deciding to take a walk, what is happening here is that my (material) brain is acting on other (equally material) parts of my body. No separate mind or soul is involved; and even if we did have such a soul, being immaterial it could not possibly interact with the brain and body to produce movement. The only way to explain voluntary actions is to say that the agent's brain is acting on their nerves and musculature; everything here is corporeal. As for my idea that I am deciding to walk, this idea is just my brain's way of registering that my action (walking) is being done from motivations arising unhindered from within my own brain. Naden is thus a compatibilist, who thinks that I am acting freely just when my 'activity proceeds, not from external compulsion, but from internal constitution' (*BT* 163). Although 'the laws which determine the conduct of a sentient being are far more complicated than those which govern chemical union and decomposition', still the difference is only one of degree, not kind (163).

Naden's view of free will is influenced by Thomas Henry Huxley, to whose work she refers. In his famous 1874 essay, 'On the Hypothesis that Animals are Automata', he argues for epiphenomenalism, treating consciousness as a causally inefficacious by-product of brain processes, 'as the steam-whistle which accompanies the work of a locomotive engine is without influence upon its machinery' ([1874] 1893: 243). 'Volition', Huxley therefore holds, is 'an emotion indicative of physical changes, not a cause of such changes' (243). We feel that we are doing something freely just when we are aware that our brains are causing us to do things without any external agencies imposing impediments. Huxley insists that

---

[42] According to Naden's 1881 poem 'The Pantheist Song of Immortality': 'Yes, thou shalt die, but these almighty forces, that meet to form thee, live for ever more;... Rejoice in thine imperishable being, one with the Essence of the boundless world' (1894: 44–5).

this is compatible with our having free will, 'for an agent is free when there is nothing to prevent him from doing that which he desires to do' (243).

The link to Huxley in turn leads us back to Carpenter, whose theory of the mind Huxley opposes. Having argued that conscious sensations are the product of molecular movements in the brain (1882: 242–3), Huxley goes on to consider three possible relations between conscious sensations and the sensorium: (1) that sensation requires the cooperation of the physical sensorium and an immaterial mental substance; (2) that the sensorium on its own produces sensation; and (3) that an immaterial mental substance has sensations of which changes in the sensorium are merely a concomitant but not a cause (268). Huxley favours the second alternative on grounds of parsimony (270). Although he does not explicitly mention Carpenter here, the first option clearly refers to Carpenter, whose views Huxley undoubtedly knew because both men were among the original twenty-six members of the (exclusively male) Metaphysical Society.

When Naden claims that we are 'self-acting machines' (*ID* 194), she refers to Huxley, and so indirectly she too is opposing Carpenter, for whom we are more than mere self-acting machines because we also have immortal souls which are the locus of our free will. Naden consistently rejects such views on which we are compounds of mortal body and immortal soul—Barker's being one such view, Cobbe's another, and Carpenter's yet another.[43] Indeed, Naden rejects these views more unequivocally than Huxley. When Huxley admits that his favoured second alternative is merely a hypothesis (1882: 269), Naden deplores his excessive 'agnosticism' and caution. She insists that the modern sciences actually '*prove* alike the real existence of the material universe and its complete homogeneity with our own being' (*ID* 200; my emphasis).

A key reason why Naden opposes dualist views like those of Barker and Carpenter is that she sees them as compromising with religion.[44] For her, the creative powers that humanity had formerly ceded to an imaginary God are really our own and the time is ripe to reclaim them. She transposes the language of God's creation of the world onto the human brain—we must learn, she says,

> to behold in the orderly arrangements of the Cosmos only a supreme glorification of [brain-]matter, the universal mother, and of man, her child ... In the grey cells of the cerebral cortex are generated ... the visible heaven, [and] the poetic sense of its beauty and harmony. (*BT* 166)

---

[43] Naden knew Carpenter's work and went on to refer to it (*MP* 81). But she used it very differently from his intentions, and very differently from Cobbe. Naden appealed to Carpenter to demonstrate how extensively the brain performs mental and ideo-motor processing—that is, she pulled Carpenter's work back in support of the thesis that any appeal to the soul is redundant.

[44] On Naden's atheism, including in her unpublished notebooks, see Stainthorp (2019: ch. 3).

Each brain creates a complete universe, Naden emphasizes: the creation is entirely our own, and no room is left for any creation by God. The brain is 'the only authentic Creator of the world as yet discovered' and 'is its own God' (*HI* 170–1).[45]

Plausibly, Naden's atheism motivates her to conjoin idealism and materialism and to highlight this by renaming hylo-zoism 'hylo-*idealism*'. Idealism, in Naden's version, supports atheism because it means that humans are sovereign creative agents; while materialism also supports atheism because it means that matter generates the full wealth and complexity of the universe with no need for God or a divine plan. By combining both currents, Naden hopes for a maximally atheist position. In stressing our sovereign agency, then, Naden is not reverting to a dualist belief in free will. On the contrary, she equates our sovereign *thinking* agency in creating an ordered experienced cosmos with the *brain's* agency in generating ideas from stimuli, which in turn exemplifies *matter's* agency in organizing itself through its own energies into complex configurations.

Hylo-idealism has problems, however. If each of us lives in our own cosmos of ideas and we cannot know how things are outside that cosmos, then how do we know about the causal-energetic processes by which the brain reacts to stimuli from the matter around it?[46] Naden gives several answers.

First, she suggests, we can only know our ideas, but we can still legitimately make inductive generalizations about laws of nature (i.e. nature insofar as it figures in our ideas). And we can generalize about the laws of how the brain works, again as we observe brains, that is, as brains appear in our ideas. Thus we can know about brain operations through science's inductive method.[47] Science's ultimate data are observations—since, after all, we can only know about our own ideas. That is, Naden's account of science is phenomenalist; she combines scientific materialism and phenomenalist epistemology. All the same, there remains a tension between her phenomenalist account of matter and her claim that brain-matter generates these same phenomena.

Second, Naden returns to the case of light acting on the retina, and clarifies that really what acts on the retina is an 'unknown force' that we call light, but where the perception of this force *as* light is an effect of the brain's metabolism. 'Beyond this [brain-metabolism] there is practically nothing, for our wildest imagination cannot overleap the boundaries of self, and depict an invisible course of light' (*BT* 159). In short, something affects the brain here, but we cannot know what this

---

[45] Although Naden's idealism owes much to Berkeley, then, her conjunction of idealism with atheism sets her far apart from him. In terms of her debt to Berkeley, though, Naden argues that he took Locke's view of perception to its logical conclusion (*ID* 56), establishing that 'we perceive nothing but our own sensations' (212). Naden further assimilates Berkeley to Protagoras ('man is the measure of all things') following Lewins ([1873] 1894: 57), who takes this assimilation in turn from George Henry Lewes's *Biographical History of Philosophy* (1857: 475–6).

[46] This criticism was made by Anonymous (1892b: 277–8), Carus (1894), and Dale (1891).

[47] A method of which Naden gave a sustained account, defending the role of induction and deduction in science, in *Induction and Deduction* (*ID*).

something may be like independently of how the brain represents it. The case of light is no different from anything else: all these forces acting on the brain are unknowable to us. We cannot even really know that they are forces: there is only void and formless chaos until the brain imposes some arrangement on it (*BT* 166).

But, Naden's critics replied, surely that must apply to the brain too, so that we cannot legitimately claim to know that there really are such things as brains, only that the world of ideas originates somehow. Here Naden's idealism undermines her materialism: because we can only know our own ideas, we cannot advance beyond these ideas to know that brains generate them. Certainly we can have ideas about brains, as we do about many things. But if ideas do not inform us about anything beyond themselves, then our ideas about brains do not inform us about how brains may be independently of the ideas.

Naden acknowledges the problem: 'If the universe be simply...a vision..., how are we to know that there is any such thing as matter?...[H]ow are we to be sure that the brain itself really exists, and that the all-generating cells are not mere illusory appearances?' (*HI* 172). She answers that, sticking within my own ideas, I find that I *actively* think and organize my experience. My ideas exhibit order. Thus: 'We are obliged to assume the existence of some active basis of thought, that is, of something which thinks.' Then, we can know that this active basis is the brain: 'having seen that sensation and motion follow upon excitation of the brain,...we are justified in restoring our thought-cells to their proud creative eminence' and in saying 'that they think, and therefore exist' (*HI* 173). In turn, for the brain to be able to think, there must be a surrounding world of matter with which it is in material-energetic interchange. 'From the material proplasm of consciousness we argue...to a material proplasm of the objects of consciousness, and therefore to a real world which existed before man was.' Unfortunately, the middle step—the claim that I know by observation that my thinking agency has its source in a material object, the brain—is problematic. For Naden takes it that, in at least this one case, observations give us access to reality in itself. But then why not say the same for other observations, and abandon the premise that 'the universe is merely a vision'?

Naden attempted other solutions, but hylo-idealism's problems remained intractable. This led her to move away from hylo-idealism to work out a new monistic philosophical standpoint, a process cut short by her early death. This standpoint was taking shape in the part of *Further Reliques* called 'Philosophical Tracts' (*FR* 134–90). For all its problems, hylo-idealism remains interesting in itself, not only for the clarity and directness of Naden's articulation and defence of it but also in substance. Naden argues that the complete dependence of thought and consciousness on the brain does not take away our freedom, creativity, or sovereignty. On the contrary, that dependence *amplifies* all of these features, both because it leaves no room for God and because it demonstrates that matter is full of creative energy. We need not defensively reassert the existence of immortal souls or immaterial wills in order to secure human freedom; freedom is most fully available if materialism is true.

3.6 Blavatsky and Besant: Explaining the Mind

In 1888, as part of their promotional campaign, the hylo-idealists sent some writings to *Lucifer*, the theosophical journal founded the previous year by Helena Blavatsky once she had settled in London. By then the theosophical movement was bedevilled by schisms and had suffered adverse publicity arising from the Coulomb affair and Hodgson report. To reassert her authority over the movement and re-establish its reputation, Blavatsky founded *Lucifer*. It featured a lively mixture of essays, fiction, translations (for instance from Giordano Bruno), reviews (for example of *Thus Spoke Zarathustra*), letters, and other miscellanea from mainly theosophical authors. Blavatsky presided over the whole, giving regular statements of theosophical position.[48]

Having received the hylo-idealists' materials, Blavatsky singled out Naden's 'extremely attractive' writing and published her short atheist piece 'Autocentricism' (signed 'C. N.') plus two hylo-idealist letters, from Lewins and George McCrie. But, signing herself 'The Adversary', Blavatsky appended a critique of hylo-idealism, her objections to which she had already sketched in late 1887 when she read Naden's 1883 essay 'What Is Religion?'[49] In these notes, subsequently published in *The Theosophist* in 1896, Blavatsky went as far as to declare that: 'Theosophy has no bitterer enemy than *Hylo-Idealism*, the great ally of materialism, today' (*MI* 9). It is clear, then, that Blavatsky both found hylo-idealism significant and regarded Naden as a serious interlocutor—which testifies to the impact that Naden and the other hylo-idealists had.

Blavatsky's central criticism of hylo-idealism was that, because it was a materialist theory, it could not explain consciousness. In fact, Blavatsky had reached this conclusion about materialism long before encountering hylo-idealism, savaging an array of scientific materialists, including both Huxley and Büchner, in *Isis Unveiled*. Blavatsky now saw hylo-idealism as the latest version of a view of mind that she already opposed. Her criticisms of the hylo-idealist version were as follows.

If we can only know our own ideas, Blavatsky says, then we cannot know about the brain; conversely, if we can know about the brain, then it cannot be true that we know only our own ideas (*LHL* 509). Hylo-idealism's materialism and idealism

---

[48] Mabel Collins was a named co-editor, but Blavatsky wrote the editorial statements and Collins re-edited what Blavatsky had written. Collins was subsequently pushed out, and Blavatsky installed Besant as co-editor instead. On these editorial power-struggles, see Ferguson (2020).

[49] Blavatsky referred to 'What is Religion?' in *Lucifer* 1.1 (1887), 72.

contradict one another. The *goal* of uniting materialism and idealism is a worthy one. But this unification should be carried out by showing that both subject and object, mind and empirical world, are merely derivative and partial forms of a more basic, all-encompassing unity (*MI* 10). The hylo-idealists instead treat both matter and ideas in turn as absolute, and this does not produce any real unity but only an inconsistent hybrid—'a modern cross-breed between misunderstood Protagoras and Büchner' (*LHL* 509). In fact, what ultimately holds hylo-idealism's materialist and idealist poles together are its 'atheism and pessimism', Blavatsky correctly recognizes, meaning by 'pessimism' the denial of immortality (*MI* 94). Blavatsky does not object to the hylo-idealists' atheism from a straightforward theist perspective; she rejects any belief in an 'unphilosophical, anthropomorphic deity' (*LHL* 511). But she does believe in a divine unity that is conceived not as a person but the ground of all things. And while she agrees with the hylo-idealists that our finite selves are not immortal, Blavatsky thinks that there is an immortal kernel in each of us, so that, after our bodies die, we can hope for progressive spiritual improvement through a series of reincarnations.

Above all, Blavatsky maintains, the hylo-idealists cannot explain consciousness on a material basis because the two orders are fundamentally different. The result is the '*absolute impossibility of explaining spiritual effects by physical causes*' (*LHL* 509). The hylo-idealists can show at most that there are constant correlations between certain brain-states and certain mental phenomena, but not *why* the former necessitate the latter. To explain, Blavatsky quotes from John Tyndall's 1868 paper 'Scientific Materialism'. This is at first sight surprising. For Tyndall had by then become infamous for his 1874 Belfast Address, in which he claimed to see in 'Matter...the promise and potency of all terrestrial Life' (Tyndall 1879: 524). That claim had become a byword for materialism and atheism (see Lightman 2011). But Blavatsky invokes Tyndall to show that even one of materialism's most notorious exponents concedes that the mind defies materialistic explanation.

Tyndall does indeed concede this. He argues in his essay 'Scientific Materialism', originally from 1868, that inanimate objects are as they are entirely because of their physical constituents and their causal interactions. Scientists can completely explain inanimate objects on this basis; no appeal to a divine architect is needed. Likewise with living entities, like a grain of corn; again, science can in principle explain everything about them, even though in practice unravelling the complex causal interactions composing some living entities may take a very long time. Tyndall might have said something similar of brain and mind—but instead he maintains that, when it comes to the mind, principled limits apply. Science informs us that certain brain-states invariably go along with certain thoughts and feelings, and vice versa. But this is only an empirical association. We cannot say why these invariably go together—why certain molecular motions in the brain cause particular mental phenomena.

Granted that a definite thought, and a definite molecular action in the brain, occur simultaneously; we... [cannot] pass, by a process of reasoning, from the one to the other. They appear together, but we do not know why. Were... [we able] to see and feel the very molecules of the brain... we should be as far as ever from the solution of the problem, 'How are these physical processes connected with the facts of consciousness?' The chasm between the two classes of phenomena would still remain intellectually impassable. Let the consciousness of love, for example, be associated with a right-handed spiral motion of the molecules of the brain, and the consciousness of hate with a left-handed spiral motion. We should then know, when we love, that the motion is in one direction, and, when we hate, that the motion is in the other; but the WHY? would remain as unanswerable as before. (Tyndall 1879: 420)

Moreover, Tyndall adds in the Belfast Address, we may not bring in religion to bridge the explanatory gap, because religion is non-cognitive, ministering to our emotional needs. Only science gives us knowledge about nature; but this knowledge has limits that we must simply accept. Thus, despite saying in the Address that he saw in matter the potential for all life, he also says that when we try to trace 'upward' the causal genesis of mind from matter we reach a limit: 'Man the *object* is separated by an impassable gulf from man the *subject*' (1879: 528).[50]

As we saw, Naden denied that there were any such limits to materialistic explanation. For her, we can explain life from complexity of material organization, and mind from further complexity in the organization of living matter. Tyndall agrees with respect to life, but not mind. Following his lead, Blavatsky contends that organic complexity would only suffice to explain consciousness if there were nothing in the latter over and above the former. But there is: nothing like the subjective, phenomenal, or first-personal quality of experience is already in the causal-energetic interactions amongst parts of matter. We are dealing with 'two different classes of phenomena' (*LHL* 509).

Blavatsky's claim that mind cannot be explained materialistically was taken up by Besant. This was a dramatic turnaround for Besant, for during her secularist period she had publicized Naden's views and worked on a translation of Büchner's *Kraft und Stoff*—combining secularism with materialism, as Naden did. Yet Besant had gnawing doubts about secularism which reached a head in 1889 when she reviewed Blavatsky's *Secret Doctrine*. Besant now converted to theosophy; amongst her motivations for doing so, she explained, were doubts about materialist explanations of life and mind. As she wrote to Bradlaugh, 'this form of Pantheism [i.e. theosophy] appears to me to promise solution of some

---

[50] Tyndall was not a transcendentalist, though, but an immanentist who believed that immanent explanation had an impassable limit. More recently, he has come to be seen as a founding figure for *mysterianism* in the philosophy of mind (e.g. Kriegel 2014: 461).

problems, *especially problems in Psychology*, which Atheism leaves untouched' (*ABA* 353; my emphasis).

Besant explains further in her 1890 essay 'Why I Became a Theosophist', published as a pamphlet. Justifying her turn to theosophy to her former secularist allies, Besant argues that if we really value free thought, then we must be prepared to consider arguments that support spiritual, religious, and metaphysical claims and accept their conclusions if the arguments are sound.[51] Furthermore, Besant says, she is as committed as ever to rejecting supernaturalism. Everything in the universe must be explained with no appeal to miracles, divine interventions, or other events contravening the laws of nature. But she had for ten years

> sought along the lines of Materialistic Science for the answer to...questions on Life and Mind...[namely] 'What is Life? What is Thought?' Not only was materialism unable to answer the question, but it declared pretty positively that no answer could ever be given. (*WT* 6)

First, Besant says, we cannot explain life from mere movements and energy transfers amongst bits of matter—from 'the blind clash of atoms and the hurtling of forces' (*WT* 7). Something in life goes beyond anything present in physical and chemical processes; Besant calls it a *sui generis* element (7). It is this novel element in life that calls for explanation, for which we appeal to its physical and chemical bases. But precisely because this element goes beyond anything in the physical and chemical domains, their workings are insufficient to account for it.

Second, we cannot explain mental phenomena from brain processes.

> Materialism traces a correlation between living nervous matter and intellection; it demonstrates a parallelism between the growing complexity of the nervous system and growing complexity of phenomena of consciousness;...it shows that certain cerebral activities normally accompany certain psychical activities. That is, it proves that...there is a close connection between living nervous matter and thought-processes. As to the *nature* of that connection knowledge is dumb. (*WT* 8; my emphasis)

As we can see, Besant is reprising arguments from Blavatsky and, indirectly, Tyndall. Besant also ridicules here the slogan of Büchner's materialist co-worker Karl Vogt that 'the brain secretes thought as the liver secretes bile'. There is no 'as' about it, Besant objects, for bile is physical and thoughts are not.

---

[51] On this aspect of Besant's argument, see Hanbery MacKay (2017).

We study the nerve-cells of the brain; we find molecular vibration; we are still in the Object World, amid form, color, resistance and motion. Suddenly there is a THOUGHT, and all is changed. We have passed into a new world, the Subject World... Between the Motion and the Thought, between the Subject and Object, lies an unspanned gulf. (*WT* 8)

However, Besant continues, the gulf between brain and mind remains uncrossable only if we assume—as scientists do—that the explanation must be materialist, that is, must proceed from lower- to higher-order phenomena. In that case, the brain–mind connection will remain mysterious, and knowledge will seem to have reached its limit here (*WT* 7). But for naturalists, everything is to be explained and nothing treated as mysterious. Anti-supernaturalism, then, pushes us to question materialism. Given Besant's above argument regarding life, to explain y from x there must be at least as much in x as in y; but if there is anything more or *sui generis* in y, then we cannot completely explain y from x. So we must see whether we can progress in explaining why life and mind emerge from matter by reversing the order of flow and starting from the *higher*-level phenomena. 'Is "spirit" the flower of "matter", or "matter" the crystallisation of "spirit"?' (*WT* 16).

For Besant, the latter view alone can satisfy our explanatory requirements. If matter derives from a spiritual element in the first place, then we can explain how life and mind emerge from matter in terms of the spiritual element's progressive *re*-emergence into forms closer to its original one. That is, we can explain mind from matter if there is already something mental in matter, all the way down. For then 'assuming intelligence is primal, the developed and dawning faculties of the human mind fall into intelligible order, and can be studied with hope of comprehension' (*WT* 16).[52] And we can explain how matter derives from this primal mental or spiritual element because we are deriving a lower-level—thinner, less complicated—phenomenon from a higher-level—richer, more complex—one. There is more in x than y, so the explanation succeeds.

Generally, then, the theosophical approach to mind is that a primary overarching unity precedes the mind/matter division. But this unity ultimately falls more on the mental or spiritual side: it is an *ideal* unity. As Besant puts it:

[T]he profound difference between Atheism and Pantheism... [is that] both posit an Existence... of which all phenomena are modes; but to the Atheist that Existence manifests as Force-Matter, unconscious, unintelligent, while to the Pantheist it manifests as Life-Matter, conscious, intelligent. To the one, life and consciousness are attributes, properties, dependent upon arrangements of matter; to the other they are fundamental, essential, and only limited in their manifestation by arrangements of matter. (*ABA* 146)

---

[52] Blavatsky made the same argument; see *IU* (I: 429).

Since the primal unity divides into matter versus spirit, the unity is not spiritual in the same way as the derivative, finite forms of spirit that differ from matter. Nonetheless, in dividing itself, the primal unity exhibits life, intelligence, and spirit: life, because it exercises activity and creativity in generating the cosmos; intelligence, because it generates the cosmos in intelligible ways; and spirit, because it is not originally material. This unity is therefore ideal.[53] Crucially, though, it is not to be identified with the Christian God but is non-personal—theosophy is a form of pantheism, not theism. As it is not a person, the unity generates the cosmos not by creation but emanation. It descends into matter, from which spirit then gradually re-emerges in an immense cosmic movement from 'involution' (spirit to matter) back through 'evolution' (matter to spirit).

Blavatsky gives a complex account of the involution/evolution movement in *The Secret Doctrine*. Within this account she identifies the human being as consisting of seven layers: (i) spirit, (ii) spiritual soul, (iii) intelligent soul or mind, (iv) animal soul, (v) astral body, (vi) vitality, and (vii) physical body (*SD* 1: 153). The individual's higher, more spiritual levels are embedded in and entangled with the lower, more physical ones. It is possible, though, for our higher selves temporarily to become free from the lower ones and act independently—which we see, Besant claims, in clairvoyance, astral travelling, thought-transference (telepathy) and mesmerism (*WT* 10–11, 23). These phenomena testify to our great untapped psychical powers, which are normally restricted by our lower physical aspects.

Levels (i) to (iii) are the immortal kernel in each individual, which undergoes successive reincarnations, whereas the 'lower quaternary' is mortal. As intelligent souls, we can be more or less submerged in the desires and feelings of our animal souls, and through *karma* this affects what future reincarnations we undergo. The more we transcend physical influences in life, the more our immortal aspect can escape future lives of physical suffering, re-enter the earth in more spiritually advanced forms, and so further humanity's ascent back to a spiritual condition. Thus, unlike Naden, Blavatsky affirms the immortality of the soul; but Blavatsky would say that theists such as Cobbe wrongly take only the *finite* individual self—the intelligent soul—to be immortal. The spirit and spiritual soul, however, are impersonal (*MI* 12), and so is the intelligent soul to the extent that it transcends the feeling soul. So what reincarnates is not personal individuality but the non-personal kernels of spiritual existence within us (see Chajes 2017: 91). Whereas Cobbe affirms personal immortality and Naden denies it, Blavatsky and Besant affirm *non*-personal immortality.

---

[53] Blavatsky speaks of 'Divine Thought...Universal Mind,' 'ONE LIFE,' and 'universal soul' (*SD* 1: 1–2), although this 'must not be regarded as even vaguely shadowing forth an intellectual process akin to that exhibited by man', for the latter processes are merely finite, discursive and changeable (*SD* 1: 1, note).

Blavatsky had many motivations for constructing her theosophical world view, just as Besant had many motivations for embracing and developing it further. Explaining how and why the mental emerges from the physical was only one factor, but it did help to motivate their position (see e.g. *SD* 1: 38). The explanation they gave was that there is a primordial spiritual life that descends into the finite material world and must then re-emerge from it, in part by assuming the guise of individual human minds and their spiritual evolution. The emergence of mental life from the brain is unmysterious because it is part of this cosmic process in which the original unity eventually regains spiritual guise, so that nothing new appears here that was not already present at the very origins of the cosmos (*SD* 1: 274).

Some readers might think that the solution—Blavatsky's elaborate cosmology—is so implausible and fantastic that it would be better simply to accept that scientific materialism has explanatory limits as Tyndall did. But we can distinguish the overall *structure* of the theosophical approach to mind—monist panpsychism—from Blavatsky's particular system. Blavatsky's and Besant's arguments for panpsychism retain merit even if one finds Blavatsky's metaphysical system too much.

3.7 The Dialectical Emergence of these Accounts of the Mind

There is an interesting dialectical progression amongst these five women's views on the mind, with each position arising out of problems in the one before it.

Lovelace inhabited a dense field of 1840s debate about the mind in which mesmerism, the unity of natural forces, and the possibility of machine thought bore on one another. She was drawn towards materialism, yet it was contested and it was not clear how to substantiate the claim that thought depends on bodily and cerebral matter, so she kept pulling back. Emerging from this field, her interlocutor Carpenter found a way to address all these issues within a comprehensive physiological theory that was avowedly dualist. Yes, the cerebrum operated automatically, like a mesmerized subject, like a thinking machine, but its operations on their own were mere 'cerebration' and they only became thought if they were regulated by conscious will. His views became definitive for mainstream respectable opinion.

The spectre of a more thoroughgoing materialism resurfaced in Germans such as Büchner—not to mention, within Britain, Martineau's *Letters*. Cobbe rose to this challenge. Taking up Carpenter's work, she attempted to reconcile theism with physiological discoveries about the brain by conceding thought to the brain but carving off a separate conscious soul.[54] Yet Cobbe conceded so much to the

---

[54] Earlier, when referring to Cobbe's particular religious system, I called it 'Theism' with a capital T; whereas here, since Cobbe is defending theism in general, I leave it uncapitalized. Admittedly the dividing line is fuzzy, since Cobbe intended her system to capture the core of Christian theism in general. The relation between Theism and theism will come up, in connection with Besant's criticisms of Cobbe, in Chapter 5.

brain—not mere 'cerebration' but actual thought and reasoning—that the soul was left with less work than ever to do, undermining the case for believing in it. The problem went beyond Cobbe's theory and pertained to British thinking about the mind right across the century: the more mental functions were shown to be performed by the brain, the less role remained for the soul. For Naden, the conclusion was clear: go with physiological findings; accept that all mental powers depend on the brain, nervous system, and body; and drop the fiction of separate mental substances or souls. If that meant abandoning traditional Christianity, so much more space was thereby opened up for sovereign human creativity.

But Naden's materialism had problems, and the one Blavatsky found most decisive was that neither Naden nor any other materialist could explain how physical brain processes gave rise to experienced thoughts—in Besant's terms, how object-world gave rise to subject-world. That is, when materialists like Naden began to deny emphatically that there were any souls or separate mental substances, this threw the full burden of explaining experienced mental phenomena onto physical brain processes. This brought into view an explanatory gap, as Blavatsky and Besant recognized, drawing upon Tyndall. Previously, mainstream theorists who granted a major role to the brain, like Carpenter and Cobbe, did not have to contend with this gap because they still believed in the soul as well as the body and attributed free will, moral agency, and subjective experience to the former. Only once the soul was stripped away did this lay bare the insufficiency of physical processes, described in scientific and objective terms, to explain the subjective quality of mental phenomena. It turned out, in hindsight, that the idea of the soul *had* been doing work after all: it bridged the gap between object-world and subject-world.

However, for Blavatsky, that did not justify a renewed dualist appeal to separate souls in addition to matter, because dualism had been conclusively undermined. Instead, what was justified was a new monism of the mental, treating matter as a diminished, involuted version of primal mind. On this basis we can explain how matter gives rise to the derivative, secondary forms of mind found in human individuals, as part of the cosmic process in which primal mind returns to itself. For the theosophists, a form of panpsychism, not a return to dualism, was the right response to the explanatory gap.

The dialectic, then, was this. The more ground was conceded to physiology, the less work remained for the soul to do, which suggested that materialism could provide a comprehensive account of mental powers. Yet the very attempt to provide that comprehensive account exposed the explanatory limits of materialism. This convinced the theosophists that we must move beyond materialism in turn but, because dualism had been surpassed, the move must be onwards to something new: panpsychism.

4
The Meaning of Evolution

4.1 Introduction

In this chapter I look at the opposed views of Julia Wedgwood, Frances Power Cobbe, and Arabella Buckley on the metaphysical, moral, and religious implications of Darwin's theory of evolution. In the early 1860s Wedgwood argued that Darwin's theory was compatible with Christian religion and morality. But *Origin of Species* (1859) left some uncertainty about how far evolutionary theory applied to human beings as moral agents. In *The Descent of Man* (1871), Darwin clarified that all aspects of human beings, including our moral feelings, are natural and evolved.[1] To Cobbe, this showed that Darwinism fatally undermined religion and morality, because it left no room for a transcendent moral law. Buckley counter-argued that Darwin's position in *Descent* was still compatible with religious belief and a pure morality of duty. Thus, for Wedgwood and Buckley, evolutionary theory cohered with religion and morality and so should be accepted, whereas for Cobbe it did not and so could only be accepted as an account of nature but not of ethics.

Inevitably, discussion of these women's positions takes place against the backdrop of the immense literature on Darwin's thought, work, and life; on Victorian responses to evolutionary theory; and on broader theories of evolution in the nineteenth century.[2] Yet voluminous as this literature is, its authors have found little room to consider women's interventions about Darwinism. Those interventions did not only concern gender and feminism.[3] As the cases of Wedgwood, Cobbe, and Buckley show, women also tackled Darwinism's metaphysical, religious, and ethical implications. These were not extraneous matters: as Robert Young has remarked, 'the scientific debate [over evolution] directly involved theological and philosophical issues. These were constitutive, not contextual' (1971: 44).

It is a commonplace that Darwin's work inflicted some serious blows upon the Christian orthodoxy of his time. According to *Origin*, the species with their

---

[1] *Descent* was largely about sexual selection, but Darwin's views on humanity in Part I of the book are my topic in this chapter.

[2] See e.g. Beer (1983), Conlin (2014), Hedley Brooke (2014: esp. ch. 8), Himmelfarb (1959), Richards (1989), and Ruse (2014). This is merely the tip of a vast iceberg of scholarship.

[3] On which, see, inter alia, Birch (2011), Brilmyer (2017), Hardman (2011), Richards (1997, 2020), and Tange (2006).

different traits have emerged through purely natural causal processes and no divine creation or planning is needed to explain them. These causal processes presuppose that the earth has existed for much longer than the book of Genesis states, at least if taken literally. On both counts, Darwin's theory threatened the then orthodox Christian account of creation. One of those who recognized and embraced this straight away was Harriet Martineau:

> [T]he theory does not require the notion of a creation; and my conviction is that Charles D. does not hold it. What a work it is! – overthrowing... revealed religion on the one hand, and Natural (as far as Final Causes and Design are concerned) on the other.
> (HM to George Holyoake, Friday 26 1859, *HMCL* 4: 208–9)

How did evolution bear on the human soul, mental powers, and morality? Darwin left this undetermined in *Origin*, yet the implication seemed fairly clear: human beings must be evolved like other animals and all human features must be the results of evolution and entirely natural. However, many Victorians alleviated these troubling implications by saying that evolution was how divine creation took place, or that evolution applied to humans only as physical beings but not as moral or spiritual agents. For instance, both Charles Lyell and Alfred Russel Wallace in different ways maintained that the higher moral and mental powers of human beings stood out irreducibly from the course of natural evolution.[4] But Darwin made clear in *Descent* that as far as he was concerned evolution *did* apply to all human traits, including our moral and mental powers. For some, such as Cobbe, that settled the case against Darwinism; yet others, such as Buckley, continued to believe that Darwinism and Christianity could be reconciled.

I have been using the word 'evolution', but it did not appear in *Origin*'s first edition. 'Evolve' did: 'from so simple a beginning endless forms most beautiful and most wonderful have been, and are being, evolved' (Darwin 1859: 490). Here Darwin used *evolve* consistently with the general senses of *evolve* and *evolution* at that time: to *evolve* meant to unfold gradually, and *evolution* was coming to denote a universal law for phenomena to develop from simple to complex over time, a meaning traceable to Martineau and on which Herbert Spencer enlarged.[5] Because

---

[4] See Lyell (1863: ch. 24) and Wallace (1869) for their respective views. Wallace stated, for instance, that 'the moral and higher intellectual nature of man is as unique a phenomenon as was conscious life on its first appearance in the world, and the one is almost as difficult to conceive as originating by any law of evolution as the other' (1869: 393; Wallace favoured a spiritualist rather than Christian explanation, however).

[5] As Martineau renders Comte, 'our social evolution is only the final term of a progression which has continued from the simplest vegetables and most insignificant animals, up through the higher reptiles, to the birds and the mammifers, and still on...' (*PP* 2: 149); much of volume 2 of her Comte edition concerns 'evolution' so conceived. Famously, for Spencer, 'evolution consists in a change from the homogeneous to the heterogeneous' (1862: 148), 'from an incoherent homogeneity to coherent heterogeneity' (325).

evolution in 1860 still had this general, not specifically Darwinian, meaning, Wedgwood discussed Darwin's theory in 1860–1 without ever saying 'evolve', 'evolution', 'evolutionism', or for that matter 'Darwinism',[6] a word that Thomas Henry Huxley coined in an important (anonymous) essay (1860: 569). In this essay, he took up Darwin's account of natural selection—that is, the process by which random variations appear in different organisms, some of which better adapt these individuals to their environments, leading more of these individuals to survive and pass their traits on, eventually stabilizing these traits in the species population. Huxley identified natural selection as the route by which evolution has taken place. Subsequent to this, *evolution* came to refer to Darwin's theory over the 1860s, so that by 1871 Cobbe and Buckley spoke freely of 'evolution', the 'theory of evolution', the 'evolution hypothesis', 'laws of evolution', 'Darwinism', and so on.[7]

As natural selection came to be understood as the process by which evolution occurred, *evolution* carried over from Martineau, Spencer, and others the sense of a progression from simple to complex. Natural selection was thus widely construed as having produced *advancement*, generating increasingly complex and developed beings over time. Darwin himself had closed *Origin* by saying that 'as natural selection works solely by and for the good of each being, all corporeal and mental endowments will tend to progress towards perfection' (1859: 490). Today, the scientific consensus is that natural selection generates mere change with no set goal, destination, or sense of ultimate improvement. But most Victorians emphasized progress, whether because it facilitated the reconciliation of Darwinism with Christianity—because species evolve naturally until the human species is sufficiently advanced to acquire further non-natural, spiritual features—or conversely because progress told against Christianity—because nature on its own generates all the advanced human powers and qualities we want, with no need for any religious factors.

How far were Wedgwood, Cobbe, and Buckley responding to one another? None of them mentions the others in their published pieces on Darwinism, but they moved in identical circles. Cobbe and Wedgwood became good friends in the 1860s,[8] when they both saw evolution as compatible with a rationally reconstructed Christianity. So did Lyell, whom Cobbe knew very well and saw regularly, often weekly, in the later 1860s. This coincided with Buckley's role as Lyell's

---

[6] Nonetheless, for simplicity, I use 'evolution' and cognates when explaining Wedgwood's views.
[7] Likewise, Darwin himself used 'evolution' in the sixth edition of *Origin* (1872: esp. 201–2).
[8] Wedgwood and Cobbe were both in the London National Society for Women's Suffrage, founded in 1867, which emerged from the Kensington Society (1865–8) with which they both had been involved. Cobbe was also good friends with Wedgwood's mother, Frances 'Fanny' Mackintosh Wedgwood, another fellow suffragist. Both Cobbe and Julia Wedgwood contributed to Butler's landmark anthology *Woman's Work and Woman's Culture* (1869) and, later, Cobbe brought Wedgwood around to anti-vivisectionism in the teeth of opposition from Wedgwood's powerful family. For more on Cobbe and Wedgwood's friendship, see Brown (2022).

secretary (and sometimes de facto research assistant). She held this position from 1864 until Lyell's death in 1875, handling much of Lyell's correspondence and regularly accompanying him and his wife to social gatherings, including with the Darwins. Darwin also knew Wedgwood, since he was her uncle; he knew Buckley, through Lyell and then in her own right; and Cobbe got to know him in the later 1860s.[9] In view of these connections and other historical evidence, I will suggest that Buckley defended Darwinism partly in reply to Cobbe; and that when Wedgwood later revisited the debates on evolution in 1897, she did so informed by Buckley. More broadly, the connections show that the three women were part of a common community of discussion.

I will begin with Wedgwood (Sec. 4.2), then Cobbe (Sec. 4.3), then I present reasons to think that Buckley was replying to Cobbe (Sec. 4.4). I then evaluate Buckley's position, bringing in her cooperative Darwinism in the 1880s, which had a major influence on overall public discussion (Sec. 4.5). Finally, I take note of Wedgwood's 1897 re-evaluation, which bears the stamp of her epistolary conversations with Victoria Welby during the intervening years (Sec. 4.6).

4.2 Wedgwood: Reconciling Evolution with Christianity

Wedgwood initially addressed evolution, science, and religion in the two-part dialogue 'The Boundaries of Science', published in *Macmillan's Magazine* anonymously in June 1860 and July 1861. But first let me locate this piece in her broader intellectual career.

Of all the women discussed in this book, Wedgwood seems to be the most completely, and unjustly, forgotten.[10] She was a member of the formidable Darwin–Wedgwood dynasty. Her father Hensleigh Wedgwood was a renowned philologist;[11] her mother, Fanny Wedgwood, was a noted intellectual, salon hostess, and great friend of Harriet Martineau; and her aunt Emma Wedgwood was Darwin's wife. Thus Julia grew up in a highly intellectual milieu. At first she tried literature, publishing two novels in her twenties (the first signed 'Florence Dawson'). But she concluded that her 'mind was "merely analytical"' (Wedgwood 1980: 262) and turned to philosophy. This was philosophy in the same broad, non-specialist sense as Martineau, who was a role model for Wedgwood; Wedgwood began to publish widely and move into the role of professional critic

---

[9] For instance, Cobbe with her partner Mary Lloyd, and the Darwins, dined chez Fanny and Hensleigh Wedgwood in April 1868 (Emma Darwin to Fanny Allen, 2 April 1868, in Litchfield 1915: 189).
[10] However, see Stevens (1998) and the welcome recent biography by Brown (2022); an earlier biography was Wedgwood (1983).
[11] On his debate about the origins of language with Max Müller, see Piattelli (2016), a debate in which Wedgwood intervened (1862), leaning more towards her father's theory.

that Martineau had famously occupied.[12] Wedgwood published at least fifty journal articles, the first few anonymously in *Macmillan's Magazine*, then many others in the *Spectator* (again anonymously) and the *Contemporary Review* (signed). The topics ranged from 'The Relation of Memory to Will' (1878) and 'Ethics and Science' (1897) to the origins of language, literature, the Bible, ancient Greek culture, contemporary theology, women's suffrage, and anti-vivisection. Some of these articles were subsequently collected into *Nineteenth-Century Teachers* (1909). Wedgwood also wrote books: her *magnum opus*, *The Moral Ideal* (1888), discussed in Chapter 6; its follow-up *The Message of Israel in the Light of Modern Criticism* (1894), an important account of Judaism's moral contribution and centrality to Western civilization in a period of growing anti-Semitism; and biographies of the Methodist John Wesley (1870) and her great-grandfather Josiah Wedgwood (unfinished when she died). In addition, she was a prolific correspondent. Her correspondence with Robert Browning from 1863 to 1870 has been published (Curle 1937); so has part of her eleven-year correspondence with Emelia Russell Gurney, which covers many philosophical and religious questions (Gurney 1902);[13] and so has part of her correspondence with Martineau (Arbuckle 1983, *HMLFW*). Extracts from her correspondence with Welby are in Cust (1929, *ELL*) and will be discussed in Sec. 4.6.

Wedgwood was highly regarded. She regularly lectured at Girton College, Cambridge, and Bedford College in London; her periodical contributions were sought after; and Darwin enlisted her help translating Linnaeus. It is remarkable how near-totally she has been forgotten, usually called a 'novelist and writer' when she is remembered at all (e.g. Harris 2011). Like others such as Martineau and Cobbe, Wedgwood's religious convictions and unusually wide-ranging interests have prevented her from fitting our inherited image of the philosopher as a professional specialist.[14]

---

[12] Wedgwood had a very close, almost filial relationship with Martineau, whom she greatly admired, as I will discuss in Chapter 6. See also Crawford (2017) on Martineau's role model status for many Victorian 'women of letters'. Wedgwood also admired Cobbe. She was upset when Robert Browning criticized Cobbe (JW to Browning, 1 November 1864, in Curle 1937: 95); and soon afterwards she dreamt that Browning, with whom she was then having an unhappy romance, was merged with Cobbe, showing the significant place Cobbe had in her psyche (JW to Browning, 18 November 1864, in Curle 1937: 102). Indeed, Brown suggests that Cobbe was Wedgwood's principal role model (2022: 276), and in Chapter 6 I will suggest that Wedgwood tried to reconcile Martineau's and Cobbe's views.

[13] 'The look of your handwriting always makes me feel thirsty... Never think I shall say "Not a word of your philosophy I beg". On the contrary, my voice would always be going into your ear if it could, saying, "Tell me some more"' (Gurney to JW, 18 September 1866, in Gurney 1902: 30). For discussion of Gurney and Wedgwood's correspondence, arguing that it 'shaped the philosophical and religious thinking of these two women, allowing them a literary space to sharpen their minds', see Currer (2020: 197–200).

[14] Wedgwood eventually reached a rapprochement with the Church of England, but she started off far from Anglican orthodoxy, aligning herself with the Christian socialism of F. D. Maurice and the heterodox theology of Thomas Erskine, who believed in universal redemption.

What unified Wedgwood's work was a philosophical belief in progress through conflict (very much like Hegel's dialectic, although Wedgwood never refers to Hegel). She began to formulate this view in 'The Boundaries of Science'. It was her first published piece of philosophy and an intervention into the burgeoning debate about Darwin's work, with over two hundred reviews and notices of *The Origin of Species* appearing at the time. Wedgwood's piece, though, was not a review but a dialogue arguing that Darwin's central claims are compatible with core Christian beliefs: that life is divinely created, the forms of the species are divinely planned, and that we have immortal souls for whose salvation God cares. To make this case, Wedgwood interpreted evolution as a progression in which the species become perfected through struggle, culminating in the production of human beings as spiritual and moral agents.

To some modern readers Wedgwood's recasting of Darwin may sound like a conservative compromise with Christianity. Yet Darwin himself was greatly impressed by 'Boundaries', even saying that Wedgwood had understood him better than anyone else (Darwin to JW, 11 July 1861, *DCP*, DCP-LETT-3206). After all, at the time he still considered evolution to be compatible with theism, as he stated at the end of *Origin* (in a passage that sounds very much like Wedgwood, as we will see):

> Thus, from the war of nature, from famine and death, the most exalted object which we are capable of conceiving, namely, the production of the higher animals, directly follows. There is grandeur in this view of life...having been originally breathed by the Creator into a few forms or into one.
>
> (Darwin 1859: 490)

Moreover, in its day, Wedgwood's 'Boundaries' was sufficiently risky and pro-Darwin that *Macmillan's* proprietor Alexander Macmillan hesitated at first to publish it. What might look conservative to us in hindsight was forward-thinking in 1860, as Wedgwood urged that Darwin's theory could and should be accepted by Christians (i.e. the vast majority of the British people at the time). Incidentally, Wedgwood's gender was not a factor in Macmillan's hesitation, as initially he did not know that the submission came from a woman (see VanArsdel 2000: 378–9). Nonetheless, the threat of criticism was all the greater for a woman in this crowded and male-dominated field. So Wedgwood concealed her gender twice over, first by publishing anonymously and second by using the dialogue form, in which the case for reconciling Darwinism and religion is made by the presumably male 'Philalethes' (lover of the truth).

Wedgwood's idea of progress-through-conflict comes into the dialogue in several ways. The first is in her claim that the species are perfected through conflict. The second is epistemological. Until now, Philalethes maintains, religion subordinated science's claims to its 'superior authority' (*BS* 1: 136); now, one-sided adherence to science is on the rise instead (1: 138); ultimately we need a synthesis that recognizes both religion and science to be legitimate within their own domains and limits—the 'boundaries' of the title. Third, this epistemological stance is reflected in the dialogue's form. In some two-person philosophical dialogues one character is the author's mouthpiece and the other a mere foil. Not so with 'The Boundaries of Science': the two interlocutors start off opposed but keep adjusting their views in mutual response until they reach a synthesis to which both assent. Admittedly, it is not a wholly even-handed synthesis but leans more towards Philalethes, who believes that religion and science can be reconciled, than Philocalos ('lover of the good'), who initially thinks that they cannot. Philalethes moves towards Philocalos, though, by accommodating nearly all the latter's religious concerns, progressively enlarging the synthesis to do so. Thus the dialogue's form, as well as its content, embodies progress-through-struggle, in an interestingly self-reflexive way.

Let us work through Wedgwood's dialogue. Because it is complex and contains much ferrying back-and-forth between Philocalos and Philalethes, I shall reorganize their exchanges into a more linear form.

At the beginning, Philocalos repudiates Darwin's discoveries because they undermine Christianity: 'If the study of the creation is to lead us away from the Creator ... then, ... the sooner that study is abandoned ... the better' (1: 138). His overarching concern is that if the gamut of life-forms, along with human intelligence, morality, and creativity, are contingent outcomes of evolution, then no room remains for God as creator of the world with a plan for how events are to go (2: 240). In addition, he fears that on the Darwinian view, human agents can never transcend nature by acting morally or in virtue of having immortal souls. Humanity is reduced to 'the product of the lower tendencies of the animal world' (1: 138). Thus Darwinian evolution entails materialism—the reduction of 'spirit' to a form of matter (1: 135; 2: 239). And since we are wholly of nature, and on Darwin's view selfish competition and sordid conflict are the sole agencies in nature, it follows that human beings can never act unselfishly (1: 134). Since science leads to these bleak conclusions, contradicting our religious and moral convictions, we are justified in setting scientific conclusions aside (2: 238).

In putting these concerns in Philocalos's mouth, Wedgwood distils the core worries that some of her contemporaries had about Darwinism: that it rules out a creator and designer God; it entails that human beings are purely material, without immortal souls; and it entails that competition, conflict, and selfishness are natural and inevitable. In short, the worries concerned God, the soul, and morality.

Philalethes tackles Philocalos's overarching worry as follows. The evolutionary theorist can accept that God creates matter and life and sets the evolutionary process underway. Science traces the *stream* of life, but not its *origin*, the spring from which it rises (2: 237). The question of origins falls outside science's proper domain, for 'it is the course of this stream with which science is exclusively occupied' (2: 237). Likewise, a builder's (i.e. God's) design is separate from the physical process of realizing it as undertaken in a workshop (i.e. natural evolution), just as the master artist's plan is separate from the work undertaken to realize it by his school (1: 134–5). The goal is different from the means to achieving it. Thus, for the evolutionary theorist, God still creates us; it is just that he creates us *through* evolution, by setting in motion the procession of life-forms out of which humanity eventually arises (2: 237–8).

Philocalos replies that Philalethes seems to be upholding a Deist view of God as a remote originator, not a living father who cares about us and offers us the hope of salvation and immortality (2: 238). God reduced to a bare causal origin doesn't give us enough of Christianity or of what we hope for from religion.

In response Philalethes enlarges his view of God's creative power. That power is ever-necessary to keep nature's forces in motion and the evolutionary process going—so God's action is ongoing, not one-off (2: 239). Furthermore, God laid 'the entire plan of organic life' in advance (2: 241). Evolution generates the details of the species, but their 'typical forms' were laid out beforehand by God. Again, then, God established the design; evolution merely handles the implementation.

Addressing Philocalos's other worries, Philalethes argues that this divine plan takes in the human species. God plans for human beings to have a 'supernatural' dimension (2: 238), with immortal souls and a distinctive capacity for virtue and altruism, so that we are 'raised above the influence of mere natural forces' (1: 135). However, although our spirit was always part of God's creation, it has only acquired outward, material manifestation as the outcome of the evolutionary process (2: 240). But this process was always intended and set up so as to allow human spirit to become realized and embodied. What Darwinism explains, then, is 'the manner in which the spirit enfolded within the bosom of nature is brought into consciousness and energy' (2: 241). This answers Philocalos's worry about God's fatherhood, showing that God was always personally concerned about us as spiritual beings; it also reassures Philocalos that, although human beings are evolved, they have moral capacities that transcend nature (1: 135). In short, for Wedgwood, natural evolution develops the physical human form to a point where it can realize the spiritual powers that God has destined for us and now infuses into us, both individually and collectively (2: 240–1).[15]

And so, Philalethes says, we need not repudiate science. Science has limits: it deals only with nature and life, not God or humans qua spiritual and moral agents, and 'Science does not...contain the elements of any decision concerning that

---

[15] Wedgwood's view is similar to Lyell's. For him 'the whole course of nature may be the material embodiment of a preconcerted arrangement', i.e., a design; and 'far from having a materialistic tendency, the supposed introduction into the earth at successive...periods of life, — sensation, — instinct, — the intelligence of the higher mammalia...— and lastly the improvable reason of Man himself, presents us with a picture of the ever-increasing dominion of mind over matter' (1863: 506).

which is *not* science' (2: 238). If scientists think their findings rule out the existence of God or spirit, they are overstepping their 'proper sphere' (2: 238). But reciprocally, scientific inquiries should not be restricted in religion's name—for whatever scientists discover, it *cannot* possibly undermine faith as long as scientists abide within their proper boundaries (1: 136). Here Philalethes takes a stance that was widespread in the first half of the nineteenth century: that science is one sphere, religion another, and that scientific inquiries are acceptable as long as they remain within their sphere.[16] Against those who think that evolutionary theory is threatening this demarcation, Philalethes replies that it still observes it, when rightly understood (2: 242).

Philocalos comes back with new objections. Surely, for knowledge to be possible at all, the universe must be coherent and our knowledge of it form an internally consistent and unified whole: 'surely, Truth is one harmonious whole' (1: 135). Therefore the several parts of our knowledge cannot possibly contradict or be at variance with one another, as Philalethes apparently says of the separate spheres of science and religion, reason and faith (2: 237). Philalethes replies that all the 'lines of Truth converge, but it is at too small an angle, and too vast a distance, for us to be able in all cases to perceive the tendency to unite' (1: 135): that is, we are not yet in a position fully to understand *how* the lines converge. But then he qualifies this, saying that we cannot avoid being drawn to consider how Darwinian evolution can be reconciled with our moral and religious inclinations (2: 238). Thus, although there are boundaries between domains, we also have to determine as well as we can how these domains cohere—which, after all, is what he is trying to do throughout.

Finally, Philocalos objects that if evolutionary struggle indeed occurs *and* God is creator and father, then it follows not only that the world is riven with conflict but, worse, that *God* has created this world pervaded with evil (2: 243). Worse still, this is not only natural evil but also moral evil, for on the evolutionary view nature is full of suffering, conflict, ruthless competition, and destruction of the weak, all of which we inherit into our natures so that we must be irredeemably sinful. How could a loving God possibly have made such a world (2: 244)?

Philalethes replies that it is precisely the conflict, wastage, and messiness of nature which show God's purpose for the world and ourselves—this 'evil agency...serve[s] as the pioneer of higher forms of being' (2: 246). Against natural theologians, for whom nature's order and harmony are the evidence that it is designed, nature's *destructiveness* evidences God's plan (2: 245). For nature is 'one vast battle-field' (2: 246), but this produces higher forms of being,

---

[16] See Winter (1997) on this 'separate spheres' doctrine with respect to science and religion—about which Martineau was characteristically scathing: 'Even theologians have got so far as to struggle to show that science and revelation can be made to agree. In this, we know, they will not succeed; but it is a testimony to the strength and consideration which science has attained' (*LLM* 249).

above all human spiritual and moral agents. Destruction is necessary for superior forms to emerge: 'failure, and suffering, and strife, and... death, are but the steps by which [man] has been raised to the height at which he finds himself' (2: 247). Thus, nature is a symbol 'of hope, of encouragement, of consolation' (2: 247): it shows us that it is through struggle and work, not peace and ease, that we gain new heights; adversity is there to spur us beyond what we could otherwise reach. This completes Philalethes's reconciliation of Christian faith with evolution.[17]

Despite Darwin's approval of Wedgwood's dialogue, readers today may well think that Wedgwood has lost some key elements of his theory. One is *contingency*. For Wedgwood the forms of the species are planned in advance by God, including the human form with its spiritual and moral capacities. This limits the room for species to come about through chance variations. Wedgwood anticipated this objection, again putting it in the mouth of Philocalos who protests that Philalethes is diverging here from Darwin himself (2: 242). Philalethes replies: 'What are *accidental* varieties – in what sense can we see the word accidental, but in that of belonging to some unknown law? And what are those varieties which are produced by some unknown law *but* the result of development?' (2: 242), where 'development' refers back to God's plan for the typical forms of species. There may be contingency in the material details of how nature realizes particular species-forms (in the 'infinitude of small deviations'; 2: 241), but *that* nature must realize these forms somehow is not contingent. Accidents happen in the service of God's plan, and they only appear accidental to us because, given the limits of our knowledge, we cannot fully comprehend the whole of the plan.[18] Arguably, though, the import of Darwin's account is very different from this: the evolutionary process might not have led to us; given only slight variations in the make-up of earlier species, life would have evolved along different lines and different species emerged. Accidents, on this view, are real and fundamental, not merely apparent and incidental.

Connected with her denial of real accidents, Wedgwood construes evolution as a *moral progression*. Competition between and within species ultimately produces creatures—humans—that are sufficiently physically complex to realize the spiritual and moral qualities and vocation that God intends for them. But, arguably, Darwin's account implies that selection pressures favour the most reproductively fit beings, who may well not be the best morally or spiritually. Cobbe vividly remembers Lyell explaining this point to her:

---

[17] See also Schaefer (2015) on this aspect of Wedgwood's views, to which Darwin's daughter Henrietta had some searching objections: 'reason tells us plainly that each life is not ordered for its own good. The most striking example of wh[ich] are those diseases which cause certain demoralisation. That they may be necessary consequences of general laws would be my explanation – but how... can we allow this to be for the good of the sufferer?' (H. Darwin 1871).
[18] Wedgwood subsequently denied the reality of accidents even more strongly; see Wedgwood (1871: 1341).

Suppose you had been living in Spain three hundred years ago [Lyell said], and had a sister who was a perfectly commonplace person... Well! your sister would have been happily married and had a numerous progeny, and that would have been the survival of the fittest; but *you* [Cobbe] would have been burnt at an *auto-da-fé*... You would have been unsuited to your environment. There! That's evolution! Good-bye! (*LFPC* 2: 405)[19]

Yet Wedgwood would not necessarily have seen her deviations from Darwin as a decisive problem. As her dialogue shows, she was not assuming the stance of a scientist per se but endeavouring to see how scientific knowledge, and religious and metaphysical convictions, could be combined into a whole. Though we cannot yet entirely comprehend that whole, we must do our best to make it out, which means adjusting our scientific *and* religious-cum-metaphysical views until they cohere, as Philalethes and Philocalos do. Readers may still object that the particular religious-and-metaphysical views Wedgwood sought to accommodate are not worth accommodating. But Wedgwood's point goes beyond those particular views: that while science has much to tell us, people cannot live by science alone, and scientific knowledge needs to be integrated, along with our moral beliefs and aspirations, into a comprehensive framework for making sense of our lives.

4.3 Cobbe on the Moral Dangers of Darwinism

In the 1860s Cobbe, like Wedgwood, saw evolution and religion as compatible. Cobbe said so in *Broken Lights* (1864: 153–6), in her autobiography (*LFPC* 406–8), and at the start of 'Darwinism in Morals' (*DM* 1–3). For Cobbe, the species having arisen by natural selection was eminently compatible with God having originated the evolutionary process. The slow emergence of order, beauty, life, and religion testified to God's creative plan. Cobbe does not seem to have been directly influenced in this by Wedgwood, but she was undoubtedly influenced by Lyell, whose position was close to Wedgwood's (Wedgwood favourably reviewed *The Geological Evidences of the Antiquity of Man*, in which Lyell stated his position).[20]

Later in the 1860s, when Darwin was working on *Descent*, Cobbe got to know him and encouraged him to read Kant, sending him the *Metaphysics of Morals*. Enthused, Darwin chose Cobbe to be one of *Descent*'s first reviewers, alongside G. J. Mivart and Wallace. Indeed, Darwin was so eager to get Cobbe's reaction that his publisher, John Murray, had to intervene to get her review postponed so that it

---

[19] These dismal implications led Lyell to deny that evolution fully applied to human beings (see Bartholomew 1973).
[20] See Wedgwood (1863).

did not appear before *Descent* itself.[21] But Cobbe's reaction was highly critical, much to Darwin's disappointment.[22] She could not accept his explanation of our moral feelings as products of evolution. To see why not, we first need to examine Darwin's account and his motivations for it.[23]

In *Descent*, Darwin maintained that, with group animals including human beings, selection pressures over time have favoured such social instincts as sympathy and the desire for others' approval (1871: vol. 2: 391–3). These are the responses out of which morality is built. Here Darwin was opposing two other views:[24] first, the sorts of compromise with religion favoured by Wedgwood, Lyell, and Wallace. For Darwin, no appeal to religion or the soul was needed to account for our moral capacities: natural laws of variation, selection, and inheritance are quite sufficient and they reliably produce our moral dispositions (vol. 2: 394–5). Thus he sought to allay the fears of those who thought that his theory ruled out human sociality and cooperation—as he wrote to Wedgwood, 'I enter my protest against your making the struggle for existence (which is sufficiently melancholy fact) still more odious by calling it "selfish competition"'.[25]

Second, Darwin thus also opposed the view that selection favoured the most competitive, selfish, aggressive individuals. One proponent of this view was William Rathbone Greg (1868). Greg argued that modern Britain was making a lamentable deviation from the law of natural selection. If natural selection was followed, as it should be, it saw to the elimination of the weak and unfit. But such modern practices

---

[21] I have detailed Cobbe's and Darwin's interactions, as well, in Stone (2022a). See Darwin to Cooke (his agent), 14 January 1871, recommending that Cobbe review *Descent*, DCP, DCP-LETT-7441; Darwin to Cooke, 30 January 1871, having Cobbe sent an advance copy of *Descent* for discussion in the *Theological Review*, DCP-LETT-7466; Murray (Darwin's publisher) to Darwin, 18 February 1871, requesting a delay of Cobbe's response, DCP-LETT-7486; Murray to Darwin, 19 February 1871, confirming that advance copies had gone to Cobbe, Mivart, and Wallace, DCP-LETT-7489.

[22] Emma Darwin to FPC, 7 April 1871, *DCP*, DCP-LETT-7666F; Emma Darwin to FPC, 14 April 1871, DCP-LETT-7684F; and Darwin to Fanny Wedgwood, 19 December 1871, DCP-LETT-8110. By this last point he said that their 'differences... [were] too fundamental ever to be reconciled'. Yet they resumed cordial relations during 1872 when discussing the minds of dogs, only to fall out again thereafter, irreparably this time, over vivisection; see Harvey (2009). Their relations deteriorated so much that by the 1890s Cobbe communicated with the Darwins only through (Julia) Wedgwood; see Emma Darwin to Laura Forster, May 1894, in Litchfield (1915: 302).

[23] The reader may wonder how Wedgwood responded to *Descent*. She wrote a critical notice of *Descent* in February, referred to by Emma Darwin (letter to JW, March 1871, *DCP*, DCP-LETT-8127). That critical notice may be the same as the 'abstract' of Darwin's ethical views that Wedgwood sent him around then (see JW to Henrietta Darwin, 1 April 1871, DCP-LETT-7651). However, Brown (2022: ch. 13) argues that Emma Wedgwood is actually referring to a review of *Descent* in the *Spectator* (namely, Anonymous 1871) and that this review is by Wedgwood. Elsewhere, however, it is attributed to Richard Holt Hutton (Tener 1973: 45); so, although Brown makes a strong case, I remain agnostic for now. Wedgwood certainly wrote 'The Natural and the Supernatural' in the *Spectator* that November, in which she reprised the arguments of 'Boundaries of Science': creation occurs through evolution; variations do not happen by chance; and nature's work offers a parable (Wedgwood 1871; see *DCP*, DCP-LETT-8080F). In short, *Descent* did not lead her to revise her views, though she did modify them by the 1890s, as we will see.

[24] Robert Richards shows that Darwin wrote the parts of *Descent* on ethics last, from 1869 onwards, in response to the following two challenges (1989: 189–90).

[25] Darwin to JW, after 1 April 1871, *DCP*, DCP-LETT-7651F.

as mild punishments, intellectual tolerance, and provision of care and charity, were allowing feeble and deficient people to flourish. Darwin argued against Greg that the sympathetic impulse to aid others *is* an outcome of natural selection that could not be checked 'without deterioration in the noblest part of our nature' (1871: vol. 1: 168).[26] Here Darwin was also opposing Francis Galton, for whom evolution had indeed exerted a selection pressure towards sympathy, clemency, and so on—but undesirably so. For Galton, our conditions as herd animals have predisposed us to mediocrity, over time filtering out excellence and exceptional individuality because as herd animals we prefer to mate with the herd's weakest, most timid, and conformist members. We have ended up 'essentially slavish', 'a mob of slaves, clinging together, incapable of self-government, and begging to be led' (1870: 357). Thus, in fact, for Galton, evolution has selected not so much for praiseworthy cooperativeness as callow conformity. His proposed solution was to take active control of the process through eugenics. In contrast, Darwin described the traits in question as the praiseworthy ones of sympathy, cooperativeness, honour, and so on, *not* mere conformity and mediocrity (Darwin 1871: vol. 1: 84–5).[27]

For Darwin, then, evolutionary theory supported morality and showed that natural selection reliably produces our most elevated and praiseworthy moral traits and practices. What was there for Cobbe to object to? She had a whole host of objections, of which I will just highlight certain key points.[28]

Cobbe thought that plausibly, contrary to Darwin, evolutionary pressures have after all disposed us to show *both* slavish conformity *and* to act selfishly, compete, and trample the weak underfoot. Cobbe referred to Galton:

Animals display affection, fidelity and sympathy. Man when he first rose above the Ape was probably of a social disposition, and lived in herds. Mr. Darwin adds that he would probably inherit a tendency to be faithful to his comrades, and have also some capacity for self-command, and a readiness to aid and defend his fellow-men. These latter qualities, we must observe, do not agree very well with what Mr. Galton recently told us of the result of his interesting studies of the cattle of South Africa [i.e. their disposition to slavish conformity], and at all events need that we should suppose the forefathers of our race to have united all the best moral as well as physical qualities of other animals. (*DM* 18)

---

[26] Darwin also thought that society would 'naturally' correct the problems of the poor needing charity, clemency (etc.), because the miseries and starvation that follow from excessive reproduction would teach the poor to exercise self-restraint (Richards 1989: 174–5; see also Darwin 1871: vol. 1: 173–9). Darwin did not, though, take what would seem the obvious step of supporting birth control. On the contrary, he refused to intercede on behalf of Charles Bradlaugh and Annie Besant in their obscenity trial, insisting that population growth should only be checked 'naturally', not voluntarily ('preventively' or 'artificially', as Besant put it), otherwise female chastity and family life would be undermined (see Peart and Levy 2008).

[27] For Galton, we should discourage the weak from procreating (*negative eugenics*) and encourage the excellent to procreate (*positive eugenics*) (Galton 1865: 319–20).

[28] For a fuller account, see Stone (2022a).

And Greg:

> Other virtues, such as that of care for the weak and aged, seem still less capable, as Mr. Mivart has admirably shown, of being evolved out of a sense of utility, seeing that savages and animals find it much the most useful practice to kill and devour such sufferers, and by the law of the Survival of the Fittest, all nature below civilized man is arranged on the plan of so doing. Mr. W. R. Greg's very clever paper in *Fraser's Magazine*, pointing out how Natural Selection fails in the case of Man in consequence of our feelings of pity for the weak, affords incidentally the best possible proof that human society is based on an element which has no counterpart in the utility which rules the animal world.

For Cobbe, the struggle to survive and obtain scarce resources has over long time bred into us instincts to compete and brutally dominate over those weaker than us. Indeed, she maintains, we see these instincts manifest all around us, in human cruelty to defenceless animals and in male violence against women. Darwin overoptimistically imagines everyone on the model of an idealized genteel Englishman (*DM* 23). But in reality what follows from evolution is 'a code of Right in which every cruelty and every injustice may form a part' (31). All these cruelties and injustices will be justified if we are to follow nature:

> Nature is extremely cruel, but we cannot do better than follow Nature; and the law of the 'Survival of the Fittest', applied to human agency, implies the absolute right of the Strong (*i.e.,* those who can prove themselves 'Fittest') to sacrifice the Weak and Unfit. (*MR* 66)

What of Darwin's argument that the traits Galton saw as mediocre conformity are actually praiseworthy concern for the good of the group? Cobbe thought that Darwin's views suffered from the same basic problem as all other versions of utilitarianism: what increases the general happiness, or the good of the whole group, is not necessarily right (*DM* 5). Or as she put it, the ideas of right and utility are different (15); there may be cases where they converge, but they can always come apart. It may serve the good of the whole group to sacrifice the weak and unfit, but doing so is still wrong (16–17). We see, then, that Cobbe regarded Darwin as a utilitarian, and so he described himself, albeit that he interpreted the good not as the general happiness but the health and strength of the species (Darwin 1871: vol. 1: 98). Cobbe saw Darwin as answering the problem of how we can ever be motivated to pursue the general happiness rather than our individual happiness. His answer is that we have evolved to be genuinely motivated by concern for others and for the common good (under the description of the health of the species) (*DM* 8–10).

Cobbe picked up on one of his examples in particular: the 'cultivated hive-bee'. For Darwin, if bees were conscious and rational, then in times when the hive is lacking in resources cultivated worker-bees would see it as their 'sacred duty' to murder their brothers, the unproductive drones. '[T]he bee, or any other social animal, would in our supposed case gain, as it appears to me, some feeling of right and wrong, or a conscience' (Darwin 1871: vol. 1: 73). This example, to Cobbe, brought into clear relief the fact that actions that serve the general good may nonetheless be wrong: murdering the least productive members may help a group to survive in lean times, but it remains impermissible (*DM* 31). Concern for the general good is one thing, morality another. As such, knowing that we have evolved to be motivated to pursue the general good does nothing to establish that we can act morally in the true sense. Acting morally depends on doing our duty for its own sake, where that duty is prescribed by the moral law and the moral law is legislated by God (as Cobbe had argued in *Intuitive Morals*). But if Darwin is right and we are entirely natural beings, then there is no such divinely legislated law. This eliminates genuine morality altogether, and so, for Cobbe:

> These doctrines appear to me simply the most dangerous... ever been set forth since the days of Mandeville. Of course, if science can really show good cause for accepting them, their consequences must be frankly faced. But it is at least fitting to come to the examination of them, conscious that... we are criticizing... theories whose validity must involve the *in*validity of all the sanctions which morality has hitherto received from powers beyond those of the penal laws.
> (*DM* 11)

Moreover, Cobbe saw the hive-bee case as showing that the evolved impulse to serve the common good of the group and the equally evolved impulse of cruelty and brutality could form a toxic combination, where we eliminate weaker members of the group and feel *justified* in doing so because they are a 'burden' (*DM* 31). As she went on to say:

> Mr. Greg has clearly expounded that our compassion for the feeble and the sickly defeats, as regards the human race, the beneficent natural law of the 'Survival of the Fittest'; and Mr. Galton considers it to involve nothing short of a menace to the civilization whence it has sprung. Nature kills off such superfluous lives among the brutes...   (*HHR* lxxv)[29]

---

[29] 'The survival of the fittest' is of course Herbert Spencer's phrase (1864: 444), although it became associated with Darwinism. Spencer himself established the association, saying that the 'survival of the fittest'—the process by which environments favour the organisms best suited to them—is 'that which Mr. Darwin has called "natural selection..."' (445).

For Cobbe, then, evolution has given us violent and brutal traits as well as the praiseworthy ones that Darwin optimistically singles out. Moreover, even his 'praiseworthy' traits are less praiseworthy than he thinks, because concern for the general welfare or the health of the species is not the same as genuine morality. The upshot is that evolutionary ethics is no real ethics at all. We need instead to recognize that all life is sacred, Cobbe proposes. And 'what, in truth, is this ever-growing sense of the infinite sacredness of human life but a sentiment tending directly to counteract the interest of the community at large?' (*HHR* lxxiv–lxxv). The sense that each individual life is sacred can only be acquired when we are educated to follow the transcendent moral law—to act against, not with, our evolved dispositions towards cruelty.

This does not mean that Cobbe rejected evolution as an account of nature. What she rejected was the extension of Darwinism to human moral feelings and practices. She stuck to the sort of reconciliation of evolution and Christianity that was popular in the 1860s, holding that humans are evolved as physical beings, but are also in touch with a divine realm that transcends nature and is the ground of moral requirements. She saw no other way of doing justice to the absolute character of moral obligations or of upholding the duty to care for the ill, weak, sick, and those in need.

4.4 Buckley Against Cobbe

Hot on the heels of Cobbe's 'Darwinism in Morals' of 1 April 1871, a defence of evolutionary theory, 'Darwinism and Religion', appeared in *Macmillan's Magazine* on 1 May, signed 'A. B.'—Arabella Buckley. She argued that evolution was compatible with conscience being God's voice within us, with the soul being immortal, and with moral action being done from pure, unselfish motives of concern for others and the common good. In short for Buckley, *pace* Cobbe, God, duty, and immortality are eminently compatible with the theory of evolution in general and the evolved status of human traits in particular. Yet Buckley's article nowhere mentioned Cobbe's name. Was it a riposte to Cobbe? As we know by now, women not mentioning each other's names does not prove that they were not responding to one another. We have to dig behind the scenes.

In this case, circumstances suggest that Buckley may well have been replying at least in part to Cobbe. Having been sent her advance copy of *Descent* on 19 February 1871, Cobbe quickly sketched out her criticisms and sent the Darwins a letter setting them out (unfortunately this letter is presently lost). Judging by Emma Darwin's reply of 25 February, the critical issues Cobbe had raised included (unsurprisingly) Darwin's elimination of a religious basis for morality. Emma commented that Darwin 'says that he knows so well how much you and many others will disapprove of the moral sense part that he will not be surprised at any degree of vigour in your attack' (Emma Darwin to FPC, 25 February 1871, *DCP*, DCP-LETT-7516F). Then, from 13 to 16 March, the Lyells, accompanied by Buckley, stayed with the Darwins. On 16 March Darwin wrote to Wallace that during this visit the group discussed Wallace's favourable review of *Descent*, published in *The Academy* on 15 March, in which (curiously) Wallace had broadly endorsed Darwin's claims about the moral sense. Darwin wrote:

> Lyell remarked that no one wrote such good scientific reviews as you, and Miss Buckley added [that] you... pick out all that is good... [H]owever much my book will hereafter be abused, as it no doubt will be, your review will console me.
> (Darwin to Wallace, 16 March 1871, *DCP*, DCP-LETT-7589)[30]

By that point Darwin knew what Cobbe was imminently going to argue—hers was some of the 'abuse' and 'vigorous attack' he feared. So the Darwins, Lyells, and Buckley might well have talked of Cobbe's criticisms, as they were evidently discussing *Descent*'s reception—and as Darwin was quite happy to sound off about Cobbe's response to others.[31] Buckley's involvement in these conversations makes it overwhelmingly likely that she read Cobbe's article.

Certainly she read other work by Cobbe. For instance, much later, she reacted angrily to Cobbe's critique of the 'Scientific Spirit of the Age' (in the *Contemporary Review*, July 1888; *SS* ch. I). Cobbe claimed that science was eclipsing all other discourses, including religion: 'We still have Religion; but she no longer claims earth and heaven as her domain, but meekly goes to church by a path over which Science has notified, "On Sufferance Only"' (*SS* 3). Buckley responded:

> M. de Laveleye's article in the *Contemporary*, with Miss Cobbe's in the same, rouse me... It is a delusion to fancy that one's own panacea is better than one's neighbour's. It riles me that people should say that there can be no religion of science and yet to give a full exposition of one's belief would be presumptuous and also one shrinks rather from laying it there for [jack]daws to peck at.... But when writers like Laveleye [and Cobbe] say that atheism and anarchy are ahead of us, one longs to 'place a creed' and see what results might follow.
> (AB to Garnett, 4 July 1888, *GFP*)

---

[30] Darwin's description of Wallace's review to Henrietta Darwin was rather different: 'I see I have had no influence on him, and his Review has had hardly any on me' (Darwin to Henrietta Darwin, 28 March 1871, in Litchfield 1915: 202).

[31] For instance, he wrote to another reviewer of *Descent*, John Morley: 'I must add that I have been very glad to read your remarks on the supposed case of the hive bee: it affords an amusing contrast with what Miss Cobbe has written in the Theolog. Rev. Undoubtedly the great principle of acting for the good of all the members of the same community, and therefore for the good of the species, would still have held sovereign sway' (Darwin to John Morley, 14 April 1871, *DCP*, DCP-LETT-7685). Morley's review appeared in the *Pall Mall Gazette*, 12 April (Morley 1871).

In short, Buckley was irked that Cobbe saw religion and science as antithetical and sided with the former. Buckley felt roused to reply showing that the two were compatible. This was in 1888—but plausibly the same was already the case in 1871.[32]

To be sure, in 1871 Buckley may well have been responding to other critics of Darwin too.[33] However, in philosophical substance Buckley's arguments speak directly to Cobbe's charges against Darwin. Buckley begins by explaining that on the theory of evolution our entire organization develops from that of animals, not only our bodily structure but also our mental powers, which differ from those of animals only in degree. These powers include our moral sense, which for Darwin is based in the social instincts that are found in many animal species and are the extension of parental and filial affections (because groups of animals form through reproduction, making group members kin). Once parental affections have arisen, natural selection reinforces them, because communities of more social and sympathetic beings are stronger, so more of their members survive and pass on their social instincts. But on the ultimate 'origin of these last [instincts] he says it "is hopeless to speculate, though we may infer that they have been to a large extent gained through natural selection"' (*DR* 46). In treating these instincts as the basis of morality, Buckley says, Darwin is upholding the reality of unselfish action for the common good:

> He takes for his text the soul-stirring words of Kant, and elevates the unselfish virtues to the highest rank to which moralists have ever assigned them. Yet many who would concede without hesitation the evolutionary origin of their bodily frame, shrink... from such a derivation of their... moral nature. They fear that if the noble gift of conscience can be traced back... to the humbler instincts, the human race will become the victims of a gross Materialism, and that all communion with God and... hope of immortality will be blotted out of our existence.
> (46)

To avert these fears, Buckley says, she will show how Darwinism is compatible with divine conscience, the immortal soul, and unselfish moral action.

---

[32] It is also relevant that in 1873, Lyell told Cobbe that he had been reading her various articles in the *Theological Review*, in which 'Darwinism in Morals' appeared (Lyell to FPC, 20 July 1873, in Lyell 1881: 451–3). Buckley transcribed this letter for Lyell; so, again, she could not possibly have been unaware of Cobbe's views.

[33] Plausibly Mivart. Although his critical review of *Descent* only came out in July 1871 (and his criticisms largely concerned sexual selection), his *Genesis of Species* came out in January 1871 and Wallace urged Buckley to read it (Wallace to AB, 2 February 1871, *WCP*, WCP5619; Wallace and Buckley maintained an extended correspondence). Mivart and Cobbe had much common ground: Mivart argued that a true understanding of what is right cannot be derived gradualistically from nature but must come from our direct relation to God's moral legislation, so that we are evolved only as physical beings (Mivart 1871: ch. 9). Buckley probably saw Mivart and Cobbe as part of a family.

Conscience. For Buckley, our social instincts build on parental and filial affections, which Darwin says have come about through natural selection. However, the laws through whose operations these instincts have arisen and been strengthened are not products of natural selection but rather govern its processes. The origin of these laws is, as Darwin admits, beyond his purview as a scientist: 'in a true spirit of philosophy, he affirms constantly the still hidden and higher law of our being' (*DR* 47). These laws cannot be 'separate entities independent of God... for then they would depend on some first cause other than God'. In short, the laws of nature must have a cause and that cause must be God, 'the Infinite and All-Perfect First Cause'. So far Buckley seems to be reprising Wedgwoodian ground: science has limits, which Darwin acknowledges rather than oversteps; he traces the effects of laws of natural selection but leaves their origin undetermined, leaving room for them to be divinely established. What Buckley adds to Wedgwood is, first, the claim that these considerations still apply post-*Descent* and, second, the implications for conscience: since natural laws are divinely established, it is no coincidence that the laws governing evolution have produced and reinforced the parental and social instincts. This has happened because God has established these laws of nature with a view to their yielding this moral result. Moreover, this means that in acting on our social instincts we are effectively doing what God wills.

This leads Buckley to a second, more direct sense in which the social instincts coincide with conscience. Here she takes it that conscience is a faculty of communing with God and apprehending the moral requirements that he lays down; Darwinism, she argues, is quite compatible with the existence of conscience so understood. But, she says, it is often thought that if our minds develop from animal minds then they cannot possibly hold commune with God. She targets the general figure of 'the intuitionist' here (*DR* 47); this includes Wallace, though Cobbe was also widely associated with intuitionism.[34] Buckley indeed seems to be challenging Cobbe's argument that if our conscience is merely an inherited prejudice, then it cannot be a faculty of grasping real moral requirements. Not so, Buckley says. A dog has more extended perceptual powers than a jellyfish, but the jellyfish having more limited powers does not mean that the dog's cannot possibly extend further; the dog's do, and they enable it to apprehend more of the reality that is there anyway. By analogy, 'the derivation of our higher faculties from animals is not necessarily any bar to revelation' (48). One might object that the cases are disanalogous because dogs see more of *natural* reality than jellyfish whereas the religious claim is that humans see more of *non-* or *super*-natural reality than non-human animals. However, Buckley continues, the dog with its naturally evolved powers can apprehend aspects of the human world, most of

---

[34] In 1865 Francis Newman was already commenting that 'Many persons suppose that the doctrine of "Intuition" is Miss Cobbe's great peculiarity' (1865: 374).

which nevertheless lies beyond its ken. Similarly, evolved human powers can enable us to apprehend the divine realm that is nonetheless beyond and higher than us. Through natural processes, we have developed advanced powers equipping us to apprehend transcendent realities and hear God's voice—as we do when we feel and act on our social impulses. Conscience can be evolved *and* be a means of apprehending divine reality.

Immortality. For Buckley, we can accept the theory of evolution and still reasonably hope for personal immortality. 'I have always contended that without a future life, this world is a mere mockery and utterly unintelligible' (AB to Garnett, 5 October 1888, *GFP*). The derivation of our faculties from those of higher animals need not prevent us from being immortal, for the higher animals may well be immortal too, as Bishop Butler argues (*DR* 48). But how do higher animals come to have immortal souls if lower animals do not? Here Buckley argues that consciousness is irreducible to physical processes and that life is irreducible to causal forces. She appeals to John Tyndall on the explanatory gap (*DR* 49). To recall (from Chapter 3), for Tyndall, we cannot explain subjective consciousness from objective causal processes. Buckley adds that the same goes for life and matter. Life is *sui generis* and the organization of living beings necessarily depends on this *sui generis* vital principle. '[T]his vitality,... being the *cause* and not the consequence of organisation, cannot be dependent on the physical organism for its existence' (49). As such, the body and all its powers can be destroyed while leaving an individual's vital principle intact, and equally the brain can be destroyed while leaving the individual's consciousness intact. Buckley takes it then that consciousness is a further intensification of vitality, so that higher animals like humans have consciousness. The theory of evolution does not tell against any of this, Buckley says, for it only tells us how life evolves once it has arisen and how the physical traits of conscious living beings evolve once there are such beings. But evolutionary theory does not itself account for either life or consciousness—nor can it, for these are *sui generis*. And so 'the most strictly materialistic view of life [i.e. Tyndall's], being obliged to start with an unknown force, cannot *disprove* a future individual existence' (50).

The moral sense. Darwin is *not* simply on the utilitarian side, Buckley contends, but rather he is reconciling utilitarianism with intuitionism. This again seems to be clearly a reply to Cobbe, especially as Buckley then sets out a criticism of utilitarianism exactly like Cobbe's—namely, that utilitarians presume that everyone is selfish, whereas genuinely moral action must be unselfish (*DR* 50). Darwin's theory, however, provides for unselfishness in the parental feeling and its extension, the social instinct. This instinct directly motivates us to act for the good of others and it is basic, immediate, and impulsive, not derived from any calculations or observations about consequences of action. 'Whether we call this instinct by the name of an intuition or not is clearly of no moment' (50–1). What matters is that it is immediate and unselfish, 'an instinct... as pure and devoid of self-seeking as the intuitionist can desire' (51). Through this instinct, 'the good of the community becomes at last the end and aim of our moral nature'.

Finally, Buckley says, we need not worry about the cultivated hive-bee—contra Cobbe, for whom the hive-bee example sounded the death-knell for Darwin's attempted evolutionary ethics, which again suggests that Buckley is replying to Cobbe. The bees, Buckley says, are still acting on their duty to the community, although what their community needs is different from what a human community needs. Thus 'an action may become a sacred duty to the community in the case of the hive-bee which we know from fact not to be the law of our being' (51).[35]

Overall, Buckley argues that our being evolved is compatible with our having consciences and immortal souls, and that Darwin unites utilitarianism with intuitionism, countering Cobbe's view that Darwin exclusively took the utilitarian side. Having also addressed the hive-bee worry, Buckley closes, 'calmly reasoning upon the evolution theory, we can establish that it neither shuts out God, degrades our conscience, ... nor diminishes the hope of immortality' (51). We can have all three and be Darwinians too.

4.5 Buckley's Moral and Religious Evolutionism

In certain ways Buckley was faithful to Darwin. She was persuaded by and expanding on his view that humans are evolved and yet still have unselfish moral impulses. We can see this fidelity clearly when Buckley later complained about Henry Drummond's 1894 book *The Ascent of Man*: 'I am only sorry that he speaks of the "struggle for others" as opposed to Darwin's views, whereas the kernel of it is all contained in the "Descent of Man". It is curious to me how [Drummond] can fail to see that [he is] but following the great master' (AB to Garnett, 26 September 1894, *GFP*). However, Buckley was much more adamant about pairing Darwinism and Christianity than Darwin was himself. By 1871 his views on religion were conflicted, and although sometimes he still said that theism and evolutionary theory could co-exist, ultimately he admitted that he had become an agnostic (Darwin to John Fordyce, 7 May 1879, *DCP*, DCP-LETT-12041). Thus, whereas Buckley says that Darwin leaves the origins of parental affection undetermined, actually he says that the 'first foundation or origin of the moral sense lies in the social instincts, including sympathy; and these instincts *no doubt were primarily gained*, as in the case of the lower animals, through natural selection' (Darwin 1871: vol. 2: 394; my emphasis). The instinct is not of 'unknown origin' as Buckley claims but undoubtedly primarily natural origin. Darwin leaves little room here for religion, whereas for Buckley, '"a philosophy of

---

[35] I have argued elsewhere, however (Stone 2022b), that Buckley was not satisfied with her own response to Cobbe here, as she revisited the issue later (Buckley 1881: 298–9).

belief has got to be constructed", that...has always been my point' (AB to Garnett, 5 October 1888, *GFP*).

Could we have a stripped-down version of Buckley's argument—closer to Darwin's own stance—in which the social instincts emerge wholly naturally, through evolution, and yet they still motivate us to act genuinely unselfishly for the good of others? In the mid-to-late 1880s some Fabian socialists took this view, notably including both Annie Besant and Beatrice Webb, whose closest friend and confidante in the mid-1880s was Buckley (Webb [1926] 1980: 293–4).[36] Influenced by Buckley, Webb referred to the 'great laws of evolution' (diary, October 1884) which have produced our sympathetic instincts, the basis of all 'the inner workings which guide the outer actions of human beings' (diary, 1883).[37] Besant did not refer directly to Buckley as far as I know, but by the mid-1880s Buckley's ideas had become part of the broad cultural mix that informed the cooperative evolutionism of Besant and other Fabians. For by then Buckley was well into her programme of popular science writing. Beginning with *A Short History of Natural Science* (1876), she authored more than a dozen books popularizing science for general and young readers. These books also disseminated the same unselfish or 'mutualist'[38] interpretation of evolution first formulated in 'Darwinism and Religion'. *Life and her Children* (1880), *Winners in Life's Race* (1882), and *Moral Teachings of Science* (1891) reached very wide audiences. Buckley was, as Thomas Dixon says, 'one of the most enthusiastic and successful communicators of Darwinian morality' (2008: 152–3). Her work contributed significantly to shaping public perceptions of evolutionary theory late in the century, and was part of the background against which the Fabians held that it was our evolved nature to cooperate with one another.[39]

But the key difference between Buckley and secular Fabians like Besant was that for Buckley religion was essential to cooperative Darwinism. In *Moral Teachings of Science*, Buckley said that we see

in our day the breaking down of old barriers, the rebellion against authority, and the confusion of men's notions of right and wrong. The very fundamental principles of religion and morality are often called in question... We live in an

---

[36] Buckley enthused about her 'most delightful days with Miss Potter' (i.e. Webb before marriage), who was 'charmingly original and just in her views... I think she will be a very remarkable woman' (AB to Garnett, 7 June 1887, *GFP*).
[37] For both entries, see Webb (1926: 119, 140–1).
[38] As Barbara Gates (1998: esp. 61; 2004) and Jordan Larsen (2017) call it.
[39] There is some excellent scholarship on Buckley's popular science writing: Boswell (2019) and Gates (1997, 1998, 2004), emphasizing Buckley's mutualism; Dixon, who sees Buckley as a faithful Darwinian and notes her contrast with Cobbe (Dixon 2008: 152–6, 177); Lightman, who brings in Buckley's spiritualism (2009: ch. 5); and Larsen (2017) who unifies these other interpretations and brings in Buckley's 'traducianism', also discussed below.

age of earnest scepticism... Now all this would not be hurtful, if belief were not needed for everyday conduct. (*MT* 4–5)

In this age of doubt, we can no longer resolve religious and moral questions by looking within and consulting our own consciences. We now need a different route: the study of nature, which proves that our instincts to be 'just and merciful, honest and unselfish' are grounded in our evolved nature (6). This evolved nature results from the workings of natural laws and forces which 'emanate from God *and would be non-existent without Him*' (16). Thus, the more we study nature, the more we find God manifest everywhere in it (16–17). Exterior scientific knowledge of laws of nature brings us safely back to the same moral teachings we used to reach along the now-discredited inward route: 'these are not really two, but only different methods of arriving at one result, namely, the knowledge of laws by which we and all the rest of nature are governed' (5). This book was written in the wake of Buckley being 'roused' by Cobbe's opposition of religion and science, which I mentioned above; against Cobbe and others of her mind, Buckley insisted that science confirms the truth of religion and puts its moral teachings on a new and sound basis.

Not everyone found Buckley's vision appealing. In 1892 Charles Sanders Peirce was unimpressed by *Moral Teachings*. The only ethic scientists need, Peirce said, is to look at the observed facts just as they are, unflinchingly. Instead, Buckley cherry-picks particular scientific findings to bolster and illustrate traditional moral beliefs. But to hold that the real 'teachings of science are necessarily sound and wholesome is... not borne out by facts, but is merely an airy optimism' (Peirce 1892: 417). To anyone who considers science's teachings impartially, they tell against Christianity and against belief in a first cause, Peirce maintained.

More can be said for Buckley's approach than Peirce allowed. To see this, let's review the intellectual options at the time in light of the Wedgwood–Cobbe–Buckley triangle. One could:

(1) see morality and Christianity as integrally linked and reject evolutionary ethics for undermining them both (Cobbe: *moral and religious anti-evolutionism*);
(2) see morality and Christianity as integrally linked but argue that both are compatible with evolutionary theory (Wedgwood) even when completely extended to all human traits and ethical feelings (Buckley) (*moral and religious evolutionism*);
(3) think that, by recognizing the social instinct, evolutionary theory supports an unselfish morality of duty with no need for religion (Besant: *secular moral evolutionism*);
(4) take evolutionary theory to undermine morality—or, more precisely, to undermine the traditional law- and duty-based universalist moral

framework of European societies—and accept or embrace this iconoclastic implication (*anti-moral evolutionism*). On such views, evolutionary theory mandates competition and letting the strong prevail (Greg) and the exceptional individuals flourish (Galton). In Germany, Nietzsche was developing the related view that, in the name of the flourishing of life, traditional moral codes that privilege the weak should be questioned.

Darwin had sought to repel such views, but Cobbe had been unconvinced. For her, authors like Galton and Greg more accurately descried the normative implications of evolutionary theory; but, because these were terrible, evolutionary ethics must be rejected. Buckley, too, was endeavouring to repel anti-moral evolutionism. She admitted that we have competitive as well as social instincts, but still declared that:

[O]ne of the laws of life which is as strong, if not stronger, than the law of force and selfishness, is that of *mutual help and dependence*... The great moral lesson taught at every step in the history of development of the animal world [is] that amidst toil and suffering, struggle and death, the supreme law of life is the law of *self-devotion and love.* (1882: 353)

But what *guarantees* that devotion and love are stronger than competition and force? Unless we can answer that question, plausibly the aggressive and brutal forces are just as strong as the benign ones if not stronger, leaving us with either anti-moral evolutionism or Cobbe's conclusion that evolutionary ethics is not a viable ethics at all. Buckley's answer had several strands. One came from 'Darwinism and Religion': natural selection for the social instincts is guaranteed because God has so established the laws of natural selection as to yield this cooperative result. As she reiterated in *Moral Teachings*, 'the very forces acting in nature, and in ourselves, emanate from God *and would be non-existent without Him*' (*MT* 16): God has so established nature's laws and forces that they necessarily produce and reinforce our cooperative instincts.

Another strand of Buckley's case that love is stronger than force came from another philosophical essay she published as 'A. B.' in 1879, 'The Soul, and the Theory of Evolution'. It advanced a view she called 'Spiritual Evolutionism' (*STE* 9). First, she rejected materialism about the mind, because of the explanatory gap between material brain processes and subjective consciousness, again referring to Tyndall (1). Second, she rejected the alternative 'spiritualist' view that God directly creates each soul, for this makes God responsible for the infant's sinful traits, its 'fierce passions' (4) (i.e. this view makes God the direct cause of evil). Another explanation for these sinful traits is the theory of reincarnation and *karma*, on which these traits are the person's punishment for their misdeeds in previous lives. But, Buckley says, we need no longer appeal to reincarnation here; we can instead explain these traits by evolutionary inheritance from the parents and earlier ancestors—the view she calls 'traducianism' (6). But doesn't this entail materialism, the reduction of soul to body? No, Buckley argues; we do have immortal souls. Life, the vital principle, is irreducible to physical objects and is indestructible (as she had argued in 'Darwinism and Religion'). Each living being shares in this universal life-principle which is passed down from parent to child in reproduction. As a living individual goes through life, its habits and experiences leave their mark and become absorbed into its vital principle (9). So this accumulated experience also becomes passed on to its offspring and descendants. Over time, this process leads to the emergence of living beings—higher animals and humans—that have richer, more developed instincts, emotions, and passions. Moreover, conscious beings pass on not merely vitality but conscious vitality to their successors, for (again as in 'Darwinism and Religion') conscious vitality is a further, irreducibly distinct level of life. The experiences of each individual therefore become literally passed on to their descendants, and to this extent all conscious beings are immortal (9).

Much could be said about this fascinating essay,[40] but I'll confine myself to its implications for our social instincts: 'from a long line of animal and savage ancestry, inherited feelings survive in us totally incompatible with the present state of civilization; and are only slowly being crushed out in the struggle for existence' (*STE* 4). This slow 'crushing out' happens as follows. As each individual goes through life, it endeavours to improve itself, to alleviate its vicious animal passions, and 'must move at least in *some* degree in the right direction (since otherwise it would soon cease to exist)' (8–9). This improvement then becomes fed back into the life-principle and subsequent generations inherit it. Later generations are therefore kinder, more social and sympathetic. In this way, contra Cobbe, our fierce, savage passions are gradually being winnowed out—spiritually and physically. We need not appeal to a transcendent law to overcome these passions; nature is overcoming them from within. That said, for Buckley, this is

---

[40] A lengthy reply defending reincarnation followed (by 'J. P. B.', 1880), then a critique of both essays from an astrological perspective by 'A. G. Trent' (1880)—actually Buckley's long-term friend and interlocutor Richard Garnett, writing pseudonymously. The *University Magazine*, in which all these essays came out, had from 1833 to 1877 been the *Dublin University Magazine* but in 1877 Keningale Cook assumed the editorship, renaming it *University Magazine: A Literary and Philosophic Review*. Cook, an esotericist, was the husband of Mabel Collins, Blavatsky's co-editor at *Lucifer*. On the *Dublin University Magazine*, see Hall (2000), who, however, is dismissive about its final philosophical stage under Cook. Buckley's essay prompted other esotericist responses elsewhere; see Larsen (2017). Interestingly too, J. P. B's response shows the unmistakeable influence of Blavatsky's defence of metempsychosis in *Isis Unveiled* (*IU* 1: 8–9). Indeed, Buckley may have been putting forward her version of 'spiritual evolution' in contrast to that of Blavatsky. Blavatsky may well have been recommended to Buckley by Wallace: Buckley and Wallace were close correspondents, as I've mentioned; Blavatsky had sent Wallace a copy of *Isis Unveiled* (HPB to Wallace, 27[?] November 1875, *WCP*, WCP3016); and Wallace regularly defended Blavatsky against those who condemned her as a fraud (see e.g. Wallace to Coues, 12 January 1891, *WCP*, WCP3452).

only possible because nature already contains a non-material life-principle and goes through a process of spiritual, not merely material, evolution.

These views placed Buckley considerably further away from Christian orthodoxy than she had been in 'Darwinism and Religion'. She still believed that the theory of natural selection needed spiritual supplementation to ensure that love was stronger than force. But now that supplement came from her picture of humanity's overall spiritual evolution.

For secularist moral evolutionists like Besant, no such spiritual supplement was needed. From evolution we inherit an evil anti-social side *and* a good social side, and the latter is inexorably winning out. As Besant explained:

> The study of Darwin...had not only convinced me of the truth of evolution, but...had led me to see in the evolution of the social instinct the explanation of the growth of conscience and of the strengthening of man's mental and moral nature.... [M]an inherits from his brute progenitors various bestial tendencies which are in course of elimination. The wild-beast desire to fight...lust...greed... [T]he anti-social tendencies are the bestial tendences in man, and...man in evolving further must evolve out of these, each also feel [ing] it part of his personal duty to curb these in himself, and so to rise further from the brute. (*ABA* 164–5)

How do we evolve out of these tendencies? For Besant, following positivism, society develops and becomes more complex and integrated through its inherent developmental laws. This strengthens our social instincts and progressively squeezes out the anti-social ones. Necessary laws of *social* evolution do the same work—shoring up the social instincts—that *spiritual* evolution does for Buckley. One way or another, though, those who wanted to get morality and cooperation out of evolution had to invoke something to strengthen the cooperative side of our evolved instinctual heritage. This was why, for Buckley, cooperative Darwinism had to go together with a religious interpretation of science.

4.6 Wedgwood's Later Reassessment

The disagreement amongst Wedgwood, Cobbe, and Buckley arose against a backdrop of considerable agreement. They all thought that religion and morality were integrally related and must be defended. Their disagreement was over whether the religion–morality couplet could or could not be conjoined with evolutionary theory. This shared assumption that religion and morality must go together may make these women's views unappealing to contemporary secularists, but I urge readers not to dismiss them too hastily. As I observed earlier, Wedgwood makes the reasonable point that all our knowledge, beliefs, and values must form a coherent whole, and that that whole has to accommodate other commitments besides scientific ones. For the sake of epistemic coherence, we may need to adjust our scientific claims, and the framing we give to them, so that they align with our other values and beliefs. As for Cobbe, she raises the important question of whether Darwinism really does support a morality of sympathy and social cooperation, as Darwin thought, or merely sanctions the survival of the fittest. And her core objection to utilitarianism—how can the utilitarian avoid sacrificing the weak or unfortunate if doing so increases the general happiness?—is, if not new, serious, and she presses it with a live sense of its practical bearings. Her concerns about Darwinism shed light, too, on Buckley's reasons for continuing to combine it with religion. Buckley fears that if evolutionary theory is construed in purely secular terms then it will follow that humanity's competitive and aggressive instincts are as strong as its social and cooperative ones. We might think that this bullet just has to be bitten and a more pessimistic, or at least mixed, view of humanity accepted. But it is, at least, understandable that Buckley was worried about this problem, especially as the anti-moral evolutionism of Greg and Galton was gaining ground.

To round off this discussion, it is interesting to look at how Wedgwood reconceived evolution, religion, and morality in 'Ethics and Science', published in the *Contemporary Review* in 1897.[41] This also helps us to connect Wedgwood and Buckley more deeply, for by then Wedgwood had read Buckley's *Moral Teachings*, yet she took a view of science and religion different from Buckley's.

In 1891 Buckley's close friend and long-time correspondent Richard Garnett sent Wedgwood a copy of *Moral Teachings*. Wedgwood replied: 'I shall read [it] with great interest, and ... I hope to write my thanks to her directly. Whether any critical notice will suggest itself to me in the perusal is a point which I can only answer afterwards' (JW to Garnett, 6 November 1891, *GFP*). I am not aware that any critical notice appeared; as Wedgwood explained to Garnett, she was increasingly avoiding reviewing to concentrate on her own writing. Yet we can register Buckley's influence on Wedgwood's argument in 'Ethics and Science'.

Reflecting back on the 'stir created by *The Origin of Species*', Wedgwood notes that the sort of compromise she championed in the 1860s could not work:

> The principle of evolution concerns the whole future as well as the past. We cannot say it was active up to a particular date and then ceased working, nor [that] ... it is true of man's bodily organs and not of his soul.... From the first it was possible to discern that the new doctrine concerned not physical life alone.
> (*NCT* 310)

---

[41] Wedgwood had continued to reflect on Darwinism in the intervening decades; see Brown (2022: ch. 13).

So ethics could not be insulated from evolutionary theory, and this explained 'the half-conscious recoil of a traditional morality from a new influence pregnant with revolution' (311). Moreover, Darwin's practice in pursuing his inquiries wherever they led him, even though they undermined his own religious faith, suggested that inquiry and experiment were the central values, taking priority over any fixed frameworks. In this way 'the world of duty...lost its landmarks' (314). However, Wedgwood says, we cannot live by experiment alone but also need some firm convictions, held on faith. So far, she reiterates Buckley's points from *Moral Teachings*: there is a new climate of questioning to which science has been central, but we need fixed faith—Buckley had spoken of belief—for practical life. But for Buckley in *Moral Teachings*, the inward route to religious and moral belief has lost credibility and now we must take the outward, scientific route back to belief—belief can and must be re-founded on science. Wedgwood, in contrast, maintains that scientific questioning and experimentation are only possible in the first place if there is some solid bedrock of belief for them to presuppose and be directed against. We cannot question without something to *be* questioned. This makes belief more fundamental than scientific inquiry:

> For it is a poor and timid claim for the beliefs that lie at the basis of all others that they may be *harmonized* with those which seem to contradict them. They must, if they be the reflex of eternal realities, stand to all other beliefs as the gnarled oak roots to the acorn. (320)

Consequently, scientific inquiry cannot be pushed and generalized to the point of undermining all faith, or it destroys the condition of its own possibility. Whereas Buckley seeks to ground religious and moral conclusions on science, Wedgwood is now arguing that science must be grounded on a prior bedrock of religious and moral conviction.

We see both continuity with and difference from Wedgwood's earlier stance. She is still trying to delimit science's boundaries. But in 1860 she sought to reconcile science and religion as parts of a coherent whole of knowledge, where each part must be refined and adjusted to fit with the other. In 1897 she sees religion as more fundamental and stresses that it is science that needs to acknowledge its dependence on religion, for if science attempts to become total and all-encompassing then it eradicates the background of settled conviction on which it relies.

Wedgwood's view that science cannot on its own provide a total framework of meaning recalls the debates about naturalism that I discussed in Chapter 2, and in particular recalls Welby's view that science is necessarily embedded in a background of meaning and significance which is the condition of possibility for scientific inquiries. The similarity between Wedgwood and Welby is no coincidence, for they corresponded about science, meaning, and religion in the 1880s. Let me take a slight detour into their correspondence, as it fills in another part of the inter-women dialogue that informed these women's published views.

Mary Everest Boole, George Boole's widow and a logician and metaphysician in her own right (see Boole 1931), knew both Wedgwood and Welby and introduced them in the early 1880s. Boole told Welby that both she (i.e. Welby) and Wedgwood were trying to 'unpick' 'the antagonism between science and religion' and to show that 'spiritual truth' and 'materialistic science' can go together (Boole to VW, 1882–5, *ELL* 90). Wedgwood then read Welby's *Links and Clues* and they began to correspond (JW to VW, 1882–5, *ELL* 96). Meanwhile, Boole continued to mediate between them, saying to Welby:

> A certain school of thinkers (which includes...Julia Wedgwood, you and me) has of late years developed the idea that truth is always positive; that between two views of any point, of which one asserts the more and the other less, the former is the right; that inclusion is truer than exclusion, affirmation than denial.
> (Boole to VW, 1885–8, *ELL* 151)

However, Boole adds, this 'positive' philosophy must acknowledge the real differences between views. Whenever one view-holder denies these differences and the other affirms them, the latter is right. She continues in the same letter:

> [T]he spirit pours out on any given age some one truth in polar-opposite-halves. Those to whom the half-truths are communicated ought...to lay their half-truths together.... 'Suppose the universe is to be divided by a line or gulf...that St. Paul is to be on one side and Mr. Darwin on the other, for all eternity. With which would you elect to spend eternity?' The question would reveal a radical double colour-blindness; and generally...help the disputants to realise the nature of their own deficiencies. (*ELL* 152–3)

In reply, Welby instead stressed the expansive, ascending movement whereby differences become absorbed in a larger whole, in light of which it transpires that they were never fully real but were only ever partial fragments. Or, metaphorically, 'the mutual colour-blindness...implies the existence of white light' (VW to Boole, 1885–8, *ELL* 153), the light in which all colours blend into one. It is a difference of emphasis but an important one: for Welby the differences are only part of a whole which is the ultimate reality, but for Boole the whole is only the unification of real differences. Wedgwood agreed more with Boole, as her subsequent letters with Welby bring out.

Welby sent Wedgwood several papers, including the one Wedgwood found most interesting, the short 1886 parable 'Heliology' (*SU* 328–30). In this parable a

Teacher who cannot perceive the sun, only the earth, is convinced that believers in the sun have fallen for an illusion, 'the myth of a sun', about which we cannot really know because it is 'beyond our faculties of perception' (329). Welby's point was that it is absurd for us to thus restrict our faculties. We can and should let ourselves rise towards the solar and cosmic levels of reality.

Wedgwood responded that the 'division line' between their views fell here:

> The experience of the individual or of the race seems...a prism breaking the white ray of light and showing it as colour,...so that, according to his position, each man sees a different portion of that which in its own nature is truly one. My vision may come upon a different part of the spectrum from yours...and then the...rays at one end of the spectrum...[and] at the other..., they, too, are a constituent of that which the eye uses whenever it is open. A wonderful parable...of the meaning and power of truth. (JW to VW, 1886–8, *ELL* 178)

The parable's meaning, to Wedgwood, was that different rays and perspectives are all constituents of the truth. The truth is the whole, but only insofar as that whole is distributed across different parts, so that 'we...find our unity as we find our fractionalness' (JW to VW, 1882–5, *ELL* 97). For Welby, the key was the greater reality towards which the parts gravitate; for Wedgwood, the key was the interplay amongst the parts, the necessity of their conflict and difference and hence the inescapable 'dislocation of our being' (JW to VW, 1885–6, *ELL* 122).

Wedgwood also discerned a second difference from Welby: 'You are in sympathy with the scientific spirit of our time in a way I never could be' (JW to VW, 1888–90, *ELL* 240). They both wanted to reconcile science and religion, but Wedgwood thought that Welby's way of doing so leaned more towards science. Was this fair to Welby? Quite possibly. After all, Welby told Besant that she revered science and was not criticizing it as such or trying to undermine it (VW to AB, 18 October 1891, *VWF*). If scientists would only acknowledge the role of meaning and significance instead of clinging to a narrow empiricism, then they could do science better—in a broader, more expansive and open-minded way. For Welby, then, reopening science onto its animating metaphysical concerns would improve science and enable it to reach new heights. In contrast, Wedgwood remained closer to her 1860s project of *delimiting* the boundaries of science. She sought to embed science in a background of faith and so establish the limits beyond which science cannot rightly pass.

This difference comes out when Wedgwood compares faith to old oak roots thrust deep underground, standing firm while surface changes come and go. Welby rejected such talk of 'grounds', 'bases', and foundations': 'there can be no "fundamental basis"...not solidity of base or fixity of status is our vital need, but moving power beyond our ken or senses' (VW to Ward, 1886–8, *ELL* 173). Welby and Wedgwood were articulating their differences in a rather metaphorical way, but the imagery sheds light on the difference between their views. Their conversation also shows how debate about evolution and science was changing as the century ended. Increasingly the task was no longer to balance the competing knowledge-claims of science and religion, but to find grounds for religion to retain a place in our lives at all—perhaps as a needed bedrock of belief or faith, or perhaps as the ultimate source of significance.

5
Religion and Morality

5.1 Introduction

In this chapter I look at the thought of Harriet Martineau, George Eliot, Frances Power Cobbe, Vernon Lee, and Annie Besant on the relation between morality and religion, which was a pivotal issue for many nineteenth-century women philosophers. For Cobbe, morality necessarily depended on religion, and Christianity in particular. For the other four, Christianity had lost credibility and morality must be put on a new non-religious basis. They found this basis in various locations: the impartial 'exterior point of view', for Martineau in the 1850s; the expanded sympathies made possible by artistic literature, for Eliot from the 1850s onwards; an honest, responsible attitude towards the conditions of collective human life, for Lee in the 1880s; and empirical science, for the secularist Besant from 1874 to 1889.

As we can see, in this debate about religion and morality, 'religion' essentially meant 'Christianity'. To be sure, these women were aware of other world religions beside Christianity—indeed, they were well-informed about and in some cases were heavily engaged with these other traditions.[1] Nonetheless, they generally saw Christianity as the most advanced religion. For Cobbe, all world religions enabled people to achieve a level of morality, but Christianity was the most advanced religion and made possible morality in the full sense. From this perspective, morality required religion in general, but fully realizing morality required Christianity in particular. Conversely, for Martineau, the next step in collective human advancement was to move on beyond Christianity but, since Christianity was the most advanced religion, this had to be a move beyond religion altogether, into secularism. Morality must be extricated and liberated both from religion in general and, in particular, from the last religion, Christianity. From both the secularist and the religionist sides, then, this debate about morality and religion centred upon Christianity.

Yet Christianity was no single thing. Due to the proliferation of Dissenting communities, and the range from 'High' to 'Low' through 'Broad' Church, nineteenth-century British Christianity encompassed many currents—such as Unitarianism, in which Martineau started out; mainstream Anglicanism, in

---

[1] This will be explored in Chapter 6.

which Eliot started out;[2] evangelicalism, in which Besant started out; and countless other permutations. So when Christianity was said to be (or not to be) the basis of morality, we might ask: *which* Christianity? Cobbe provided a clear answer that I will use to anchor the ensuing discussion. For her, morality depended on the rationally reconstructed nucleus of Christianity—'simple theism'—which lay at the heart of all its variations, even those that had 'corrupted' its promise (*FW* 798):

> [B]y the word Religion I mean definite faith in a Living and Righteous God; and, as a corollary therefrom, in the survival of the human soul after death. In other words, I mean by 'religion' that nucleus of simple Theism which is common to every form of natural religion, of Christianity and Judaism; and, of course, in a measure also to remoter creeds. (*FW* 797)

What about the diversity on the secularist side? Were Martineau, Eliot, Lee, and Besant *agnostics* or *atheists*? Martineau and Eliot are often classed as agnostics; Lee affiliated herself with 'unbelief' and 'secular morality'; Besant openly avowed atheism. But the difference was less than we might assume. Atheism and agnosticism, which we now see as distinct, often converged at the time, as in Martineau's view that because we cannot know anything about God, we have no grounds for believing in him at all. One might add that by the same token we have no grounds for positively denying that God exists. But while conceding this in principle, nineteenth-century agnostics generally emphasized our lack of grounds for *belief*, while reciprocally most atheists so formulated their position as to draw it close to agnosticism. For instance, Besant admitted that before publishing her essay 'On the Nature and Existence of God' she corrected its 'vulgar error that the Atheist says "there is no God"', to say instead that 'the atheist says he can find no acceptable evidence that there is a God' (*ABA* 139).[3] Atheism and agnosticism thus existed on a continuum. For shorthand, I will use the word 'secularism' to encompass this whole continuum (the word was coined in 1851 by George Holyoake, as I discuss briefly in Sec. 5.6). 'Free thought' was the political wing of this continuum, along which people campaigned for the freedom to think and express non-religious ideas and for associated civil and political freedoms, for instance to serve in Parliament or in court cases without having to swear a religious oath.

The fact that so many prominent women—Martineau, Eliot, Lee, Besant— adopted versions of secularism in the later century may seem to support the

---

[2] Although Eliot's background was Anglican, she went through an evangelical phase in her adolescence; see, inter alia, Fleishman (2010: ch. 1) and Lovesey (2013).

[3] In the essay in question, Besant considered, and rejected as irrational, Henry Mansel's Kantian case that our lack of knowledge about God creates space for faith (see Mansel [1858] 1867). She argued that Mansel has conclusively shown that no knowledge of God is possible, and yet he retreats from his own conclusion and wheels in 'faith' as a *deus ex machina* (*MPA* 123–30).

idea that the nineteenth century was the era of secularization. For much of the twentieth century 'the reigning paradigm for understanding religion under the condition of modernity' was this notion of 'the secularization of the European mind in the nineteenth century' (Rasmussen, Wolfe, and Zachhuber 2017: 1).[4] But, as Rasmussen et al. continue:

> Much was missed by this paradigm. For through various realignments...continuing across the nineteenth century, Christianity...not only endured as a vibrant intellectual tradition within an increasingly pluralistic world, but also contributed decisively to a wide range of conversations, movements, and transformations across all spheres of modern intellectual, cultural, and social history. (1)

That is, as the nineteenth century went on, belief did not straightforwardly *secularize* so much as it *pluralized*. Christianity remained a major presence and took ever-new forms, while alongside it new forms of belief grew up such as spiritualism, Christian Science, and theosophy. Indeed, it is striking that of the twelve women discussed in this book no less than five had some leanings towards 'alternative' spiritual currents: mesmerism (Martineau, Lovelace); spiritualism (Buckley, Blavatsky); and theosophy (Blavatsky, Besant). There also arose new forms of non-belief that fell within the secularist continuum. But even these were not always so anti-religious as one might think. Besant admitted of herself, 'if "morality touched by emotion" be religion, then...I was the most religious of Atheists' (*ABA* 157). More specifically, she carried across from her evangelical background 'a quasi-Christian messianic drive to change the world' (Leland 2021: 311).[5] Thus Christianity sometimes remained a background presence even in new and ostensibly secular forms of belief.

On the theme of religion and morality, many of our five women explicitly engaged with one another. Eliot and Martineau were close friends in the early 1850s, having both journeyed through Higher Criticism to positivism and reached the similar view that society must now progress beyond religion. Yet these two women ultimately reached quite different views on secular morality. Even so, Cobbe grouped Martineau and Eliot together as 'virtuous agnostics' and explicitly criticized them both. Cobbe and Lee were friends, and epistolary and textual evidence suggests that Cobbe was the model for the pro-religious character in the dialogue in which Lee defended 'responsible unbelief'. Cobbe explicitly replied to Lee's dialogue, and Lee wrote another dialogue in response. Besant, too, explicitly criticized Cobbe; indeed, Besant's secularism was shaped by her turn

---

[4] The phrase 'secularization of the European mind' is Owen Chadwick's (1975); advocating the secularization thesis, see also Bruce (2002).

[5] Leland is referring to Wessinger's (1988) account of Besant's 'progressive messianism'.

against Cobbe's Theism.[6] Women thus referred to one another more openly than with the topics covered in earlier chapters. Women felt more able to name one another's names apropos of morality and religion because this was an area in which women were taken to have authority as women. In this field, one could refer to women without sacrificing one's credibility.

The chapter proceeds chronologically through Martineau's version of secularism in her *Autobiography* (Sec. 5.2); Eliot's view that literature affords a new secular basis for morality because it expands our sympathies (Sec. 5.3); Cobbe's criticisms of 'magnanimous atheism' (Sec. 5.4); Lee's debate with Cobbe (Sec. 5.5); and Besant's critiques of Cobbe (Sec. 5.6). Finally, I will pull out some overarching issues that emerge from these debates (Sec. 5.7).

5.2 Martineau and the Exterior Point of View

Martineau's *Autobiography* was published in 1877 after she died, although she had written it back in 1855, believing that she was going to die soon. When she did not, she held the *Autobiography* from publication for fear of controversy—which indeed came when the book finally appeared, for in it Martineau extolled atheism's intellectual, personal, and moral merits.

She wrote the *Autobiography* as a positivist, and this shapes how she portrays her philosophical development in the book (see Petersen 1986). Allegedly, she advanced from morbid, gloomy childhood religiosity (1802–19), through youthful metaphysical fogs (1819–39), to adulthood and the joyful daylight of science (1839–), when she finally threw off religion's baleful influence.[7] She depicted herself as having evolved inexorably towards atheism. Crucially, Martineau's journey was free of the doubts, torments, soul-searching and anguish of the typical Victorian crisis of faith. On the contrary, for Martineau, leaving religion behind meant *escaping* from gloomy fogs, doubts, and anguish into a sunlit realm of happiness, tranquillity, and serenity. It was religion and metaphysics, not their abandonment, that provoked uncertainty and torment. The exit from religion brought overwhelming relief and liberation from a heavy burden.[8]

---

[6] Besant highlights Cobbe's importance for her in her *Autobiography* (*ABA* 107, 131–2), *Autobiographical Sketches* (*AS* 62, 85, 95), *My Path to Atheism* (*MPA* vii–viii, 113–14), as well as the two essays discussed here, 'The True Basis of Morality', originally from 1874, and 'A World Without God', from 1885. As late as *The Basis of Morality* (1915) Besant was still tacitly signalling Cobbe's importance by identifying the five stages of morality as revelation, *intuition*, utility, (spiritual) evolution, and mysticism. These reprise Besant's own stages: evangelicalism, Theism, secularism, theosophy, and Hindu mysticism.
[7] Also notably, in her *Autobiography* Martineau repeatedly calls herself a philosopher and talks about the evolution of her philosophical views (e.g. *HMA* 1: 103–11, 158, 426). See also Meyers (1980) on how the *Autobiography* narrates 'the making of a female philosopher'.
[8] As Odile Boucher-Rivalain remarks, Martineau narrates not a 'painful crisis of faith' but 'boundless enthusiasm over her new condition as an agnostic' (2012: 24). This was part of what made the narrative so controversial.

Martineau felt released from the self-judging, self-scrutinizing form of subjectivity in which, since childhood, she had been constantly monitoring and mentally punishing herself for transgressions. She was trapped in a narrow preoccupation with her own mental states (*LLM* 222). In addition, abandoning religion at last allowed Martineau to be fully rationally consistent, whereas previously she had been in a constant intellectual struggle, plagued by religious doubts—especially about the problem of evil—yet feeling that she must retain a belief in divine government and try to reconcile it with the existence of evil (*HMA* 1: 108–9).

Martineau portrayed the final stages of her 'transition from religious inconsistency and irrationality to free-thinking strength and liberty' as follows (*HMA* 2: 182). In the 1840s many people she knew died, heightening her sense of the 'apparent cruelty and injustice of the scheme of "divine government"' (184). Wrestling with the problem to no avail, she came to see that she was trying vainly to use her intellect on matters beyond its scope. Actually 'our mere human faculty' does not equip us to 'understand the scheme, or nature, or fact, of the universe, any more than the minnow in the creek, ... can comprehend the perturbations caused in his world of existence by the tides' (186). To be sure, we can understand *some* things: by making repeated observations we can generalize to invariant laws of nature. But we cannot know about any overarching plan or cause that may underlie and orchestrate these laws. Indeed, because this is beyond the reach of our knowledge, we have no grounds to believe that any such plan or cause is at work at all. Neither, therefore, have we any basis for thinking that we—human beings—are at the centre of the universe or that everything is set up so as to produce us. We are part of the universe but not its destination or *telos*, and realizing this:

> We find ourselves suddenly living and moving in the midst of the universe, – as a part of it, and not as its aim and object. We find ourselves living, not under capricious and arbitrary conditions, unconnected with the constitution and movements of the whole, but under great, general, invariable laws, which operate on us as a part of the whole. (*PP* 1: xiv)

All we can know is that the universe follows invariable laws which, being general and invariable, act on us too: we fall under the same laws as everything else in the universe.

Here we have reached 'the true exterior point of view' (*HMA* 2: 217). It is the view of human beings from the outside (from 'the point of view of the universe' as Sidgwick would put it; [1874] 1907: 382). From the torments of the first-person perspective, terribly concerned about the state of our own souls and the consistency of our edifice of beliefs, we have escaped into a calm, detached, external standpoint on which humanity is one natural phenomenon amongst others. At last, Martineau says, she had got out of the prison of my own self, wherein I had formerly sat trying to interpret life and the world, – much as a captive might undertake to paint the aspect of Nature from the gleams and shadows and faint colours reflected on his dungeon walls. I had learned that, to form any true notion whatever of any of the affairs of the universe, we must take our stand in the external world.

(*HMA* 2: 333–4)

And 'the relief is like that of coming out of a cave full of painted shadows under the free sky, with the earth open around us to the horizon' (*LLM* 219). The allusion to Plato could hardly be any plainer: religious and metaphysical perspectives, and 'anxious solicitude about my own "salvation"' (222), trap the self in Plato's cave. Extricating ourselves from these illusions, we leave the cave and enter the sunlight of actual reality.

Simultaneously, Martineau relinquished belief in the afterlife and personal immortality. She had already come to find them intellectually incredible, but had not yet been prepared to abandon them emotionally:

I had long given up, in moral disgust, the conception of life after death as a matter of compensation for the ills of humanity, or a police and penal resource of 'the divine government'. I had perceived that [regarding] the...immortality of the soul...we were wholly without evidence...But I still resorted, in indolence and prejudice, to...the instinctive and universal love of life, and inability to conceive of its extinction.   (*HMA* 2: 186)

Her love of life had compelled her to believe that, somehow, her soul would survive the death of her body. But now she recognized this dogged clinging to life as 'selfish'. It is selfish morally, for if I believe I will be rewarded for virtue in the afterlife, then I am motivated to act virtuously merely for my own posthumous benefit (i.e. in my own long-term self-interest). In addition, this clinging is selfish perspectivally, for it is a refusal to quit the first-person perspective from which my non-existence is inconceivable. But from the exterior point of view, everyone does begin and end while the universe rolls on regardless. Having adopted this perspective,

I feel no reluctance whatever to pass into nothingness, leaving my place in the universe to be filled by another. The very conception of *self* and *other* is, in truth, merely human, and when the self ceases to be, the distinction expires.

(*HMA* 2: 207)

Martineau had by no means lost her love of life, she insisted. One can relish life without having to fear death. In fact, the exterior perspective enhances our appreciation of life, bringing us to a humble-minded recognition of all that the universe achieves through its own workings.

But can we really adopt this detached, exterior standpoint on our own lives? My death may be of infinitesimal significance from a cosmic perspective, but that does not show that it is possible or desirable for me, this living being, to take up that perspective. We might find more plausible Spinoza's position that 'Every single thing endeavors as far as it lies in itself to persevere in its own being' (2018: 101, E3P6) and that therefore 'a person is determined to do those things' 'that serve his preservation' (103, E3P9). Even though this might seem to dovetail with Martineau's determinism, she did not consider these apparent counter-claims to her position—she had little time for Spinoza, of whose system she wrote in 1830 that its 'chief importance is derived from the mystery with which it is invested, and to which alone...it owes its reception by any rational mind'. She proceeded to lambast Spinoza's 'ambiguous terms, his false assumptions, his identical propositions, and inaccurate definitions' ([1830] 1836c: 246).[9]

What did, positively, influence Martineau in thinking that we can and should adopt the exterior standpoint? A plausible candidate is the 1773 essay 'Against Inconsistency in our Expectations' by Anna Barbauld, about which Martineau enthused in 'Female Writers on Practical Divinity', and which was 'admired, both as English prose and wisdom literature, for a full century' (McCarthy and Kraft 2002: 186). Barbauld blended Unitarianism with Stoicism, arguing that the path to a contented life is to avoid forming unrealistic desires that cannot be satisfied, and instead to train and educate one's desires in recognition of the invariant laws regulating the universe. Barbauld said:

[U]pon an accurate inspection, we shall find, in the moral government of the world,...laws as determinate, fixed, and invariable as any in Newton's Principia.... The man, therefore, who has well studied the operations of nature... will acquire a certain moderation and equity in his claims upon Providence.

(Barbauld [1773] 2002: 187)

Admittedly, as this passage shows, Barbauld still believed in providence and a moral government of the world, both notions that Martineau came to reject. But the secularist Martineau still shared with Barbauld the idea that we can and should rise above painful disappointment and dissatisfaction by coming to locate ourselves within a world of consistent and invariant laws.

From all this we can see that, for Martineau, atheism was an *attitude to life* as much as a belief:

---

[9] There was no English translation of Spinoza's *Ethics* in 1830 but this would have been no obstacle to Martineau, who had studied Latin both at school and home. Eliot produced the first English translation in 1856, though it remained unpublished until the twentieth century.

[T]he best state of mind was to be found... in those who were called philosophical atheists.... [They] were the most humble-minded in the presence of the mysteries of the universe, the most equable in spirit and temper..., the most devout in their contemplation of the unknown, and the most disinterested in their management of themselves, and their expectations from the human lot. (*HMA* 2: 189)

The atheist state of mind is the best because atheists do not falsely inflate their own importance and place in the universe. Appreciating that they are only one small piece of the jigsaw, they are raised above narrow, selfish preoccupations and can act with genuine disinterest.

For Martineau, then, naturalism and atheism go hand in hand with morality. This is because naturalism leads us to the exterior viewpoint on life, which elevates us to act in impartial, unselfish, and disinterested ways that benefit everyone and not merely our own selves. Far from undermining morality, atheism encourages it; it is Christianity that turns the self in upon itself and leads us falsely and selfishly to exaggerate our individual importance.

5.3 Eliot: Literature and the Expansion of Sympathy

I now turn to a woman far better known than most of the others discussed in this book: George Eliot. Virtually every aspect of Eliot's thought and work has been extensively examined.[10] What I hope to add here is, first, to situate Eliot as contributing to broader debates about religion and morality; second, to identify her unique contribution to these debates, that of moving artistic literature into the space supporting morality which religion had formerly occupied;[11] and, third, to put this unique contribution into conversation with the views of other women, particularly Martineau.

I highlight Martineau because she and Eliot moved in the same overlapping radical liberal circles from the 1840s through the 1850s.[12] Eliot 'venerated' Martineau and loved Martineau's fiction.[13] Yet after a meeting in April 1845 they had no further contact until 1852, when they became very friendly. For a while in the early 1850s the two enjoyed a 'considerable intimacy' (Cross 1885: vol. 1: 196). Martineau described Eliot's 1852 visit as 'a vast pleasure' (HM to John Chapman, 29 October 1852, *HMCL* 3: 247). Reciprocally, Eliot was keen to feature Martineau's writing in the *Westminster Review*, calling her 'a *trump*—the only English woman that possesses thoroughly the art of writing' (GE to the Brays and

---

[10] On the philosophical side of Eliot's work overall, see Anger (2019).
[11] Gatens has argued this too (2009: 73).
[12] On these common circles, see e.g. Ashton (2006) and Postlethwaite (1984).
[13] See GE to Martha Jackson, 21 April 1845, *GEL* I: 189; GE to Mrs Bray, 25 May 1845, *GEL* I: 192.

Sara Hennell, 2 June 1852, *GEL* II: 32). Unfortunately, Martineau abruptly ended the friendship in 1854 because she disapproved of Eliot's relationship with George Henry Lewes. Even so, Eliot continued to admire Martineau and the two followed one another's work for years afterwards.[14]

Because of the two women's common intellectual context in the 1840s and 1850s and their parallel intellectual trajectories, there are certain similarities between their accounts of how duty can stand without religion. We see this from Frederick Myers's famous description of Eliot speaking in 1873:

> She, stirred somewhat beyond her wont, and taking as her text the three words which have been used so often as the inspiring trumpet calls of men – the words *God, Immortality, Duty* — pronounced, with terrible earnestness, how inconceivable was the *first*, how unbelievable the *second*, and yet how peremptory and absolute the *third*. Never, perhaps, have sterner accents affirmed the sovereignty of impersonal and unrecompensing law. (Myers [1881] 1917: 62)

Admittedly, Myers's remarks are part of the mythologization of Eliot that was by then well underway. But they still point towards her common ground with Martineau: namely that, for Eliot too, morality needs to be set on a non-religious foundation, and the idea of impersonal law plays a part in this. Yet on the detail there is considerable difference between the two women's views.

To unearth this, let us trace how Eliot, like Martineau, became convinced that the religious frameworks that formerly underpinned morality had ceased to be believable. Eliot's doubts about orthodox Christianity were first prompted by Charles Hennell's 1838 *Inquiry concerning the Origin of Christianity*. Hennell argued that the Gospels contain a mix of truth and fiction, and by sifting the former from the latter he reconstructed the historical reality of the life of Jesus, thereby endeavouring to re-establish Christianity on a basis of natural reason rather than miracle ([1838] 1841: vi–vii). Eliot then proceeded to read Strauss and Feuerbach, two giants of German religious criticism whose work she translated. Strauss, like Hennell, distinguished the historical truths in the Gospels from mythical and symbolic interpretations and accretions, especially regarding miracles, although compared to Hennell Strauss found a higher proportion of myth to history (see Eliot 1846; Hennell [1838] 1841: xii). Feuerbach went even further. For him, religion and Christianity arose because we have projected human qualities and powers onto gods and then worshipped these qualities and powers in alienated form. This was necessary at earlier stages of human consciousness, but now the time has come to reclaim our powers and celebrate humanity directly, including our capacity to love one another and our physical bodies (see Eliot 1854).

---

[14] See e.g. *GEL* II: 127, 405, 430.

Through her engagement with these authors, Eliot lost her faith. She came to think, in agreement with Feuerbach, that 'the immediate object and the proper sphere of all our highest emotions are our struggling fellow-men and this earthly existence' (GE to F. D'Albert-Durade, 6 December 1859, GEL III: 231). And as she later put it,

> the fellowship between man and man which has been the principle of development, social and moral, is not dependent on conceptions of what is not man: and ... the idea of God, so far as it has been a high spiritual influence, is the ideal of a goodness entirely human (i.e. an exaltation of the human).
> (GE to Mrs Ponsonby, 10 December 1874, GEL VI: 98)

That is, the true purpose of morality is to meet people's needs and enhance their earthly well-being.[15] To the extent that religion has had a beneficial moral influence, this is entirely because of this secular content secreted within it, the 'fellowship between man and man'. But insofar as religion has secreted this content and constrained inter-human fellowship to pass by way of God, its influence has never been wholly beneficial. To realize the moral element in Christianity fully, it needs to be extricated from religion.[16]

Eliot's Strauss translation came out anonymously in 1846, and Martineau read it (LLM 221–2). Simultaneously she was developing her own historical critique of religion, expressed in *Eastern Life* of 1848.[17] Along parallel routes, then, both women relinquished their faith over the 1840s and then gravitated to positivism, for its vision of the necessary intellectual progression from theology through metaphysics to secularism spoke very concretely to them.[18] However, Eliot was more concerned than Martineau about how we can *feel* emotions of sympathy and concern for other human beings without a religious background to inculcate them, in however distorted and alienated a form. Martineau did not find this problem so pressing because, for her, moral actions stem primarily from rational principles.[19]

---

[15] As Julia Wedgwood explained Eliot's views to Victoria Welby: 'George Eliot once said to me that she thought morality ... began whenever one animal felt the need of another' (JW to VW, 12 December 1886, *ELL* 122).

[16] As Rohan Maitzen (2014) points out, for Eliot, 'people's religious beliefs are much less important than—and may even impede—their capacity for sympathy. Thus her novels often feature clergymen of imperfect faith, like Mr Irwine in *Adam Bede*, or imperfect behaviour, like Mr Farebrother in *Middlemarch*, whose flaws ... highlight that theirs is a fundamentally human benevolence. Dinah may be devout, but the good she does is attributable to her, not to God'.

[17] As Caroline Roberts notes, Martineau's *Eastern Life* had more impact at the time and was the best-known British work of religious criticism up to that point (Roberts 2002: 155–6).

[18] On Eliot's sympathy with positivism, see, inter alia, Scholl (2012) and Wright (1981).

[19] Martineau recognized that she and Eliot differed on this point, and she criticized Eliot's 'sentimentalism' (HM to Charles Holt Bracebridge, 21 November 1859, *HMCL* 4: 205). As Margaret Walters and Valerie Sanders have observed, Martineau always upheld 'an impassable division between the personal and the impersonal, between—on the one hand—discipline, principle, duty, the rational mind; and on the other, passion' (Walters 1976: 336 and Sanders 1986: xv).

As we have seen in earlier chapters, Martineau believed that the rational principles that should govern our actions are supplied by the invariant laws regulating the universe. In her earlier work, she thought that these laws descended from God; in her later work, she dispensed with God and thought that the highest level of knowledge to which we can rise is that of the laws of the universe. But in both phases she thought that it is by adhering to these laws that we can transcend selfish impulses and so act morally.

For Eliot, on the other hand, it is always emotions from which we act,[20] and so if we are to overcome selfishness this must be from an *emotional* source other than self-interest. That source is sympathy. Consider her well-known objection to maxims and general moral rules from *The Mill on the Floss*:

> All people of broad, strong sense have an instinctive repugnance to the men of maxims; because such people early discern that the mysterious complexity of our life is not to be embraced by maxims, and that to lace ourselves up in formulas of that sort is to repress all the divine promptings and inspirations that spring from growing insight and sympathy. And the man of maxims is the popular representative of the minds that are guided in their moral judgment solely by general rules, thinking that these will lead them to justice ... without ... the insight that comes from ... a life vivid and intense enough to have created a wide fellow-feeling with all that is human.   (*MF* 371)[21]

Reliance on rules is undesirable because it suppresses sympathy, which is the real basis of morality.

What is Eliot's view of sympathy? One way of conceptualizing it comes from T. H. Irwin (2013: 280–1), who breaks down sympathy as Eliot conceives it into *cognitive* sympathy, the imaginative grasp of what another person feels in a given situation (what in the twentieth century began to be called *empathy*);[22] *affective* sympathy, the tendency to feel what that other person feels; and *practical* sympathy, treating the other in a way that takes their interests into consideration. For Eliot, each of these dimensions of sympathy flows out of the one preceding it. In particular, what Irwin calls practical sympathy is at the root of morality because

---

[20] On the pervasive reality of the emotions in human life, Eliot says, for example: 'Men may dream in demonstrations, and cut out an illusory world in the shape of axioms, definitions, and propositions ... [T]he unemotional intellect may carry us into a mathematical dreamland where nothing is but what is not' (Eliot [1876] 2010: bk IV: 363). The passage reflects the influence of Lewes's claim that 'thinking is really a Mode of Sentience, a particular form of the general activity named Feeling' (1879: vol. 2: 10).

[21] This passage has been taken to show that Eliot is a moral particularist; Dancy calls Eliot the 'Patron Saint of Particularists' (Dancy 1993: 70; for discussion, see Fessenbecker 2018). I see Eliot more as a proponent of the ethics of sympathy (see also e.g. Burdett 2020). Relatedly, Albrecht (2020) reconceives Eliot's sympathy ethics in terms of a 'communion imperative'. See also the account of Eliot as a moral realist by Henberg (1979).

[22] *Empathy* was coined to better translate the German *Einfühlung*, previously translated *sympathy*; Schliesser (2015: 3).

one acts morally just when one acts unselfishly to enhance the other person's good. Eliot shares with Martineau this idea that properly moral action is unselfish or altruistic. While this equation became very widespread in later nineteenth-century Britain, Eliot and Martineau were both influenced in making it by Comte—in fact, the English word 'altruism' was coined by Lewes in one of his articles expounding Comte.[23] However, for Martineau, we achieve unselfishness by rising above the emotions through a rational grasp of universal laws, whereas Eliot thinks that altruistic action must still be motivated by the emotions. How, then, do we get from selfish emotional motivations to unselfish ones? Eliot's answer is: Through the imagination. For her, we can only be unselfishly concerned for the other person's good if we first apprehend what that good is from their independent perspective, and for this we need the imagination, with which we apprehend things from the other person's point of view (this is what Irwin called cognitive sympathy). We then come to feel as the other feels and become motivated to pursue the other person's good, making the transition from self-interested feelings to other-concerned ones.

For Eliot, therefore, the post-religious basis of morality lies in that which cultivates our power to imagine things from other people's perspectives: imaginative literature. As she puts it in the anonymous 1856 essay 'The Natural History of German Life', in one of the main statements of her aesthetic vision:

> The greatest benefit we owe to the artist, whether painter, poet, or novelist, is the extension of our sympathies. Appeals founded on generalisations and statistics require a sympathy ready-made, a moral sentiment already in activity; but a picture of human life such as a great artist can give, surprises even the trivial and the selfish into that attention to what is apart from themselves, which may be called the raw material of moral sentiment. (*NHGL* 54)

Admittedly, not all literature does this; Eliot denounces 'silly novels by lady novelists' (see Eliot 1856). The literature has to be constructed in the right way.

Above all, the literary work has to be 'realist': it must present the reality of the characters with which it deals. But what does this mean? During the 'aside' in *Adam Bede* that is another of Eliot's major aesthetic statements, she says of realism: 'It is for this rare, precious quality of truthfulness that I delight in many Dutch paintings.... I find a source of delicious sympathy in these faithful pictures of a monotonous homely existence' (*AB* 287). This still might not sound very illuminating, but the animating contrast is with didactic literature, of which Martineau's *Illustrations of Political Economy* were a central instance—perhaps *the* central instance. Thus Eliot clarifies: 'The thing for mankind to know is, not

---

[23] Lewes (1852: 618); see also Dixon (2008: 1). For Comte, '"altruism"... refers to selfless or other-regarding instincts, motives, or emotions' (Dixon 2008: 4).

what are the motives and influences which the moralist thinks *ought* to act on the labourer or the artisan, but what are the motives and influences which *do* act on him' (*NHGL* 54). And in *Adam Bede*: 'These fellow-mortals, every one, must be accepted as they are' (*AB* 286). A realist work depicts the real motives and concerns of characters without mixing in value judgements. This contrasts with Martineau's *Illustrations* in which, invariably, characters who fail or refuse to act on the necessary economic laws of life end up suffering as a result; the iron laws of political economy teach them a moral lesson.

Because Eliot on the other hand set out to depict people as they are, Martineau complained of her *Scenes of Clerical Life* that it 'leads one through moral squalor as bad as Dickens's physical squalor...I am sure it is bad art in both, – and in all such cases' (HM to Henry Reeve, 25 December 1859, *HMCL* 4: 207). Martineau went on to regard *Adam Bede* as bad art too, telling one of her correspondents about a conversation she had had with Eliot: for Eliot, 'true delineation is good art.... Being asked whether men on a raft eating a comrade would be good in art, she was silent' (HM to Reeve, 7 May 1861, *HMCL* 4: 274).[24] Martineau was an aesthetic moralist, as these letters make clear: she thought that art must be morally edifying to be aesthetically good. One should not simply delineate people committing bad actions without portraying them undergoing some sort of punishment or suffering as a direct consequence. From Eliot's perspective, though, the artist's task with the men on the raft is to bring out the desperation that drives them to cannibalism, arousing our sympathy for them in their dilemma of needing to commit a terrible act simply to survive. Contra Martineau, for Eliot 'true delineation' *fosters* morality because it expands our powers of sympathy. For this expansion to happen, we must put our moral rules and judgements into abeyance so as to pay attention to what the people represented actually feel and why they are acting as they are. To sympathize we must observe, and to observe we must put away the maxims, like Philip Wakem in the *Mill on the Floss*, who 'was given to observing individuals, not to judging of them according to maxims, and [so] no one knew better than he that all men were not like himself' (*MF* 190).

To understand why characters are feeling and acting as they are, we also need literary works to show us how their feelings and motivations are produced as causal effects of the social wholes to which the characters belong. This is where the conception of law comes into Eliot's thought. Like Martineau, she regards society as a whole, evolving and progressing necessarily under inexorable laws of motion (*PWR* 4–5). More broadly still, Eliot speaks of 'the great conception of universal regular sequence, without partiality and without caprice' (Eliot 1865: 55). These invariable regularities apply to the mind: 'that Mind presents itself

---

[24] Martineau softened when *Middlemarch* came out; she regarded it as a great advance (HM to unknown correspondent, 29 August 1873, *HMCL* 5: 321).

under the same condition of invariableness of antecedent and consequent as all other phenomena... I agree' (GE to Charles Bray, 15 November 1857, *GEL* II: 403). Consequently, all our actions are determined by motives, and motives are determined by prior causal chains. Nonetheless, Eliot rejects necessarianism: 'necessitarianism – I hate the ugly word' (GE to Mrs Ponsonby, 19 August 1875, *GEL* VI: 166). Eliot is instead a compatibilist. She distinguishes causation from compulsion, taking it that our actions are free when we perform them not under external duress but from motives arising internally within our minds (GE to Mrs Ponsonby, 10 December 1874, *GEL* VI: 98; see also Levine 1962).[25]

Because motives are causally determined by outer circumstances, the literary work can only show us why people feel as they do by depicting them as members of social wholes. Eliot does this most successfully in *Middlemarch* of 1872, which presents us with a panorama of characters drawn from different social strata. The reader comes to appreciate how these characters each feel, think, and act as they do because of the social forces shaping their past experiences and so, over time, their dispositions. For instance, we see how Rosamond Vincy acts as she does—vain, self-centred, preoccupied with her social standing—because she has been brought up to see climbing the social ladder as her number-one goal. We come to feel pity for her rather than simple condemnation. Invariant law thus figures quite differently in Eliot's picture from Martineau's. Eliot invokes laws to explain and make intelligible characters' actions and so arouse our sympathy for them, whereas in the *Illustrations* Martineau uses laws to distribute rewards and punishments to characters and so demonstrate to readers that the right way to act is on invariant laws.[26]

However, if the novel is to explain characters' actions and motivations by tracing them to invariable laws and social forces, this might suggest that the novel is taking the exterior point of view. For instance, the narrator of *Middlemarch* asks: 'Will not a tiny speck very close to our vision blot out the glory of the world, and leave only a margin by which we see the blot? I know no speck so troublesome as self' (Eliot [1872] 2016: 302). This might imply that the panoramic work of literature, told by an 'omniscient' narrator, stands back from all these 'specks'—the selves of the characters—and takes a higher viewpoint that transcends them all. Perhaps Eliot, like Martineau after all, thinks that the ultimate basis of morality is a knowledge of invariant laws and how individuals fall under them, where we overcome selfishness by rising to this disinterested and universal perspective.

---

[25] Of course, as we saw in Chapter 2, such necessarians as Priestley and the earlier Martineau were compatibilists. But by the 1850s Martineau had moved over to hard determinism, which likely influenced Eliot to identify necessarianism with hard determinism rather than the compatibilism that she favoured.

[26] In an important way, though, Martineau's *Illustrations* prefigured and made possible Eliot's aesthetic project: the *Illustrations* were about ordinary working people. Martineau was one of the first authors to put ordinary working people centre stage. Eliot shared this conviction that literature should depict ordinary people (*NHGL* 53–5). On this similarity, see Sanders (1986: ch. 1).

But although Eliot does sometimes employ devices in which the narrator stands back and surveys the whole scene, for the vast majority of her novels we move in and out of, and inhabit, each character's perspective in turn. To effect this she abundantly uses 'free indirect speech', in which the narrator blends their perspective seamlessly into that of each character in turn.[27] Many others such as Jane Austen and Elizabeth Gaskell had used free indirect speech before, but Eliot gives it philosophical significance as the means by which we come to see things from many points of view so that our sympathies are expanded. Or as she puts it: 'Art is the nearest thing to life; it is a mode of amplifying experience and extending our contact with our fellow-men beyond the bounds of our personal lot' (*NHGL* 54). With literature's aid, we can come to experience the world as others experience it, to feel what they feel. This is not the point of view of the outside but that of many insides.

As we saw earlier, for Eliot: 'A picture of human life such as a great artist can give, surprises even the ... selfish into that attention to what is apart from themselves, which may be called the raw material of moral sentiment' (*NHGL* 54). Literature, then, gives us only the 'raw material' of moral sentiment. We still need to get from sympathy for fictional characters to practical manifestations of sympathy for others in real life. But this transition happens almost automatically, because literature develops in us dispositions and habits of sympathy which we inevitably transpose onto the real people around us. In addition, Eliot's realism is again relevant here. By showing us realistic characters located in a social world obeying the same laws and at the same stage of historical evolution as our own, as *Middlemarch* does, the novel helps us to recognize similar types of people around us and to see comparable social forces at work in their dispositions and actions, fostering our sympathy for them.

We can now see that Myers's characterization of Eliot was not altogether accurate. The stern emphasis on rational principles with which Myers credits her would have better fitted Martineau. Eliot, in contrast, was an ethical sentimentalist. For her, literature needs to replace religion as the basis of morality because morality rests on sympathy, sympathy requires imagination, and literature cultivates imaginative sympathy with others. The amplified perspectives fostered by literature are worked up from 'raw material' into real moral sentiment when we transfer them from the fictional realm into social life.

Finally, Eliot thought that literature should displace religion as the source of morality in another way too. Julia Wedgwood points this out in her insightful 1881 essay, 'The Moral Influence of George Eliot' (*NCT* 225–41). As we saw, through her reading of Feuerbach, Eliot came to think that the needs and desires of ordinary, finite, embodied human beings are at the heart of ethics. This

---

[27] My thanks to Patrick Fessenbecker for clarifying to me the importance of free indirect speech in Eliot's work; see Fessenbecker (2021: 287).

conviction, Wedgwood says, pervades Eliot's novels. The characters with whom Eliot most arouses our sympathies are the ordinary ones—not exalted or exceptional individuals but everyday people pursuing mundane concerns, seeking happiness, yet caught up haplessly in chains of cause and effect beyond their control. Eliot immerses us in the finite world and the this-worldly hopes and aspirations of its inhabitants. When these characters do have religious feelings and hopes, Eliot treats them as part of the motivational furniture of the secular world, rather than placing the secular world in any relation to a divine world. Eliot does away with any transcendent axis; she concentrates our attention horizontally on this life and on characters whose attentions are likewise horizontally focused upon their this-worldly relationships with one another. This, Wedgwood says, is another reason why Eliot is determined to focus her novels on ordinary people—so as to keep our orientation horizontal. Literature is the vehicle through which Eliot reorientates our attention and energies away from the religious domain and towards secular life.[28]

5.4 Cobbe's Case Against Atheism

Cobbe wrote 'Magnanimous Atheism' (1877) in response to Martineau's *Autobiography*, opposing a swathe of secular moralists, including Martineau and Eliot as well as the arch-positivist Frederic Harrison.[29] Cobbe opposed them because ever since *Intuitive Morals* she had believed that moral obligations derive from an absolute moral law, which presupposes a divine legislator, without whom the law would not be absolute—if we were the legislators, then we could take the law away again whenever it suited us (*IM* 10–11). Cobbe therefore thought that Martineau's and Eliot's secularism would inevitably destroy any possibility of morality. They believed otherwise of course, but Cobbe thought they were wrong. Some of her main arguments against them were as follows.

Personal immortality. Martineau was content that the universe should roll on without her after she died, but Cobbe objects that we have good reasons to fear death: it threatens to part us forever from those we love (*AM* 794). We need to believe in an afterlife to reassure us that the separation is only temporary. We also need this belief to reconcile us to the sufferings, and moral failings and injustices, we see around us. Cobbe had argued in *Intuitive Morals* that we can only reconcile God's having made us for virtue with the fact that people are often vicious if we all have immortal souls that go on making moral progress after we die (*IM* 39–43).

---

[28] Wedgwood was implicitly criticizing Eliot, for she took the aspiration towards a transcendent horizon to be integral to human life and history, as we will see in Chapter 6.
[29] Here Cobbe describes Martineau and Eliot as atheists and later, in 'Agnostic Morality', she would classify them as agnostics. This typifies how atheism and agnosticism were run together at the time.

Without this conviction, our moral strivings will come to seem futile given all the evils we see in the world. For Cobbe, then, we need a religious framework to make suffering tolerable and give us hope (*MA* 46–52). Ironically, Martineau would deprive us of the religious perspective that we need if we are to feel the calm equanimity about death that she advocated.

Selfishness and posthumous rewards. Martineau contended that Christianity reduces virtue to selfishness by motivating people to act virtuously only for the sake of rewards in the afterlife. Cobbe objects that this is a misunderstanding: 'when Agnostics boast of the superior disinterestedness of the virtue they inculcate over that of religious men, they think (and cannot divest themselves of the early acquired habit of thinking) of religion as of this kind of labor-and-wages system' (*MA* 24). In fact, the posthumous 'reward' for a virtuous life is not happiness in a material sense, because in the afterlife we will no longer be embodied.[30] The only posthumous reward for virtue is more virtue. This will only make us happy if we already value virtue for its own sake, and we can only learn to do that on a Christian basis.

To understand why Cobbe thinks this, we must go back to her moral theory. For Cobbe, we must do what is right just because it is right. We must also do what is right because God legislates it, but, since God is righteous, he legislates what is right anyway, so obedience to God and to the right converge (*IM* 53). However, Cobbe's strong emphasis that the moral law is right in itself and on doing duty for duty's sake can create the impression that her moral theory extols empty rule-following, since the right is not to be done for the sake of securing any good. But her response to Martineau shows that, for Cobbe, the duty to do what is right for its own sake generates a duty to reshape one's character and desires—to cultivate the virtues, such as 'purity, truth, temperance and contentment' (*MA* 58). I must cultivate these traits so that I will reliably be motivated to obey the moral law. Once I have these traits, obeying the law will make me happy. So there is a place for the good life in Cobbe's theory, but we attain a virtuous and happy life only by first doing what is right for its own sake.

Virtue presupposes a Christian culture. Cobbe praises Martineau and Eliot as highly virtuous individuals (e.g. *MA* 46; *AM* 792), but their virtue does not show that morality has no need of religion. Rather, these two women were only able to be virtuous because they were steeped in Christianity. Biography aside, their philosophical ideas bear out Cobbe's point. Martineau's exterior point of view remained indebted to Unitarianism, as we saw; and, although Eliot claimed to be extracting the secular kernel—human-to-human fellowship—from the Christian shell—divine-to-human relations, the kernel still owed much to the shell. The idea that we act morally just when we escape narrow selfishness, see things as other

---

[30] Cobbe had argued in 'The Life After Death' that disembodied personal survival was more intelligible than the idea that we will have new kinds of spiritual bodies in the afterlife (*HHR* 1–120).

people see them, and help others to reach the goods for which they are struggling, sounds suspiciously like the Christian ideal of selfless love. For Eliot, however, that ideal had always been at root secular—'the idea of God, so far as it has been a high spiritual influence, is the ideal of a goodness entirely human' (GE to Mrs Ponsonby, 10 December 1874, *GEL* VI: 98). From this Feuerbach-influenced perspective it was not unselfish concern for others that was indebted to Christianity, but Christianity that had given a distorting religious slant to an unselfish concern for others that is 'entirely human'. Cobbe, though, denies that there is any such ahistorical human-to-human fellowship. Our different ways of treating one another and levels of sympathy with and hostility towards one another have a history, and they have changed historically in tandem with different religious outlooks (*HHM* 155–7). Arguably, then, those who would extract a secular core from the Christian wrapping are really only extracting one part of the historical edifice of Christianity from the rest of it, but where the part ultimately still belongs to this whole fabric. Hence, Cobbe concludes, Martineau, Eliot, and other virtuous agnostics 'are yet obeying the great impetus of religion, and running along the rails laid down by our forefathers' (*MA* 64).

Cobbe makes a key concession, however: that she has not shown that atheism is false but that the moral consequences of it becoming widely adopted would be disastrous. We might wonder whether this is exactly the sort of appeal to consequences that Cobbe professes to oppose. If in fact we are to pursue the truth for its own sake, then perhaps by Cobbe's own standards the truly virtuous stance is to adopt atheism simply because it is true, regardless of the consequences. This became the basis of Vernon Lee's response to Cobbe.

5.5 The Lee–Cobbe Debate

Vernon Lee was from an English family but was born and raised in mainland Europe. She belongs in this book because she published in British print and periodical culture, and engaged in the English-speaking debates that took place in the British journals. She came to acclaim with her first book *Studies of the Eighteenth Century in Italy* (1880), swiftly followed by *Belcaro: Sundry Essays on Aesthetical Questions* (1881). By then she had already adopted her pseudonym, feeling 'sure that no one reads a woman's writing on art, history or aesthetics with anything other than unmitigated contempt' (VL to Mrs Jenkin, 18 December 1878, *SLVL* 1: 244). Like Eliot, Lee retained the masculine pseudonym long after being exposed as a woman. She had an ideal of 'true women...women without woman's instincts and wants, sexless – women made not for man but for humankind' (Lee 1884: vol. 2: 309). The persona of Vernon Lee allowed her to approximate to this ideal.

Having made her name, Lee began to spend regular periods in England from the 1880s onwards, while retaining Italy as her base. She became part of the aestheticist social circles which included Walter Pater, the expatriate Henry James, and the ubiquitous later-century presence, Mary Ward (a.k.a. Mrs Humphry Ward). Lee affiliated herself with aestheticism in her 1881 essay 'Ruskinism', stating that beauty and goodness are categorically distinct:

> beauty is a quality independent of goodness, independent sometimes to the extent of hostility.... Beauty, in itself, is neither morally good nor morally bad; it is aesthetically good, even as virtue is neither aesthetically good nor aesthetically bad, but morally good. (*Bel* 210)

However, Lee began to distance herself from aestheticism with her 1884 novel *Miss Brown*, 'a scathing satire of the Aesthetic movement and its London devotees' (Maxwell and Pulham 2006: xvii).[31] Lee now looked for ways to maintain that art and ethics—or, as she preferred to put it, beauty and goodness—were necessarily connected, without returning to the aesthetic moralism of figures such as Martineau. Lee theorized beauty–goodness relations in successive ways, broadly holding that the more beautiful an artwork is the more it conduces to various forms of moral goodness in the recipient (see e.g. Lee 1896).

Lee's vexed relations with aestheticism and particularly the male aestheticists have received scholarly attention.[32] But it is rarely noted that Lee also admired and took up a position relative to Cobbe. Lee and Cobbe first met and became friends in Italy in 1878, after which point Lee eagerly visited Cobbe when in England (see *SLVL* 1). Their exchanges informed Lee's dialogue 'The Responsibilities of Unbelief: A Conversation of Three Rationalists', published in the *Contemporary Review* in May 1883.

This was one of numerous philosophical dialogues that Lee wrote in the earlier 1880s, several of which were published in the *Contemporary Review* and were collected in *Baldwin: Being Dialogues on Views and Aspirations* (1886). The topics

---

[31] Wedgwood reviewed *Miss Brown*. Lee arranged this review, being eager to get Wedgwood's view because Wedgwood was one of her role models of a woman-as-critic (VL to Mr Bunting, 30 December 1884, *SLVL* 1: 616, and see *SLVL* 1: 605). Wedgwood had taken Martineau as a role model, and now Lee did the same with Wedgwood (though Lee admired Martineau's 'fine career' too; VL to Linda Villari, 30 July 1879, *SLVL* 1: 253–4). However, Wedgwood's review was not favourable. She found *Miss Brown* overly intellectual, preferring Lee's non-fiction and saying that the issues dealt with in *Miss Brown* would have been better addressed non-fictionally. In the novel, Wedgwood wrote, Lee 'exhibits the debasing influence of the worship of *beauty*' in its male protagonist Walter Hamlin (Wedgwood 1885: 749), who treats wicked and horrifying things as being just as valuable as beautiful or admirable ones, so long as they arouse sensuous thrills and are interesting rather than commonplace. Lee intended to critique Hamlin. However, Wedgwood objected, by making this flawed character her protagonist, Lee despite herself presumed that a depiction of something interesting (i.e. Hamlin) had aesthetic value despite being morally unedifying. Further, by addressing the relation between art and ethics in a novel, Lee reduced it to the purely aesthetic matter that she said it was not: 'It is impossible to look on such subjects as she has touched merely from the point of view of art; the very degradation of the world she paints is that it has ceased to look on any subject from any other point of view' (749).

[32] See e.g. Maxwell and Pulham (2006) and Zorn (2003).

ranged beyond aesthetics: *Baldwin* addressed secularism, life after death, the problem of evil, the purpose of art and literature, anti-vivisectionism, evolutionary theory, and pessimism. The main interlocutor throughout was Baldwin, Lee's mouthpiece, of whom, she said, 'I agree in all his ideas' (*B* 13).

In 'The Responsibilities of Unbelief' Baldwin's interlocutors are Rheinhardt and Vere. Rheinhardt is an irreverent, flippant atheist who regards all religion as baleful dross and sees only good in its demise. Rheinhardt holds that if morality goes under with religion as it must, then so much the better, for the loss of both liberates us to concentrate on pursuing intellectual and aesthetic pleasure—he is both an aestheticist and an amoralist. Lee portrays him unsympathetically, as taking a belittling, mocking attitude to important concerns; this is part of her critique of aestheticism. Rheinhardt eventually bows out of the conversation, unable to engage with the serious matters discussed by the other two. The heart of the dialogue unfolds between Vere, who holds on to religious beliefs for their moral and emotional consolations, and Baldwin, who urges sober atheism and confronting the secular truth, harsh as it is.

Vere, I suggest, represents Cobbe. There is direct evidence of this in Lee's correspondence. In June 1883, just after 'Responsibilities' had come out, Lee reported that she had received a 'most strange letter from Miss Cobbe,...I had written solely about her views of God and an afterlife and cannot conceive what in the world she means' (VL to Matilda Paget, 30 June 1883, *SLVL* 1: 428). Whatever Cobbe's 'strange letter' said, it must be 'Responsibilities' to which Lee refers when saying that she had written about Cobbe's religious views—so that it must be Cobbe whom Vere represents. And in June 1883 Lee said that Cobbe's response to her dialogue (discussed below) had confirmed her view that 'persons of Miss Cobbe's mode of thinking', by making 'appeals to the emotional and moral feelings...may entirely divert half emancipated and wavering minds from scientific beliefs' (VL to Thomas Escott, 7 June 1883, *SLVL* 1: 417).[33]

Furthermore, Vere expresses many views that Cobbe held. Vere maintains that religion has subjective value; it may be false objectively, but it answers to our subjective needs (*B* 47). We need something to hope for and a sense of overarching meaning to console us for suffering. In particular, it is horrifying that those we love should be annihilated at death; love leads us inevitably to hope for an afterlife and to trust that God would not have made us capable of love without giving us immortal souls (*B* 53). Cobbe had argued just this: if we have loved anyone enough to want to go on being with them, we cannot fail to desire immortality: 'not to

---

[33] Moreover, Baldwin took up the position of the sober atheist in contrast to that of the jubilant atheist, which Cobbe had criticized and associated with Martineau. Cobbe described Martineau's agnosticism as being at 'the *jubilant* stage' (*AM* 783; my emphasis). Lee must have known of Cobbe's criticisms of Martineau, for in 1879 Lee said that she had at last read Martineau's *Autobiography* and encountered at first hand her '*jubilation* at the discovery that she had no soul and consequently no afterlife' (VL to Linda Villari, 30 July 1879, *SLVL* 1: 253–4; my emphasis).

desire to meet again the being we profess to love supremely seems to be a contradiction' (*MA* 69).

Baldwin answers that 'increasing truth is the law of increasing good'—that is, really to increase the amount of good in the world, we must first believe what is in fact the case; it is cowardice not to do so (*B* 48). Moreover, he tells Vere, he too has undergone the horrors of bereavement. He suffered horribly when a friend of his died. But, looking to nature for consolation, he found it indifferent. Even so we must face facts: nature *is* indifferent.

Vere protests: surely Baldwin cannot be saying that we are to act in accordance with nature, for 'this same Nature...is for ever committing evil greater than any of us can commit' (62). Nature is merely 'the battlefield or the playground of physical forces, without thought or conscience' (60); the only standard of action it supplies is one of cruelty, caprice, and chaotic destruction. Vere's concerns here recall Cobbe's satire of the 'morals of evolution'—'Nature is extremely cruel, but we cannot do better than follow Nature' (*MR* 66)—and her fear that a moral code derived from evolution would be one 'in which every cruelty and every injustice may form a part' (*DM* 39).

Baldwin replies that nature is indifferent, but not cruel or evil, for nature cannot rightly be regarded under moral lights at all or attributed any moral properties (*B* 66-7). Indeed, he came through his crisis over his friend's death by realizing that he had been wrongly looking for moral qualities in nature. But he did not retreat from nature to the supernatural—as Vere is recommending—but delved into the scientific study of nature, determined to recognize nature for what it really is. This further reinforced his recognition that morality is nowhere to be found in nature.

But neither, Baldwin continues, is morality of divine origin (*pace* Vere and Cobbe). Morality is an exclusively human phenomenon, made by humans to enable them to live together. Because morality is a human *creation*, its proper *object* of concern is humanity; being made *by* human agents, it must be made *for* human agents. Thus its aim and object is human welfare, or the general happiness. Moral rules, then, are rules that tell us how best to increase the general happiness (*B* 67-8). Or as Baldwin puts it in the next dialogue 'The Consolations of Belief', 'Morality is a necessity grown out of social life, [and] the only duties of man are towards the mortal creatures of the present and future' (117). Our duty is not to serve the moral law for its own sake or for the sake of our souls in the afterlife, but to contribute to improving human lives in this world.

Of course, Baldwin continues, it is tempting to embrace consolatory illusions, but doing so is 'mean and cowardly'. We are responsible not only for increasing the general happiness but also for facing the truth. However, the truth once confronted proves less lonely and harsh than we feared. Having appreciated that morality is a human institution that allows us to live together and help one another, we come to experience ourselves as part of an immense evolutionary process in which the human species is advancing along with its moral institutions:

... [T]he school of philosophy to which I adhere has traced all the distinctions of right and wrong to the perceptions, enforced upon man by mankind, ... of the difference between such courses as are conducive to the higher development and greater happiness of men, and such other courses as are conducive only to their degradation and extinction. Such a belief, so far from ... making me doubt of my own moral nature, brings home to me that I am but a drop in the great moral flood called progress; ... that my morality is an essential contribution to the morality of millions of creatures who will come after me ... (B 78)

The loss of religion, then, does not leave us isolated in a meaningless world. On the contrary, it reveals in a new way how we are bound together with others—free from the illusions of the divine world, we rejoin the human world and find ourselves reunited with one another.

In 'Responsibilities', then, Lee locates herself with neither Rheinhardt's aestheticism nor Vere's Cobbeian theism but with a third alternative: secular ethics. For Lee, secularism does not entail amoralism or immorality but puts morality on a new basis as the human institution that cements our collective life, a position that involved a loose alliance of utilitarianism and evolutionary theory.

Cobbe replied with 'Agnostic Morality' in the *Contemporary Review* in June 1883. Cobbe heralds Baldwin's 'sober sadness' as being a step up from Martineau's jubilation (AM 783), but she makes several objections. Baldwin can find no divine presence or moral norms in nature because he is looking in the wrong place; he should look to the inner world of spirit and conscience (784). Instead, approaching the inner world from an external, third-person standpoint, he reduces conscience to a depository of inherited impulses registering what, contingently, has been useful to the human species over time. But, Cobbe maintains—as she had argued previously apropos of Darwin—the ideas of duty and utility are distinct. We have duties to do things that are not and have never been useful; for instance, to show compassion for the weak, infirm, and frail. And there are things that would be useful to the human race—namely to sacrifice the weak, infirm, and frail—that are nonetheless wrong (789).

According to Cobbe, Baldwin is wrong to consider it a 'moral tonic' that there is no afterlife and that the only arena in which we can do good is this world; actually, this is morally enervating (792). If there is no afterlife, then everyone's life will soon be over without a trace, however well or ill that life has gone and however rightly or wrongly the person has acted. Moral actions and distinctions will lose their weight and the moral importance of life will be diminished. This is not to say that we should believe in the afterlife merely as a fiction that throws an enhancing veil over this life. Rather: 'That love which invents immortality is ... the pledge and witness of immortality. It is the Infinite stirring within the finite breast' (794). We only long for immortality because there really is an immortal kernel within us that strains beyond our mortal limitations.

Perhaps most decisively, Cobbe argues that Baldwin's responsibilities to pursue the truth and further the happiness of others depend on the Christianity that he rejects. Baldwin urges honesty and truthfulness; these are personal virtues. We do have a duty to develop virtues of character, Cobbe agrees, but that duty depends on the moral law, for virtues of character are the qualities and capacities that enable us to realize the moral law and that come about when we follow and internalize it (*DW* lec. II). Only if there is a transcendent moral law, legislated by God, can we have an obligation to value truth for its own sake whatever the consequences, and a concomitant obligation to develop the character trait of truthfulness. Overall, Cobbe concludes, 'Vernon Lee feels deeply the "responsibilities of unbelief". But are not such sentiments the last failing wail of melody from a chord already snapped?' (*AM* 790). And since in fact the chord has snapped—because Lee has rejected the keynote, Christianity—Baldwin's outlook is doomed to collapse into Rheinhardt's nihilistic indifference to all values.

The conversation did not end there. Lee immediately penned a reply. The *Fortnightly Review* rejected it (*SLVL* 1: 417–18, 1: 454–5), so she rewrote it as 'The Consolations of Belief', in which Baldwin defended sober atheism again, this time against Agatha who represented Cobbe. Lee then sent it to the *Contemporary Review*, who again rejected it (*SLVL* 1: 514). Eventually it became the second dialogue in *Baldwin*.[34]

I have only ventured a very little way here into Lee's huge body of work. But the parts of it that we have looked at bear on her broader oeuvre in significant ways. In particular, the ethical stance that Lee began to develop in these dialogues with Cobbe went on to inform the consequentialist and evolutionary connection she made between beauty and goodness in 'Art and Life' (1896). Here she argued that beautiful artworks foster altruism, a sense of harmony, and a flourishing life in the individuals who experience them. The more beautiful an artwork is, the better its consequences for human happiness, our treatment of one another, and our sense of belonging together; beautiful artworks foster the ongoing evolution of human connectedness. In this way the exchange with Cobbe was important for the development of Lee's aesthetic thought.[35]

---

[34] As Lee says, the dialogue 'was suggested to me by Miss Cobbe's remarks on my previous paper' (VL to Mr Bunting, 1 March 1884, *SLVL* 1: 508). See also Donald (2019: 196–7) on the Cobbe–Agatha equation. Agatha, like Vere, says many things that Cobbe said. I discuss Lee's 'Consolations of Belief' in Stone (2022b). The third *Baldwin* dialogue, 'Of Honour and Evolution', was also a rejoinder to Cobbe, arguing that evolutionism provided a basis for anti-vivisectionism, whereas Cobbe thought evolutionism justified vivisection as part of the 'survival of the strongest'.

[35] Lee continued to write on ethical topics, bringing out *Althea: A Second Book of Dialogues on Aspirations and Duties* in 1894. Cobbe may, moreover, have influenced Lee in moving away from aestheticism. Cobbe loved *Miss Brown*, unlike most readers recognizing that it broke ranks with aestheticism. Late in 1884 Lee was still protesting, 'I cannot join in your animosity against aestheticism', which 'has on the whole been a most healthy and useful movement' (VL to FPC, December 1884, *SLVL* 1: 608). But by 1886 Lee was asking Cobbe to introduce her to more practical people than the 'aesthetes, with whom I have broken entirely' (VL to FPC, 26 April 1886, *SLVL* 2: 26–7).

5.6 The Besant–Cobbe Debate

Cobbe's religious stance came in for criticism from Besant during the latter's secularist phase. We have looked before at some of Besant's philosophical grounds for converting to theosophy in 1889; now we move back to her earlier secularist period. This in turn had been preceded by an evangelical phase. Besant then underwent a crisis of faith, but she managed to preserve her religious convictions by turning to the Theism of Cobbe and like-minded others in the early 1870s (*ABA* 106–7). Yet Besant's doubts returned again, exacerbated by reading Comte. In 1874 she took the plunge, joined the National Secular Society, and became an atheist. She understood atheism very similarly to Martineau: because all knowledge derives from the senses, we cannot possibly know about God, but therefore we have no grounds for affirming that he exists at all. 'The position of the Atheist is a clear and a reasonable one: "I know nothing about 'God,' and *therefore I do not believe in Him* or in it [my emphasis];...I am without God"' (*ABA* 145).

The similarity to Martineau registers a historical continuity. The National Secular Society had come about through the long-term efforts of George Holyoake, although he then lost control of the society to Charles Bradlaugh, whom Besant joined at the helm from 1874 onwards. Back in the late 1840s and early 1850s Holyoake had been close to Martineau. Like her, he was influenced by positivism, and he co-founded *The Leader* with Lewes and others. Earlier still, in 1846, Holyoake had founded the journal *The Reasoner*, in which he introduced the word 'secularism' in 1851. He did so in the context of defending Martineau and Atkinson's *Letters on the Laws of Man's Nature and Development*, an exceptional stance at the time. Holyoake maintained that 'secularism' was the best word for Martineau's stance in that book. She was *not* a dogmatic atheist but a secularist, Holyoake said, and in turn admirers of Martineau had grounds to embrace secularism (Holyoake 1851a: 363, 1851b: 88, 1852a: 34, 1852b: 88).[36] Martineau reciprocated by defending Holyoake when he faced criticism in the American press. She said that:

> The adoption of the term Secularism is justified by its including a large number of persons who are not Atheists, and uniting them for action which has Secularism for its object, and not Atheism. On this ground...the use of the name Secularism is found advantageous. (Martineau 1853: 186)

Elsewhere Martineau stated: 'I am, in fact, (if one must take a name) a *secularist*' (HM to Charles Kingsley, 27 June 1851, *HMCL* 3: 236).[37] However, as we have

---

[36] On Holyoake, Martineau, and secularism, see also Zuckerman and Shook (2017).
[37] See also HM to Holyoake, 17 May 1854 and 15 February 1855, *HMCL* 3: 320–1 and 349. When she expected to die soon, Martineau looked into the option of a secularist funeral.

seen, she also called herself a philosophical atheist. Thus, for Martineau, secularism and atheism shaded together, whereas Holyoake was trying to distinguish the former from the latter. Two decades later Bradlaugh and Besant again pulled them together,[38] which was one source of their disagreement with Holyoake, who was still striving for a more moderate position.

Having joined the Society, Besant signalled her new-found atheism with a talk in September 1874, 'The True Basis of Morality'. This was published as a pamphlet first by Bradlaugh's secularist ally Charles Watts and then, in 1882, by the Freethought Publishing Company, which Besant and Bradlaugh established in 1877.[39] Because Besant was here turning against her former inspiration Cobbe, she used much of the essay to criticize Cobbe's intuitionism and argue that utilitarianism provides a better and more scientific foundation for morality.

Besant argues that intuition is merely subjective and cannot inform us about objective moral truths. We can tell that intuition is subjective from the fact that people find completely different things intuitive in different times, places, and cultures. So, 'is there any particular reason why *our* intuition should be *the* intuition?' (*TBM* 7). Cobbe's answer—according to Besant—is that the intuitions of modern civilized Europeans are the right ones (8). But why are they right? Besant replies that they are 'the result of transmitted moral tendencies ... [that] arise from our ancestors having done [certain] actions for generation after generation' (8). That is, these 'intuitions' are our inherited moral responses, embodying accumulated human experience of what has proven useful to the social group over long periods of time. In other words, the moral principles to which Cobbe appeals are actually right because they provide reliable guidance about what most increases the general happiness. The explanation for why these 'intuitions' should be followed is utilitarian, *pace* Cobbe whose assertion that they are intuitive is just that—a bare assertion. Utilitarianism, unlike Cobbe, offers a reasoned and scientific approach—where the method of science is observation, induction, and deduction (9). We start by gathering repeated observations about human beings, from which we frame the inductive generalization that everyone wants happiness, from which we deduce that the right thing to do is whatever increases the general happiness. This provides a scientific basis for morality, which is more secure than the old religious one because God's existence is uncertain and contested. In

---

[38] All this raises the question of whether Besant was influenced by Martineau, especially as Besant published *Auguste Comte: His Philosophy, His Religion, and His Sociology* in 1885, apparently following in Martineau's footsteps. Yet although Besant drew readily on Lewes's expositions of Comte, she only referred to Martineau when extolling her as one of the century's great intellectual women alongside Mary Somerville, Eliot, Harriet Taylor Mill, and Cobbe (*AC* 17; *AS* 333).

[39] On Besant's talk and its history, see *ABA* 153–6 and Nethercot (1960: 81). Watts and Bradlaugh divided over the birth-control pamphlet, which led Bradlaugh and Besant to found the Freethought Publishing Company so as to wrest control of secularist publishing away from Watts. The birth-control pamphlet also further estranged Holyoake from Bradlaugh and Besant. Like so many political movements, secularism was beset by schisms.

contrast, we *can* know about human beings, and what they do and want, since these are matters we can observe with our senses (14–16).

Besant's arguments might strike us as simplistic, but more charitably we can view her as bold and direct. Furthermore, it was very common in the nineteenth century to regard utilitarianism as an empirical and inductive approach to morality—as Mill did as well, for instance, aligning utilitarianism with the 'inductive school' as opposed to the 'intuitive' one ([1861] 1998). Utilitarianism's empirical basis was often seen as a selling-point. Besant merely stated this view with characteristic frankness.

Cobbe heard Besant present 'The True Basis of Morality', was 'greatly offended', and 'would have left...had not the speaker been a woman', Besant recalled (*AS* 161–2). Besant's new-found atheism flowed into the rising tide of secularism about which Cobbe had been concerned in 'Magnanimous Atheism'. She tried once again to stem the tide in 'A Faithless World' of 1884. Cobbe framed this essay, though, in explicit opposition to James Fitzjames Stephen, not Besant, although Cobbe did include a passing reference to Bradlaugh. Why did she not mention Besant? The answer comes out when Cobbe explains in 1894 why she changed the publisher of her autobiography. Her initially intended outlet was also bringing out Besant's autobiography, 'a woman I specially dread – & with whom it would be too good fire for my enemies to bracket me in the reviews' (FPC to Sarah Wister, 7 June 1894, quoted in Williamson 2005: 193). Cobbe's reputation was by now embattled by her anti-vivisectionism; she needed to distance herself from the even more controversial 'Red Annie'. This exemplifies the overall pattern for women to bolster their own contested credibility by referencing men, not other women—and in Stephen's case, a very authoritative figure and bastion of the legal and intellectual establishment.[40]

Cobbe takes issue with Stephen's claim that abandoning Christianity would make little difference to us and leave life's many goods unaffected (*FW* 796). It is easy to take this view at the moment, Cobbe says, because a Christian culture remains in place. The individual can think they have left it behind while failing to appreciate how thoroughly the surrounding social world remains shaped by Christianity. It will take over a thousand years of atheism before its devastating consequences will be plain to see.

> Atheists have hitherto been like children playing at the mouth of a cavern of unknown depth. They have run in and out, and explored it a little way, but always within sight of the daylight outside...Not till the way back to the sunshine has been lost will the darkness of that cave be fully revealed. (*FW* 799)

---

[40] On Stephen, see Smith (1988).

Cobbe deliberately uses the cave metaphor in the opposite way to Martineau. For the latter, we escape the cave of religious illusions and torments into the daylight of science and happiness. Conversely, for Cobbe, it is atheists who are leading us out of the sunlight of God's love into a dark, cold cave. For both, following Plato, the cave represents illusion and the sunlit outer world represents truth; but Cobbe locates that truth with religion whereas Martineau locates it with science.[41]

These cave/sunlight metaphors lead into Cobbe's central arguments. Stephen had referred to life's many goods. Cobbe replies that these are all finite and single whereas religion, like the sun, offers an overall perspective on life's meaning. Without this religious horizon, life will be belittled and people will have nothing to aspire to; human life will be reduced to the body, either to hedonistic bodily pleasures or the misplaced worship of bodily health that Cobbe called 'hygeiolatry'; nature will be disenchanted; art will become trivial and obscene; people will seek ease, not challenges, virtue, or self-improvement; moral choices will become unimportant: 'the temperature of all moral sentiments will fall so considerably when the sun of religion ceases to warm them that not a few will perish of cold' (*FW* 804). Suffering will become unbearable because we will have nothing better to hope for, and love will become intolerably painful and be eschewed because we will have no hope of being reunited with our loved ones after death. The atheist future, in short, is very bleak indeed.[42]

Besant subjects this essay to merciless critique in her 1885 essay 'A World Without God: A Reply to Miss Frances Power Cobbe', published as a free-standing pamphlet by Bradlaugh and Besant's Freethought Publishing Company. Recalling Baldwin's rejoinder to Vere, Besant argues that even if religion does provide a total framework of meaning, that framework is still false and so it must be rejected (*WWG* 6–7). Indeed, as well as being false, the framework is damaging. Far from encouraging us to act morally and unselfishly, it effectively discourages moral action as pointless, by teaching us that life is a vale of tears and that people's sufferings must be part of God's plan. Conversely: 'There is every hope of righting earth's wrongs and of curing earth's pains if the reason and skill of man which have already done so much are free to do the rest' (20). It is *atheism*, not Christianity, that fosters hope and an active spirit of improvement. Indeed, Cobbe herself admits that many atheists act morally; surely 'the obvious conclusion ... is that the two thing[s], belief and conduct, are not causally related' (8), rather than that the conduct rests on unacknowledged belief as Cobbe maintains.

Moreover, Besant continues, much of the institutional social fabric that Cobbe fears would disintegrate without Christianity will survive and be repurposed to

---

[41] Nietzsche, like Martineau, compares religion's persistence to the dark cave, and its demise to dawn and daylight: 'After Buddha was dead people showed his shadow for centuries afterwards in a cave, an immense frightful shadow. God is dead: – but ... there will perhaps be caves for millenniums yet, in which people will show his shadow' ([1882] 2001: sec. 108).

[42] For a more detailed account, see Stone (2022a).

serve the Religion of Humanity; churches, for instance, will become places for celebrating humanity's powers; social duties will still be inculcated. Many of the goods and values that Cobbe thinks will wither and die without a religious background will actually flourish when freed from religion. Art will flourish, having returned to its real inspiration, nature; literature will reach new heights, no longer having to refer constantly back to the Bible. Altruistic acts will be done not for posthumous rewards to the self but directly for others, to increase their happiness and that of the whole group. Love between humans will flourish, relieved from dismal assumptions about sin. Human life overall will flourish, for we will all be concentrating on this life and on making it better (13–16).

Finally, one of Besant's most telling arguments is the following. Previously, Cobbe distinguished her 'system of Theism' from the primitive violence of the Bible and from the Church's historic injustices and hierarchies (see Cobbe 1864). Now, however, Cobbe is endorsing much of the institutionalized Christendom that she formerly rejected—for example, she now portrays the Bible as the source of all English literature and churches as the centre of community life. After all, she now takes the view that Christianity is our total horizon of meaning, and this is only plausible if 'Christianity' means *not* rationally reconstructed Theism but the whole of institutionalized Christendom (*WWG* 3–4, 7). But, as Cobbe herself had previously recognized, the latter is rife with immorality, injustice, and oppression; it is not a viable foundation for morality. Cobbe can either have a rationally reconstructed and morally purified Christianity, but then it does not furnish our whole horizon of life and value; or she can have a Christendom that furnishes our whole horizon, but then it is replete with immorality.

Either way, Besant concludes, Cobbe cannot rightly claim that morality depends necessarily on Christianity. If Christianity is chiselled down to Cobbeian Theism, then this specific framework cannot plausibly be said to be underpinning everybody's lives. Conversely, if Christianity is an all-encompassing horizon, then it encompasses much immorality, suffering, and inequality. All things considered, morality would be best set free from Christianity, and so Besant reasserts Martineau's joyful atheism: 'This joyous, self-reliant facing of the world with the resolute determination to improve it is characteristic of the noblest Atheism of our day' (*ABA* 167).

5.7 Evaluation and Comparison

As we have seen, one of Cobbe's central criticisms of Martineau and Eliot was that their ostensibly secularist ethical standpoints remained tacitly dependent on Christianity. I agreed that, indeed, Martineau's exterior point of view owed much to Unitarianism, and that although Eliot understood her ethic of unselfish sympathy to be the (secular) kernel secreted *within* Christianity, plausibly it remained part *of* Christianity. So, whereas Eliot tried to extract the secular moral core from the religious wrapping, Cobbe instead sought to extract the 'simple Theist' and moral core of Christianity from its institutional distortions. But this strategy had its own problems. To defend the claim that morality requires Christianity from secularist challenges and criticisms, Cobbe progressively expanded her account of the centrality of Christianity until eventually, against Stephen, she maintained that the whole of meaningful life, culture, and evaluation presupposes a Christian background. As Besant pointed out, this was only plausible if 'Christianity' meant institutionalized Christendom, not merely 'simple Theism'. But institutionalized Christendom, as Cobbe herself admitted, had perpetrated much injustice, oppression, and violence. This confirmed to Besant that, after all, the way to bring about the world's moral improvement was to throw off this entire religious legacy.

Yet this does not settle the case against Cobbe, who had other arguments for her view, one of which, as we saw, concerned truth. Against Lee, Cobbe insisted that the value of truth depends on Christianity: it is God's moral law that obliges us to seek the truth irrespective of consequences and to cultivate the virtue of truthfulness (*MA* 58). The epistemic virtue of truth is in the end a moral virtue, for Cobbe. As she put it: 'Many a man who is an Atheist as regards God holds... a noble faith in Truth *as* Truth, a firm conviction that nothing can be better than truth' (45)—a conviction that only makes sense against a Christian background.

Here there was a surprising convergence between Cobbe and Nietzsche. For him, too, the value of truth was part of our inherited moral-religious framework. It was because people formerly believed in a 'true world'—of God, moral values, moral laws, souls, the afterlife—behind the sensory world that they were determined to seek out the truth behind sensory appearances (1997: 23–4). The ideal of truth continued to animate science, Nietzsche maintained; although its religious underpinnings had been cut away, the ideal retained force and it remained a legacy of Christianity (Nietzsche [1887] 2006: 109–13). Nietzsche and Cobbe also agreed that morality and Christianity were inextricable. For Nietzsche:

> G. Eliot. – They have got rid of the Christian God and now think that they have to hold on to Christian morality more than ever. That is an English consistency; we do not wish to hold it against little moralistic females à la Eliot. In England, every time you take one small step towards emancipation from theology you have to reinvent yourself as a moral fanatic... For the rest of us, things are different. When you give up Christian faith, you pull the rug out from under your right to Christian morality as well.... Christianity is a system, a carefully considered, *integrated* view of things.... If you break off a main tenet, the belief in God, you smash the whole system along with it... Christian morality... stands or falls along with belief in God.   (Nietzsche [1889] 1997: 53)

Cobbe concurred, up to a point:

> They [virtuous agnostics] have imagined that they had merely to choose between morality *with* religion, or morality *without* religion. But the only choice for them is between morality and religion together, or the relinquishment both of morality and religion. (*AM* 793)

But the fundamental difference was that for Cobbe we must retain Christianity and morality both, whereas for Nietzsche the two were doomed to go under together.[43]

In sneering at 'little moralistic females', however, Nietzsche failed to appreciate that women theorized religion and morality from a particular social standpoint. Women's social role was to be guardians of morality, and because their right to speak and philosophize was contested, they turned this role to their advantage, to say that their philosophizing was urgently needed *because* of their greater moral seriousness or more acute sympathies. For instance, faced with criticisms that her animal advocacy was mere feminine sentimentality, Cobbe replied:

> I do not in the smallest degree object to finding my appeals on behalf of animals treated as womanly. I claim, as a woman... the better right to be heard in such a cause than a man... If my sex has a 'mission' of any kind, it is... to soften this hard world. (1895: 497)

Cobbe based her claim to speak on her feminine 'mission' to improve the world morally. Or consider Martineau's reaction to Mill's argument in *On Liberty* that there should be no legal penalty for experiments in living as long as these do not harm others:

> Mill does not reject the penalty of *opinion* on self-regarding vices... [and] it would be *too* unnatural to suppress the involuntary movements of sympathy and antipathy in regard to purity and corruption, – sobriety and intemperance etc.... he does not interfere with interior sentiment in regard to everybody's personal conduct. (HM to R. P. Graves, 20 May 1859, *HMCL* 4: 173)

That is, for Martineau it was important that while enjoying personal liberty we could still apply 'penalties of opinion' and pass moral judgement upon one another's actions. She approached Mill as the moralist that she had always been;

---

[43] Of course, what Nietzsche expected to supersede morality is open to many interpretations: amoralism; ethics as distinct from morality; living aesthetically rather than morally; living by individual values rather than universal rules; and a plethora of other possibilities. Some of these interpretive options push Nietzsche back closer to the ideas of this-worldly flourishing endorsed by Eliot, Lee, and Besant.

for being a moralist, she took it, qualified her to speak, in defiance of those who had doubts about intellectual women.

To return to Nietzsche, Cobbe, and truth, although they both saw Christianity, morality, and the value of truth as intertwined, this was not in quite the same sense. For Nietzsche these formed an interwoven historical assemblage, but one that was now in ruins and must be superseded. In contrast, for Cobbe the edifice was not merely historical but also captured the truth about reality and value. The two agreed, though, that one could not simply detach the value of truth from this broader framework and treat it as a stand-alone value, as secularists such as Besant and Lee tried to do (and not only Besant and Lee—today, for example, Richard Dawkins opposes the God *delusion* in the name of truth; see Dawkins 2006). Without some underpinning framework, it is not clear why we should value truth over illusion at all; and if truth *is* nonetheless valued, it is probably because we still tacitly accept some part of the old religious-cum-metaphysical framework despite ourselves.

Take Besant, who went on to write: 'I ask no other epitaph on my tomb but SHE TRIED TO FOLLOW TRUTH' (*WT* 31). As she moved through her successive standpoints—evangelical (pre-1872), Theist (1872–4), secularist (1874–89), and theosophist (1889–)—the unifying factor was the quest for truth.[44] When she was a Theist, Besant believed that 'our God is the God of truth, and ... therefore the honest search for truth can never be displeasing in His eyes' (*ABA* 124). When she was a secularist, she then held that: 'If Truth is not loved for her own pure sake, ... then we are not worthy to be Secularists, we have no right to the proud title of Freethinkers' (*ABA* 163; the National Secular Society's motto was, in fact, 'We Search for Truth'). And Besant had doubts, which grew rather than abated over her secularist period, about whether morality and the value of truth could be adequately sustained on a secular basis. These doubts, in the end, drew her back to religion to provide a basis for these values—although the religion to which she now turned was not Christianity but theosophy.[45]

If Besant's trajectory bears out Cobbe's and Nietzsche's position on the value of truth, the fact that she moved on to an 'alternative' religion rather than back to Christianity raises important further issues. In these debates about whether morality requires religion, the religion in question was Christianity, as I noted at the start of this chapter. Christianity was privileged because it was taken to be the most advanced religion, both by secularists like Martineau and by religionists like Cobbe. Yet they did not simply assume the superiority of Christianity unthinkingly. Martineau, Cobbe, and others put forward complex theories of

---

[44] Bevir (1999) likewise finds a continuity and logic in Besant's changes of mind. For an excellent account of interpretations of Besant's intellectual journey, see Leland (2021).
[45] Subsequently, however, Besant went on to recover the kernels of esoteric truth hidden within Christianity; see Besant (1898).

the progression of world-historical religions, maintaining that the progression so far led up to Christianity—whether the next step was secularism (for Martineau), the further expansion of Christianity (Cobbe), or the reconciliation of Christianity with secular science (as Julia Wedgwood proposed). Helena Blavatsky, however, put forward a very different account of the sequence of world religions, which demoted Christianity and vindicated theosophy in its place. In the background of the debates about religion and morality, then, were debates about the meaning and direction of world history, and I turn to these in Chapter 6.

6
Progress in History

6.1 Introduction

This chapter is on the accounts of progress in history developed by Harriet Martineau in the 1840s, Frances Power Cobbe in the 1860s, and Julia Wedgwood and Helena Blavatsky in the 1880s. Their accounts share three key features: they believe in a world-historical progression culminating in modern Europe; they think this has moved through a sequence of stages of civilization tied to different world religions and belief systems; and, broadly, they hold that the sequence has run from ancient East to modern West. All these women thus construct metanarratives about the grand sweep of historical movement.

There are also important differences. One is whether the progression is culminating in secularism (Martineau), Christianity (Cobbe), the synthesis of secular science and Christianity (Wedgwood), or the recovery of ancient spiritual wisdom within theosophy (Blavatsky). A second difference is which world religions are included and in what order: ancient Egypt is the original religious culture for Martineau, but Cobbe and Wedgwood replace Egypt with ancient India, while Blavatsky vacillates: she restores Egypt to originary status in *Isis Unveiled* (1877), but ultimately relocates Egypt as a descendant of India in *The Secret Doctrine* (1888). A third difference is how unequivocally the historical movement is seen as one of advancement. Blavatsky qualifies this most heavily, while Wedgwood is most firmly in favour.

Clearly, women contributed to philosophy of history in nineteenth-century Britain. It is well-known that in this period philosophy took a historical turn, with a new recognition that the entirety of thought, ideas, human life, and indeed nature have a history. Generally, though, German-speaking theorists of history receive the lion's share of interpretive attention, especially Hegel and Marx. How far did these two influence our four women? Only Blavatsky was definitely influenced by Hegel; she invoked his philosophy of history in support of her account of spiritual evolution (*SD* 1: 50–1, 640–1).[1] Wedgwood viewed history as progressing through conflict, and this seems to be so clearly Hegelian that Sue

---

[1] Referring to Sibree's 1857 translation of Hegel's *Lectures on the Philosophy of History*, Blavatsky endorsed Hegel's idea that history is moving towards a goal, the full unfolding and self-consciousness of spirit. Elsewhere she equated her 'primal mind' with Hegel's absolute (*SD* 1: 16) and agreed with him that nature progressively spiritualizes itself (1: 257).

Brown concludes: 'Her view of history relied on a Hegelian dialectic' (2002: 442). Yet I have found no positive evidence that Wedgwood read Hegel.[2] Nor have I found any evidence that Hegel influenced Martineau,[3] while Cobbe emphatically rejected Hegel's mere 'dialectic subtleties' in favour of Kant's 'true transcendentalism' (*IM* ix, 48). Marx's historical materialism influenced these women even less, not only in that none of them referred to Marx,[4] but also in that all their accounts of history were, broadly, idealist. They understood historical progression in terms of religious and metaphysical belief systems (i.e. in the realm of ideas).[5] To that extent at least, their philosophies of history were closer to Hegel than Marx.

Who, then, did influence these women? Martineau's earlier thought in the 1820s and 1830s was influenced by Scottish Enlightenment histories of successive economic stages, and these still indirectly informed her developmental account of history's 'great guiding Ideas' in the 1840s (*EL* 208). Cobbe framed her theory in particular opposition to positivism, according to which societies inexorably move from religious to metaphysical to 'positive' and secular stages; she recast the progression as leading to Christianity instead. The influences on Wedgwood's philosophy of history are difficult to reconstruct because she referred almost entirely to 'primary' works—ancient Greek and Roman literature, early Christian writings, and so on—and no modern interpretive accounts. Blavatsky, for her part, drew on a wealth of esoteric and occult literature, while like Cobbe she reacted against positivism (see Rudboeg 2012). It is also worth noting a respect in which all these women departed from other prominent British theories of historical progress of this period. All four women measured progress in respect of religion-and-morality, *not* science and intellectual understanding—in contrast to accounts of the 'progress of the intellect' (Mackay 1850), of progress in our understanding of physical laws and control of nature (Buckle 1857–61), and of progress in scientific and rational inquiry (Lecky 1869).[6] Because these women emphasized religion-and-morality, the work of Max Müller, the founder of

---

[2] Wedgwood had read Kant, for she tried unsuccessfully to persuade Darwin to read the *Critique of Pure Reason* (Brown 2022: 153).

[3] Pichanick says that Martineau's historical theory in *Eastern Life* 'suggests that she had read... Hegel with whom the idea of religious evolution is usually associated' (1980: 178), but this hardly seems conclusive.

[4] Although Marx lived in Britain from 1849 to 1883, he seems not to have become well-known in the country as a theoretician until after his death. For instance, in her 1883 diary, Beatrice Webb recorded meeting 'Miss [Eleanor] Marx in the refreshment rooms [of the British Library]. Daughter of Karl Marx, socialist writer and refugee' ([1926] 1980: 302)—Marx at the time still needed introduction, whereas Eleanor was better known. In 1887, Annie Besant disparaged *Capital*'s opening chapter as 'pure metaphysics' (Besant 1887: 2)—an indication that his work was now becoming known, although for Besant 'this quagmire of contradictions and bad metaphysics is no safe foundation for modern Socialism'.

[5] In Martineau's case this was a departure from her earlier, more materialist work, as I will explain.

[6] Wedgwood argues that Buckle overestimated 'the domain of the intellect': '"The great danger of the present day", says Comte... "is the dream of a reign of Mind"' (*NCT* 364). And Cobbe thought that

comparative religion, was important for Cobbe, Wedgwood, and—albeit with more criticisms—Blavatsky.

How far were these women responding to one another? Cobbe explicitly formed her Christian view of progress in opposition to Martineau's secular one. Wedgwood knew Martineau very well besides being friends with Cobbe, and Wedgwood's correspondence and published work suggest that she was seeking to reconcile their secular and Christian perspectives. Blavatsky did not refer to the others, but she vehemently opposed materialistic science as personified by two figures above all—Thomas Henry Huxley, whose views were indirectly linked to Martineau's, as we've seen before, and Darwin, a central antagonist for Cobbe. Thus Blavatsky was, at least, intervening into the same field of discourse as the other women.[7] As usual, then, a mixture of overt and indirect filiations was at work.

I have described these women as doing philosophy of history, but only Wedgwood explicitly described her project in these terms (*MI* vii–x, 150). Martineau advanced her historical theory through a narrative of Eastern travel,[8] and Blavatsky advanced her theory within the framework of her theosophical system. Cobbe's essays on this topic might be seen as contributing to anthropology or comparative religion as much as philosophy, especially as she was influenced by E. B. Tylor, one of the founding anthropologists. As we have seen repeatedly in this book, nineteenth-century women's philosophizing largely preceded disciplinary divisions and it would be anachronistic to insist upon them too forcefully. These women's historical metanarratives are certainly philosoph*ical* even if they are not philosoph*y* in a demarcated sense.

Because these women narrated historical progress in terms of world religions, their accounts were entangled with questionable assumptions about Eurocentrism, Orientalism, and the justification of European colonialism and the British Empire. Blavatsky's case was the most ambiguous, but Martineau, Cobbe, and Wedgwood all placed modern Europe at the summit of progress so far, with Britain at the summit of the summit. This raises a question about why we should read these accounts today, for readers may understandably feel that these

---

the rise of science and its practical concomitant, vivisection, threatened to undermine our religious and moral progress: 'either the moral progress of Europe itself must be arrested and recede far back behind the point attained at the Christian era, or Vivisection must cease' (*MR* 271).

[7] Moreover, Blavatsky surely knew of both Martineau and Cobbe. Martineau had been famous for propounding the very kind of materialism that Blavatsky denounced, while Cobbe was the leading anti-vivisectionist, and Blavatsky joined the anti-vivisectionist cause with 'Have Animals Souls?' (1886). Besant later came round to the cause too (see Besant 1903). Indeed, anti-vivisection and theosophy became overlapping movements (see Viswanathan 2011). A key intermediary figure was Anna Kingsford, who was an anti-vivisectionist and a theosophist, and had contestive relations with both Cobbe and Blavatsky (see Vyvyan 1969 and Stone 2022b). Given these connections, Blavatsky could not possibly have been unaware of Cobbe's work.

[8] As Elizabeth Bohls has remarked, travelogues 'gave women writers the opportunity to engage with philosophical concepts without trespassing on the more forbidding territory of the treatise' (1995: 6).

projects of ranking world civilizations are best forgotten. I think that it is still worth mapping out these historical metanarratives, for three reasons. The first is simply to recognize that women contributed to theorizing historical progress in the period, however problematically at times. The second reason is that, in order to understand the social world we live in and why it exhibits the global and racial inequalities that it does, it is useful to remember and understand the internal logic of the discourses that have helped to shape this world. These discourses are not merely part of the past but remain active in forming the world today. We should not brush them under the carpet. The third reason is that although these women's metanarratives were, in part, a rationalization of European imperialism, they also contained ambiguities and fissures. This is most true of Blavatsky's narrative; for her, the Europeans were at the nadir of their developmental cycle and could only advance spiritually by relearning ancient wisdom from the East. These ambiguities in Blavatsky's view of progress amplify ambiguities that are also present in the other accounts. As such, these women's metanarratives not only rationalized European colonialism but also opened up possibilities for contesting it.

With these clarifications in mind, I will now move chronologically through Martineau's account of progress (Sec. 6.2), to Cobbe's (Sec. 6.3), Wedgwood's (Sec. 6.4) and Blavatsky's accounts (Sec. 6.5), before drawing out the structural parallels, significant differences, and ambiguities regarding Eurocentrism (Sec. 6.6).

6.2 Martineau and *Eastern Life*

First let me place Martineau's treatment of progress in history within her intellectual development. We saw in earlier chapters how Martineau gradually renounced her faith, a process that was completed when she published the *Letters on the Laws of Man's Nature and Development* with Henry George Atkinson in 1851. But there was a key step in this process that we have so far skipped over: her travels in Egypt and the Near East in the later 1840s, which she pinpointed in her *Autobiography* as the decisive turning-point convincing her of the need to move beyond Christianity. Specifically, Martineau toured Egypt, Sinai, Palestine, and Syria from late 1846 to mid-1847. By then, such tours had become fashionable, and several thousand Europeans had taken them. Florence Nightingale took one shortly after Martineau,[9] and Cobbe would follow suit, unaccompanied, in 1857-8. Several travellers published accounts of their journeys. Martineau's *Eastern Life* (1848) was one such account—but it also contained 'one of the most searching philosophical accounts of Egyptian travel in English'

---

[9] On Nightingale's tour and its impact on her theological views, see Calabria (1996).

(Gange 2013: 109). Indeed, Martineau conceived it as a work of philosophy and not simply as travel writing (HM to Henry Crabb Robinson, 8 June 1848, *HMCL* 3: 111). She used the travel narrative to narrate a necessary progression in which religion was ultimately destined to be superseded.

Martineau's travels, she said, transformed her perception of the 'genealogy... of the old faiths, – the Egyptian, the Hebrew, the Christian and the Mohammedan' (*HMA* 2: 279). Seeing the places, monuments, artefacts, and rituals linked to these faiths, in a geographical order that mirrored their chronological emergence, revealed to her the *necessity* of the 'passage' and 'progress' through these faiths (2: 280). It was a necessary course of progression which she had already mystically foreseen in 1845:

> I *saw* the march of the whole human race, past, present and to come, through existence, and their finding the Source of Life. Another time, I *saw* all the idolatries of the earth coming up to worship at the ascending series of Life-fountains, while I discovered these to be all connected, – each flowing down unseen to fill the next...
> (HM to Richard Monckton Milnes, 22 February 1845, in Martineau 1990: 108)

But if Martineau had already formed her core concept of a progressive sequence of world-religions before her Eastern travels—even though those travels put flesh on the concept's bones—then what sources initially inspired her to conceive of these 'Life-fountains'? The likely answer is Scottish Enlightenment histories on which societies inevitably pass through successive stages of economic, social, and political development, particularly Adam Smith's 'four stages' theory. Martineau's first *Illustration of Political Economy*, 'Life in the Wild', dramatized this theory, depicting a group of European settlers in South Africa who rebuild their civilization from scratch, making an accelerated journey from hunter-gathering to basic animal husbandry to agriculture before finally rejoining commercial society with a flourish (*IPE* 1).[10]

In *Eastern Life*, Martineau transformed these economic stages into stages of religious and philosophical thought, and her account implied that the next step in this series of stages was to move beyond religion altogether. She decided not to state this openly, but her book's 'infidel tendency' was nonetheless visible to her intended publisher, John Murray, who rejected the book on this account.[11] In fact, however, Martineau did not narrate a simple linear rise up the series of religions.

---

[10] On Smith's theory, see Okan (2017) and Smith ([1776] 1904: vol. 2, bk. V). Schematically, Smith's stages are hunting, pastoral, agricultural, and commercial societies. On Martineau's knowledge and use of these Scottish histories, see Klaver (2007), Palmeri (2016: esp. 70–3), and *IPE* 1: xv–xvi.

[11] On Murray's reaction, see HM to Edward Moxon, 1 March 1848, *HMCL* 3: 88. The 'infidel tendency' was also apparent to several reviewers who found the book incendiary and objectionable; see Gange (2013: 110) and Roberts (2002: ch. 6).

She told a more complicated historical story: one side traced an upward progression towards secularism; the other side stressed the Egyptian roots of all European culture.

The latter side is to the fore in Part 1 on ancient Egypt, which occupies nearly half the book. Here Martineau argues that ancient Egypt's culture, religion, and philosophy lie at the origin of Western civilization. They are the source from which ancient Greece, Judaism, and Christianity arose, and the matrix of belief within which contemporary Christian Europe remains unknowingly located. Egyptian 'religious philosophy', for Martineau, centred on belief in a single God. The 'Egyptian priests upheld the doctrine of the unity of God... The leading point of belief of the Egyptians... was that there was One Supreme, – or, as they said, only one God' (*EL* 100).[12] Yet the ruling caste of priests monopolized knowledge of God's unity while fostering belief in polytheism, myth, ritual, and symbolism in the common people. Another aspect of Egyptian religious philosophy was the preoccupation with life and death, which reflected Egypt's environment, with its sharp contrast between the abundant Nile (life) and arid desert (death). The constant awareness of potentially imminent death led to a belief in 'the Immortality of the Soul, and rewards and punishments in the afterlife' (85), and to a belief that all life and organized living bodies are sacred—hence the practice of mummification, including of sacred animals.

Egyptian religious philosophy, Martineau argues, shaped ancient Greek philosophy, Judaism, and Christianity. Greek civilization 'unquestionably derived' from Egypt (91). Egyptian ideas especially influenced Greek philosophy, she explains: Thales studied in Egypt with the priests, as did other pre-Socratics including Pythagoras. His belief in immortal souls undergoing successive reincarnations was essentially Egyptian and influenced Plato, who spent time in Egypt too. Thus ancient Greece, the supposed foundation-stone of Western civilization, was at its core Egyptian.

As for Judaism, Martineau continues, Moses was an Egyptian, educated amongst its priestly caste, from whom he acquired the belief in monotheism. His revolutionary move was to abandon theocracy and disseminate belief in a single god to his people, along with belief in a divinely legislated moral law. These ideas of one god and a divine law were Egyptian: 'the great doctrine of a Divine Moral Government was the soul alike of the practical legislation of Moses and the speculative philosophy of Plato' (85).

Through these Greek and Judaic routes, and by direct influence, Egypt also lies at the origins of Christianity. The story of Christ's death and resurrection derives

---

[12] We may wonder whether Martineau is projecting proto-Christian monotheism onto the ancient Egyptians, who prima facie were polytheists. The mid-fourteenth-century BC ruler Akhenaten introduced monotheism, but this was short-lived. That said, earlier on, the Egyptian pantheon did contain a chief deity—first Ra, later Amun or Amun-Ra. So if Martineau's claim about Egyptian monotheism simplifies things, it is not completely without foundation.

from the mythology of Osiris; the creation story in Genesis derives from Egyptian creation myths; ideas of immortal souls and bodily resurrection come from Egypt and reappear, inter alia, in Paul's talk of the resurrection of our spiritual bodies. Overall: 'It cannot be overlooked...how large was the Egyptian element, in comparison with every other...The Hebrew mind was fed by the Egyptian incessantly' (*EL* 374). Ultimately, Martineau concludes, ancient Egypt is 'the key' to Western civilization.

These claims make clear that Martineau subscribes to what Martin Bernal in *Black Athena* calls the 'ancient model', according to which ancient Greek culture derived from Egyptian influence (Bernal 1987). One of the model's key exponents was Herodotus, to whom Martineau refers copiously, endorsing his view that Greece began as an Egyptian colony. Many Europeans accepted the ancient model up until the mid-nineteenth century, Bernal shows,[13] but then the 'Aryan model' supplanted it. On the Aryan model, Greek culture essentially derived from later influences from incoming Indo-European—'Aryan'—peoples. The Aryan model took hold, Bernal argues, because on the ancient model Western civilization stems from Africa; but, according to the racial hierarchy that became entrenched over the nineteenth century, Africans are black and black people are uncivilized; so Africans cannot possibly have originated Western civilization.

Martineau does not unambiguously see the Egyptians as black. She maintains that in their iconography the Egyptians depicted themselves in dark red, distinguished from Asiatics, Northerners (painted white) and Africans (painted black) (*EL* 161). Martineau herself categorizes the Egyptians as 'Nubian' in ethnic terms, with 'dark bronze' skin (86) (i.e. half-way between African and Mediterranean).[14] Still, for Martineau the Egyptians were not straightforwardly white and so it follows that Western civilization did not originate with white Europeans. This decentring of white Europeans is an interesting feature of Martineau's account, along with her consistent description of the Egyptians as having a 'religious philosophy'—she has no qualms at all about recognizing non-Europeans as doing philosophy.

Martineau chastises her European contemporaries for viewing Egyptian culture as primitive, deficient, and impoverished. She insists that all major faiths are noble and should be approached respectfully, sympathetically, and with an open mind. After all, Christianity's core ideas of monotheism and moral law stem from Egyptian religion in the first place: 'historical and philosophical knowledge...

---

[13] Although Bernal sadly fails to acknowledge Martineau's contribution to this body of thought. Indeed, few women make it into *Black Athena* at all.

[14] *Pace* Barrell (1991), who claims that Martineau regarded the Nubians as black and that she was consequently troubled about black people having originated Western culture. On the contrary, Martineau was happy to recognize black people as culture-originators; she wrote a biography of the Haitian revolutionary leader Toussaint L'Ouverture to bring 'into full notice the intellectual and moral genius of as black a negro as was ever seen' (*HMA* 2: 160).

reveal the origin and sympathy and intermingling of the faiths of men, so that each may go some way in the interpretation of the rest' (356). Martineau effectively offers Christians a choice: condemn Egyptian religion as superstitious idolatry, but then Christianity must be condemned too; or concede their affinities, and then Egyptian religion must be as noble as the Christianity that descends from it.

So far, Martineau seems not to be extolling the advanced state of modern Europe at all. Rather, she appears to be asserting the continuity between ancient and modern cultures and questioning Christianity's claim to be more advanced than other world religions. However, the progress-orientated side of her views comes out in Parts 2 to 4 of *Eastern Life*.

Part 2 is on Judaism. She argues that Moses attempted to democratize monotheism and establish a pure moral law. Yet the Jews were too immured in the pre-existing superstitious mind-set of popular Egyptian culture to take up his innovations. Hence Judaism fell back into ritual observances and practices, the letter not the spirit of the law. In addition, Moses's God became the tutelary deity of the Jews—another particular, not universal, deity. Moses had tried to purify the noble kernel of Egyptian religion from the baser elements mixed with it: the combination of a secretive priesthood with popular polytheism, idolatry, and rituals. Over time these base elements had led Egyptian religion to decline, as the people grew increasingly superstitious and the priests increasingly secretive. Against this background, Moses initiated a progressive advance; yet his purified faith fell back into superstition and ritual.

In Part 3, on Christianity, Martineau places Jesus in a context where the Jewish faith had fallen into superstition and was facing challenges from sects like the Essenes, whose concern with the moral law Jesus took even further. He sought to purify monotheism, eliminate superstitious rituals, simplify doctrine, and re-centre religious behaviour around universal moral principles. Against Pharisaic law-worship, he envisaged a spiritual kingdom that would render the law redundant. Again, his purification effort failed. People began to 'overlay the simple teachings of Jesus with mysteries and allegories and fables' (*EL* 413). These were of Egyptian origin, for Egypt remained the central cultural influence (373–4). Myths about Osiris (and his Greek analogue Pan) were superimposed onto Jesus, hence the growing preoccupation with Jesus's miraculous birth, death, and resurrection rather than his teachings and accomplishments in life. Jesus's attempted reorientation towards moral conduct in life became overlaid with doctrines about the soul's fate in the afterlife. This was consolidated in the Alexandrian, Platonized form of Christianity which remodelled this new religion in light of earlier Egyptian beliefs.

Martineau's account of Christianity is influenced by Higher Criticism (*LLM* 221–2) and makes a key contribution to it, filtering out the historical Jesus from the myths subsequently imposed on him. Martineau gives this history/myth distinction her unique twist: the historical element was Jesus's attempt to purify monotheism and morality; the mythical element was the superimposition of Egyptian-derived myths and rituals. By now, however, Martineau seems to have reversed her earlier positive evaluation of Egypt, for she is effectively blaming Egyptian culture for dragging Christianity back down into superstition and myth. 'Till the religion taught by Jesus is purged of its Egyptian, Greek, Assyrian and Pharisaic accretions and adulterations... its failure in regenerating the world will remain what it now is', Martineau says (*EL* 430). She laments the 'superstitions which were engrafted upon Christianity at Alexandria, and... which debase the religion until this day' (383).

Martineau has been widely understood to be saying in *Eastern Life* that Christianity is merely the last mythology that must now be discarded. That is, her argument is often taken to be that: (1) modern Europeans must leave primitive Egyptian ways behind; (2) Christianity is a mere Egyptian relic; so (3) modern Europeans must jettison Christianity. Many of her contemporaries took issue with the presumed anti-Christianity (premise 2), while some recent readers object to her pejorative and Eurocentric judgements about Egypt (premise 1).[15]

However, both groups of readers are seeing only one side of Martineau's whole argument. The other side is that Christianity inherits *not only* the mythical, ritualistic, superstitious aspects of Egypt but *also* its noble faith in one god and divine moral government (*EL* 383–4, 400). In trying to purify these ideals, Jesus sought to *realize* the valuable core of Egyptian religion more fully than the Egyptians had done themselves. *This* respect in which Christianity remains Egyptian does not debase the progeny but ennobles ancestry and progeny alike, for 'the great guiding Ideas of mankind are the more... venerable for having wrought for some thousands of years longer than we had imagined' (208). Overall, for Martineau, Christianity *is* debased by the superstitions it inherits from Egypt, *but* it retains a noble core inherited from Egypt as well.

We can now set out Martineau's overall conception of historical progress. The original Egyptian religion was a hybrid of noble faith and base superstition. Historical progress across the world religions has occurred with their successive attempts to purify the noble from the base components. But the base components have such tenacious hold that each attempt falls back into superstition—although not before rising to greater purity than the stage before it (*EL* 466; see also *HMA* 2: 287). That is, each time around, the core noble ideas are raised to greater purity— for instance, from Egyptian monotheism-in-polytheism to Judaic monotheism-with-titulary-God to Christian pure monotheism. Christianity is thus the highest stage so far.[16] By implication, the contemporary task is to purify Christianity of its

---

[15] See David (1987: 70–3) and Melman (1992: 237).

[16] A major qualification concerns Islam, with which Martineau deals in Part 4 of *Eastern Life*. Martineau wants to avoid what would seem the natural conclusion that Islam makes yet another

residual superstitions, rituals, and myths, thereby releasing its moral potential. To do this, though, would not be simply to purge Christianity of Egyptian residues; it would also fulfil the potential contained in Egyptian belief.

This is where the secularist implication comes into Martineau's narrative. For her, Christianity today remains completely imbued with myths, such as ideas about Jesus's divine origins and resurrection and about the immortal soul and the afterlife. If the Christian religion was purified of myth, it would not remain *as a religion* at all. To purify Christianity would be to secularize it. If the noble core of monotheism was extricated from mythic belief in a creator God who is imagined as a person, what would be left? Martineau answers: The recognition that the universe is law-governed throughout, and that its laws form a unity and hold invariably, but where we cannot possibly know about any creative agency or first cause 'behind' these laws (*HMA* 2: 184, 290). If we likewise demythologize the idea of divine moral government, what will remain is the idea that we must strive for moral perfection and render society a perfect fraternity, the secular version of Christ's spiritual kingdom.

These twin ideas of 'the infinite'—of the universe as an ordered, law-governed whole and of moral perfection—underlie all religion, Martineau says (*SA* 3: 225). These are the pure kernels in all faiths, their fundamental great 'Ideas', which have always been secular implicitly, though they have taken a religious form by being mixed with myth, superstition, and ritual. Through the historical progression of the world-religions, these Ideas have been extricated more and more from their mythic accretions. The next step will be to cease to 'personify' the infinite or derive moral obligations from a divine legislator, thereby extricating the Ideas so fully from myth that they cease to be religious at all (*HMA* 2: 280). This will be the innovation of the modern West, which to date has only ever received Ideas from the East (i.e. ultimately, from Egypt). Now it is the West's time to originate, which it must do by moving past religion altogether (*EL* 488).

6.3 Cobbe on the World Religious Progression

In Chapter 5 I looked at Cobbe's criticisms of Martineau's secularism in the 1877 essay 'Magnanimous Atheism'. Those criticisms were rooted in Cobbe's long-running intellectual differences with Martineau.[17] As part of these differences, in

---

purifying effort and is the most advanced religion yet. Her solution is to say that Islam reduces the moral law to empirical precepts, in order to adapt it to the passionate 'Oriental' character. Hence, Islam is supposedly a step backwards compared with Christianity.

[17] In Chapter 2, I noted that Cobbe and Martineau never met. The reader may wonder whether Martineau knew or ever responded to any of Cobbe's work. Tantalizingly, Elizabeth Jesser Reid (founder of Bedford College) wrote to Martineau concerning a letter in the *Daily News*: 'It was written by Miss Cobbe, whose name I conclude you know though probably not her book [i.e. *Intuitive Morals*].

the 1860s and 1870s Cobbe gave a historical account of the development of religion and morality which she formed in opposition to Martineau's narrative in *Eastern Life*. Cobbe was not only opposing Martineau but also positivism more broadly, for the positivists held that societies necessarily progress from religion to metaphysics to secularism, a view Cobbe rejected.[18] Though Martineau had not yet embraced positivism in *Eastern Life*, she already saw the religious-and-metaphysical progression as moving on to secularism, and so, for Cobbe, Martineau's account and that of the positivists were of a piece.

Cobbe first read and took notes on *Eastern Life* while she was researching religious history in 1851–2 (Mitchell 2004: 76). *Eastern Life* inspired Cobbe to make her own eleven-month tour of Egypt, the Eastern Mediterranean, and Europe in 1857–8 and to produce her 1864 travel narrative *Cities of the Past* (*CP* 2, 6). Here she maintained that the religions of ancient Egypt and ancient Greece, Judaism, and Islam approximate to Christianity, of which they contain anticipatory 'traces' (*CP* 6–7). Their substance, 'the simple relation of creature and Creator' (59), is most fully developed in Christianity—not, as Martineau had it, in secularism. Cobbe went on to elaborate and defend this conviction by organizing the world-religions into a progressive sequence culminating in Christianity. This was in a series of essays on comparative religion from the 1860s, several of which were included in *Darwinism in Morals, and Other Essays* (see *DM* chs 7–10).[19]

Cobbe summed up her view in 'The Evolution of Morals and Religion' of 1872 (*DM* ch. 14). The earliest religious stage is *animism*, in which invisible powers are attributed to natural phenomena. These powers operate capriciously, not morally. 'Only through a long upward course... can the savage be brought to the level whereon he can have any comprehension of goodness' (*DM* 393).[20] This upward course next yields *polytheism*, notably that of the ancient Greeks and Romans. Here the gods are seen to administer a system of justice, but morality is still understood merely in terms of positive rules requiring external compliance. Next, the religions of *partial holiness*, above all Judaism and Hinduism, apprehend God or the gods as good and, to a degree, loving. Yet this is not fully separated from the requirement to obtain divine love or favour through external compliance with rules or through membership of certain ethnic groups (i.e. the Jews or the Brahmins). Finally, we reach *full holiness* with Christianity, which recognizes a

---

We have all a great friendship for her & admire her earnest & humane spirit' (Reid to HM, 27 November 1860, *HM*, HM/128). Unfortunately, Martineau's letters replying to Reid are lost, so we do not know what Martineau had said about Cobbe (Logan 2007: xxiv).

[18] See e.g. Cobbe (1869) and, for discussion, Stone (2022a).

[19] To specify, the essays are, under their final titles, 'The Sacred Books of the Zoroastrians' (1865, *ESS* 89–146), 'A Pre-Historic Religion' (1869), 'The Religions of the World' (1868), 'The Religions of the East' (1868) and 'The Religion and Literature of India' (1870). The last four are all in *Darwinism in Morals*.

[20] Cobbe's concept of animism was informed by the work of the anthropologist E. B. Tylor (1871).

single God who loves everyone alike and whose love supplies a model of moral action. All are included in the community of subjects loved by God.

Cobbe, then, sees religion and morality having evolved indissolubly together; to that extent she agrees with Martineau. She also concurs with Martineau in taking an idealist view of history. For Martineau in *Eastern Life*, 'the history of Ideas is the only true history' (*EL* 122). Likewise, Cobbe states in 1868 that ideas, especially religious ideas, are the main drivers of change in human life (*DM* 235–6). However, Cobbe emphasizes more unequivocally than Martineau that the later stages improve on the earlier ones. For Cobbe, it is only in the retrospective light of the final whole that the earlier stages become intelligible as its incomplete parts. Christianity's 'full holiness' extends beyond and includes Judaism's 'partial holiness', which extends beyond but includes classical positive rules, which extend beyond but include animistic negotiation with capricious powers.

Unlike Martineau, then, Cobbe's emphasis is more that the earlier stages embody *partial* truth than that they embody *truth*. Even so, for Cobbe those stages do embody truth, albeit partially—as she metaphorically puts it, 'there are no *azoic* rocks in the geology of man's religion' (*ESS* 91). As such, these earlier religious systems deserve respect; after all, the genuine Christian spirit is one of universal community and inclusiveness (*DM* 239–41). The germinal truth latent in all religions, their common 'substance', is the intuitive sense of dependence on God. At first, within animism, God is merely apprehended as a 'dimly discerned Power' (236). Still, this idea of dependence is present from the start, and it eventually becomes completely and explicitly worked out in Christianity.[21]

Thus Cobbe, like Martineau, sees the succession of world-religions as progressively realizing an embryonic truth that was there at the start of history. But for Martineau that truth was essentially secular, consisting in ideas of a law-governed universe and moral community. For Cobbe, the truth is essentially religious, consisting in the feeling of dependence on the divine. Being essentially religious, this truth finds its fullest development in the Christian idea of a loving God. Whereas for Martineau successive attempts to purify the 'great guiding Ideas' of their religious wrappings have kept falling back into religion, for Cobbe successive religions get better and better at articulating and realizing the original, and intrinsically religious, meaning of our dependence on the divine.

Another difference between Cobbe and Martineau is that Cobbe includes more world-religions in her progression. She classifies the world's major faiths into two

---

[21] Cobbe knew of Hume's naturalistic explanation of religion in his *Natural History of Religion*; she mentions Hume amongst the writers on religion she read during her youthful crisis of faith (*LFPC* 1: 86). For Hume, 'the first ideas of religion arose...from a concern with regard to the events of life, and from the incessant hopes and fears, which actuate the human mind' (Hume [1757] 1956: 27). Supposing that there are agencies behind these events provides a 'coping mechanism' (Ferreira 1995). Evidently, Cobbe disagrees; she thinks that 'primitive' people already have the dawning sense of a real divine power.

triads (*ESS* 89–146). In the East, the primal religion is Hinduism which spawns two variations, Buddhism and Zoroastrianism. In the West, the primal religion is Judaism, which spawns Islam and Christianity. Most twentieth-century accounts of comparative religion include five world religions; Cobbe has six, because she includes Zoroastrianism. Treating Zoroastrianism as a sixth major world faith was common in the nineteenth century (see e.g. Müller 1867: xi–xii). For Cobbe, Zoroastrianism is important as the channel by which religious progression moves from East to West, from India to Persia. As she sees it, the Zoroastrians reacted against Hinduism's degradation into ritual by re-emphasizing moral conduct, and Judaism inherited this advancement. Unfortunately, Judaism then stagnated back into ritual; but Christianity took up the renewal of morality in turn. Thus, within Cobbe's two triads, Zoroastrianism and Christianity are symmetrical counterparts. Zoroastrianism advances over Brahminism in re-emphasizing moral action rather than ritual, and Christianity advances over Judaism in the same respect (*CP* 7; *ESS* 91).

It is notable that Cobbe's progression is not straightforwardly chronological, since she ranks ancient Greek and Roman polytheism below the Eastern religions. This is because Cobbe orders the belief-systems not by time but proximity to Christianity. For her, Christianity's most direct sources lie in the series of world-religions running from Brahminism through Zoroastrianism to Judaism. As this series runs up to Christianity, and anticipates it in 'partial holiness', the whole series lies ahead of the classical cultures. Martineau had displaced the classical civilizations from the supreme status they were acquiring for many Europeans by arguing that these civilizations were fundamentally derivative of Egypt. Cobbe displaces the classical civilizations in a different way from Martineau, but she displaces them all the same.

Egypt, though, has dropped out of Cobbe's account, another major difference from Martineau and one that is emblematic of a broader transition in nineteenth-century European thought, in which Egypt lost its status as the originating religious culture to India. Bernal argues that this change had racial motivations: India was favoured because it was seen as the ancestral site of both the Indo-European language family and the supposed corresponding 'Aryan' race (Bernal 1987: 229). Thus, the rise of India instead of Egypt was key to the Aryan model. Indeed, Cobbe states that: 'By the Aryan and Semitic races has the progress of the world been carried on' (*DM* 249). She notes that Egypt has a doubtful pedigree because its language is related to that of the 'Hottentots' (249), who are only at the level of animism in her historical scheme. Hinduism, she insists, is spiritually much closer to Christianity than the 'enigmatical, half-comprehensible' Egyptian ideas of the *Book of the Dead* (271).

Müller was a central figure in the displacement of Egypt by India. Cobbe enthusiastically reviewed his 1867 collection *Chips from a German Workshop*, Vol. 1, and she developed her view of the world-religions in dialogue with Müller.

In *Chips*, Müller identified Christianity as the highest religion, up to which the others lead, although the seeds of true religion—feelings of dependency on the divine, intuitions of moral goodness, and hopes for a better life—pre-exist everywhere. These seeds are only fully realized in Christianity; the goal of comparative religion was to show this, proving that Christianity fulfils the aspirations animating all religions. Clearly these views influenced Cobbe, and so did Müller's demotion of Egypt. For him: 'We are by nature Aryan, Indo-European...: our spiritual kith and kin are to be found in India, Persia, Greece, Italy, Germany; not in Mesopotamia, Egypt, or Palestine' (Müller 1867: 4–5).

In highlighting the originary status of India, Müller praised the original Vedic faith but sharply distinguished it from Hinduism's contemporary degenerated reality. Cobbe agreed that the originally pure Vedic faith had long since decayed (*DM* 227). Owing to the supposedly diminished condition of present-day India, Cobbe was comfortable with British rule there. This was in keeping with Orientalist ideology: generally, the more India was deemed noble and pure *in the past*, the more it was judged stagnant and degraded *today*, effectively justifying British rule (Said [1978] 1991). Even so, Cobbe objected to the attempts of missionaries to impose Christianity on India, arguing that Indians have a rightful attachment to their own traditions (*BS* 201). Instead, she supported indigenous movements to reform Hinduism and bring it closer to the 'moral excellence' of Christ's teachings and the simplicity of monotheism. She particularly praised the monotheistic Hindu movement the Brahmo Samaj and the 'healthy, active *moral spirit*' of its leading figure Ram Mohun Roy (*BS* 204–5). Indeed, she declared of another leading Brahmo Samajist with whom she became friends, Keshub Chunder Sen, that 'at any other age of the world, [he] would have taken his place with such prophets as... Gautama' (*LFPC* 2: 179–82).

Overall, Cobbe gave Hinduism the status of original religion while keeping Christianity at the top of the historical progression. For her, it was in Christianity that the noble kernel of ancient Hinduism was finally realized. In giving India and not Egypt this original status, Cobbe was once more working out her differences from Martineau. Martineau had claimed that the noble truths at the core of the religious progression were fundamentally secular by way of her account of ancient Egypt. By making India into the beginning of the chain of major world religions instead, Cobbe was able to banish the spectre of atheism and trace an unbroken religious line up to Christianity.

6.4 Wedgwood and *The Moral Ideal*

Published to acclaim in 1888, *The Moral Ideal* was Wedgwood's magnum opus, setting out her philosophy of history. A four-hundred-page book on which she worked for nearly twenty years, it gives an ambitious account of the formative ingredients of modern European civilization. Wedgwood's central thesis is that the progression of world civilizations is moving towards not secular science or Christianity alone but the synthesis of both: the combination of a scientific acceptance of natural reality with a Christian horizon of aspiration.

I believe that, amongst other motivations for Wedgwood's project, she was negotiating between Martineau and Cobbe. Earlier in this book I suggested that Martineau was Wedgwood's role model of an intellectual woman. Wedgwood and Martineau had a long and close relationship. Wedgwood's mother Fanny was Martineau's close friend and confidante, and aged six Wedgwood followed in her mother's footsteps and entered into correspondence with Martineau. The friendship blossomed, so much so that Wedgwood has been described as the childless Martineau's substitute daughter (Todd 2003: 17). Once Martineau was cured of her illness in the mid-1840s, Wedgwood regularly visited her and they 'had many passionate discussions on theology, literature, politics, and social reform' (Wedgwood 1983: 82). They kept up their correspondence until Martineau's death.[22] Not surprisingly, Wedgwood knew most if not all of Martineau's work.[23]

Of particular relevance here, Wedgwood read *Eastern Life* and appreciated but rejected its secularist implication. In 1875 she adversely compared John Stuart-Glennie's 1875 book *Pilgrim-Memories* to *Eastern Life*, saying that the former was 'modelled on Miss Martineau's book of Eastern travel, but...the writer is entirely without that power...which raises that work, whatever we may think of the views set forth in it, to the first rank' (*NCT* 362). Moreover, Wedgwood remarked that the books shared the goal of pairing 'sketches of Eastern travel and theories of philosophy'. Thus, Wedgwood appreciated the philosophical dimension of *Eastern Life* and its secularism, although clearly she did not agree with it.

Wedgwood also read Martineau's *Autobiography*, fiercely defending Martineau from her correspondent Jane Gourlay:

I am sorry to say I disagree with [you]...especially about Miss Martineau....Great minds, to which the Scriptures are familiar, do not reject Christianity for want of a few words to sweep away misunderstandings. What is there to show *you* the nature of Christianity that H M and G E [Eliot] have not possessed?...In H M's case I think you so underrate the enormous importance of her denial of immortality *and her delight* in the thought.

(JW to Jane Gourlay, 12 April 1878, W/M 447)

---

[22] Some of their letters are in *HMLFW* (34–7, 45–8, 65–9, 149–55, 306–7).
[23] For example, Martineau discussed the controversy about *Letters* with Wedgwood, evidently presupposing her knowledge of the book (HM to JW, 4 May 1857, *HMLFW* 151–4). Martineau in turn kept up with Wedgwood's writing: she knew Wedgwood was 'Florence Dawson' (HM to Fanny Wedgwood, 27 August 1858, *HMLFW* 166) and praised Wedgwood's Wesley biography for its 'sagacity, dispassionateness, power of justice, power of analysis, power of appreciation' (HM to JW, 2 July 1871, *HMLFW* 306).

Given that Wedgwood and Cobbe were good friends, one wonders whether Wedgwood's final sentence shows the influence of Cobbe's 'Magnanimous Atheism', published in October 1877.

On the one hand, then, Wedgwood thought that Martineau's secularism must be taken seriously along with her reasoning for it, which was spelt out most fully in *Eastern Life*, as we've seen. Martineau was a 'great mind' who must be reckoned with. On the other hand, Wedgwood herself remained a Christian. In particular she believed, like Cobbe, that aspiration towards an ideal depends upon Christianity. Wedgwood's formulations of the link between aspiration and Christianity in *The Moral Ideal* are so close to Cobbe's that I suspect they reflect the latter's influence (although the influence may have gone both ways).[24] Wedgwood observed, for instance, 'I should better have described my aim had I called the book a History of Human Aspiration' (*MI* xx), while for Cobbe, in a secular world 'the life of Aspiration will be lived no more' (*FW* 804). Since the essay in which Cobbe said this, 'A Faithless World', appeared in the same July 1884 issue of the *Contemporary Review* as Wedgwood's review of recent fiction, Wedgwood would undoubtedly have read Cobbe's piece. Putting all this together, when Wedgwood portrayed history as moving towards the reconciliation of secular science and Christian aspiration, plausibly she was trying to synthesize the conflicting perspectives of Martineau and Cobbe. This was only part of what she was doing in this ambitious book, but it was one strand.

With this background in mind, let us now look at Wedgwood's account of history. She begins her narrative in ancient India whose outlook, she claims, was monistic: the cosmos is orderly, unified, harmonious, and good, and evil is merely a transitory appearance, not ultimately real. But each of the ideas of oneness and difference that were amalgamated here needed to be developed in its own right. Buddhism took forward the unity and denial of the reality of difference. Zoroastrianism took forward the reality of evil and thus construed existence as a battleground between good and evil, our task being to conquer evil through our actions. In reaction to these rival faiths, India stagnated, while Persia, because of its focus on action, initiated history proper (*MI* 61). But now the two preceding principles—the unity of good and evil (India) and their difference (Persia)—had to be united. This yielded ancient Greek culture, whose principle was the unity of opposites: the elastic and supple holding-together of differences, the balance of contending forces (in the *Oresteia*, for example, when the bloodthirsty Erinnyes are accepted into the pantheon and so become the benign Eumenides; 89–90).

---

[24] Wedgwood admired much of Cobbe's work, and, reciprocally, Cobbe read and praised *The Moral Ideal*; see Brown (2022: 494, 614). For example, Wedgwood was 'greatly interested' in Cobbe's essay on life after death (in *HH* 1–61), originally published in 1872; see JW to Ellen Tollet, 22 October 1872, *W/M* 401.

Notably, Egypt has no place in Wedgwood's account; neither do the rest of Africa nor the Arab world. While the grounds for omitting the latter are unclear, Africa and its 'races' are allegedly prehistorical.[25] Wedgwood sees herself as narrating the history of the 'Aryan' race (viii) (i.e. the historical race). She leans on Müller's view of ancient India as the seed of 'Aryan' culture, and indeed is heavily indebted to Müller for her account of India and Persia. However, Wedgwood also sees a discontinuity between the India–Persia axis and ancient Greece, and this discontinuity offers a 'prophetic rehearsal of modern Europe' (146):

> Classical Greece is modern Europe on a tiny scale... It presents that platform of culture above barbarism which Europe, and that greater England which forms a vast appendix to Europe, present in contrast to the African and Asian populations. (118)

Accordingly Wedgwood regards Greece as the pivotal 'nation' in world history (107). Unlike Cobbe, then, Wedgwood places classical Greece above Hinduism, Buddhism, and Zoroastrianism in the progression. In Wedgwood's work the hierarchy of civilizations has stabilized into a dismayingly familiar pattern: India originates 'Aryan' culture, Persia initiates history proper, and Greece makes the key break from barbarism into culture which marks the start of Europe and is realized in the British Empire.

However, Wedgwood's detailed account of the classical Greeks is more interesting and foregrounds their differences from modern Europeans. The Greeks had no concept of the individual as a separate self rather than a citizen; as such, for the Greeks, virtue *was* duty to the state; liberty was not the 'opportunity for individual development' but the bond that unites people into a city (104–5); and to the extent that any kind of individual liberty was recognized, it consisted not in freedom from interference but having 'a share in a corporate unity' (31). This form of political life flowed out of the central Greek principle, the balance of forces and unification of differences; it was also bound up with Greece's central limitation. Because liberty was co-extensive with citizenship, non-citizens—women, foreigners, slaves, artisans—were denied liberty, and citizenship meant manliness. Thus, Wedgwood in no way sees the ancient Greeks as a model for modern Europeans. She sees the emergence of modern liberty (i.e. 'opportunity for individual development') as positive, and necessarily tied to an improvement in women's status (104).

---

[25] However, in the second, substantially revised, edition of *The Moral Ideal* from 1907, Wedgwood added an initial chapter 'Egypt, The Earliest Nation'. She also expanded the feminist conclusions of the book with a final chapter 'Male and Female Created He Them' (see Wedgwood 1907). Since this edition post-dates 1900 I shall not consider it here, but the changes are indicative once again of the unstable relations between Egypt and India in British historical narratives of this era.

Through Greece's exclusion of women, slaves, and others, mastery and slavery were compacted together with liberty within its culture, and now each had to be developed more explicitly (147). This led to ancient Rome, in which citizenship in the state was at once subjection to it. The Roman state became a unitary form imposed on heterogeneous individuals; this was the reign of order. As the state expanded its power over more and more individuals in their ever-greater diversity, Rome became an empire and kept expanding. But, concomitantly, the *individual self* began to emerge in its own right (199), and individuality and citizenship were no longer conflated. This was reflected in Stoicism, where an ideal of virtue as conformity to the outer realm of law was accompanied by an idea of peace and freedom in the inner realm. This new idea of the self as an intrinsically isolated individual with its own interiority was fundamental for Europe's future.

Besides Greece and Rome, the third decisive strand for Christian Europe was Judaism, which for Wedgwood arose in reaction against Persia. Where the Zoroastrians saw an active struggle between good and evil, Judaism effected a 'moral revolution' (263): it denied the evil principle and insisted that only the good is real. But this good was still conceived in light of the Zoroastrian focus on moral action, therefore as a moral law, laid down by a divine lawgiver who also creates a law-governed universe. To do good was now to obey the divine law; to assert one's own will against that law was to do wrong. Here Wedgwood finds the germ of the idea that selfishness is bad (274). But Judaism denied the existence of any evil principle, so the existence of the selfish will presented a problem: how could evil possibly stem from an all-good and all-powerful creator?

Greek, Roman, and Jewish currents converged into early Christianity, which addressed the problem of evil using elements of these several currents. The Gnostic solution drew on the Greek idea that material differences, to the extent that they fall outside the elastic unity, are bad. Accordingly, matter is evil; but, still, only God is ultimately real; thus God 'falls' into matter through a long series of emanations (302). In the end, then, Gnosticism failed fully to treat evil as a principle in its own right. That idea still remained to be developed, as it was in Manichaeanism. This took up the Zoroastrian good/evil moral divide once again and remodelled it into a metaphysical dualism (321). On the resulting view matter, nature, and the body are evil; virtue consists in resistance to nature and material impulses. Wedgwood sees this as a profound ethical shift: natural human impulses, feelings, and desires became seen as evil, and the human will as evil if it chose to succumb to them. This shift, crystallized by Augustine, drew together the Greek idea that material differences are bad, the Roman idea of the separate self, and the Jewish idea that self-assertion is wrong, yielding an idea of the 'abysmal depths of personality' (366-7): that we are full of deep-seated evil impulses constantly needing to be rooted out.

According to Wedgwood, such were the founding ideas of European Christendom after the demise of the Roman Empire. These ideas went along with an other-worldly era in which only a monastic life of renunciation counted as virtuous, and everything else was sinful (370). The degradation of social and political life was accepted as an inevitable concomitant of the sinfulness of the world. Because sexual desire was regarded as sinful, the family and women were devalued. The feminine side of life could not be totally eradicated, however, and it returned in the worship of Mary and in a celebration of the 'womanly virtues' of love, chastity, and humility (379). But then stern Calvinist creeds restored the earlier Christian preoccupation with sin. To this extent 'Protestantism, ... which is often regarded as a step forward in the progress from the age of undoubting faith to the age of critical reason, was in reality a step backwards' (384).

Against this background, Wedgwood regards the secularization of modern Europe as a positive development. The value of this life has been restored, and nature recognized as necessary and good. It is acknowledged that we are necessarily embodied, that all our powers depend on our embodiment, and that our natural impulses need and ought to be gratified (387). Science has been central to these developments, showing that nature is wondrously complex and creative (379–81). Because women are associated with nature, this new acceptance of nature and natural desires has brought in more positive attitudes to women.

Nevertheless Wedgwood does not want Christianity to be abandoned. We must retain Christianity in order to have ideals to strive towards, a 'Beyond' to aspire to, she maintains, like Cobbe:

> Men think in our day that this centre [the whole for which we strive] can be found in the ideal of Humanity. They have yet to learn that no ideal is possible if that which is idealized know no Beyond.... Virtue must be a refracted ray from something above Virtue; duty must be the aspect, visible in our dense atmosphere, of a higher excellence extending far beyond it. (*MI* 393)[26]

But we should not go back to being hostile to life and nature. On the contrary, our next step must be to reconcile Christian aspiration with the acceptance of nature, natural life, and impulses. How? Through the sexual relation: for here we can relate to someone who is other, 'beyond' us as the member of a different sex, but to whom we relate *within* natural life:

> [T]he mutual love of man and woman is an expression of the fact that it contains something which is not mutual, something which does not merely invert all

---

[26] Similarly, Cobbe endorses 'the attribution of our moral ideas...to the teaching of a Being immeasurably above us, a theory which represents conscience as a ray shot down from the sun' (*MA* 19). And on aspiration: 'Human nature, ever pulled two ways by downward and by aspiring tendencies, cannot afford to lose all the aid which religious ideas offer to its upward flight...elevation, aspiration, and reverence...have their root in religion' (*FW* 802).

self-centred feeling... but which supplies self with a complement and teaches men concession to needs they do not feel. (374–5)

Equal relations between the two sexes provide the model of how to relate to what is beyond the self while doing so within, not against, one's natural life. Thus, the next phase in history is to balance natural reality and aspirational ideal, science and Christianity; and this entails placing sexual relations on an equal and mutually respectful basis, and revaluing the domestic realm as key to ethical life (377–8).[27]

Wedgwood's incredibly ambitious narrative is full of insight; I have only touched upon the bare bones of its rich content. Amongst its interesting features, Wedgwood makes feminism integral to her account of history, seeing sexual equality as crucial to the next stage of world history. Her idea that sexual difference offers a way to integrate the spiritual and the natural startlingly anticipates the recent work of Luce Irigaray ([1990] 1996). Wedgwood integrates her stance on evolutionary theory as well, as expressed in 'The Boundaries of Science' in 1860–1. In *The Moral Ideal* she argues that evolutionary theory rescues nature from the Manichaean charge of being altogether evil, by showing that the suffering and destruction involved in life's evolution are necessary for its eventual perfection: nature improves itself through conflict. In this way evolutionary theory provides the best solution yet to the problem of evil, by showing that evil is necessary for the good (*MI* 330). Further, evolutionary theory has shown how completely we are natural, evolved beings and therefore how damaging the Augustinian denial of natural life is. On both counts evolutionary theory has effected the moral rehabilitation of nature.

Furthermore, Wedgwood sees historical progression as being dialectically structured. India's component ideas had to be unfolded into their inherent opposition, in Persia; then the Indian and Persian principles needed to be united, in Greece; then Greece's combined elements had to be unfolded into their opposition, in Rome; and so on up until today when science and Christianity need to be reconciled. The overall pattern is that each civilizational stage is organized by a ruling principle containing elements that need to unfold in their own right. Once unfolded, these 'partial truths' then need to be reintegrated (*MI* 330). This yields new syntheses comprising many elements that again need to be unfolded and then reintegrated. Thus, the historical stages become richer and more complex over time, and the whole truth is a living, developing organism

---

[27] Wedgwood argued that only the Jewish tradition had recognized the ethical importance of family life, and that modern Europe had much to learn from the Jews. Indeed, she felt she had not given Judaism enough coverage in *The Moral Ideal* (Wedgwood 1894: 6). Hence, her next book was *The Message of Israel*, which, stressing the 'keen pathos, the vivid dramatic interest, the profound spiritual teaching' of the Jews (15), made a pointed departure from the rise of anti-Semitism in Britain at the time (on which, see Terwey 2012).

(48–9). All this recalls Hegel's dialectical account of world-history, yet Wedgwood seems to have rediscovered the dialectic quite independently.

For Martineau, history had to progress beyond Christianity, whereas for Cobbe history had reached its final stage in Christianity. On Wedgwood's middle way, the next stage is to reconcile scientific naturalism with Christian aspiration. However, Wedgwood also sees Christianity as the fullest expression of the universal human aspiration that has driven all world history. She says, 'the history of aspiration is the clue to all history' (*MI* ix). The 'aspiration' is to go beyond what is given, beyond the existing state of affairs—to render ideas more developed and coherent than they are already, to reconcile conflicting ideas, and so advance closer to the whole. Whereas we might see this aspiration as deriving from the nature of rationality (as Hegel does), Wedgwood thinks that the aspiration 'beyond' is intrinsically religious. The urge to improve ourselves is a religious urge, for her, and Christianity is the religion that most fully realizes this aspirational impulse, by conceiving God as both the ideal 'beyond' and the complete whole for which we are working:

> Man can strive towards no virtue in which he does not feel the sympathy of God.
>
> He must feel himself in some sense a fragment, if ever he is to discover his true oneness.... Man, if we judge him by history, knows himself only so far as he turns towards the eternal Other of the human spirit; he finds his true Unity only as he finds a larger Unity which makes him one with himself and with his brother man. (*MI* 393–4)

That is, the idea of God as a whole of which we are merely parts, a divine whole towards which we keep endlessly reaching, expresses and guides our aspiration to make our ideas whole and coherent. To this extent Wedgwood's synthesis of science and religion is not even-handed. Religion is one side of the synthesis *and* is what guides and motivates us to forge a synthesis in the first place.[28]

6.5 Blavatsky and Spiritual Evolution

Martineau and Cobbe made grand tours of the Middle East, but Blavatsky's international travels were far more extensive and occupied most of her adult life. Originally from Russia, from the 1850s onwards she travelled around

---

[28] This relates back to Wedgwood's disagreement with Welby, discussed in Chapter 4. As we saw there, although both women sought to reconcile science and religion, Wedgwood said to Welby: 'You are in sympathy with the scientific spirit of our time in a way I never could be' (JW to VW, 1888–90, *ELL* 240). Wedgwood in the end put more weight on religion; in *The Moral Ideal*, she did so through the idea of aspiration.

Europe, the Near East, Egypt, India, Tibet, North America, Canada, and parts of the Far East. The five countries where she stayed longest were Russia (1858–63), Egypt (1870–2, where she established a Spiritualist Society), the USA (1873–8, where she co-founded the Theosophical Society in 1875), India (1879–84, where the Theosophical Society moved its headquarters and where she established *The Theosophist* in 1879), and finally England (1887–91). By her own account she also sojourned with the Masters in Tibet from 1868 to 1870.[29] These quite exceptional travels gave Blavatsky a deep knowledge of many of the world's religious and spiritual traditions. She does not, though, seem to have known Martineau's, Cobbe's, or Wedgwood's work on these religions. Making comparisons will have to fall to us. But first we should lay out Blavatsky's complicated perspective on progress, focusing primarily on *The Secret Doctrine*, which as we know was her final and most comprehensive work, completed in London and published in 1888.

Martineau, Cobbe, and Wedgwood all held versions of the prevailing Victorian view that European civilization stood at the summit of progress so far. They measured progress respectively in terms of secularization (Martineau), Christian love (Cobbe), and reconciliation between science and religion (Wedgwood). In contrast, Blavatsky distanced herself from the dominant view of progress: 'Our age, we say, is *inferior* in wisdom to any other ... Where then is the wisdom of our modern age?... We bow before *ancient* wisdom, while refusing absolutely to see any of it in our modern civilisation' (1890: 2). She traced modern culture's degeneracy to its outdated theological dogmas and its 'crass and illogical materialism' (*SD* 1: xx).[30] She proposed instead a return to ancient wisdom, saying of the *Secret Doctrine*: 'The aim of this work may be thus stated:... to rescue from degradation the archaic truths which are the basis of all religions; and to uncover... the fundamental unity from which they all spring' (1: viii). For Blavatsky, these archaic truths told the true history of the cosmos and humanity, but this wisdom had become degraded, with modern culture deteriorating ever further away from these ancient insights. She presented herself as recovering these insights, specifically from the ancient Tibetan Book of Dzyan, of which *The Secret Doctrine* was allegedly a translation, commentary, and elaboration.[31]

The idea of recovering ancient wisdom was a core part of the esoteric tradition, by which Blavatsky was greatly influenced. Western esotericists usually traced this

---

[29] For judicious accounts of her travels, see Godwin (2013: 15–17) and Goodrick-Clarke (2004: 2–6).

[30] Blavatsky especially excoriated Comte and the positivists, accusing them (with the Religion of Humanity) of using a regressive view of women to paste a spiritual veneer over their crass materialism (*IU* 1: 75–83). She called the positivists 'pseudo-philosophers... with sometimes no better right to be regarded as scholars than the possession of an electrical machine' (*IU* 1: 74). Yet, in lamenting the wave of positivism that swept over England in the 1850s, she managed to avoid mentioning Martineau.

[31] In saying 'allegedly' I do not mean to endorse Müller's claim that Blavatsky invented the Book of Dzyan wholesale (Müller 1893: 767–8). On the contrary, David Reigle and Nancy Reigle (1999) have identified various textual sources on which Blavatsky was drawing. Rather, I am highlighting Blavatsky's use of the familiar nineteenth-century strategy to portray herself as a mere commentator and translator.

ancient wisdom back to the ancient Egyptians, along with the Persians and Jews. Esotericists claimed that this wisdom, largely lost to Christendom, had been kept alive through secret traditions such as neo-Platonism, Gnosticism, and Rosicrucianism. Blavatsky shifted the locus of the original wisdom further East—to India and the surrounding regions (see Hanegraaff 2013: 41).

At the same time, as Blavatsky's interpreters have pointed out, she had a distinctly modern idea of evolution. Nicholas Goodrick-Clarke (2004: 1–20) and Garry Trompf (2013), for instance, describe Blavatsky as having an all-embracing evolutionary cosmology. It was not evolution in Darwin's sense but, as Blavatsky said, *spiritual* evolution, encompassing everything in the universe, not only biological life-forms. As well as having this comprehensive theory of cosmic evolution, Blavatsky believed that the evolutionary process went through recurring cycles. This cyclical element enabled her to claim that there was an ancient wisdom more spiritually advanced than modern scientific materialism. As Tim Rudboeg has put it, 'to vindicate the ancients and to prove that they possessed significant knowledge, she was . . . forced to construct an alternative [cyclical] view of progress' (2012: 176). Because of this cyclical conception of progress, Blavatsky ended up challenging the Western hierarchy of world religious cultures and raising the standing of the ancient East compared to the modern West. Let us examine this step by step.

Cosmic evolution. For Blavatsky, successive universes periodically appear, expand, unfold, then disappear again.[32] Each contains chains of planetary globes, with seven in each chain and the fourth always being the densest and most material—including the Earth, which is the fourth of the sevenfold 'earth chain'. Waves of what Blavatsky calls 'monads' make their ways through these globes, in journeys thus comprising seven rounds. Very roughly, a monad is a kernel of spiritual existence; it is not simply another word for 'person' but is the inner essence contained within each person.[33] The monads, presently in their fourth round, on the Earth, enter into and move through a succession of seven 'root-races'. Each root-race is housed on a particular continent, each of which gets destroyed as the monads move into the next root-race. The sequence has run through the Polarian, Hyperborean, Lemurian, and Atlantean root-races and has come to the present, Aryan root-race, with the last two root-races still to come in the future. Each root-race develops one of the seven principles of the

---

[32] Although for simplicity I am presenting Blavatsky's views simply as claims, she is synthesizing a huge range of ideas from esotericism, comparative religion, and spiritual traditions.

[33] '"Pilgrim" is the appellation given to our Monad . . . during its cycle of incarnations. It is the only immortal and eternal principle in us' (*SD* 1: 16). Blavatsky draws on Leibniz ('Leibnitz conceived of the Monads as elementary and indestructible units'; 1: 179), though she maintains that the monads are emanations of universal mind rather than separate units (1: 628–30)—more like droplets of water in a lake than self-contained entities. Determining how exactly Blavatsky's conception of monads relates to that of Leibniz (or others who use the concept) is beyond the scope of this chapter.

'individualized monad': physical body, vital body, astral body, animal body, mind or intellect (*manas*), intuitive or spiritual soul, and spirit.[34] The seven root-races and principles line up so that it is the (fifth) Aryan root-race that develops (the fifth principle) *manas*, the intellect.

To add to the complexity of this account, each root-race contains seven sub-races and each sub-race contains seven family-races, each further ramifying into innumerable offshoots some of which correspond to 'nations' (*SD* 2: 198, 434). Blavatsky is rather cryptic about the identity of the seven Aryan sub-races,[35] although a few points are relatively clear: the people of ancient India are first;[36] the 'Teutonic' people of Europe, the so-called 'white conquerors', are fifth and last so far[37]—that is, modern Europeans are the fifth sub-race of the fifth root-race; and two further sub-races are to come. She hints that the intermediate links in the chain of Aryan sub-races run through ancient Chaldea, Egypt, and Homeric Greece.[38]

Cyclical evolution. The monads must ultimately move through all these stages in a sequence of reincarnations governed by the law of karma. All, more or less slowly, will advance into the more highly evolved root-races that are to come and that will be governed by the principles of intuitive soul and spirit. Overall, then: 'The whole order of nature evinces a progressive march towards a higher life' (*SD* 1: 277). This 'progressive march' notwithstanding, nowhere in cosmic evolution do we find simple linear ascent. Rather, the entire cosmos follows a pattern of first 'involution', descent into matter, then 'evolution', emergence back to spirit; this is the 'law of descent into materiality and re-ascent into spirituality' (1: 417); 'the one absolute, ever acting and never erring law, which proceeds on the same lines from one eternity...to another...plunging Spirit deeper and deeper into materiality, and *redeeming it through flesh* and liberating it' (2: 88). Thus as the monads move through the root-races, they descend into the depths of materiality, which occurs

---

[34] At times Blavatsky says that really the monad is only spirit and spiritual soul (1: 177) or only these two plus *manas* (1920: 91); but while the monads are 'descended' into material shape, they assume the other four more material layers as well (*SD* 1: 620). See also my discussion of this aspect of Blavatsky's system in Chapter 3, Sec. 3.6.

[35] Not so later theosophists, who made efforts to pin them down. Besant connected the five Aryan sub-races so far to Hinduism, Egypt, Zoroastrianism, the ancient Greeks and Romans, and the Teutonic Christians in 'Theosophy: Immediate Future' (1911).

[36] Koot Hoomi in *Esoteric Buddhism* speaks of 'India, as one of the first and most powerful offshoots of the mother race' (i.e. the Aryan race); and refers to 'the highest people now on earth (spiritually) [who] belong to the *first sub-race of the Aryan root-race*, and those are the Aryan Asiatics' (Sinnett 1883: 68, 70; my emphasis).

[37] See, again, Koot Hoomi: 'the highest race (physical intellectuality) is the last sub-race of the fifth – yourselves, the white conquerors' (Sinnett 1883: 70).

[38] At an 1889 meeting of the Blavatsky Lodge she referred to 'the divine dynasties in which every ancient nation – India, Chaldea, Egypt, Homeric Greece, etc. – has preserved the tradition in some form or another' (2014: 295). On the Egyptians as the second sub-race, see *SD* 2: 750; on the Greeks and Romans as the fourth, *SD* 2: 436. Blavatsky dates all these 'sub-races' much earlier than is conventional for their respective civilizations, because in her views the civilizations that we know of are merely late-stage survivals.

with the third Lemurian and fourth Atlantean races. Having reached the densest point of materialization during the Atlantean phase they have now begun to re-ascend towards spirit: we have 'crossed the equatorial line and [are] cycling onward on the spiritual side' (2: 301). The mid-point is crossed mid-way through the evolution of the Atlantean root-race because this is halfway through the seven stages to be traversed.

The same cyclical descent/ascent, involution/evolution pattern occurs between and within the sub-races. The first Aryan sub-race was the people of ancient India. Being the first sub-race, they are the proximate source of the ancient wisdom that needs recovery—although the Indians did not invent that wisdom but learnt it from the surviving members of the previous Atlantean root-race, who in turn had inherited it from still earlier root-races, a chain of transmission ultimately going back to the very first monads on earth. But once the Indians had elaborated this wisdom their culture declined. The next sub-race rediscovered it but then declined too. Blavatsky had already theorized this process in *Isis Unveiled*: one after another each empire descends to its lowest point, whereupon things begin to rise again, peaking in a new empire, 'the height of its attainment being, by this law of ascending progression through cycles, somewhat higher than the point from which it had before descended' (*IU* 1: 34). That is, each civilization in turn recovers the wisdom of the one before it, only to degenerate, with the next civilization then rediscovering the wisdom of its predecessor and in doing so coming back at a slightly higher level, and so on repeatedly. Each one comes back somewhat higher because: 'Everything in the universe progresses steadily in the Great Cycle, while incessantly going up and down in the smaller cycles' (1: 257). Because of this 'Great Cycle' a gradual *overall* ascent occurs. The 'Great Cycle' is that of the entire Aryan root-race, which is slowly working out its principle *manas*, and so thinks through and elaborates the original wisdom somewhat more completely with each recovery. Through this whole cycle, we move closer to the emergence of the next root-race, and concomitantly to the advance from *manas* to intuition and spirit's further re-emergence from matter.

But how does this sit with Blavatsky's view of the dire state of modern European civilization and its degenerate, exhausted state? After all, she pessimistically remarks that 'The cycle is truly at its lowest point' (*IU* 1: 622). The 'cycle' in question is the life-cycle of the European sub-race, which is at its lowest point, 'the acme of materiality' (*SD* 1: 610). Earlier in the cycle of this sub-race, Christ and his followers recovered much of the ancient wisdom of earlier civilizations; but then this wisdom was lost once more, preserved only in esoteric traditions while Church and state fossilized and decayed. Blavatsky thus weaves in a Higher-Critical contrast between the 'pure teachings of Jesus' and 'their debasement into pernicious ecclesiastical systems' (*IU* 2: iv), sounding for a moment surprisingly like Martineau. But for Blavatsky this debasement reflects the inexorable law of descent into materiality—now at its nadir, hence the dominance of the materialistic science that she associates with Darwin, Huxley, Tyndall et al. Positively, though, because we are at the ebb of the descending arc, we are poised for a new beginning, a new sub-race, and a new recovery of the ancient wisdom at a higher level than before. Thus, to quote in full the above remark from *Isis Unveiled*: 'The cycle is truly at its lowest point, *and a new era is begun*'; likewise, Blavatsky says that: 'The cycle has almost run its course, *and a new one is about to begin*' (*IU* 1: 38; my emphases). She saw the glimmerings of the new sixth sub-race emerging in North America, due to its 'strong admixture of various nationalities' (*SD* 2: 444). Reflexively, Blavatsky's own work is conveniently placed within this vast cyclical movement. Located in Europe at the end of its cycle, yet widely travelled and having learnt from a mix of nationalities and cultures, Blavatsky is perfectly placed to recover the ancient wisdom, state it with new systematicity, and thereby hasten the monads onward.

Ancient wisdom. Blavatsky reconceives progress in a way that makes sense of the idea of an ancient wisdom. The ancients *did* know more than us, because we are at a decayed point in the life-cycle of the European sub-race. Although we are further along the evolutionary course of the Aryan root-race and so of the whole cosmos than the people of ancient India or Egypt, they were at higher points in their own sub-racial cycles when they grasped the original wisdom, elements of which have secretly come down to us. Thus the original wisdom is *universal*. All peoples of all root- and sub-races have access to it during the high-points of their cycles. Hence this wisdom forms the basis of all religions and it is the fundamental unity from which all religious cultures spring (*SD* 1: viii). Moderns like Blavatsky may be best placed to elaborate this wisdom, but its core elements have been available to all peoples across the eras. This is partly because the wisdom comes down from the very first monads on earth, and partly because all seven principles of the self, including mind, are present in all monads, even though mind is only fully developed by the Aryan Europeans.

The chain of world religious cultures. Blavatsky shares with her contemporaries the idea that humanity has passed through successive civilizations each centred on its religious beliefs. In the *Secret Doctrine*, despite the vagueness about the Aryan sub-races, broadly they follow the now-familiar movement from East to West—from India through the Middle East to ancient Egypt to ancient Greece and Rome and finally Christian Europe. Blavatsky's Aryan root-race thus corresponds to Müller's Aryan or Indo-European civilization, though he identified it on a linguistic basis. It is also noteworthy that Blavatsky includes *both* India and Egypt. In *Isis Unveiled*, which still owed more to esotericism, she stressed the ancient Egyptian source of the ancient wisdom, whereas in *The Secret Doctrine* she relocates Egypt as a tributary of India.[39] This reflects the wider shift, noted earlier,

---

[39] To be fair, in *Isis*, Blavatsky already hinted that Egyptian lore derived from ancient India (*IU* 1: 625–7), but this hint was developed much more fully in *Doctrine*.

in which India displaced Egypt as the 'original civilization' in nineteenth-century British culture. Müller, who was key to that shift, influenced Blavatsky to relocate Egypt as an offshoot of India.[40] Even so, she still gives Egypt considerable importance, for although the ancient Egyptians were only recovering Indian wisdom, the Greeks and Christians in turn were only recovering Egyptian wisdom. Thus, in the *Key to Theosophy*, she refers to 'Christian theology, borrowed from the Egyptian and Greek exoteric systems of the Gnostics' ([1889] 1920: 65), and—like Martineau—she agrees with Herodotus that ancient Greece fundamentally derived from Egypt. In short, Blavatsky incorporates the older emphasis on Egypt into the newer India-centred picture.

Despite sharing the widely held idea of the Indo-European progression from East to West, Blavatsky complains that 'History – or what is called history – does not go further back than the fantastic origins of our fifth [European] sub-race' (*SD* 2: 351). In contrast, Blavatsky not only embeds the Europeans in the history of the whole Aryan race but also embeds the whole evolution of the Aryan race in the broader 'cosmogenesis' and 'anthropogenesis'. Although Blavatsky castigates standard histories of Europe as 'fantastic', from these more standard perspectives it is *The Secret Doctrine* that is fantastic—with its account of geological cataclysms, the lost civilization of the Atlanteans, the evolution from the first ethereal root-races to giants and cyclops, the 'fall' of the Lemurians into sexual reproduction, and the emergence of primates as a result of Lemurians interbreeding with animals. But she would reply that this only looks fantastic because of the restricted sights and narrow scientism of modern Europeans, who dismiss as mere 'myth' much of the real history of the cosmos.

Blavatsky's abundant talk of root-*races*, sub-*races*, the *Aryan* race, and so on, is troubling. But we should clarify straightaway that for Blavatsky the Aryan root-race includes the Semites (*SD* 2: 47). Hers is not a discourse of Aryans versus Semites. Even so, she appears to be propagating a typically high-Victorian hierarchical racial taxonomy. She has her defenders, such as James Santucci: 'The Theosophical explanation of race... should be considered to be entirely separate and apart from the discourses of race common in the eighteenth and nineteenth centuries' (2008: 39). Race is, at least, not a straightforwardly biological category for Blavatsky, who after all rejects materialistic science. Instead, she defines the Aryan root-race spiritually, in terms of *manas*. Admittedly, she says that spiritual

---

[40] Blavatsky's agreements and disagreements with Müller are many and complicated (see Lubelsky 2016). To pick out a few key points: Against Müller, she regards linguistic facts as derivative of more fundamental spiritual principles. Müller is right to apprehend the Aryans as a unity, but under the misleading dominance of analytical materialism he focuses on external linguistic details rather than inner spiritual principles (i.e. the unity of *manas*) (*SD* 2: xxxi–xxxii). Moreover, Müller mistakenly regards Eastern religions as *approximating* to the truths of Christianity, whereas for Blavatsky, Christianity has at best—and only at best—*rediscovered* the original wisdom of the East (2: xxxvii). Finally, Müller has a mistaken commitment to scholarly neutrality; the proper standpoint for gaining wisdom is to be an adept, an insider (2: xxx).

differences necessarily manifest themselves in corresponding physical features, including skin colours (*SD* 2: 249); but these physical features are secondary.

That her conception of race is spiritual and cultural rather than biological is not much of a defence, though. Saying that some races are culturally and spiritually inferior to others is no more defensible than saying that some races are biologically inferior to others. The more important point is that Blavatsky explicitly denies that any races are inferior, spiritually or otherwise. From a theosophical standpoint, 'the reason given for dividing humanity into superior and inferior races falls to the ground and becomes a fallacy' (*SD* 2: 425). This is because for the theosophist all peoples can apprehend the original wisdom and can reach it through their various traditions: 'the *Gnosis*... was never without its representatives in any age or country' (*IU* 2: 38). Wisdom is not a Western preserve.

Unfortunately, there is a more negative side to this story as well. Blavatsky's Aryan root-race does not include the African or Asiatic peoples, who are leftovers, respectively, from the (third) Lemurian and (fourth) Atlantean root-races. This is partly why Blavatsky spends so long detailing the achievements and failings of those two earlier root-races: they have ongoing relevance because much of the world's population still descends from these root-races. But therefore Asiatic and African people are less advanced, for these root-races realize the more corporeal aspects of the monad rather than *manas*. To be sure, because of civilizational cycles, the Lemurians and Atlanteans had points when they were more spiritually advanced than later Aryan sub-races are now. As such, Lemurians and Atlanteans also apprehended the original wisdom, and indeed Asians (i.e. Atlanteans) passed it on to Indians. But the surviving descendants of Lemurians and Atlanteans are not now at those advanced points. Rather, they are merely the last 'remnants of once mighty races, the recollection of whose existence has entirely died out of the remembrance of the modern generations' (*SD* 2: 445). Blavatsky speaks especially pejoratively about the Aboriginal people of Australia, classing them as a remnant of the Lemurians, 'a very low sub-race' that is already dying out (2: 197, 332). Overall, Africans and Asians count as mere relics of superseded phases in cosmic evolution, while the story is moving onward on the Aryan and ultimately European side. These claims about the African and Asian peoples directly contradict Blavatsky's principle that it is fallacious to divide humanity into superior and inferior races; unfortunately, she fails to adhere to her own principle consistently.

Reconfiguring the hierarchy of civilizations. When it comes to the hierarchy *within* the Aryan root-race—amongst its sub-races—Blavatsky's views present much more of a challenge to Eurocentrism. For by positioning ancient India as the oldest surviving source of ancient wisdom, Blavatsky dramatically raises India in status. That said, this remains a move within Orientalist discourse, for she emphasizes the insights of ancient India, by comparison to which modern India counts as degraded. 'None is older than [India] in esoteric wisdom and civilisation, however fallen may be her poor shadow – modern India' (Blavatsky 1879: 5).

Moreover, Blavatsky sees Europeans like herself as best placed to recover, gather, and restate the insights of ancient India, for Europeans are further advanced along the chain of Aryan sub-races (*SD* 2: 301). *But*, crucially, Europeans can only advance by learning from the wisdom-traditions of other parts of the world, particularly ancient India. To move on, Europeans must look outside their own orbit, and look to India above all. In practice, this means learning from the adepts in India who have kept the original traditions alive. Hence Blavatsky went to Tibet to learn from the Masters; presented herself as channelling the teachings of Morya and Koot Hoomi; and styled *The Secret Doctrine* as a mere commentary on the Book of Dzyan.

As we saw in Chapter 1, many of Blavatsky's British contemporaries were unsettled by her idea that modern Europeans should take instruction from Easterners. If her claims to have learnt from the Masters were genuine, then the hierarchy of epistemic authority would be destabilized. For their part, conversely, Indian nationalists found theosophy a useful weapon. Modern India might be stagnant, they conceded, but the British Raj had exacerbated that: it had depleted India's native cultural traditions by imposing the degenerate modern materialism favoured by the British, *and* it had exploited India's resources because of its preoccupation with material growth. Theosophy thus provided grounds for arguing that India must rejuvenate and reorganize itself around its own traditions and its more original, superior wisdom.

In sum, Blavatsky's theosophy had ambivalent racial implications and she revalued India upon a still-Orientalist basis. But there was enough ambivalence and revaluation in her picture to aid Indian nationalists in their struggle for independence.[41]

6.6 Comparisons and Colonialism

As I remarked at the start of this chapter, our four women's accounts of historical progress share three key features: there has been a world-historical progression culminating in modern Europe; this progression has passed through a sequence of stages of civilization tied to different world religions and belief systems; and the whole sequence has moved from ancient East to modern West. We can now enlarge on the differences.

Religion. For Martineau, the progression so far has culminated in Christianity and must now move on beyond Christianity, the last religion, into secularity. In contrast, for Cobbe, the progression has culminated *in* Christianity and further

---

[41] For more on this, see Bevir (2003) and Lubelsky (2012).

progress can only come from the deepening and extension of Christian sentiments, not from their overcoming. On Wedgwood's middle position, the next step is to synthesize secular science with Christian ideals. Blavatsky, too, presents her next step, theosophy, as the 'synthesis' of science, religion, and philosophy (the subtitle of *Secret Doctrine*). But this is a very different synthesis to Wedgwood's. For Blavatsky, the true elements in modern science and Christianity can only be rescued if they are reinterpreted in light of ancient wisdom. Hence the subtitle of *Isis Unveiled*: the 'master-key to the mysteries of ancient and modern science and theology'.

The sequence of world belief systems. Table 6.3 shows that the taxonomies grew more complicated as the century went on and demonstrates how the status of ancient Egypt was contested, with India replacing it as primal civilization over the century. This change was linked to the rise of the 'Aryan' paradigm, the idea of the Indo-Europeans as a single civilizational continuum. Meanwhile, ancient Greece gradually stabilized into position as the key source of European civilization. Martineau had treated it as a mere offshoot of Egypt and Cobbe ranked it beneath all the major world faiths. Wedgwood then elevated it to be Europe's foundation-stone. Although Blavatsky returned Greece to being merely one of Egypt's tributaries, the foundationalist picture of Greece, of which Wedgwood's view was an instance, was the one that became established and standard. Furthermore, for Cobbe and Wedgwood, Africa and the Far East did not figure in world history. Blavatsky did accommodate these peoples, albeit only as residues of the earlier root-races that preceded the Aryans. But she still had considerable respect for those earlier root-races and their civilizations, and gave them considerable attention as part of the cosmic evolution.

How far has the course of civilizations been an advancement? Blavatsky travelled furthest from that view. For her, each stage rediscovers the wisdom of its predecessors only to decay and degenerate before the next stage recovers the ancient wisdom again, so that ultimately that wisdom is carried through from very ancient times, indeed from the root-races before the Aryans. Yet since each recovery improves on the recoveries before it, a gradual spiritual ascent still occurs. Martineau had a not dissimilar view: each world-religion attempts to purify the noble kernel of the one before it and rescue that kernel from base superstitions, but then the new religion falls back into superstition in turn, from which the next religion again attempts to extricate the truth before sinking back down again, and so on. Nonetheless, each rescue attempt rises higher in the purifying scale than the one before it, so that a gradual ascent takes place. Cobbe distilled this structure as the 'strange law of human progress whereby all human races, and mayhap all human individuals, ascend as it were in spiral lines, coming round again in each revolving period somewhere near, yet above, the past' (*BS* 203).

Despite crystallizing this 'spiral view', Cobbe conceived each stage more firmly as an improvement on its predecessor than Martineau or Blavatsky did.

Table 6.3 Accounts of the successive world civilizations

Martineau			Egypt	Judaism	Christianity	Secular science
Cobbe	Primitive animism	Classical civilizations	Hinduism	Zoroastrianism	Judaism	Christianity
Wedgwood	Hinduism	Zoroastrianism	Classical Greece and Rome	Judaism	Christianity	Science
Blavatsky	Earlier root-races	First Aryan sub-race: Ancient India (Hinduism and Buddhism)	Egypt (?)	Chaldea (?)	Ancient Greece and Rome (?)	Fifth Aryan sub-race: Teutons/ Europe
						Synthesis of Christianity and science
						New sub-races and root-races

Wedgwood was more unequivocal still and so replaced the spiral with the zigzag: 'Men make their way up the mountain of truth, as up every other mountain, by a perpetual zig-zag. The progress of Science is the result of oscillation between opposites' (*MI* 167). Each civilizational stage realizes opposed ideas that had been compacted together and then reunites them—first the zig, then the zag, then their unity. As history progresses, then, we reach ever wider syntheses; our schemes of ideas and values become ever more developed and encompassing, or so Wedgwood thought.

On *Eurocentrism*, just as Blavatsky was the most critical of modern Europe, she also differed from the other women over Eurocentrism and Orientalism. As we have seen, Blavatsky revalued Indian religion, and this motivated some Indian nationalists to make common cause with theosophy and vice versa. Even so, Blavatsky contrasted the noble wisdom of ancient India and its current deteriorated state. Similarly for Martineau, although ancient Egypt was the source of a noble wisdom, contemporary Egypt and the East generally were degenerate and stagnant, because the components of base superstition in their religious traditions had prevailed over time. For Cobbe, too, ancient India was noble but its current reality was fallen and stagnant, while for Wedgwood, 'the Vedic belief took in instincts and emotions which later seem to have withered away' (*MI* 7).

Although Blavatsky shared this Orientalist theme—the stagnancy and degeneration of the East—she combined it with the idea that the modern West was *also* degenerate, in some ways more so than the East. Martineau, Cobbe, and Wedgwood did not think this, and as such their Orientalist claims tied in with their broad support for European colonialism and the British Empire. Martineau wrote extensively on matters of imperial politics, and supported the empire so long as it either advanced 'barbarous' countries or helped formerly great ones to rejuvenate themselves; however, she thought that once colonies had left 'minority' status they should become independent, and that the purpose of colonization must be strictly to guide colonized countries to advancement, not to exploit them economically.[42] Cobbe's views were less qualified: she was comfortable with British rule in India; she upheld the civilizing power of European culture; and she firmly opposed Irish independence (see Cobbe 1866). Wedgwood, too, described Europe, England, and 'greater England' as the platform of culture against barbarism. For instance, she thought that British rule was needed in India because the stagnancy of its culture, and its monistic denial of the reality of evil, meant that there was no culture of hard work—for there was no recognition of any real adversity for work to overcome (*MI* 29–30).

---

[42] See, on Martineau and empire, Dzelzainis and Kaplan (2010) and Logan (2004a; 2010: esp. 9, 12); on Cobbe and empire, see Hamilton (2006: 125–43), Peacock (2002: ch. 3), and Suess (2016).

These women's pro-empire views were connected, not accidentally but structurally, to their Eurocentric accounts of history as progressing through a series of stages culminating in modern Europe. For as Shohat and Stam argue, Eurocentrism and colonialism have been closely connected in general:

> Eurocentrism... emerged as a discursive rationale for colonialism... Although colonialist discourse and Eurocentric discourse are intimately intertwined, the terms have a distinct emphasis. While the former explicitly justifies colonial practices, the latter embeds, takes for granted and 'normalises' the hierarchical power relations generated by colonialism and imperialism, without necessarily even thematizing these issues directly. (Shohat and Stam [1994] 2014: 2)

We see these connections in *Eastern Life*, for example, where Martineau sketches at the end how the world-historical progression has moved from East to West and is destined to advance onwards in the West. Egyptian culture has long since stagnated, and the torch of dynamism has passed to modern Europe, she maintains (*EL* 488; see also Rees 1992: 41–5). By implication, the British Empire was justified insofar as it spread advanced Western thinking to Eastern regions that had become stuck at lower historical levels and could not pull themselves up by their own momentum. Likewise, for Cobbe, advancement has passed along the line of world-religions, moving from East to West and concluding with Christianity, which is most advanced because of the universality of its moral concern. As such, she thought that the British Empire was justified inasmuch as it diffused this Christian spirit.

There are some qualifying factors. The first concerns *imperialism and race*. Although Blavatsky's theory was the most ambiguous over imperialism, she came closest to articulating a race theory, albeit one very different from the scientific orthodoxy of the time. Conversely, both Martineau and Cobbe expressed opposition to racism and they were active abolitionists, Martineau especially. Anti-slavery was at the heart of her analysis of American society in the later 1830s:

> [T]here appears to be a mockery somewhere, when we contrast slavery with the principles and the rule which are the test of all American institutions: – the principles that all men are born free and equal; that rulers derive their just powers from the consent of the governed; and the rule of reciprocal justice. This discrepancy between principles and practice needs no more words.
> (*SA* 2: 312–13)

Martineau therefore advocated a total and immediate end to slavery. For Martineau and Cobbe, though, the British Empire and anti-racism went together, odd as this might sound to us today. They saw the empire as drawing formerly separated communities together, encouraging cultural and racial mixing, spreading commerce and the exchange of ideas, and breaking down the barriers to universal moral concern.[43] This was an over-optimistic view of the empire, to say the least. Moreover, general statements of opposition to racism could co-exist with ongoing acceptance of racist stereotypes, as we see at times in Cobbe's work (e.g. 1863).

However, there were other British women at the time who were more critical of the empire—Annie Besant, for one. Besant's relations with imperialism are a complex topic, exceeding the scope of this book and falling largely outside its nineteenth-century time-frame. Even so, it is useful here to briefly note their contours, so as to indicate that women were not all of one mind on the issue of empire.[44] During her secularist and positivist phase, Besant was highly critical of British exploitation of India. After converting to theosophy, she moved to India in 1893. This had religious rather than political motivations, stemming from her theosophical belief that India was where the ancient wisdom remained most alive. Initially, therefore, Besant was focused on the need to recover India's native spiritual wisdom:

> India's coming means the spiritualising of humanity; India's thinking means the lifting of thought on to a higher level; India's prosperity shall be the justification of religion, the justification of philosophy, as part of the life of a nation; and the world shall be redeemed from materialism because India is awake.
> (Besant [1910] 1917: 27)

But just as Blavatsky's revaluation of Indian wisdom inevitably took on a political colouring, likewise Besant could not keep these spiritual considerations apart from political ones. In 1913 she 'threw off all restraints and plunged herself into Indian political activism' (Fix Anderson 2002: 32). Once again, theosophy and Indian nationalism flowed together. Yet despite becoming central to Indian nationalism and briefly serving as president of the Indian National Congress (1818–19), Besant ultimately envisaged an expanded more holistic empire in which India, Britain, and other regions would exist as cooperating parts of a whole (see Besant 1916b). She opposed Gandhi's campaign of civil disobedience, and became increasingly accepting of a limited devolution of power. For these reasons, she became side-lined within the nationalist movement and it flowed on past her.

Besant's relations to British imperialism show, in fact, that the difference between imperial supporters and critics was not absolute. After all, Martineau, too, believed that Britain should withdraw from its territories as soon as they had attained majority. A supporter of the empire could be a qualified critic, while a

---

[43] On all these points see, for example, Martineau (1838: 206–20). On Cobbe's combination of anti-slavery with pro-imperialist views, see Carrera (2020).
[44] For some accounts, see Bevir (1998, 2003), Dinnage (1986), and Fix Anderson (2002).

critic could be a qualified supporter. And this reflects the fact that colonialist discourses contained instabilities and ambiguities—as did anti-colonialist ones.

This leads to a second area of ambiguity in these women's theories of history: how *Europe's relations with other civilizations* were conceived. To articulate how and why European civilization was most advanced, Martineau, Cobbe, and Wedgwood had to engage intellectually with other world civilizations. Accordingly, all three informed themselves heavily about non-European religious and philosophical belief-systems: ancient Egyptian philosophy for Martineau, non-Western religions for Cobbe, and the nexus of ancient Judaea, Greece, and Rome for Wedgwood. They did not hesitate to identify these belief-systems as being genuinely philosophical and religious. Admittedly, they learnt about other cultures in order to arrange them in a series culminating in modern Europe. This was quite unlike Blavatsky, who learnt about them in order to identify a perennial wisdom lost to modern Europe which it needed to recover. But, either way, all four women studied these cultures and knew considerably more about them than most professional Western philosophers in the twentieth century.

Furthermore, none of these women treated Europe as a self-contained entity. There has been a tendency in modern Western reflection on history to do just that, a pattern that Enrique Dussel (1995) has forcefully criticized. History has been reduced to the movement from classical Greece to the Roman Empire and its fall into medieval stagnation, followed eventually by modernization and progress through the Reformation, the French Revolution, and the industrial and technological revolutions. Here Europe is considered in complete isolation from its relations to the world—even though Europe's material economic dominance over other regions underpinned many of the modernizing developments being celebrated.

Again, it was Blavatsky who most sharply rejected the sort of self-contained picture that Dussel criticizes. She explicitly complained that what Europeans typically regard as history is merely one small part of the whole history of the world and all its races. But the other three women, too, in various ways saw Europe as being intrinsically related to and emerging out of non-European cultures and 'the East'. For Martineau, European culture fundamentally derived from ancient Egypt; for Cobbe, Christianity realized the seeds inherent in all world-religions; for Wedgwood, modern Europe elaborated and synthesized ideas originating in India, Persia, Judaea, and the ancient Mediterranean. They all concurred that modern Europe depended on and was internally constituted by its 'others'. Indeed, it was these instabilities within Eurocentric narratives of the kind developed by Martineau, Cobbe, and Wedgwood which made it possible for Blavatsky to articulate her much more ambivalent narrative. These women's metanarratives of historical progress were more than mere rationalizations of the European imperial project; they opened up lines of thought that destabilized that project as well.

Conclusion

After writing a book one inevitably feels painfully conscious of how much had to be left out of it. I could have said far more about the twelve women included here, and often they could have appeared under additional topics besides those where I featured them—for instance, Mary Shepherd and Victoria Welby could have appeared in relation to mind, Annie Besant on naturalism, Helena Blavatsky and Vernon Lee on evolution, or Julia Wedgwood on religion and morality. And that is only for the topics that I covered: these women wrote about many other topics as well, such as animal welfare, slavery, feminism, language, aesthetics, and welfare. Hopefully, though, one thing this book has made clear is that women did not only address practical, value-facing topics such as feminism and animal welfare, important as those topics are. Women wrote across the full spectrum of philosophical questions, just like their male contemporaries. And, in addition to the women discussed in this book, there were many, many other women doing philosophy in Britain at the time. No doubt the more all this is explored, the more limitations will be exposed in my narrative. But I hope to have at least shown others that there is a rich field here for further inquiry.

What can we take from the work of these nineteenth-century women philosophers in Britain? In many ways their work offers an inspiring model of how to do philosophy. Most of these women were not specialists; they addressed diverse audiences that were sometimes very wide indeed and sometimes consisted of fellow partisans in a common political, religious, or intellectual endeavour. This affected how these women wrote: sometimes their writing was direct, plain, and straightforward; or bold and ambitious; or 'writerly', packed with vivid examples and literary connections; sometimes it was intended to persuade and arouse, showing great rhetorical verve. Being generalists, these women did not lose sight of the big questions and they wrote with a sense of the live importance and urgency of the matters they addressed.

What can we learn for our practice as historians of women in philosophy? As we set about recovering women in the nineteenth century, we should not be deterred by finding them badged as 'writers' or 'reformers'. These catch-all terms reflect the fact that nineteenth-century women frequently do not fit our inherited image of the professional philosopher—or, indeed, that of the specialist of any specific discipline, hence such suitably vague and expansive labels as 'writer' and 'reformer'. When one finds a woman described in scholarly literature as a 'writer', it is usually worth taking a closer look; some of what she wrote may turn out to have been philosophy. Nor should we be misled by women calling themselves 'popularizers', 'educators', 'translators', and so on. As we have seen, these commonly served as screen-words behind which women surreptitiously got on with original philosophizing.

We should not expect these women to have been doing professional philosophy *avant la lettre*. Some of them, like Shepherd and Welby at times, may have been doing things that come relatively close to professional philosophy as it exists in the twenty-first century. But we should not demand this of everyone; rather, we should be open to other forms of philosophizing as well, given that the bulk of nineteenth-century philosophizing occurred in the generalist periodical culture. Partly for this reason, we can learn a great deal from the large body of scholarship, crossing many disciplines, on nineteenth-century culture, society, politics, science, history, and letters. Much of this scholarship is philosophically relevant.

We cannot recover nineteenth-century women philosophers without also recovering their male contemporaries who have likewise fallen from view, as with George Henry Lewes, William Benjamin Carpenter, Robert Lewins, Charles Babbage, and others. Nevertheless, I encourage others to attend to the intellectual relations amongst women in their own right, moving beyond the practice of restoring a particular woman by placing her in relation only to her male interlocutors. We should not be put off by women's paucity of explicit references to one another in their published work. As we have seen, because of patriarchal constraints at the time, women frequently reached for the 'disappearing ink' when they wrote. They deliberately made themselves and other women invisible. It is quite sad to see women of the period do this again and again—sad because every time a woman referred only to male interlocutors, wanting understandably to put herself in the right intellectual company, she nonetheless contributed to ensuring that other subsequent women would make the same judgement and would therefore not refer to her work. A strategy that made sense for individual women unfortunately helped to consolidate the invisibility of women philosophers as a group.

To make visible what has been invisible, we need to approach women's published work with knowledge of the relevant constraints and contextual factors: anonymity, periodical culture, scholarly practice and conventions at the time, and the role of footnotes as 'historically conditioned echoes of the scholarly, cultural and ideological forces of their time' (Garritzen 2020). Additional sources such as correspondence, and historical scholarship about intellectual and social networks, can fill in the traces of inter-women influence that women frequently obscured in their published work.

Women may have covered over their tracks, but they were there. Their exclusion from nineteenth-century philosophical and intellectual life was far less complete than stereotypes about the period may have led us to expect. A huge body of nineteenth-century women's philosophical writing lies waiting, ready to be integrated into our narratives about the philosophy of this period and receive the investigation, interpretation, and analysis that it deserves.

Bibliography

Alarabi, Nour (2012). Constance Naden's Philosophical Poetry. *Literature Compass* 9: 848–60.
Albrecht, Thomas (2020). *The Ethical Vision of George Eliot*. London: Routledge.
Allard, James (2014). Early Nineteenth-Century Logic. In W. J. Mander, ed., *The Oxford Handbook of British Philosophy in the Nineteenth Century*. Oxford: Oxford University Press.
Anger, Suzy (2019). George Eliot and Philosophy. In George Levine and Nancy Henry, eds, *The Cambridge Companion to George Eliot*. 2nd edn. Cambridge: Cambridge University Press.
Anonymous (1840). Principles of General and Comparative Physiology [review]. *Edinburgh Medical and Surgical Journal* 53 (1 Jan.): 213–28.
Anonymous (1871). Mr. Darwin's Descent of Man [second notice]. *Spectator* (18 Mar.): 319–20.
Anonymous (1873). Unconscious Fallacy of 'Unconscious Cerebration'. *College Courant* (15 Mar.): 121–2.
Anonymous (1891). Mrs Annie Besant. *Boston Evening Transcript* (9 Apr.): 4.
Anonymous (1892a). Vivisection. *The Times* (7 Oct.): 6.
Anonymous (1892b). A New Philosophy [review of Naden's *Induction and Deduction* and other works]. *Journal of Mental Science* 38: 275–9.
Anonymous (1894). Record of Events: The Institute of Journalists. *Englishwoman's Review* 223 (15 Oct.): 28–48.
Armstrong, Isobel (2021). *Monthly Repository* (1806–1838). *Nineteenth-Century Serials Edition*. https://ncse.ac.uk/headnotes/mrp.html.
Arnold, Matthew (1887). Up to Easter. *Nineteenth Century* 21 (123): 629–43.
Ashton, Rosemary (1980). *The German Idea: Four English Writers and the Reception of German Thought, 1800–1860*. Cambridge: Cambridge University Press.
Ashton, Rosemary (2006). *142 Strand: A Radical Address in Victorian London*. London: Vintage.
Atalić, Bruno and Stella Fatović-Ferenčić (2009). Emanuel Edward Klein—The Father of British Microbiology and the Case of the Animal Vivisection Controversy of 1875. *Toxicologic Pathology* 37 (6): 708–13.
Atherton, Margaret (1996). Lady Mary Shepherd's Case Against Berkeley. *British Journal for the History of Philosophy* 4 (2): 348–66.
Babbage, Charles (1838). *The Ninth Bridgewater Treatise. A Fragment*. 2nd edn. London: Murray.
Babbage, Charles ([1837] 1989). On the Mathematical Powers of the Calculating Engine. In *The Works of Charles Babbage*, ed. Martin Campbell-Kelly, vol. 3. New York: New York University Press.
Baillie, Joanna (1798). Introductory Discourse. In *A Series of Plays in which it is attempted to delineate the Stronger Passions of the Mind*. London: T. Cadell and W. Davies.

Barbauld, Anna Letitia ([1773] 2002). Against Inconsistency in our Expectations. In *Anna Letitia Barbauld: Selected Poetry and Prose*, ed. William McCarthy and Elizabeth Kraft. Ontario, CA: Broadview Press.
Barker, A. T., ed. (1923). *The Mahatma Letters to A. P. Sinnett from the Mahatmas M. & K. H.* London: T. Fisher Unwin.
Barker, J. H. (1881). Life and its Basis. *Journal of Science* (3rd series) 3: 1–10.
Barrat, Alain (2005). George Henry Lewes's *Comte's 'Philosophy of the Sciences'*. *George Eliot–George Henry Lewes Studies* 48-9: 19–26.
Barrell, John (1991). Death on the Nile: Fantasy and the Literature of Tourism 1840–1860. *Essays in Criticism* 61 (2): 97–127.
Bartholomew, Michael (1973). Lyell and Evolution. *British Journal for the History of Science* 6 (3): 261–303.
Barton Scott, J. (2009). Miracle Publics: Theosophy, Christianity, and the Coulomb Affair. *History of Religions* 49 (2): 172–96.
Battersby, Christine (1989). *Gender and Genius*. London: The Women's Press.
Beer, Gillian (1983). *Darwin's Plots*. Cambridge: Cambridge University Press.
Beeton, Isabella (1861). *The Book of Household Management*. London: S. O. Beeton.
Bergès, Sandrine (2015). On the Outskirts of the Canon: The Myth of the Lone Female Philosopher, and What to Do about It. *Metaphilosophy* 46 (3): 380–97.
Bernal, Martin (1987). *Black Athena: The Afroasiatic Roots of Classical Civilization*, vol. 1. New Brunswick, NJ: Rutgers University Press.
Besant, Annie (1887). Marx's Theory of Value. *Pall Mall Gazette* (24 May): 2.
Besant, Annie (1898). *Esoteric Christianity*. London: Theosophical Publishing.
Besant, Annie (1903). *Against Vivisection*. Benares: Theosophical Publishing.
Besant, Annie (1911). *Theosophy: Immediate Future*. London: Theosophical Publishing.
Besant, Annie (1914). *India and the Empire*. London: Theosophical Publishing.
Besant, Annie (1916a). *India: A Nation; A Plea for Self-Government*. London: Theosophical Publishing.
Besant, Annie (1916b). Theosophy and Imperialism. *The Theosophist* 37: 477–82.
Besant, Annie ([1910] 1917). *The Birth of New India*. Adyar: Theosophical Publishing.
Bevir, Mark (1998). In Opposition to the Raj: Annie Besant and the Dialectic of Empire. *History of Political Thought* 19 (1): 61–77.
Bevir, Mark (1999). Annie Besant's Quest for Truth: Christianity, Secularism and New Age Thought. *Journal of Ecclesiastical History* 50: 62–93.
Bevir, Mark (2003). Theosophy and the Origins of the Indian National Congress. *International Journal of Hindu Studies* 7: 99–115.
Birch, Catherine Elizabeth (2011). Evolutionary Feminism in Late-Victorian Women's Poetry. PhD thesis, University of Birmingham. https://etheses.bham.ac.uk/id/eprint/3024/1/Birch11PhD.pdf.
Blavatsky, Helena Petrovna (1879). What Are the Theosophists? *The Theosophist* 1 (1): 5–7.
Blavatsky, Helena Petrovna (1886). H. P. Blavatsky on Precipitation and Other Matters. Letter from Blavatsky to Constance Wachtmeister (Jan.). https://universaltheosophy.com/hpb/hp-blavatsky-on-precipitation-and-other-matters/.
Blavatsky, Helena Petrovna (1886). Have Animals Souls? *The Theosophist* 7: 243–9.
Blavatsky, Helena Petrovna (1888). Lodges of Magic. *Lucifer* 3: 89–93.
Blavatsky, Helena Petrovna (1890). The Dual Aspect of Wisdom. *Lucifer* 7: 1–9.
Blavatsky, Helena Petrovna (1920). *The Key to Theosophy*. 3rd revised edn. London: Theosophical Publishing.

Blavatsky, Helena Petrovna (2004). *The Letters of H. P. Blavatsky: Volume 1, 1861–1879*, ed. John Algeo. New York: Quest Books.
Blavatsky, Helena Petrovna (2014). *The Secret Doctrine Dialogues: H. P. Blavatsky Talks with Students*. Los Angeles, CA: The Theosophy Company.
Blinderman, C. and D. Joyce (1998). *The Huxley File*. http://aleph0.clarku.edu/huxley/.
Boddice, Rob (2011). Vivisecting Major: A Victorian Gentleman Scientist Defends Animal Experimentation, 1876–1885. *Isis* 102 (2): 215–37.
Bohls, Elizabeth A. (1995). *Women Travel Writers and the Language of Aesthetics, 1716–1818*. Cambridge: Cambridge University Press.
Bolton, Martha (2011). Causality and Causal Induction: The Necessitarian Theory of Lady Mary Shepherd. In Keith Allen and Tom Stoneham, eds, *Causation and Modern Philosophy*. London: Routledge.
Bolton, Martha (2021). Mary Shepherd. In Edward N. Zalta, ed., *Stanford Encyclopedia of Philosophy* (Spring 2021 edition). https://plato.stanford.edu/archives/spr2021/entries/mary-shepherd/.
Boole, Mary Everest (1931). *Collected Works*, 4 vols, ed. E. M. Cobham. London: C. W. Daniel.
Boos, Florence S. (2017). *Memoirs of Victorian Working-Class Women*. Dordrecht: Springer.
Boswell, Michelle (2019). Buckley, Arabella. In Lesa Scholl, ed., *The Palgrave Encyclopedia of Victorian Women's Writing*. Basingstoke: Palgrave Macmillan.
Boucher-Rivalain, Odile (2012). Harriet Martineau (1802–1876), from Unitarianism to Agnosticism. *Cahiers victoriens et édouardiens* 76: 27–43.
Bourne Taylor, Jenny (2000). Fallacies of Memory in Nineteenth-Century Psychology: Henry Holland, William Carpenter and Frances Power Cobbe. *Victorian Review* 26: 98–118.
Bourne Taylor, Jenny and Sally Shuttleworth, eds (1998). *Embodied Selves: An Anthology of Psychological Texts 1830–1890*. Oxford: Clarendon Press.
Boyle, Deborah (2017). Expanding the Canon of Scottish Philosophy: The Case for Adding Mary Shepherd. *The Journal of Scottish Philosophy* 15 (3): 275–93.
Boyle, Deborah (2018). Introduction to *Lady Mary Shepherd: Selected Writings*, ed. Deborah Boyle. Bristol: Imprint Academic.
Boyle, Deborah (2020). Mary Shepherd on Mind, Soul, and Self. *Journal of the History of Philosophy* 58 (1): 93–112.
Boyle, Deborah (2021a). Mary Shepherd on the Meaning of 'Life'. *British Journal for the History of Philosophy* 29 (2): 208–25.
Boyle, Deborah (2021b). Lady Mary Shepherd: A Snapshot. *Philosopher's Magazine*. https://archive.philosophersmag.com/snapshot-lady-mary-shepherd/.
Boyle, Deborah (2021c). Elizabeth Hamilton's *Memoirs of Modern Philosophers* as a Philosophical Text. *British Journal for the History of Philosophy* 29 (6): 1072–98.
Braid, James (1846). *The Power of the Mind Over the Body: An Experimental Inquiry into the Nature and Cause of the Phenomena Attributed by Reichenbach and Others to a 'New Imponderable'*. London: John Churchill.
Brake, Laurel (2021). The Leader (1850–1859), *Nineteenth-Century Serials Edition*. https://ncse.ac.uk/headnotes/ldr.html.
Brake, Laurel and Marysa Demoor (2009). *Dictionary of Nineteenth-Century Journalism in Britain and Ireland*. London: Academia Press.
Brandreth, Mary Elizabeth Shepherd (1886). *Some Family and Friendly Recollections of 70 Years*. Westerham: C. Hooker.

Bressey, Caroline (2010). Victorian 'Anti-Racism' and Feminism in Britain. *Women: A Cultural Review* 21 (3): 279–91.
Bressey, Caroline (2012). Reporting Oppression: Mapping Racial Prejudice in *Anti-Caste* and *Fraternity*, 1888–1895. *Journal of Historical Geography* 38 (4): 401–11.
Bressey, Caroline (2013). *Empire, Race and the Politics of Anti-Caste*. London: Bloomsbury.
Brilmyer, S. Pearl (2017). Darwinian Feminisms. In Stacy Alaimo, ed., *Gender: Matter*. New York: Macmillan.
Bringsjord, Selmer, Paul Bello, and David Ferrucci (2001). Creativity, the Turing Test, and the (Better) Lovelace Test. *Minds and Machines* 11: 3–27.
Broad, Jacqueline (2003). *Women Philosophers of the Seventeenth Century*. Cambridge: Cambridge University Press.
Brown, Stuart (2014). The Professionalization of British Philosophy. In W. J. Mander, ed., *The Oxford Handbook of British Philosophy in the Nineteenth Century*. Oxford: Oxford University Press.
Brown, Sue (2022). *Julia Wedgwood, The Unexpected Victorian: The Life and Writing of a Remarkable Female Intellectual*. London: Anthem.
Bruce, Steve (2002). *God is Dead: Secularization in the West*. Oxford: Wiley-Blackwell.
Buckle, Henry Thomas (1857–61). *History of Civilisation in England*. London: Parker.
Buckley, Arabella (1881). *Life and Her Children*. London: E. Stanford.
Buckley, Arabella (1882). *Winners in Life's Race*. London: E. Stanford.
Buckley, Arabella and W. J. Robertson (1891). *High School History of England*. Toronto: Clark.
Bullivant, Stephen (2016). Defining 'Atheism'. In Stephen Bullivant and Michael Ruse, eds, *The Oxford Handbook of Atheism*. Oxford: Oxford University Press.
Burdett, Carolyn (2020). Sympathy–Antipathy in Daniel Deronda. *19: Interdisciplinary Studies in the Long Nineteenth Century* 0 (29). https://doi.org/10.16995/ntn.1983.
Burdon-Sanderson, J., et al. (1873). *Handbook for the Physiological Laboratory*. London: J. & A. Churchill.
Burton, Antoinette (1994). *Burdens of History: British Feminists, Indian Women, and Imperial Culture, 1865–1915*. Chapel Hill: The University of North Carolina Press.
Buurma, Rachel Sagner (2007). Anonymity, Corporate Authority, and the Archive. *Victorian Studies* 50 (1): 15–42.
Byron, George Gordon (1976). *Letters and Journals, Volume V: 'So late into the night,' 1816–1817*, ed. Leslie Marchand. Cambridge, MA: Harvard University Press.
Byun, Jiwon (2017). Thomas Henry Huxley's Agnostic Philosophy of Science. PhD thesis, University of British Columbia.
Caine, Barbara (1993). *Victorian Feminists*. Oxford: Oxford University Press.
Calabria, Michael D., ed. (1996). *Florence Nightingale in Egypt and Greece: Her Diary and 'Visions'*. Albany, NY: SUNY Press.
Capern, Amanda L. (2008). Edith Thompson (*pseud.* Evelyn Todd) (1848–1929). *Oxford Dictionary of National Biography*. https://doi.org/10.1093/ref:odnb/64832.
Carlisle, Clare, ed. (2019). *Spinoza's Ethics*, trans. George Eliot. Princeton, NJ: Princeton University Press.
Carpenter, William Benjamin (1837). On the Voluntary and Instinctive Actions of Living Beings. *Edinburgh Medical Surgical Journal* 48 (1 July): 22–44.
Carpenter, William Benjamin ([1844] 1845). *Principles of Human Physiology*. 2nd edn. Philadelphia, PA: Lea & Blanchard.
Carpenter, William Benjamin (1852). *On the Influence of Suggestion in Modifying and directing Muscular Movement, independently of Volition*. London: Royal Institution of Great Britain.

Carpenter, William Benjamin (1855). *Principles of Human Physiology*. 5th edn. Philadelphia, PA: Lea & Blanchard.
Carpenter, William Benjamin (1871). The Physiology of the Will. *Contemporary Review* 17: 192–217.
Carrera, María José (2020). Frances Power Cobbe on Brutes, Women, and the Irish (Human) Landscape: Ethics, Environment, and Imperialism. *Estudios irlandeses* 15: 31–41.
Carus, Paul (1894). Monism and Henism. *The Monist* 4: 228–47.
Chadwick, Owen (1975). *The Secularization of the European Mind in the Nineteenth Century*. Cambridge: Cambridge University Press.
Chajes, Julie (2017). Reincarnation in H. P. Blavatsky's 'The Secret Doctrine'. *Correspondences* 5: 65–93.
Claeys, Gregory (2010). *Imperial Sceptics*. Cambridge: Cambridge University Press.
Claggett, Shalyn (2010). Harriet Martineau's Material Rebirth. *Victorian Literature and Culture* 38 (1): 53–73.
Class, Monika (2012). *Coleridge and Kantian Ideas in England, 1796–1817*. London: Bloomsbury.
Cobbe, Frances Power (1857). *Religious Duty*. London: Longmans.
Cobbe, Frances Power (1863). *The Red Flag in John Bull's Eyes*. London: Emily Faithfull.
Cobbe, Frances Power (1864). *Broken Lights: An Inquiry into the Present Condition and Future Prospects of Religious Faith*. London: Trübner.
Cobbe, Frances Power (1866). The Fenian 'Idea'. *Atlantic Monthly* 17: 572–7.
Cobbe, Frances Power (1869). The Final Cause of Woman. In Josephine Butler, ed., *Woman's Work and Woman's Culture*. London: Macmillan.
Cobbe, Frances Power (1881). The Medical Profession and its Morality. *Modern Review* (Apr.): 296–328.
Cobbe, Frances Power (1888). The Education of the Emotions. *Fortnightly Review* 43: 223–36.
Cobbe, Frances Power (1895). The Ethics of Zoophily. *Contemporary Review* 68: 497–508.
Colby, Vineta (2003). *Vernon Lee: A Literary Biography*. Charlottesville: University of Virginia Press.
Coleman, William Emmett (1895). The Sources of Madame Blavatsky's Writings. In *A Modern Priestess of Isis* by Vsevolod Sergyeevich Solovyoff. London: Longmans, Green, and Co.
Colley, Linda (2009). *Britons: Forging the Nation 1707–1837*. 3rd edn. New Haven, CT: Yale University Press.
Collini, Stefan (1993). *Public Moralists: Political Thought and Intellectual Life in Britain, 1850–1930*. Oxford: Oxford University Press.
Conley, John (2000). Madame de Sablé's Moral Philosophy. In Cecile T. Tougas, ed., *Presenting Women Philosophers*. Philadelphia, PA: Temple University Press.
Conlin, Jonathan (2014). *Evolution and the Victorians*. London: Bloomsbury.
Cook, Chris (2005). *The Routledge Companion to Britain in the Nineteenth Century, 1815–1914*. London: Routledge.
Corbeil, Patrick John (2019). Grounding Non-Theological Morality: The Victorian Secularist Movement, Secular Ethics, and Human Progress. *Secularism and Nonreligion* 8. https://secularismandnonreligion.org/articles/10.5334/snr.93/.
Cornwallis, Caroline Frances (1841). *Philosophical Theories and Philosophical Experience*. London: Pickering.
Cornwallis, Caroline Frances (1864). *Selections from the Letters of Caroline Frances Cornwallis*. London: Trübner.

Cox, R. G. (2005). The Cornhill Magazine. *The Victorian Web*. https://victorianweb.org/periodicals/cornhill/cornhill.html.
Craft, William (1860). *Running a Thousand Miles for Freedom*. London: W. Tweedie.
Cranston, Sylvia (1992). *H. P. B.: The Extraordinary Life and Influence of Helena Blavatsky*. New York: Putnam's Sons.
Crawford, Iain (2017). Harriet Martineau: Women, Work and Mid-Victorian Journalism. In Joanne Shattock, ed., *Journalism and the Periodical Press in Nineteenth-Century Britain*. Cambridge: Cambridge University Press.
Crockett, Alasdair (1998). A Secularizing Geography? Patterns and Processes of Religious Change in England and Wales, 1676–1851. PhD thesis, University of Leicester.
Cross, John (1885). *George Eliot's Life: As Related in Her Letters and Journals*, 3 vols. London: Blackwood and Sons.
Curle, Richard, ed. (1937). *Robert Browning and Julia Wedgwood: A Broken Friendship as Revealed by Their Letters*. New York: Stokes.
Currer, Rebekah Julia Fairgray (2020). Dissent, Discussion and Dissemination: The Strategies of the Kensington Society in the Mid-Victorian Women's Movement. PhD thesis, University of Melbourne.
Dabby, Benjamin (2017). *Women as Public Moralists in Britain*. London: Boydell & Brewer.
Dabydeen, David and Paul Edwards (1991). *Black Writers in Britain 1760–1890*. Edinburgh: Edinburgh University Press.
Dale, R. W. (1891). Constance Naden. *Contemporary Review* 59: 508–22.
Dancy, Jonathan (1993). *Moral Reasons*. Oxford: Blackwell.
Darwin, Charles (1859). *On the Origin of Species by Means of Natural Selection*. London: Murray.
Darwin, Charles (1871). *The Descent of Man*, 2 vols. London: Murray.
Darwin, Charles (1872). *The Origin of Species*. 6th edn. London: Murray.
Darwin, Henrietta (1871). Journal entry, 26 March. https://www.darwinproject.ac.uk/henrietta-darwins-diary.
David, Deirdre (1987). *Intellectual Women and Victorian Patriarchy*. Basingstoke: Macmillan.
Davidoff, Leonore (1973). *The Best Circles: Society, the Season, and Etiquette*. London: Croom Helm.
Davidson, Catherine (1998). Preface: No More Separate Spheres! *American Literature* 70 (3): 443–63.
Davies, Emily (1866). *The Higher Education of Women*. London: Strahan.
Dawkins, Richard (2006). *The God Delusion*. London: Bantam.
De Morgan, Augustus (1837). *The Elements of Algebra*. London: Taylor & Walton.
De Morgan, Augustus (1849). *Trigonometry and Double Algebra*. London: Taylor, Walton & Malbery.
Delorme, Shannon (2014). Physiology or Psychic Powers? William Carpenter and the Debate over Spiritualism in Victorian Britain. *Studies in History and Philosophy of Biological and Biomedical Sciences* 48 (A): 57–66.
Dilke, Emilia (1869). Art and Morality. *Westminster Review* 35: 149–84.
Dilke, Emilia (1873). The Use of Looking at Pictures. *Westminster Review* 44: 415–23.
Dinnage, Rosemary (1986). *Annie Besant*. Harmondsworth: Penguin.
Dixon, Joy (2001). *Divine Feminine: Theosophy and Feminism in England*. Baltimore, MD: Johns Hopkins University Press.
Dixon, Thomas (2008). *The Invention of Altruism: Making Moral Meanings in Victorian Britain*. Oxford: Oxford University Press.

Dockrill, D. W. (1971). T. H. Huxley and the Meaning of 'Agnosticism'. *Theology* 74: 461–77.
Donald, Diana (2019). *Women Against Cruelty: Protection of Animals in Nineteenth-Century Britain*. Manchester: Manchester University Press.
Drew, John (2017). Dickens and the Middle-Class Weekly. In Joanne Shattock, ed., *Journalism and the Periodical Press in Nineteenth-Century Britain*. Cambridge: Cambridge University Press.
Duncan, David, ed. (1911). *The Life and Letters of Herbert Spencer* [reissue]. London: Williams & Norgate.
Dussel, Enrique (1995). *The Invention of the Americas: Eclipse of 'the Other' and the Myth of Modernity*, trans. Michael D. Barber. New York: Continuum.
Dzelzainis, Ella and Cora Kaplan, eds (2010). *Harriet Martineau: Authorship, Society and Empire*. Manchester: Manchester University Press.
E. V. N. (1870). Latent Thought. *Spectator* (12 Nov.): 1349–50.
Easley, Alexis (2004). *First Person Anonymous: Women Writers and Victorian Print Media, 1830–70*. Farnham: Ashgate.
Easley, Alexis, Clare Gill, and Beth Rodgers, eds (2019). *Women, Periodicals and Print Culture in Britain, 1830s–1900s*. Edinburgh: Edinburgh University Press.
Eastern Hermit (1878). Ivy-Leaves. *Fraser's Magazine* 17: 259–68.
Eliot, George, trans. (1846). *Life of Jesus* by David Friedrich Strauss. London: Edward Chapman and William Hall.
Eliot, George [Marian Evans], trans. (1854). *The Essence of Christianity* by Ludwig Feuerbach. London: Edward Chapman and William Hall.
Eliot, George (1856). Silly Novels by Lady Novelists. *Westminster Review* 66: 442–61.
Eliot, George (1865). The Influence of Rationalism. *Fortnightly Review* 1: 43–55.
Eliot, George ([1876] 2010). *Daniel Deronda*. New York: Open Road Integrated Media.
Eliot, George ([1872] 2016). *Middlemarch*. New York: Open Road Integrated Media.
Eliot, Simon (n.d.). Introduction. *Aspects of the Victorian Book*. British Library. https://www.bl.uk/collections/early/victorian/pu_intro.html.
Ellegård, Alvar (1971). The Readership of the Periodical Press in Mid-Victorian Britain: II. Directory. *Victorian Periodicals Newsletter* 4 (3): 3–22.
Engledue, W. C. (1843). *Cerebral Physiology and Materialism*. London: Watson.
Essinger, James (2014). *Ada's Algorithm*. London: Gibson Square.
Evans, Samantha, ed. (2017). *Darwin and Women: A Selection of Letters*. Cambridge: Cambridge University Press.
Fantl, Jeremy (2016). Mary Shepherd on Causal Necessity. *Metaphysica* 17 (1): 87–108.
Faraday, Michael (1846). Thoughts on Ray Vibrations. *Experimental Researches in Electricity* 3: 447–52.
Ferguson, Christine (2020). The Luciferian Public Sphere: Theosophy and Editorial Seekership in the 1880s. *Victorian Periodicals Review* 53 (1): 76–101.
Ferguson, Moira (1992). *Subject to Others: British Women Writers and Colonial Slavery*. London: Routledge.
Ferreira, M. Jamie (1995). Hume's 'Natural History': Religion and 'Explanation'. *Journal of the History of Philosophy* 33 (4): 593–611.
Ferris, Ina (2012). The Debut of *The Edinburgh Review*, 1802. *BRANCH: Britain, Representation and Nineteenth-Century History*. http://www.branchcollective.org/?ps_articles=ina-ferris-the-debut-of-the-edinburgh-review-1802.
Fessenbecker, Patrick (2018). Sympathy, Vocation, and Moral Deliberation in George Eliot. *ELH* 85 (2): 501–32.

Fessenbecker, Patrick (2021). The Fragility of Rationality: George Eliot on Akrasia and the Law of Consequences. *British Journal for the History of Philosophy* 29 (2): 275–91.
Fix Anderson, Nancy (2002). 'Mother Besant' and Indian National Politics. *Journal of Imperial and Commonwealth History* 30 (3): 27–54.
Fleishman, Avrom (2010). *George Eliot's Intellectual Life*. Cambridge: Cambridge University Press.
Folescu, M. (2021). Mary Shepherd on the Role of Proofs in our Knowledge of First Principles. *Noûs* (early view). https://doi.org/10.1111/nous.12365.
Forbes-Macphail, Imogen (2013). The Enchantress of Numbers and the Magic Noose of Poetry. *Journal of Language, Literature and Culture* 60 (3): 138–56
Foucault, Michel ([1969] 1998). What is an Author? In James Faubion, ed., *Aesthetics, Method, and Epistemology*. New York: New Press.
Francis, Mark (2007). *Herbert Spencer and the Invention of Modern Life*. London: Routledge.
Froude, James Anthony (1851). Materialism – Miss Martineau and Mr. Atkinson. *Fraser's Magazine* 43: 418–34.
Fryer, Peter (1984). *Staying Power: The History of Black People in Britain*. London: Pluto Press.
Fulton, Richard D. (2016). Richard Holt Hutton: A Retrospective. *Nineteenth-Century Prose* 43 (1–2): 135–50.
Galton, Francis (1865). Hereditary Talent and Character. Part Two. *Macmillan's Magazine* 12: 318–27.
Galton, Francis (1870). Gregariousness in Cattle and in Men. *Macmillan's Magazine* 23: 353–7.
Gange, David (2013). *Dialogues with the Dead: Egyptology in British Culture and Religion, 1822–1922*. Oxford: Oxford University Press.
Gardner, Catherine Villanueva (2013). *Empowerment and Interconnectivity: Toward a Feminist History of Utilitarian Philosophy*. University Park, PA: Penn State University Press.
Garritzen, Elise [ms footnote] (2020). The Masked Historian: Publishing History Anonymously in Victorian Britain. *Clio's Footnotes* blog. https://cliosfootnotes.wordpress.com/2020/04/.
Gatens, Moira (2008). Marian Evans, George Henry Lewes and 'George Eliot'. *Angelaki* 13 (2): 33–44.
Gatens, Moira (2009). The Art and Philosophy of George Eliot. *Philosophy and Literature* 33: 73–90.
Gates, Barbara T. (1997). Revisioning Darwin with Sympathy: Arabella Buckley. In Barbara T. Gates and Ann B. Shteir, eds, *Natural Eloquence: Women Reinscribe Science*. Madison: University of Wisconsin Press.
Gates, Barbara T. (1998). *Kindred Nature: Victorian and Edwardian Women Embrace the Living World*. Chicago, IL: University of Chicago Press.
Gates, Barbara T. (2004). Buckley [married name Fisher], Arabella Burton (1840–1929). *Dictionary of National Biography*. https://doi.org/10.1093/ref:odnb/54371.
Gerzina, Gretchen (2003). *Black Victorians/Black Victoriana*. New Brunswick, NJ: Rutgers University Press.
Gjesdal, Kristin and Dalia Nassar, eds. (2022). *Oxford Handbook of Nineteenth-Century Women Philosophers in The German Tradition*. Oxford: Oxford University Press.
Gleadle, Kathryn (1998). *The Early Feminists: Radical Unitarians and the Emergence of the Women's Rights Movement, 1831–51*. London: Palgrave.

Godwin, Joscelyn (2013). Blavatsky and the First Generation of Theosophy. In Olav Hammer and Mikael Rothstein, eds, *Handbook of the Theosophical Current*. Leiden: Brill.

Gokcekus, Samin (2019). Elizabeth Hamilton's Scottish Associationism: Early Nineteenth-Century Philosophy of Mind. *Journal of the American Philosophical Association* 5 (3): 267–85.

Goodman, Russell B. (2015). *American Philosophy Before Pragmatism*. New York: Oxford University Press.

Goodrick-Clarke, Nicholas, ed. (2004). *Helena Blavatsky: Western Esoteric Masters*. Berkeley, CA: North Atlantic Books.

Gray, Beryl (2000). George Eliot and the *Westminster Review*. *Victorian Periodicals Review* 33 (3): 212–24.

Gray, Jeremy (2014). Some British Logicians. In W. J. Mander, ed., *The Oxford Handbook of British Philosophy in the Nineteenth Century*. Oxford: Oxford University Press.

Gray, Lesley Frances (2018). Interdisciplinary Perspectives on Mesmer and His Legacy. PhD thesis, University of Kent. https://kar.kent.ac.uk/73400/.

Green, Christopher D. (2001). Charles Babbage, the Analytical Engine, and the Possibility of a 19th-Century Cognitive Science. In C. D. Green, M. Shore, and T. Teo, eds, *The Transformation of Psychology*. Washington, DC: American Psychological Association.

Green, Christopher D. (2005). Was Babbage's Analytical Engine Intended to Be a Mechanical Model of the Mind? *History of Psychology* 8 (1): 35–45.

Greg, William Rathbone (1868). On the Failure of 'Natural Selection' in the Case of Man. *Fraser's Magazine* 78: 353–62.

Gregory, William (1846). Abstract of 'Researches on Mesmerism and on Certain Allied Subjects', by Baron von Reichenbach. London: Taylor and Walton.

Gurney, Emelia Russell (1902). *Letters of Emelia Russell Gurney*, ed. Mary Ellen Gurney. London: Nisbet.

Haight, Gordon, ed. (1969). *George Eliot and John Chapman*. 2nd edn. Hamden, CT: Archon Books.

Hall, Wayne (2000). *Dialogues in the Margin: A Study of the Dublin University Magazine*. Washington, DC: Catholic University of America Press.

Hamilton, Elizabeth (1801). *Letters on Education*. Bath: R. Cruttwell.

Hamilton, Susan (2006). *Frances Power Cobbe and Victorian Feminism*. New York: Palgrave.

Hamilton, Susan (2012). 'Her Usual Daring Style': Feminist New Journalism, Pioneering Women, and Traces of Frances Power Cobbe. In F. Elizabeth Gray, ed., *Women in Journalism at the Fin de Siècle*. London: Palgrave.

Hamilton, Susan (2015). '[T]o Bind Together in Mutual Helpfulness': Genre and/as Social Action in the Victorian Antivivisection Press. *Journal of Modern Periodical Studies* 6 (2): 134–60.

Hanbery MacKay, Carol (2009). A Journal of Her Own: The Rise and Fall of Annie Besant's Our Corner. *Victorian Periodicals Review* 42: 324–58.

Hanbery MacKay, Carol (2017). A Spiritual Materialist Turns Material Spiritualist: Annie Besant Rewrites Her Secularist Years, 1889 and 1891. *BRANCH: Britain, Representation and Nineteenth-Century History*. https://branchcollective.org/?ps_articles=carol-hanbery-mackay-a-spiritual-materialist-turns-material-spiritualist-annie-besant-rewrites-her-secularist-years-1889-and-1891.

Hanegraaff, Wouter J. (2012). *Esotericism and the Academy: Rejected Knowledge in Western Culture*. Cambridge: Cambridge University Press.

Hanegraaff, Wouter J. (2013). *Esotericism: A Guide for the Perplexed.* London: Bloomsbury.
Hannan, Leonie (2016). *Women of Letters: Gender, Writing and the Life of the Mind in Early Modern England.* Manchester: Manchester University Press.
Hardman, Philippa (2011). Darwin, Becker & Sexual Equality. *Darwin and Gender: The Blog.* https://darwinandgender.wordpress.com/2011/07/08/darwin-becker-sexual-equality/.
Hardwick, Charles S., ed. (1978). *Semiotics and Significs: Correspondence Between Charles S. Peirce and Lady Victoria Welby.* Bloomington: Indiana University Press.
Harris, Jose (2011). Wedgwood, (Frances) Julia (1833–1913). *Oxford Dictionary of National Biography.* https://doi.org/10.1093/ref:odnb/52808.
Harrison, Brian (1973). Review Article: The 'Wellesley Index' and the Historian. *Victorian Periodicals Newsletter* 6 (3–4): 52–9.
Harrison, Vernon (1997). *H. P. Blavatsky and the SPR: An Examination of the Hodgson Report of 1885.* Pasadena, CA: Theosophical University Press.
Harvey, Joy (2009). Darwin's 'Angels': The Women Correspondents of Charles Darwin. *Intellectual History Review* 19 (2): 197–210.
Hatfield, Gary (2010). Philosophy and Psychology. In Dean Moyar, ed., *The Routledge Companion to Nineteenth-Century Philosophy.* New York: Routledge.
Haynes, Renée (1982). *History of the Society for Psychical Research: 1882–1982.* London: Macdonald.
Hedley Brooke, John (2014). *Science and Religion: Some Historical Perspectives.* Cambridge: Cambridge University Press.
Henberg, M. C. (1979). George Eliot's Moral Realism. *Philosophy and Literature* 3 (1): 20–38.
Hennell, Charles ([1838] 1841). *An Inquiry concerning the Origin of Christianity.* 2nd edn. London: Allman.
Higgitt, Rebekah and Charles Withers (2008). Science and Sociability: Women as Audience at the British Association for the Advancement of Science, 1831–1901. *Isis* 99 (1): 1–27.
Hill, Michael and Susan Hoecker-Drysdale, eds (2001). *Harriet Martineau: Theoretical and Methodological Perspectives.* London: Routledge.
Himmelfarb, Gertrude (1959). *Darwin and the Darwinian Revolution.* Garden City, NY: Doubleday.
Hodgson, Richard (1894). The Defence of the Theosophists. *Proceedings of the Society for Psychical Research* 9: 129–59.
Hoecker-Drysdale, Susan (1992). *Harriet Martineau: First Woman Sociologist.* Oxford: Berg.
Hoecker-Drysdale, Susan (1995). The Enigma of Harriet Martineau's Letters on Science. *Women's Writing* 2 (2): 155–65.
Hoecker-Drysdale, Susan (2001). Harriet Martineau and the Positivism of Auguste Comte. In Michael Hill and Susan Hoecker-Drysdale, eds, *Harriet Martineau: Theoretical and Methodological Perspectives.* London: Routledge.
Hollings, Christopher, Ursula Martin, and Adrian Rice (2017). The Early Mathematical Education of Ada Lovelace. *BSHM Bulletin: Journal of the British Society for the History of Mathematics* 32 (3): 221–34.
Holton, Sandra Stanley (2001). Segregation, Racism and White Women Reformers: A Transnational Analysis, 1840–1912. *Women's History Review* 10 (1): 5–26.
Holyoake, George (1851a). New Work by Miss Martineau and Mr. Atkinson. *The Reasoner* 10: 363.
Holyoake, George (1851b). Reply to 'On the Word Atheist'. *The Reasoner* 11: 88.
Holyoake, George (1852a). Fulfilment of Demands. *The Reasoner* 12: 33–6.

Holyoake, George (1852b). The Religious Character of the 'Weekly Dispatch'. *The Reasoner* 12: 49–51.
Huber, Irmtraud (2022). The Unity of Thought and Thing: Collapsing Mind-Matter Boundaries in the Poetry and Prose of Constance Naden. *European Journal of English Studies* 26 (1): 85–104.
Hughes, Linda K. (2009). Review of *Frances Power Cobbe: Victorian Feminist, Journalist, Reformer*, by Sally Mitchell, and *Frances Power Cobbe and Victorian Feminism*, by Susan Hamilton. *Victorian Studies* 51 (3): 588–92.
Hughes, Linda K. (2012). On New Monthly Magazines, 1859–60. *BRANCH: Britain, Representation and Nineteenth-Century History*. http://www.branchcollective.org/?ps_articles=on-new-monthly-magazines-1859-60.
Hume, David ([1757] 1956). *The Natural History of Religion*, ed. H. E. Root. London: A. & C. Black.
Hunter, Shelagh (1995). *Harriet Martineau: The Poetics of Moralism*. Aldershot: Scolar Press.
Hutton, Richard Holt (1869). The Theological Statute at Oxford. *Spectator* (29 May): 642–3.
Hutton, Richard Holt (1870a). Miss Cobbe on Latent Thought. *Spectator* (5 Nov.): 1314–15.
Hutton, Richard Holt (1870b). Pope Huxley. *Spectator* (29 Jan.): 135–6.
Hutton, Richard Holt (1874). Latent Thought. *Contemporary Review* 24: 201–11.
Hutton, Sarah (2015). 'Blue-Eyed Philosophers Born on Wednesdays': An Essay on Women and History of Philosophy. *The Monist* 98 (1): 7–20.
Hutton, Sarah (2019). Women, Philosophy and the History of Philosophy. *British Journal for the History of Philosophy* 27 (4): 684–701.
Huxley, Thomas Henry (1854). Science. *Westminster Review* 61: 254–70.
Huxley, Thomas Henry (1860). Darwin on the Origin of Species. *Westminster Review* 17: 541–70.
Huxley, Thomas Henry (1869). The Scientific Aspects of Positivism. *Fortnightly Review* 5: 653–70.
Huxley, Thomas Henry (1871). Mr Darwin's Critics. *Contemporary Review* 18: 443–76.
Huxley, Thomas Henry (1879). *Hume*. London: Macmillan.
Huxley, Thomas Henry (1882). *Science and Culture, and Other Essays*. London: Macmillan.
Huxley, Thomas Henry (1886). The Evolution of Theology: An Anthropological Study. *Nineteenth Century* 19: 485–506.
Huxley, Thomas Henry ([1874] 1893). On the Hypothesis that Animals are Automata, and its History. In *Selected Works*, vol. 1. New York: Appleton.
Huxley, Thomas Henry (1899). *Evolution and Ethics, and Other Essays*. New York: Appleton.
Huxley, Thomas Henry et al. ([1884] 2021). Agnosticism: A Symposium. In Naomi Hetherington and Clare Stainthorp, eds, *Nineteenth-Century Religion, Literature and Society: Disbelief and New Beliefs*. London: Routledge.
Irigaray, Luce [1990] (1996). *I Love to You: Sketch of a Possible Felicity within History*, trans. Alison Martin. London: Routledge.
Irwin, T. H. (2013). Sympathy and the Basis of Morality. In Amanda Anderson and Harry E. Shaw, eds, *A Companion to George Eliot*. Oxford: Blackwell.
J. P. B. (1880). Traducianism and Metempsychosis. *University Magazine* 5: 155–66.
Jacyna, L. S. (1983). Immanence or Transcendence: Theories of Life and Organization in Britain, 1790–1835. *Isis* 74: 310–29.
Jameson, Anna (1832). *Characteristics of Women: Moral, Poetical, and Historical*. 2 vols. London: Saunders & Otley.

Jameson, Anna ([1848–64] 1892). *Sacred and Legendary Art*. 6 vols. Boston, MA: Houghton Mifflin.

Jameson, Robert (1987). Purity and Power at the Victorian Dinner Party. In Ian Hodder, ed., *The Archaeology of Contextual Meanings*. Cambridge: Cambridge University Press.

Janssen, Flore (2017). Talking about Birth Control in 1877: Gender, Class, and Ideology in the Knowlton Trial. *Open Cultural Studies* 1 (1): 281–90.

Johns, Alessa (2014). *Bluestocking Feminism and British-German Cultural Transfer, 1750–1837*. Ann Arbor: University of Michigan Press.

Johnston, Judith (1997). *Anna Jameson: Victorian, Feminist, Woman of Letters*. Aldershot: Scolar Press.

Kaplan, Fred (1975). *Dickens and Mesmerism*. Princeton, NJ: Princeton University Press.

Kaufman, Matthew H. (2008). William Gregory (1803–58): Professor of Chemistry at the University of Edinburgh and Enthusiast for Phrenology and Mesmerism. *Journal of Medical Biography* 16 (3): 128–33.

Kelley, Philip and Ronald Hudson, eds (1984–91). *The Brownings' Correspondence*. 12 vols. Winfield, KS: Wedgestone Press.

King, Andrew, Alexis Easley, and John Morton, eds (2016). *The Routledge Handbook to Nineteenth-Century British Periodicals and Newspapers*. London: Routledge.

Kingsford, Anna and Edward Maitland (1882). *The Perfect Way, or the Finding of Christ*. New York: Scribner & Welford.

Klaver, Claudia C. (2007). Imperial Economics: Harriet Martineau's *Illustrations of Political Economy* and the Narration of Empire. *Victorian Literature and Culture* 35 (1): 21–40.

Kosits, Russell D. (2018). Carpenter, William Benjamin. *Complete Dictionary of Scientific Biography*. https://www.encyclopedia.com/people/history/historians-miscellaneous-biographies/william-benjamin-carpenter.

Kriegel, Uriah (2014). Mysterianism. In Tim Bayne et al., eds, *The Oxford Companion to Consciousness*. Oxford: Oxford University Press.

La Vergata, Antonello (1995). Herbert Spencer: Biology, Sociology and Cosmic Evolution. In Sabine Maasen, Everett Mendelsohn, and Peter Weingart, eds, *Biology as Society, Society as Biology*. New York: Springer.

Lachman, Gary (2012). *Madame Blavatsky: The Mother of Modern Spirituality*. London: Penguin.

Lacy, Lisa McCracken (2017). *Lady Anne Blunt in the Middle East: Travel, Politics and the Idea of Empire*. London: I. B. Tauris.

Landy, David (2020a). Shepherd on Hume's Argument for the Possibility of Uncaused Existence. *Journal of Modern Philosophy* 2 (1): 1–14.

Landy, David (2020b). A Defense of Shepherd's Account of Cause and Effect as Synchronous. *Journal of Modern Philosophy* 2 (1): 1–15.

Larrabee, Mary Jeanne (2006). 'I Know What a Slave Knows': Mary Prince's Epistemology of Resistance. *Women's Studies* 35 (5): 453–73.

Larsen, Jordan (2017). The Evolving Spirit: Morals and Mutualism in Arabella Buckley's Evolutionary Epic. *Notes and Records* 71: 385–408.

Lazari-Radek, Katarzyna de and Peter Singer (2014). *The Point of View of the Universe: Sidgwick and Contemporary Ethics*. Oxford: Oxford University Press.

Lecky, William Edward Hartpole (1869). *History of European Morals from Augustus to Charlemagne*. London: Longmans, Green and Co.

Lee, Vernon (1882). Vivisection: An Evolutionist to Evolutionists. *Contemporary Review* 41: 788–811.

Lee, Vernon (1884). *Miss Brown: A Novel*. 3 vols. London: Blackwood.
Lee, Vernon (1896). Art and Life. Parts I–III. *Contemporary Review* 69: 658–70 and 813–25, 70: 59–73.
Leland, Kurt (2021). 'Friendly to All Beings': Annie Besant as Ethicist. *British Journal for the History of Philosophy* 29 (2): 308–26.
Levine, George (1962). Determinism and Responsibility in the Works of George Eliot. *PMLA* 77 (3): 268–79.
Levine, Philippa (1990). 'The Humanising Influences of Five O'Clock Tea': Victorian Feminist Periodicals. *Victorian Studies* 33 (2): 293–306.
Lewes, George Henry (1845–6). *A Biographical History of Philosophy*. 4 vols in two books. London: Knight.
Lewes, George Henry (1851). Letters on Man's Nature and Development and Martineau's Letters on Man [review]. Part one, *Leader* 2 (1 Mar.): 201–3 and part two, *Leader* 2 (8 Mar.): 227–8.
Lewes, George Henry (1852). Contemporary Literature of France. *Westminster Review* 58: 614–30.
Lewes, George Henry (1853). *Comte's Philosophy of the Sciences*. London: H. G. Bohn.
Lewes, George Henry (1857). *Biographical History of Philosophy*. Enlarged, revised edn. London: Parker.
Lewes, George Henry (1879). *Problems of Life and Mind*. London: Trübner.
Lewins, Robert (1869). *On the Identity of the Vital and the Cosmical Principle*. Lewes: Bacon.
Lewins, Robert ([1873] 1894). *Life and Mind: On the Basis of Modern Medicine (Materialism)*, ed. W. Stewart Ross. London: Stewart & Co.
Lewins, Robert ([1887] 2020). Extracts from Humanism *versus* Theism; or Solipsism (Egoism) = Atheism. In a Series of Letters. In Naomi Hetherington and Clare Stainthorp, eds, *Disbelief and New Beliefs*. London: Routledge.
Lewis, Sarah (1839). *Woman's Mission*. New York: Wiley & Putnam.
Lidwell-Durnin, John (2020). William Benjamin Carpenter and the Emerging Science of Heredity. *Journal of the History of Biology* 53: 81–103.
Lightman, Bernard (1987). *The Origins of Agnosticism: Victorian Unbelief and the Limits of Knowledge*. Baltimore, MD: Johns Hopkins University Press.
Lightman, Bernard (2002). Huxley and Scientific Agnosticism. *British Journal for the History of Science* 35: 271–89.
Lightman, Bernard (2009). *Victorian Popularizers of Science*. Chicago, IL: University of Chicago Press.
Lightman, Bernard (2011). On Tyndall's Belfast Address, 1874. *BRANCH: Britain, Representation and Nineteenth-Century History*. https://www.branchcollective.org/?ps_articles=bernard-lightman-on-tyndalls-belfast-address-1874.
Lightman, Bernard (2016). Popularizers, Participation and the Transformations of Nineteenth-Century Publishing: From the 1860s to the 1880s. *Notes and Records* 70: 343–59.
Lillehammer, Hallvard (2010). Methods of Ethics and the Descent of Man: Darwin and Sidgwick on Ethics and Evolution. *Biology and Philosophy* 25: 361–78.
Litchfield, Henrietta, ed. (1915). *Emma Darwin: A Century of Family Letters*. London: Murray.
Loader, Helen (2019). *Mrs Humphry Ward and Greenian Idealism*. London: Palgrave.
Loewenberg, Bert James and Ruth Bogin, eds (1976). *Black Women in Nineteenth-Century American Life*. University Park, PA: Penn State University Press.

Logan, Deborah (2002). *The Hour and the Woman: Harriet Martineau's 'Somewhat Remarkable' Life*. Ithaca, NY: Cornell University Press.

Logan, Deborah, ed. (2004a). *Harriet Martineau's Writings on the British Empire*, 5 vols. London: Pickering & Chatto.

Logan, Deborah (2004b). Introduction to Martineau, *Illustrations of Political Economy: Selected Tales*. Ontario, CA: Broadview Press.

Logan, Deborah (2007). General Introduction to Harriet Martineau, *Collected Letters*, vol. 1. London: Pickering & Chatto.

Logan, Deborah (2009). 'I Am, My Dear Slanderer, Your Faithful Malignant Demon': Harriet Martineau and the *Westminster Review*'s Comtist Coterie. *Victorian Periodicals Review* 42 (2): 171–91.

Logan, Deborah (2010). *Harriet Martineau, Victorian Imperialism, and the Civilizing Mission*. Farnham: Ashgate.

Lolordo, Antonia (2019). Mary Shepherd on Causation, Induction, and Natural Kinds. *Philosophers' Imprint* 19: 1–14.

Lolordo, Antonia (2020). Introduction to Mary Shepherd, *Essays on the Perception of an External Universe*. Oxford: Oxford University Press.

Lovesey, Oliver (2013). Religion. In Margaret Harris, ed., *George Eliot in Context*. Cambridge: Cambridge University Press.

Lubelsky, Isaac (2012). *Celestial India: Madame Blavatsky and the Birth of Indian Nationalism*. Sheffield: Equinox.

Lubelsky, Isaac (2016). Friedrich Max Müller vs. Madame Blavatsky: A Chronicle of a (Very) Strange Relationship. In Julie Chajes and Boaz Huss, eds, *Theosophical Appropriations*. Beer Sheva: Ben Gurion University of the Negev Press.

Lyell, Charles (1863). *The Geological Evidences of the Antiquity of Man*. London: Murray.

Lyell, Mrs, ed. (1881). *Life, Letters and Journals of Sir Charles Lyell, Bart*. London: J. Murray.

Lyons, Sherrie (1999). *Thomas Henry Huxley: The Evolution of a Scientist*. Lanham, MD: Rowman & Littlefield.

Lyons, Sherrie (2012). A Most Eminent Victorian: Thomas Henry Huxley. *Cahiers victoriens et édouardiens* 76: 85–104.

McCarthy, William and Elizabeth Kraft, eds (2002). *Anna Letitia Barbauld: Selected Poetry and Prose*. Ontario, CA: Broadview Press.

Mackay, Robert William (1850). *The Progress of the Intellect*. London: Chapman.

McRobert, Jennifer (n.d.). Philosophical Research on Mary Shepherd (1999–2005). https://philarchive.org/archive/MCRMSA-2.

Maitzen, Rohan (2014). Realism and Research in *Adam Bede*. British Library, Discovering Literature: Romantics and Victorians. https://www.bl.uk/romantics-and-victorians/articles/realism-and-research-in-adam-bede#.

Mander, W. J. (2011). *British Idealism: A History*. Oxford: Oxford University Press.

Mander, W. J., ed. (2014). *Oxford Handbook of British Philosophy in the Nineteenth Century*. Oxford: Oxford University Press.

Mander, W. J. (2020). *The Unknowable: A Study in Nineteenth-Century British Metaphysics*. Oxford: Oxford University Press.

Mansel, Henry Longueville ([1858] 1867). *The Limits of Religious Thought*. 5th edn. London: Murray.

Manvell, Roger (1976). *The Trial of Annie Besant and Charles Bradlaugh*. London: Elek.

Martineau, Harriet ([1831] 1836a). On the Duty of Studying Political Economy. *Miscellanies* 1: 272–87.

Martineau, Harriet ([1832] 1836b). Theology, Politics, and Literature. *Miscellanies* 1: 191–200.
Martineau, Harriet ([1830] 1836c). Crombie's Natural Theology. *Miscellanies* 2: 236–68.
Martineau, Harriet (1838). *How to Observe Morals and Manners*. London: Knight.
Martineau, Harriet (1853). Letter, *The Liberator* (Boston) (25 Nov.): 186.
Martineau, Harriet (1990). *Selected Letters*, ed. Valerie Sanders. Oxford: Oxford University Press.
Martineau, James (1851). Mesmeric Atheism. *Prospective Review* 26: 224–62.
Martineau, James (1888). *A Study of Religion*. Oxford: Clarendon Press.
Maxwell, Catherine and Patricia Pulham (2006). *Vernon Lee: Decadence, Ethics, Aesthetics*. London: Palgrave.
Meiklejohn, J. M. D., trans. (1855). *Critique of Pure Reason* (Kant). London: Bohn.
Meir, Natalie Kapetanios (2005). 'A Fashionable Dinner Is Arranged as Follows': Victorian Dining Taxonomies. *Victorian Literature and Culture* 33 (1): 133–48.
Melman, Billie (1992). *Women's Orients: English Women and the Middle East, 1718–1918*. Ann Arbor: University of Michigan Press.
Mermin, Dorothy (1993). *Godiva's Ride: Women of Letters in England, 1830–1880*. Bloomington: Indiana University Press.
Meyers, Mitzi (1980). Harriet Martineau's *Autobiography*: The Making of a Female Philosopher. In Estelle Jelinek, ed., *Women's Autobiography: Essays in Criticism*. Bloomington: Indiana University Press.
Midgley, Clare (1992). *Women Against Slavery: The British Campaigns, 1780–1870*. New York: Routledge.
Midgley, Clare, ed. (1998). *Gender and Imperialism*. Manchester: Manchester University Press.
Mill, John Stuart (1869). *The Subjection of Women*. London: Longmans, Green, Reader and Dyer.
Mill, John Stuart ([1873] 1981). Autobiography. In *The Collected Works of John Stuart Mill, Volume I*, ed. John M. Robson and Jack Stillinger. London: Routledge and Kegan Paul.
Mill, John Stuart ([1861] 1998). *Utilitarianism*, ed. Roger Crisp. Oxford: Oxford University Press.
Mineka, Francis E. (1944). *The Dissidence of Dissent: The Monthly Repository, 1806–1838*. Chapel Hill: University of North Carolina Press.
Mitchell, Sally (2004). *Frances Power Cobbe: Victorian Feminist, Journalist, Reformer*. Charlottesville: University of Virginia Press.
Mivart, St George Jackson (1871). *On the Genesis of Species*. New York: Appleton.
Moore, James R. (1987). The Erotics of Evolution. In George Levine, ed., *One Culture: Essays on Science and Literature*. Madison: University of Wisconsin Press.
More, Hannah (1799). *Strictures on the Modern System of Female Education with a View to the Principles and Conduct of Women of Rank and Fortune*, 2 vols. London: T. Cadell Jun. and W. Davies.
Morley, John (1871). Mr. Darwin on Conscience. *Pall Mall Gazette* 13: 1358–9.
Morrison, Mark S. (2008). The Periodical Culture of the Occult Revival: Esoteric Wisdom, Modernity, and Counter-Public Spheres. *Journal of Modern Literature* 31 (2): 1–22.
Moyar, Dean, ed. (2012). *Routledge Companion to Nineteenth-Century Philosophy*. New York: Routledge.
Moynagh, Maureen and Nancy Forestell, eds (2011). *Documenting First Wave Feminisms: Volume 1: Transnational Collaborations and Crosscurrents*. Toronto: University of Toronto Press.

Müller, Max (1867). *Chips from a German Workshop*, vol. 1. London: Longmans, Green & Co.
Müller, Max (1893). Esoteric Buddhism. *The Nineteenth Century* 33: 767–88.
Myers, Frederic ([1881] 1917). George Eliot. In *George Eliot: The Mill on the Floss*. Harvard Classics Shelf of Fiction, vol. IX. Cambridge, MA: Harvard University Press.
Myers, Norma (1996). *Reconstructing the Black Past: Blacks in Britain 1780–1830*. London: Routledge.
Naden, Constance (1894). *Complete Poetical Works*. London: Bickers & Son.
Nethercot, Arthur Hobart (1960). *The First Five Lives of Annie Besant*. Chicago, IL: University of Chicago Press.
Nethercot, Arthur Hobart (1963). *The Last Four Lives of Annie Besant*. Chicago, IL: University of Chicago Press.
Newman, Francis (1865). Capacities of Women. *Westminster Review* 84: 353–80.
Nietzsche, Friedrich ([1889] 1997). *Twilight of the Idols*, trans. Richard Polt. Indianapolis: Hackett.
Nietzsche, Friedrich ([1882] 2001). *The Gay Science*, trans. Josefine Nauckhoff. Cambridge: Cambridge University Press.
Nietzsche, Friedrich ([1887] 2006). *On the Genealogy of Morality*, trans. Carol Diethe. Cambridge: Cambridge University Press.
Okan, Ecem (2017). How Did It All Begin? Adam Smith on the Early and Rude State of Society and the Age of Hunters. *European Journal of the History of Economic Thought* 24: 1247–76.
O'Neill, Eileen (1998). Disappearing Ink: Early Modern Women Philosophers and Their Fate in History. In Janet A. Kourany, ed., *Philosophy in a Feminist Voice*. Princeton, NJ: Princeton University Press.
O'Neill, Eileen (2005). Early Modern Women Philosophers and the History of Philosophy. *Hypatia* 20 (3): 185–97.
Onslow, Barbara (2000). *Women of the Press in Nineteenth-Century Britain*. London: Palgrave.
Oppenheim, Janet (1985). *The Other World: Spiritualism and Psychical Research in England, 1850–1914*. Cambridge: Cambridge University Press.
Oppy, Graham and David Dowe (2020). The Turing Test. In Edward N. Zalta, ed., *The Stanford Encyclopedia of Philosophy* (Winter 2020 edition). https://plato.stanford.edu/archives/win2020/entries/turing-test/.
Owen, Alex (1989). *The Darkened Room: Women, Power, and Spiritualism in Late Victorian England*. Chicago, IL: University of Chicago Press.
Paget, V. (1883). The Transformations of Chivalric Poetry. *National Review* 2: 341–53.
Palmeri, Frank (2016). *State of Nature, Stages of Society: Enlightenment Conjectural History and Modern Social Discourse*. New York: Columbia University Press.
Paoletti, Cristina (2011). Restoring Necessary Connections: Lady Mary Shepherd on Hume and the Early Nineteenth-Century Debate on Causality. *I Castelli di Yale* 11: 47–59.
Papineau, David (2021). Naturalism. In Edward N. Zalta, ed., *The Stanford Encyclopedia of Philosophy* (Summer 2021 edition). https://plato.stanford.edu/archives/sum2021/entries/naturalism/.
Patterson, George (1884). The Collapse of Koot Hoomi. *Madras Christian College Magazine* Sept.: 199–215 and Oct.: 289–317.
Peacock, Sandra J. (2002). *The Theological and Ethical Writings of Frances Power Cobbe, 1822–1904*. Lewiston, NY: Edwin Mellen.

Peart, Sandra J. and David M. Levy (2005). Happiness, Progress and the 'Vanity of the Philosopher'. Parts 1 and 2. *The Library of Economics and Liberty.* https://www.econlib.org/library/Columns/y2005/PeartLevymalthus.html.
Peart, Sandra J. and David M. Levy (2008). Darwin's Unpublished Letter at the Bradlaugh-Besant Trial. *European Journal of Political Economy* 24 (2): 343–53.
Peirce, Charles Sanders (1892). Review of Buckley, *Moral Teachings of Science. The Nation* 54 (June): 417.
Petersen, Linda H. (1986).*Victorian Autobiography: The Tradition of Self-Interpretation.* New Haven, CT: Yale University Press.
Peterson, M. Jeanne (1989). *Family, Love, and Work in the Lives of Victorian Gentlewomen.* Bloomington: Indiana University Press.
Petrilli, Susan, ed. (2009). *Signifying and Understanding: Reading the Works of Victoria Welby and the Signific Movement.* Berlin: De Gruyter.
Petrilli, Susan (2015). Sign, Meaning, and Understanding in Victoria Welby and Charles S. Peirce. *Signs and Society* 3 (1): 71–102.
Piattelli, Michela (2016). 'Language is our Rubicon': Friedrich Max Müller's Quarrel with Hensleigh Wedgwood. *Publications of the English Goethe Society* 85 (2–3): 98–109.
Pichanick, Valerie (1980). *Harriet Martineau, the Woman and Her Work, 1802–76.* Ann Arbor: University of Michigan Press.
Pickering, Mary (2017). Auguste Comte and the Curious Case of English Women. In Andrew Wernick, ed., *The Anthem Companion to Auguste Comte.* New York: Anthem.
Pietarinen, Ahti-Veikko (2013). Christine Ladd-Franklin's and Victoria Welby's Correspondence with Charles Peirce. *Semiotica* 196: 139–61.
Postlethwaite, Diana (1984). *Making It Whole: A Victorian Circle and the Shape of their World.* Columbus: Ohio State University Press.
Priestley, Joseph (1777a). *Disquisitions Relating to Matter and Spirit.* London: J. Johnson.
Priestley, Joseph (1777b). *The Doctrine of Philosophical Necessity Illustrated.* London: J. Johnson.
Priestley, Joseph ([1788] 1812). *A General View of the Arguments for the Unity of God; and Against the Divinity and Preexistence of Christ.* New edn. London: Johnson & Co. and Eaton.
Prince, Mary (1831). *The History of Mary Prince.* London: Westley and Davis.
Rasmussen, Joel D. S., Judith Wolfe, and Johannes Zachhuber (2017). Introduction to the *Oxford Handbook of Nineteenth-Century Christian Thought.* Oxford: Oxford University Press.
Rectenwald, Michael (2017). Mid-Nineteenth-Century Secularism as Modern Secularity. In Ryan T. Cragun, Christel Manning, and Lori L. Fazzino, eds, *Organized Secularism in the United States.* Berlin: De Gruyter.
Reed, Edward S. (1998). *From Soul to Mind: The Emergence of Psychology from Erasmus Darwin to William James.* New Haven, CT: Yale University Press.
Rees, Joan (1992). *Writings on the Nile: Harriet Martineau, Florence Nightingale, Amelia Edwards.* London: Rubicon Press.
Reigle, David and Nancy Reigle (1999). *Blavatsky's Secret Books: Twenty Years' Research.* San Diego, CA: Wizards Bookshelf.
Remond, Sarah Parker ([1862] 1942). The Negroes in the United States of America. *Journal of Negro History* 27 (2): 216–18.
Richards, Evelleen (1997). Redrawing the Boundaries: Darwinian Science and Victorian Women Intellectuals. In Bernard Lightman, ed. *Victorian Science in Context.* Chicago, IL: University of Chicago Press.

Richards, Evelleen (2020). *Embryos, Monsters, and Racial and Gendered Others in the Making of Evolutionary Theory and Culture*. London: Routledge.
Richards, Robert (1989). *Darwin and the Emergence of Evolutionary Theories of Mind and Behavior*. Chicago, IL: University of Chicago Press.
Richardson, Sarah (2013). *The Political Worlds of Women: Gender and Politics in Nineteenth Century Britain*. London: Routledge.
Rilett, Beverley Park (2016). George Henry Lewes, the Real Man of Science Behind George Eliot's Fictional Pedants. *George Eliot–George Henry Lewes Studies* 68 (1): 4–24.
Roberts, Caroline (2002). *The Woman and the Hour: Harriet Martineau and Victorian Ideologies*. Toronto: University of Toronto Press.
Robinson, Ainslie (2000). Stalking Through the Literary World: Anna Jameson and the Periodical Press, 1826–1860. *Victorian Periodicals Review* 33: 165–77.
Rogers, Dorothy (2005). *America's First Women Philosophers*. New York: Bloomsbury.
Rogers, Dorothy (2021). *Women Philosophers*, 2 vols. New York: Bloomsbury.
Rogers, Dorothy and Therese Boos Dykeman, eds (2004). *Women in the American Philosophical Tradition 1800–1930*. Hypatia 19: 2.
Rogers, Dorothy and Therese Boos Dykeman, eds (2012). *Contributions by Women to Nineteenth-Century American Philosophy: Frances Wright, Antoinette Brown-Blackwell, Marietta Kies*. Lewiston, NY: Edwin Mellen.
Rose, Jonathan (2001). *The Intellectual Life of the British Working Classes*. New Haven, CT: Yale University Press.
Rubery, Matthew (2010). Victorian Print Culture, Journalism and the Novel. *Literature Compass* 7 (4): 290–300.
Rudboeg, Tim (2012). H. P. Blavatsky's Theosophy in Context: The Construction of Meaning in Modern Western Esotericism. PhD thesis, University of Exeter. https://ore.exeter.ac.uk/repository/handle/10871/9926.
Ruse, Michael (2014). Evolution and Ethics in Victorian England. In W. J. Mander, ed., *The Oxford Handbook of British Philosophy in the Nineteenth Century*. Oxford: Oxford University Press.
Ruston, Sharon (2005). *Shelley and Vitality*. London: Palgrave.
Ryall, Anka (2000). Medical Body and Lived Experience: The Case of Harriet Martineau. *Mosaic* 33 (4): 35–53.
Said, Edward ([1978] 1991). *Orientalism*. Harmondsworth: Penguin.
Salenius, Sirpa A. (2016). *An Abolitionist Abroad: Sarah Parker Remond in Cosmopolitan Europe*. Amherst: University of Massachusetts Press.
Sanders, Valerie (1986). *Reason over Passion: Harriet Martineau and the Victorian Novel*. Basingstoke: Palgrave Macmillan.
Sanders, Valerie and Gaby Weiner, eds (2017). *Harriet Martineau and the Birth of Disciplines: Nineteenth-Century Intellectual Powerhouse*. London: Routledge.
Santucci, James A. (2008). The Notion of Race in Theosophy. *Nova Religio* 11 (3): 37–63.
Saville, John, ed. (1970). *A Selection of the Social and Political Pamphlets of Annie Besant*. New York: A. M. Kelley.
Schaefer, Donovan (2015). The Science of Life. In Joel Rasmussen, Judith Wolfe, and Johannes Zachhuber, eds, *Oxford Handbook of Nineteenth-Century Christian Thought*. Oxford: Oxford University Press.
Schliesser, Eric, ed. (2015). *Sympathy: A History*. Oxford: Oxford University Press.
Schmitz, H. Walter (2013). Taking Stock of the Published Correspondence of Victoria Lady Welby. *Ars Semeiotica* 36 (3–4): 203–26.

Schneewind, Jerome B. (1977). *Sidgwick's Ethics and Victorian Moral Philosophy*. Oxford: Clarendon Press.
Scholl, Lesa (2012). George Eliot, Harriet Martineau and the Popularisation of Comte's Positive Philosophy. *Literature Compass* 9 (11): 764–73.
Schopenhauer, Arthur ([1844] 1966). *The World as Will and Representation*. 2nd edn. Trans. E. F. J. Payne. New York: Dover Press.
Schroeder, Janice (2012). On the *English Woman's Journal*, 1858–64. *BRANCH: Britain, Representation and Nineteenth-Century History*. http://www.branchcollective.org/?ps_articles=janice-schroeder-on-the-english-womans-journal-1858-62.
Seacole, Mary ([1857] 2005). *The Wonderful Adventures of Mrs Seacole in Many Lands*. Harmondsworth: Penguin.
Semple, John W., ed. and trans. (1836). *The Metaphysic of Ethics* (Kant). Edinburgh: T. Clark.
Senate House Library (n.d.). List of Books in the Lady Welby Library. https://archive.senatehouselibrary.ac.uk/sites/default/files/files/blogs/LadyWelbyLibrary.pdf.
Seymour, Miranda (2018). *In Byron's Wake: The Turbulent Lives of Lord Byron's Wife and Daughter: Annabella Milbanke and Ada Lovelace*. New York: Simon and Schuster.
Shapiro, Lisa (2004). Some Thoughts on the Place of Women in Early Modern Philosophy. In Lilli Alanen and Charlotte Witt, eds, *Feminist Reflections on the History of Philosophy*. Dordrecht: Kluwer.
Shattock, Joanne (1989). *Politics and Reviewers: The Edinburgh and the Quarterly in the Early Victorian Age*. Leicester: Leicester University Press.
Shattock, Joanne, ed. (2017). *Journalism and the Periodical Press in Nineteenth-Century Britain*. Cambridge: Cambridge University Press.
Shohat, Ella and Robert Stam ([1994] 2014). *Unthinking Eurocentrism*. 2nd edn. London: Routledge.
Sidgwick, Eleanor (1885). On Physical Tests, and the Line Between the Possible and Impossible. *Journal of the Society for Psychical Research* 1: 430–2.
Sidgwick, Henry (1872). Cobbe, *Darwinism in Morals and Other Essays* [review]. *The Academy* 3: 230–1.
Sidgwick, Henry ([1874] 1907). *Methods of Ethics*, ed. E. E. C. Jones. London: Macmillan.
Sinnett, A. P. (1883). *Esoteric Buddhism*. London: Trübner.
Skorupski, John (1993). *English-Language Philosophy 1750 to 1945*. Oxford: Oxford University Press.
Smiles, Samuel (1905). *Autobiography of Samuel Smiles*, ed. Thomas Mackay. New York: Dutton.
Smith, Adam ([1776] 1904). *An Inquiry into the Nature and Causes of the Wealth of Nations*, ed. Edwin Cannan, 2 vols. London: Methuen.
Smith, K. J. M. (1988). *James Fitzjames Stephen: Portrait of a Victorian Rationalist*. Cambridge: Cambridge University Press.
Smith, Mary (1892). *The Autobiography of Mary Smith, Schoolmistress and Nonconformist*. London: Bemrose & Sons.
Smith, Philip E, II (1978). Robert Lewins, Constance Naden, and Hylo-Idealism. *Notes & Queries* 25: 303–9.
Spencer, Herbert (1862). *First Principles*. London: Williams & Norgate.
Spencer, Herbert (1864). *The Principles of Biology*. London: Williams & Norgate.
Spicer, Finn (2011). Intuitions in Naturalistic Philosophy. Unpublished paper presented at Lancaster Philosophy research seminar.

Spinoza, Baruch (2018). *Ethics*, trans. Matthew Kisner. Cambridge: Cambridge University Press.
SPR (1885). Report of the Committee Appointed to Investigate Phenomena Connected with the Theosophical Society. *Proceedings of the Society for Psychical Research* 3: 201–7.
SPR ([1883] 2021). Statement of Aims and Objectives. https://www.spr.ac.uk/statement-aims-and-objectives-1883.
Stainthorp, Clare (2017). Constance Naden: A Critical Overview. *Literature Compass* 14 (8). https://doi.org/10.1111/lic3.12401.
Stainthorp, Clare (2019). *Constance Naden: Scientist, Philosopher, Poet*. Berlin: Peter Lang.
Stedman Jones, Gareth and Gregory Claeys, eds (2013). *Cambridge History of Nineteenth-Century Political Thought*. Cambridge: Cambridge University Press.
Stein, Dorothy (1985). *Ada: A Life and a Legacy*. Cambridge, MA: MIT Press.
Steinbach, Susie (2012). Can We Still Use 'Separate Spheres'? British History 25 Years After *Family Fortunes*. *History Compass* 10 (11): 826–37.
Stern, Robert (1998). Nineteenth-Century Philosophy. *Routledge Encyclopedia of Philosophy*. https://www.rep.routledge.com/articles/overview/nineteenth-century-philosophy/v-1.
Stevens, L. Robert (1998). Intertextual Constructions of Faith: Julia Wedgwood. In Julie Melnyk, ed., *Women's Theology in Nineteenth-Century Britain*. New York: Routledge.
Stewart, Lindsey (2020). 'Count it all Joy': Black Women's Interventions in the Abolitionist Tradition. *British Journal for the History of Philosophy* 29 (2): 292–307.
Stone, Alison (2022a). Introduction. In Alison Stone, ed., *Frances Power Cobbe: Essential Writings of a Nineteenth-Century Feminist Philosopher*. Oxford: Oxford University Press.
Stone, Alison (2022b). *Frances Power Cobbe*. Cambridge: Cambridge University Press.
Stone, Alison, ed. (2011). *Edinburgh Critical History of Nineteenth-Century Philosophy*. Edinburgh: Edinburgh University Press.
Stott, Anne (2003). *Hannah More: The First Victorian*. Oxford: Oxford University Press.
Stout, G. F. (1896). *Analytic Psychology*, 2 vols. London: Allen & Unwin.
Suess, Barbara A. (2016). Colonial Bodies and the Abolition of Slavery: A Tale of Two Cobbes. *Slavery & Abolition* 37 (3): 541–60.
Superson, Anita (2013). Review of Catherine Villanueva Gardner, *Empowerment and Interconnectivity*. *Notre Dame Philosophical Reviews*. https://ndpr.nd.edu/reviews/catherine-villanueva-gardner-empowerment-and-interconnectivity-toward-a-feminist-history-of-utilitarian-philosophy/.
Sutherland, John (1986). 'Cornhill's' Sales and Payments: The First Decade. *Victorian Periodicals Review* 19 (3): 106–8.
Tange, Andrea Kaston (2006). Constance Naden and the Erotics of Evolution. *Nineteenth-Century Literature* 61 (2): 200–40.
Taylor Mill, Harriet (1851). Enfranchisement of Women. *Westminster Review* 59: 149–61.
Taylor, Barbara (1983). *Eve and the New Jerusalem: Socialism and Feminism in the Nineteenth Century*. New York: Pantheon.
Taylor, Michael W. (2007). *The Philosophy of Herbert Spencer*. London: Continuum.
Tener, Robert H. (1973). R. H. Hutton: Some Attributions. *Victorian Periodicals Newsletter* 6 (2): 1–65.
Tennyson, Alfred (1847). *The Princess*. London: Moxon.
Terwey, Susanne (2012). British Discourses on 'the Jew' and 'the Nation' 1899–1919. *Quest: Issues in Contemporary Jewish History* 3: 111–28.
Thain, Marion (2003). 'Scientific Wooing': Constance Naden's Marriage of Science and Poetry. *Victorian Poetry* 41: 151–69.

Thain, Marion (2011). Birmingham's Women Poets: Aestheticism and the Daughters of Industry. *Cahiers victoriens et édouardiens* 74: 37–57.
Thayer, Horace (1968). *Meaning and Action: A Critical History of Pragmatism*. New York: Bobbs-Merrill.
Thomas, Gillian (1985). *Harriet Martineau*. Boston, MA: Twayne.
Tjoa, Hock Guan (1978). *George Henry Lewes: A Victorian Mind*. Cambridge, MA: Harvard University Press.
Todd, Barbara (2003). Elisabeth Sanders Arbuckle, Harriet Martineau and the Wedgwood Circle. *Martineau Society Newsletter* 18: 17–20.
Toole, Betty (1991). Ada, an Analyst and a Metaphysician. *ACM SIGAda Ada Letters* 11 (2): 60–71.
Torgersen, Beth (2017). Harriet Martineau, Victorian Sciences of Mind and the Birth of Psychology. In Valerie Sanders and Gaby Weiner, eds, *Harriet Martineau and the Birth of Disciplines*. London: Routledge.
Towheed, Shafquat (2006). The Creative Evolution of Scientific Paradigms: Vernon Lee and the Debate over the Hereditary Transmission of Acquired Characters. *Victorian Studies* 49 (1): 33–61.
Trent, A. B. (1880). The Soul and the Stars. *University Magazine* 5: 334–46.
Trompf, Garry W. (2013). Theosophical Macrohistory. In Olav Hammer and Mikael Rothstein, eds, *Handbook of the Theosophical Current*. Leiden: Brill.
Tucker, D. H., George Unwin and Philip Soundy (2020). History of Publishing. *Encyclopedia Britannica*. https://www.britannica.com/topic/publishing.
Turing, A. M. (1950). Computing Machinery and Intelligence. *Mind* 59: 433–60.
Tylor, Edward B. (1871). *Primitive Culture*, 2 vols. London: Murray.
Tyndall, John (1879). *Fragments of Science*. 5th edn. London: Longmans, Green & Co.
Uckelman, Sara (2019). Review: 'An Advance Sheet' by Jane Barlow. *SFF Reviews*. https://sffreviews.com/2019/01/21/review-an-advance-sheet-by-jane-barlow/.
Utke, Allen (1994). Michael Faraday's Concept of Ultimate Reality and Meaning. *Ultimate Reality and Meaning* 17 (3): 167–83.
Valente, K. G. (2010). Giving Wings to Logic: Mary Everest Boole's Propagation and Fulfilment of a Legacy. *British Journal for the History of Science* 43 (1): 49–74.
VanArsdel, Rosemary (2000). 'Macmillan's Magazine' and the Fair Sex: 1859–1874. Part One. *Victorian Periodicals Review* 33 (4): 374–96.
VanArsdel, Rosemary (2010). Victorian Periodicals: Aids to Research: A Selected Bibliography. 10th edn. *The Research Society for Victorian Periodicals*. https://rs4vp.org/resources/vanarsdel-bibliography/.
Vickery, Amanda (1993). Golden Age to Separate Spheres? A Review of the Categories and Chronology of English Women's History. *The Historical Journal* 36 (2): 383–414.
Victorian Web (n.d.). Victorian Periodicals Mentioned in the Victorian Web. http://www.victorianweb.org/periodicals/periodicals.html.
Villanueva Gardner, Catherine (2012). *Empowerment and Interconnectivity: Towards a Feminist History of Utilitarian Philosophy*. University Park, PA: Penn State University Press.
Visram, Rozina (1986). *Ayahs, Lascars and Princes: The Story of Indians in Britain 1700–1947*. London: Routledge.
Visram, Rozina (2002). *Asians in Britain: 400 Years of History*. London: Pluto Press.
Viswanathan, Gauri (2011). 'Have Animals Souls?': Theosophy and the Suffering Body. *PMLA* 126 (2): 440–7.
Vyvyan, John (1969). *In Pity and in Anger*. London: Michael Joseph.

Waithe, Mary Ellen, ed. (1987). *A History of Women Philosophers*, 4 vols. Dordrecht: Springer.
Walker, David (2018). Periodicals in Transition: Politics and Style in Victorian Higher Journalism. PhD thesis, University of Arkansas.
Wallace, Alfred Russel (1869). Geological Climates and the Origin of Species. *Quarterly Review* 126: 359–94.
Waller, Ralph (2014). The Philosophy of James Martineau. In W. J. Mander, ed., *The Oxford Handbook of British Philosophy in the Nineteenth Century*. Oxford: Oxford University Press.
Walters, Margaret (1976). The Rights and Wrongs of Women: Mary Wollstonecraft, Harriet Martineau, Simone de Beauvoir. In Juliet Mitchell and Ann Oakley, eds, *The Rights and Wrongs of Women*. Harmondsworth: Penguin.
Ward, James (1886). Psychology. In *Encyclopaedia Britannica*, vol. 20. 9th edn, Edinburgh: Black.
Watts, Ruth E. (1980). The Unitarian Contribution to the Development of Female Education, 1790–1850. *History of Education* 9 (4): 273–86.
Webb, Beatrice ([1926] 1980). *My Apprenticeship*. Cambridge: Cambridge University Press.
Webb, R. K. (1960). *Harriet Martineau: A Radical Victorian*. New York: Columbia University Press.
Wedgwood, Barbara (1980). *The Wedgwood Circle, 1730–1897: Four Generations of a Family and Their Friends*. London: Studio Vista.
Wedgwood, Barbara (1983). A Critical Study of the Life and Works of Julia Wedgwood. PhD thesis, UCL. https://discovery.ucl.ac.uk/id/eprint/1546145/1/Wedgwood_281729.pdf.
Wedgwood, Julia (1862). The Origin of Language. *Macmillan's Magazine* 7: 54–60.
Wedgwood, Julia (1863). Sir Charles Lyell on the Antiquity of Man. *Macmillan's Magazine* 7: 476–87.
Wedgwood, Julia (1871). The Natural and the Supernatural. *Spectator* (4 Nov.): 1340–2.
Wedgwood, Julia (1885). Fiction. *Contemporary Review* 47: 747–54.
Wedgwood, Julia (1894). *The Message of Israel in the Light of Modern Criticism*. London: Isbister & Co.
Wedgwood, Julia (1907). *The Moral Ideal*. New and revised edn. London: Kegan Paul, Trench, Trübner & Co.
Weiner, Gaby and Valerie Sanders, eds (2017). *Harriet Martineau and the Birth of Disciplines: Nineteenth-Century Intellectual Powerhouse*. London: Routledge.
Welby, Victoria (1852). *A Young Traveller's Journal of a Tour in North and South America During the Year 1850*. London: Bosworth.
Welby, Victoria (1907). Time as Derivative. *Mind* 16: 383–400.
Welby, Victoria (1909). Mr. McTaggart on the 'Unreality of Time'. *Mind* 18: 326–8.
Wellek, René (1931). *Immanuel Kant in England, 1793–1838*. Princeton, NJ: Princeton University Press.
Wellesley Index (2006–21). W.E.H. Wellesley College August 29, 1965 Introduction. http://wellesley.chadwyck.co.uk/marketing/well_intro.jsp.
Wessinger, Catherine (1988). *Annie Besant and Progressive Messianism, 1847–1933*. Lewiston, NY: Edwin Mellen.
Wheatley, Vera (1957). *The Life and Work of Harriet Martineau*. London: Secker & Warburg.
Wheeler, Anna Doyle and William Thompson (1825). *Appeal of One Half the Human Race*. London: Longmans.

Whewell, William (1840). *Philosophy of the Inductive Sciences*, 2 vols. London: Parker.
Williamson, Lori (2005). *Power and Protest: Frances Power Cobbe and Victorian Society*. London: Rivers Oram Press.
Wilson, Carol Shiner and Joel Haefner, eds (1994). *Re-Visioning Romanticism: British Women Writers 1776–1837*. Philadelphia: University of Pennsylvania Press.
Wilson, Jessica (2022). On Mary Shepherd's *Essay upon the Relation of Cause and Effect*. In Eric Schliesser, ed., *Neglected Classics of Philosophy II*. Oxford: Oxford University Press. http://individual.utoronto.ca/jmwilson/Wilson-Shepherd-on-Causation.pdf.
Wilson, Matthew (2019). Rendering Sociology: On the Utopian Positivism of Harriet Martineau and the 'Mumbo Jumbo Club'. *Journal of Interdisciplinary History of Ideas* 16. https://journals.openedition.org/jihi/281.
Winter, Alison (1995). Harriet Martineau and the Reform of the Invalid in Victorian England. *The Historical Journal* 38 (3): 597–616.
Winter, Alison (1997). The Construction of Orthodoxies and Heterodoxies in the Early Victorian Life Sciences. In Bernard Lightman, ed., *Victorian Science in Context*. Chicago, IL: University of Chicago Press.
Winter, Alison (1998). A Calculus of Suffering: Ada Lovelace and the Bodily Constraints on Women's Knowledge in Early Victorian England. In Christopher Lawrence and Steven Shapin, eds, *Science Incarnate*. Chicago, IL: University of Chicago Press.
Winter, Alison (2000). *Mesmerized: Powers of Mind in Victorian Britain*. Chicago, IL: University of Chicago Press.
Witt, Charlotte (2006). Feminist Interpretations of the Philosophical Canon. *Signs* 31 (2): 537–52.
Witz, Anne (1992). *Professions and Patriarchy*. London: Routledge.
Wolfe, Charles T. and Falk Wunderlich (2020). Joseph Priestley: Materialism and the Science of the Mind. *Intellectual History Review* 30 (1). https://doi.org/10.1080/17496977.2020.1690356.
Wood, Allen and Songsuk Susan Hahn, eds (2011). *Cambridge History of Philosophy in the Nineteenth Century*. Cambridge: Cambridge University Press.
Woolley, Benjamin (1999). *Ada Lovelace: Bride of Science*. London: Macmillan.
Wright, T. R. (1981). Eliot and Positivism: A Reassessment. *Modern Language Review* 76 (2): 257–72.
Wright, T. R. (1986). *The Religion of Humanity: The Impact of Comtean Positivism on Victorian Britain*. Cambridge: Cambridge University Press.
Young, Robert M. (1971). Darwin's Metaphor: Does Nature Select? *The Monist* 55: 442–503.
Young, Robert M. (1985). *Darwin's Metaphor: Nature's Place in Victorian Culture*. Cambridge: Cambridge University Press.
Zorn, Christa (2003). *Vernon Lee: Aesthetics, History, and the Victorian Female Intellectual*. Athens: Ohio University Press.
Zuckerman, Phil and John R. Shook (2017). Introduction: The Study of Secularism. In Phil Zuckerman and John R. Shook, eds, *Oxford Handbook of Secularism*. Oxford: Oxford University Press.

Index

Note: Tables are indicated by an italic "*t*" and notes are indicated by "n" following the page numbers.

For the benefit of digital users, indexed terms that span two pages (e.g., 52–53) may, on occasion, appear on only one of those pages.

Abolitionist (journal) 36–7
academia and professional life
   professionalization as constraint on men 45–6, 54
   professionalization as constraint on women 42–7, 53–4
   professionalization and specialization 22, 42–4
   professional specialist or expert 44
   specialist academic journals 25–7, 42–4
   women in academia 23, 27–8
   women's exclusion from professional life 2, 23
Adams, Charles 46
aesthetics
   Cobbe, Frances Power 3
   Eliot, George 175–6, 177n.26, 178
   Lee, Vernon 4–5, 182, 186
   Lee, Vernon and aestheticism 4–5, 181–3, 186n.35
   Martineau, Harriet 176
Agnostic Annual (journal) 27*t*, 76n.31
agnosticism
   agnosticism and atheism as a continuum 165, 179n.29
   agnosticism/atheism distinction 7n.12, 165
   Eliot, George 165–7, 173, 180–1
   Huxley, Thomas Henry 7n.12, 11, 76, 122
   Martineau, Harriet 76, 165–7, 167n.8, 180–1, 183n.33
Albrecht, Thomas 174n.21
'alternative' spiritual currents 166, 194–5,
   see also Christian Science; mesmerism; spiritualism; theosophy
Andrieu, Jules 30n.22
Anglicanism 164–5
animal welfare 231
   1876 Cruelty to Animals Act 46–7
   Cobbe, Frances Power 3, 31
   see also vivisection
animism 100n.2, 120–1, 206–8, 226*t*
Anscombe, G. E. M. 1
Anti-Caste (journal) 17–18
Arendt, Hannah 1

Aristotelian Society 29–30
Arnold, Matthew 32
Arrowsmith, Jane 73–4
associationism 69–70
atheism
   agnosticism and atheism as a continuum 165, 179n.29
   agnosticism/atheism distinction 7n.12, 165
   Besant, Annie 14–15, 165–6, 187–91
   Cobbe, Frances Power 3, 7–8, 179–81, 189–90, 192
   'dogmatic'/'suspensive' atheism 7n.12
   Lee, Vernon 4–5, 14–15, 183, 186
   Lee, Vernon: 'responsible unbelief' 7–8, 14–15, 166–7, 186
   Martineau, Harriet 2–3, 7–8, 36, 66, 74–6, 79, 97, 167–71, 179, 187–8, 199–200, 205
   morality and 7–8, 171
   Naden, Constance 5, 118–19, 123
   negative atheism 76
   philosophical atheism 75, 187–8
   popular/philosophical atheism 75–6
   positive atheism 76n.32
   secularism/atheism distinction 7n.12
Athenaeum (journal) 27*t*, 108
Atkinson, Henry George 2–3, 56–7
   Martineau, Harriet and 2–3, 73–4, 108
   phreno-mesmerism 73–4
   see also Martineau and Atkinson: *Letters on the Laws of Man's Nature and Development*
Augustine of Hippo 152–3
Austen, Jane 37–8, 45–6, 178
Austin, Sarah 33n.31
authorship: anonymity and signature 37–42
   anonymity 2n.4, 8, 21–2, 27–8, 37–40, 42, 136–8, 232
   Blavatsky's anonymity 39
   citation and referencing practices (nineteenth-century) 8, 40–2, 53n.66, 58, 91, 232
   Eliot's anonymity 30–2, 39, 173–5
   Eliot's pseudonym 5n.9, 27–8, 40
   fiction writing 37–8

authorship: anonymity and signature (*cont.*)
  initialled authorship 2n.4, 8, 21–2, 39–40
  journals 38–9
  Lee's pseudonym 5n.9, 39–40, 181
  male anonymity 40
  male pseudonyms 34, 138
  Martineau's signatures 34–5, 39, 67
  Naden's pseudonym 39, 119
  non-fiction writing 37–8
  philosophical books 37–8
  pseudonymity 2n.4, 8, 21–2, 27–8, 37, 40, 42, 138
  signed authorship 2n.4, 21–2, 38–40
  Wedgwood, Julia 136–8
  women's constrained philosophical participation 40, 42

Babbage, Charles 232
  'analytical engine' 102–3, 104n.11, 113
  'difference engine' 101–3
  Lovelace, Ada and 3, 99, 101–2
  Ninth Bridgewater Treatise 105n.13
  Shepherd, Mary and 8–9
Baillie, Joanna 19, 33n.28, 107n.20
Bain, Alexander 16n.22, 44–6
Balfour, Arthur 50–1
Barbauld, Anna Letitia 19, 34–5, 170
Barker, J. H. 120–2
Barlow, Jane 50–1
Barrell, John 202n.14
Battersby, Christine 33n.28
Beauvoir, Simone de 1
Bedford College (London) 22–3, 137
Beecher, Catharine 55
Berkeley, George 2, 123n.45
Bernal, Martin 202, 208
Besant, Annie 15–16, 231
  anti-vivisectionism 198n.7
  atheism 14–15, 165–6, 187–91
  biographical information 4, 16–19, 53
  birth-control debate 24–5, 35
  Comte, Auguste and 95, 187
  editorial work 25–7, 36–7
  empirical science 164
  epitaph 194
  evangelicalism 166, 187, 194
  Fabian socialism 4
  imperialism 229–30
  India 4, 18–19, 229
  intuitionism 188–9
  materialism 100, 127–9, 132
  omitted in 'public moralists' account 2n.4
  panpsychism 13, 98, 131
  philosophy of mind 98, 100, 125–31

  positivism 4, 158, 229
  publication in journals 27*t*, 39
  as public figure/speaker 2n.4, 53, 188
  religion and morality 14–15, 36, 164, 187–91
  secularism 4, 7–8, 14–15, 36–7, 100, 127, 164–7, 187–8, 194, 229
  secular moral evolutionism 155, 158
  theism 4, 187, 194
  theosophy 4, 14, 94–5, 100, 127–31, 166, 194, 229
  trial 24–5, 35, 145n.26
  utilitarianism 4, 188–9
  see also women's filiations/relationships
Besant, Annie: works
  Autobiographical Sketches (AS) 167n.6
  Autobiography, An (ABA) 127–9, 165–6, 167n.6, 187, 191, 194
  Fruits of Philosophy, The (co-edited with Bradlaugh) 24–5
  My Path to Atheism (MPA) 167n.6
  'True Basis of Morality, The' (TBM) 167n.6, 188–9
  Why I Became a Theosophist (WT) 128–30
  'World Without God, A' (WWG) 190–1
Blackwell, Elizabeth 47n.49
Blackwood's Magazine 26*t*, 27*t*
Blaettler, Christine 1n.1
Blavatsky, Helena Petrovna 15–16, 231
  anonymity 39
  anti-vivisectionism 198n.7
  biographical information 3, 16–19
  Britain 3n.8, 216–17
  Coulomb affair 22, 49–53, 125
  Eastern religion and philosophy 18–19
  evolutionary cosmology 130–1, 218
  fraud and imposture accusations 22, 49–53
  Hegel, Georg Wilhelm Friedrich and 196–7
  Hodgson report 22, 49n.56, 50–3, 125
  hylo-idealism, critique of 14, 125–6
  immortality 130
  India 18–19, 49, 216–18, 220–4, 227
  influence by 3
  initialled authorship 39–40
  Lucifer (journal) 3n.8, 25–7, 27*t*, 39, 125
  'Mahatma Letters' 49–52
  materialism 100, 125–7, 132
  metempsychosis 157n.40
  monism 131–2
  Müller, Max and 221–2
  panpsychism 13–14, 98, 131–2
  philosophy of mind 98, 100, 125–31
  positivism 197–8, 217n.30
  progress in history 15, 196–9, 216–25, 227–8, 230

publication in journals 27t
race 222-4, 228
racial and imperial politics 52-3
reincarnation 125-6, 130
Russian origins 3n.8, 18-19, 216-17
spiritual evolution 3, 15, 131, 196-7, 216-24
spiritualism 48-9, 166
spiritual philosophy outside academic respectability 22
theosophy 3-4, 7, 14, 18-19, 36, 49, 130-1, 166, 194-5, 224-5
travels 216-17
see also women's filiations/relationships
Blavatsky, Helena Petrovna: *The Secret Doctrine* (SD) 95n.59, 127-8, 216-17
  ancient wisdom 217-18, 220-1, 224-5
  Aryan root-race 218-24
  Aryan sub-races 219-24
  chain of world religious cultures 221-2
  cosmic evolution 218-19
  cyclical evolution 219-21
  India and Egypt 221-2
  progress in history 15, 196, 217-22, 224-5
  reconfiguring the hierarchy of civilizations 223-4
  theosophy 3, 130, 224-5
  Tibetan Book of Dzyan and 217, 223-4
Blavatsky, Helena Petrovna: works
  'Have Animals Souls?' 198n.7
  Isis Unveiled (IU) 50-1, 125, 157n.40, 196, 217n.30, 220-2, 224-5
  Key to Theosophy 221-2
  'Modern Idealism, Worse than Materialism' (MI) 125-6, 211, 214, 216, 225-7
  'To Dr Lewins, and the Hylo-Idealists at Large' (LHL) 125-7
  see also Blavatsky, Helena Petrovna: *The Secret Doctrine*
Bohls, Elizabeth 198n.8
Bolton, Martha 60n.5, 62
Boole, Mary Everest 50-1, 161
Boucherett, Jessie 27n.17
Boucher-Rivalain, Odile 167n.8
Boyle, Deborah 59, 62
Bradlaugh, Charles 100, 187-90
  Fruits of Philosophy, The (co-edited with Besant) 24-5
  trial 145n.26
Braid, James 110-11
Brain: A Journal of Neurology 42-3
Brake, Laurel 9n.14, 32, 38, 45
Bressey, Caroline 17n.25, 18n.29
Britain 2n.5
  black and ethnic minority population 17-18
  literacy 24-5
  Victorians 2n.4, 15, 18-19, 31, 135
  working class 16-18
  see also print culture
British Empire 17-18, 198-9, 212, 227-30
British Journal of Psychology 42-3
British Psychological Society 42-3
British Quarterly Review (journal) 27t
Broad, Jacqueline 6
Brontë, Anne 34
Brontë, Charlotte 34
Brontë, Emily 34
Brown, Sue 137n.12, 144n.23, 196-7
Browning, Elizabeth Barrett 30
Browning, Robert 136-7
Büchner, Ludwig 99-100, 125-6, 131-2
  Kraft und Stoff 114, 127-8
Buckley, Arabella
  biographical information 4, 19
  Darwin, Charles and 41, 148-9, 153-4
  as educator 33-4
  evolution 4, 14, 133, 135-6, 155
  evolution: Buckley against Cobbe 148-53, 155
  evolutionary theory and cooperative morality 4, 14, 153-9
  Garnett, Richard and 8-9, 41-2, 157n.40, 159
  immortality 152-3, 156-7
  invisibility 8-9
  Lyell, Charles and 41, 135-6
  popular science books 4, 39, 154
  publication in journals 27t, 39
  science and religion 149-50, 160
  spiritual evolutionism 156-8
  spiritualism 166
  see also women's filiations/relationships
Buckley, Arabella: works
  'Darwinism and Religion' (DR) 148, 150-2, 154, 156-8
  High School History of England 41-2
  Life and her Children 154
  Moral Teachings of Science (MT) 154-6, 159-60
  Short History of Natural Science, A 154
  'Soul, and the Theory of Evolution, The' (STE) 156-8
  Winners in Life's Race 154
Buddhism 207-8, 211-12, 226t
Butler, Josephine 2n.4, 18n.30, 46, 135n.8
Byron, Annabella (Lovelace's mother) 23n.5, 101-2, 106, 108-9, 114n.29
Byron, George Gordon 33n.28
Bywater, Ingram 45-6

Caine, Barbara 1n.1
Carlyle, Thomas 83

Carpenter, William Benjamin 111–14, 232
  'automatic' action/'excito-motor' 106–8, 112
  Cobbe, Frances Power and 7, 10–11, 14, 46–7, 47n.49, 99–100, 114–16, 131–2
  dualism 7, 14, 112
  Lovelace, Ada and 106–7, 110–11, 113, 131
  materialism 107, 109–11
  mesmerism 110–11, 113
  philosophy of mind 106–7, 111–14
  physiology of mind 106–7, 111–12, 122, 131
  Principles of General and Comparative Physiology 107
  Principles of Human Physiology 106–7, 111
  thinking automaton 113
  'unconscious cerebration' 99, 112–14, 131
  volitional/voluntary/automatic action distinction 112
causation
  Cobbe, Frances Power 42, 82–8, 97
  God as first cause 64–5, 67–8, 71–3, 151
  Lewes, George Henry 84–5
  Martineau, Harriet 13–14, 57–8, 66–73, 81
  Shepherd, Mary 13–14, 42, 56–66, 68, 71, 82
Cavendish, Margaret 1
Chadwick, Owen 166n.4
Chambers, Robert 9n.17
Chapman, John 25–7, 30–1
Christianity 226t
  nineteenth-century British intellectual life 166
  Besant, Annie, evangelicalism 166, 187, 194
  Cobbe, Frances Power 164–5, 180–1, 186, 189, 191–2, 197–8, 206–9, 216, 224–5, 228, 230
  Darwin, Charles 133–4
  evolution as compatible with Christian belief 4, 14, 133–5, 138–43, 148, 150–5
  Hennell, Charles 172
  Higher Criticism 3, 166–7, 203–4, 220–1
  Martineau, Harriet 201–5, 216, 224–5
  Müller, Max 208–9
  religion and morality 164–5, 173, 191–2, 194–5
  Wedgwood, Julia 137n.14, 211, 213–16, 224–5
Christian Science 50n.58, 166
Church of England 12, 137n.14
Church Quarterly Review (journal) 27t, 90n.55
Cobbe, Frances Power 15–16
  abolitionism 18, 228
  aesthetics 3
  animal welfare 3, 31
  anti-naturalism 13–14, 56–8, 81–8, 97
  anti-vivisectionism 36–7, 46–8, 135n.8, 189, 197n.6
  atheism 3, 7–8, 179–81, 189–90, 192
  biographical information 3, 16–19
  Carpenter, William Benjamin and 7, 10–11, 14, 46–7, 47n.49, 99–100, 114–16, 131–2
  causation 42, 82–8, 97
  Christianity 164–5, 180–1, 186, 189, 191–2, 197–8, 206–9, 216, 224–5, 228, 230
  comparative religion 198, 206–9
  Darwin, critique of 14–15, 28, 41, 133–4, 143–9, 158–9
  death 48
  dualism 7, 13–14, 86–8, 98, 116–17
  editorial work 33–4
  evolution 3, 14, 28, 135–6, 143–8, 155, 184
  feminism 3, 31
  Hume, critique of 86, 207n.21
  immortality and afterlife 14–15, 86, 88, 130, 179–80, 183–5
  influence by 3, 15–16
  intuitionism 82–4, 151–2, 188–9
  as 'journalist' 31–2
  Lewes, critique of 84–6
  Lloyd, Mary and 19
  materialism 99, 116–17
  metaphysics 86–7
  Nietzsche/Cobbe convergence 192–4
  philosophy of mind 7, 10–11, 13, 98, 100, 114–17
  positivism 197–8, 205–6
  progress in history/world religious progression 15, 196–8, 205–9, 216, 225, 227, 230
  publication in journals 3, 27t, 30–2
  publishing career 11n.21, 39
  religion and morality 7–8, 14–15, 114, 133, 164, 167, 179–92, 207
  rise and fall of 22, 46–8, 53
  Theism/theism 36, 82–3, 86–7, 131–2, 164–7, 191–2
  topics addressed by 3, 31
  travels 199–200, 206
  'unconscious cerebration'/thought 98–9, 114–17, 131–2
  women's education 22n.4
  as writer 3, 34, 39, 55
  see also women's filiations/relationships
Cobbe, Frances Power: *Darwinism in Morals and Other Essays* (DM) 143, 145–7, 184, 206–8
  'Darwinism in Morals' 28
  'Dreams as Instances of Unconscious Cerebration' 114–15
  'The Evolution of Morals and Religion' 206–7
  'Unconscious Cerebration' 114–16
Cobbe, Frances Power: *Essay on Intuitive Morals* (IM) 3, 14–15, 31–3, 38–9, 179–80
  experimentalism 82–3

intuitionism 82–4
Kantianism 32–3, 82–3, 86, 196–7
naturalism and morality 81–2
theism 82–3, 86–7
Cobbe, Frances Power: moral theory 3, 14–15, 32–3, 81–8, 179–81, 185–6
Cobbe: omitted in 'public moralists' account 2n.4
God as moral legislator 83, 86–7, 179–80, 186
moral epistemology 3
morality 34–5, 39
moral law 179, 186, 192
moral responsibility 117
virtue 179–81, 186, 192
Cobbe, Frances Power: works
'Agnostic Morality' (AM) 179n.29, 185–6, 193
'Brahmo Samaj, The' (BS) 209, 225
Broken Lights 31, 36, 143
Cities of the Past (CP) 206
'Faithless World, A' (FW) 164–5, 189–90, 211, 214n.26
Hopes of the Human Race, Hereafter and Here (HHR) 147–8, 180n.30
Life of Frances Power Cobbe, by Herself (LFPC) 143, 209
'Magnanimous Atheism' (MA) 81–2, 86n.45, 179–81, 183–4, 189, 192, 205–6, 211, 214n.26
'Medical Profession and its Morality, The' 47
Modern Rack: Papers on Vivisection, The (MR) 146, 184, 197n.6
Scientific Spirit of the Age, The (SS) 149
Studies New and Old of Ethical and Social Subjects (ESS) 206n.19, 207–8
see also Cobbe, Frances Power: *Darwinism in Morals and Other Essays*; Cobbe, Frances Power: *Essay on Intuitive Morals*
Coleman, William 53n.66
Coleridge, Samuel Taylor 83, 114–15
Collini, Stefan 2n.4
Collins, Mabel 25n.15, 39
colonialism 18, 227, 229–30
European colonialism 198–9, 227–8
comparative religion 197–8, 206–9, 218n.32
compatibilism 13, 67–8, 78, 121, 176–7
Comte, Auguste 79, 174–5
Besant, Annie and 95, 187
Course of Positive Philosophy 2–3, 79
critique of 80n.36, 91
Lewes, George Henry and 85, 174–5
Religion of Humanity 80, 91
Contagious Diseases Acts 18n.30, 35, 47n.49
Contemporary Review (journal) 26t, 27–8, 27t
Cobbe, Frances Power 31, 149, 185, 211

Lee, Vernon 182–3, 186
signed authorship 38–9
Wedgwood, Julia 39, 136–7, 159, 211
Conway, Anne 1
Cook, Eliza 27n.17
Cornhill Magazine 25, 26t, 27t, 31
Cornwallis, Caroline Frances 5n.10
Small Books on Great Subjects series 23–4
Coulomb, Emma and Alexis (Coulomb affair) 22, 49–53, 125
Craft, Ellen and William 17n.25
Crockett, Alasdair 12
Curran Index 38n.36
Cust, Nina 89n.50, 136–7

Dabydeen, David and Paul Edwards 17n.25
Daily News (journal) 27t, 30–1, 205n.17
Dancy, Jonathan 174n.21
Darwin, Charles
agnosticism 153–4
Buckley, Arabella and 41, 148–9, 153–4
Christianity and 133–4
Cobbe's critique of 14–15, 28, 41, 133–4, 143–9, 158–9
creation doctrine and 133–4
'cultivated hive-bee' 147, 153
Darwinism 135
Descent of Man 14, 41, 92, 133, 143
Descent of Man, reviews by Wallace, Mivart, and Cobbe 41, 143–4, 148–9, 150n.33
morality and evolution 144–5, 148–9
natural selection 135, 142, 144–5, 151
Origin of Species 14, 133–5, 159
religion and morality 133, 144
theism 138, 153–4
utilitarianism 146, 152–3, 158–9
Wedgwood, Julia and 8–9, 137–8, 144
see also evolution
Darwin, Emma (Julia Wedgwood's aunt and Darwin's wife) 136–7, 148–9
Darwin, Henrietta (Darwin's daughter) 142n.17
Davidoff, Leonore 29n.20
Davies, Emily 22n.4
Dawkins, Richard 194
Delap, Lucy 1n.1
Demoor, Marysa 32, 38
De Morgan, Augustus 11–12, 22–3, 101–3, 106
De Sablé, Mme 45–6
Descartes, René 6–7, 13, 116
De Sévigné, Mme 45–6
digital archives 5
Dixon, Thomas 154
Doyle Wheeler, Anna 5n.10

Drew, Catherine 31n.25
Drummond, Henry: *The Ascent of Man* 153–4
dualism
  Carpenter, William Benjamin 7, 14, 112
  Cobbe, Frances Power 7, 13–14, 86–8, 98, 116–17
  Lovelace, Ada 14, 98
  Naden, Constance 100, 120–2, 131–2
  'orthodox dualism' 100n.2, 120–1
  Shepherd, Mary 65–6
Dussel, Enrique 230

Easley, Alexis 40
Echo (journal) 27t, 31
Edinburgh Review (journal) 19, 25, 26t, 27t
  anonymity 38–9
  essay/review form 28
  Martineau, Harriet 30, 39
Eliot, George (Mary Ann Evans) 1–2, 2n.4, 15–16
  aesthetics 175–6, 177n.26, 178
  agnosticism 165–7, 173, 180–1
  anonymity 30–2, 39, 173–5
  biographical information 3, 16–17, 19
  education 22–4
  influence by 3
  'Law of Progress' 15, 30–1, 89n.53
  laws 176–7
  Lewes, George Henry and 19, 171–2, 174n.20
  literature 24n.12
  literature and the expansion of sympathy 164, 167, 171–9
  married to John Cross 19
  morality 14–15, 34–5
  morality and sympathy 14–15, 174
  mythologization of 172
  positivism 89n.53, 166–7
  pseudonym 5n.9, 27–8, 40
  publication in journals 27t, 30–2, 39
  realism 175–6, 178
  religion and morality 36, 164, 167, 171–9
  secularism 165–6, 178–9
  secular morality 166–7, 179–81, 191–2
  sympathy: cognitive, affective, practical 174–5
  topics addressed by 3
  translation of Feuerbach 3, 28, 33–4, 172, 178–81
  translation of Spinoza 3, 33–4, 170n.9
  translation of Strauss 3, 33–4, 39, 172–4
  as writer 3, 34
  see also women's filiations/relationships
Eliot, George: works
  Adam Bede (AB) 173n.16, 175–6
  Eliot as novelist 3, 178–9

George Eliot Letters, The (GEL) 74, 171–3, 176–7, 180–1
Middlemarch 31, 173n.16, 176n.24, 177–8
Mill on the Floss, The (MF) 174, 176
'Natural History of German Life, The' (NHGL) 175–6, 178
novels: 'free indirect speech' 178
novels: ordinary people in 177n.26, 178–9
'Prospectus of the Westminster and Foreign Quarterly Review' (PWR) 31, 89n.53
Scenes of Clerical Life 176
Elisabeth of Bohemia 1
Elliotson, John 104, 108
empirical science 47, 55
  Besant, Annie 164
  empirical scientific methods 13–14, 51–2, 91, 97
  naturalism and 56–7, 97
  philosophy and 57, 64–6, 79, 88
  Welby, Victoria 41–2, 92–3, 96–7
  see also science
Engledue, William 99–100, 104, 112–13, 115–18
Englishwoman's Review (journal) 26t
Enlightenment 19–20, 34–5, 56–7, 66–7
  Scottish Enlightenment 197–8, 200
Eurocentrism 15, 198–9, 223–4, 227–8, 230
evolution 14, 133–6, 231
  anti-moral evolutionism 155–6, 158–9
  Buckley, Arabella 4, 14, 133, 135–6, 155
  Buckley, Arabella: evolutionary theory and cooperative morality 4, 14, 153–9
  Buckley against Cobbe 148–53, 155
  Cobbe, Frances Power 3, 14, 28, 135–6, 143–8, 155, 184
  Cobbe's critique of Darwin 14–15, 28, 41, 133–4, 143–9, 158–9
  as compatible with Christian belief 4, 14, 133–5, 138–43, 148, 150–5
  creation doctrine and 133–4
  critique of 14–15, 28, 133
  evolution, meanings of 134–5
  Lee, Vernon 4–5, 182–3, 186n.34, 231
  Lyell, Charles 134–6, 140n.15, 142–3, 149
  Martineau, Harriet 134–5
  moral and religious anti-evolutionism 155
  moral and religious evolutionism 155
  morality and 134, 144–5, 148, 151, 155–6, 160
  natural selection 135–6, 142–5, 150–1, 158
  religion and morality 133, 158–9
  secular moral evolutionism 155, 158
  Spencer, Herbert 134–5, 147n.29
  'survival of the fittest' 147n.29, 158–9
  Wedgwood, Julia 4, 14, 133, 135–43, 155, 158–63

women philosophers' filiations 135–6, 148–53, 158–9
  see also Darwin, Charles

Faraday, Michael 110, 118
Fawcett, Henry 30n.22
feminism 1n.1, 28, 45–6, 133, 231
  Cobbe, Frances Power 3, 31
  Wedgwood, Julia 4, 212n.25, 214–15,
  see also gender-related issues; patriarchy
Feuerbach, Ludwig 173
  Eliot's translation of 3, 28, 33–4, 172, 178–81
Folescu, M. 60n.5, 64n.8
Foot, Philippa 1
Fortnightly Review (journal) 26t, 27t, 30n.22, 38, 186
Foster, Michael 47
Foucault, Michel 38
Fraser's Magazine 26t, 27t, 31, 146
Freethought Publishing Company 100, 188, 190

Galton, Francis 46–7, 144–7
  anti-moral evolutionism 155–6, 158–9
Gardner, Catherine Villanueva 42n.44, 55
Garnett, Richard 8–9, 41–2, 157n.40, 159
Garritzen, Elise 232
Gaskell, Elizabeth 178
gender-related issues 19
  Cobbe, Frances Power 193
  gender biases 5–6, 138, 181
  gender constraints 2, 16n.22, 23
  see also feminism; patriarchy; 'separate spheres' ideology; women; women's education
Girton College (Cambridge) 22–3, 44, 137
Gnosticism 213, 217–18, 221–2
God
  as Creator 138–9, 141, 205–6
  as first cause 64–5, 67–8, 71–3, 151
  as moral legislator 83, 86–7, 179–80, 186
Goodrick-Clarke, Nicholas 218
Gourlay, Jane 210
Green, Thomas Hill 1–2, 11, 44, 104n.10
Greg, William Rathbone 144–7
  anti-moral evolutionism 155–6, 158–9
Greig, Woronzow 108–9
Gurney, Edmund 50–1
Gurney, Emelia Russell 136–7

Hall, Spencer T. 73–4, 108
Hamilton, Elizabeth 19–20, 70n.21
Hamilton, William 43–4
Harrison, Frederic 89n.54, 179
Hays, Mary 19–20

Hegel, Georg Wilhelm Friedrich 12–13, 45–6, 196–7
  Blavatsky, Helena Petrovna and 196–7
  Wedgwood, Julia and 138, 196–7, 215–16
  Welby, Victoria and 94n.58
Hemans, Felicia 33n.28
Hennell, Charles: *Inquiry concerning the Origin of Christianity* 172
Hermit, Eastern 42–3
Herodotus 202, 221–2
Hill, Octavia 2n.4
Hinduism 206–9, 212, 219n.35, 226t
history of philosophy
  male/female philosophers interaction in 6–9, 11–12
  as series of conversations 6–7
  women in 55
  women's omission in 6–7, 11, 49
Hodgson, Richard: Hodgson report 22, 49n.56, 50–3, 125
Holyoake, George
  Martineau, Harriet and 76n.33
  secularism 76n.33, 165, 187
  secularism/atheism distinction 7n.12, 187–8
Home, Allan 49
Horsley, Victor 47–8, 51
Hughes, Linda 11n.21
Hume, David
  Cobbe's critique of 86, 207n.21
  Martineau's critique of 71
  Natural History of Religion 207n.21
  Shepherd's critique of 2, 55, 58, 68, 71, 86
Hutton, Richard Holt 76n.30, 113, 117, 144n.23
  as 'journalist' 32
Hutton, Sarah 6
Huxley, Thomas Henry 11, 30n.22, 58, 198
  agnosticism 11, 76, 122
  agnosticism/atheism distinction 7n.12
  critique of 90–1
  Darwinism 135
  empiricism 90–1
  free will 121–2
  'Mr. Darwin's Critics' 41
  Naden, Constance and 100n.2, 121–2
  naturalism 57–8
  'On the Hypothesis that Animals are Automata' 121–2
  positivism 90–1
  Science and Culture, and Other Essays 100n.2
  theory of mind 121–2
  Welby, Victoria and 41–2, 89–91
hylo-idealism 45
  Blavatsky's critique of 14, 125–6
  Naden, Constance 5, 14, 98, 118–20, 123–5

hylo-zoism
  Lewins, Robert 14, 117–19
  Naden, Constance 120–1

immanentism 110–11, 117–18, 127n.50
immortality and afterlife
  Blavatsky, Helena Petrovna 130
  Buckley, Arabella 152–3, 156–7
  Cobbe, Frances Power 14–15, 86, 88, 130, 179–80, 183–5
  Lee, Vernon 182–3
  Martineau, Harriet 169, 179–80, 183n.33
  Naden, Constance 130
  philosophy of mind 98
  Shepherd, Mary 65
Impey, Catherine 17–18
India 208–9, 227
  Aryan model 208, 212, 225
  Besant, Annie 4, 18–19, 229
  Blavatsky, Helena Petrovna 18–19, 49, 216–18, 220–4, 227
  Indian independence 4, 18, 224, 229
  Indian National Congress 18–19, 229
  Theosophical Society headquarters 4, 49–50, 216–17
  theosophy and Indian nationalism 18, 224, 227, 229
  Wedgwood, Julia 211–12, 215–16
induction 13–14
  Martineau, Harriet 13–14, 70, 74–5
  Naden, Constance 5, 123
intuitionism 151–3
  Besant, Annie 188–9
  Cobbe, Frances Power 82–4, 151–2, 188–9
  Wallace, Alfred Russel 151–2
Ireland 2n.5, 18–19, 30, 35
Irigaray, Luce 215
Irwin, T. H. 174–5
Islam 204n.16

James, Henry 181–2
Jameson, Anna 5n.10, 33n.31, 41
Johnston, Judith 46n.48
Johnstone, Christian Isobel 27n.17
Jones, E. E. Constance 44
journalism 31–2
  female 'journalists' 31–2
  higher journalism 32, 45
Journal of the Anthropological Institute 27t
Journal of Science 27t, 119
journals *see* print culture
Judaism 226t
  Cobbe, Frances Power 15, 206–8

Martineau, Harriet 15, 201–5
Wedgwood, Julia 4, 136–7, 213, 215n.27

Kant, Immanuel 72, 82n.37, 83, 143–4
  Cobbe, Frances Power and 32–3, 82–3, 86, 196–7
  Martineau, Harriet on 72, 83
Kierkegaard, Søren Aabye 38n.37
Kingsford, Anna 95n.59, 198n.7
Knowledge (journal) 27t
Knowlton, Charles: *The Fruits of Philosophy* 24–5
Koot Hoomi 52, 219, 223–4

Ladd-Franklin, Christine 89n.51
Lawrence, William 65
Leader (journal) 27t, 39, 45, 85–6, 187
Lee, Vernon
  aestheticism 4–5, 181–3, 186n.35
  aesthetics 4–5, 182, 186
  afterlife 182–3
  Anstruther-Thomson, Kit and 19
  'Art and Life' 4–5
  atheism 4–5, 14–15, 183, 186
  biographical information 4–5, 16–19, 181
  Britain 3n.8, 181–2
  evolution 4–5, 182–3, 186n.34, 231
  pseudonym 5n.9, 39–40, 181
  publication in journals 27t, 181
  religion and morality 36, 164, 167, 181–7, 192
  'responsible unbelief' 7–8, 14–15, 166–7, 186
  secularism 165–6, 182–3
  secular morality 165, 185
  'a sort of art-philosophy' 4–5
  topics addressed by 182–3
  utilitarianism 4–5, 185
  vivisectionism 4–5, 182–3, 186n.34
  writings 53
  see also women's filiations/relationships
Lee, Vernon: *Baldwin* (B) 182–3
  'Consolations of Belief, The' 184, 186
  'Of Honour and Evolution' 186n.34
  'Responsibilities of Unbelief: A Conversation of Three Rationalists' 182–5
Lee, Vernon: works
  Althea: A Second Book of Dialogues on Aspirations and Duties 186n.35
  'Art and Life' 186
  Belcaro (Bel) 4–5, 181–2
  Miss Brown 182, 186n.35
  'Ruskinism' 181–2
  Selected Letters of Vernon Lee, 1856-1935 (SLVL) 181–3, 186
  Studies of the Eighteenth Century in Italy 181
  see also Lee, Vernon: *Baldwin*

Leibniz, Gottfried Wilhelm 218n.33
Le Lotus (theosophical journal) 27t
letters 10, 28–30, 232
 as appropriate medium for women 28–9
 as philosophical writing 28–9, 89
Lewes, George Henry 11, 45, 58, 187, 232
 Biographical History of Philosophy 79, 85–6
 causation 84–5
 Cobbe's critique of 84–6
 Comte, Auguste and 174–5
 Comte's Philosophy of the Sciences 85
 'dogmatic'/'suspensive' atheism 7n.12
 Eliot, George and 19, 171–2, 174n.20
 as 'journalist' 32, 45
 Martineau/Lewes differences 85n.44
 naturalism 57–8
 positivism 57–8, 85, 90–1
Lewins, Robert 117–18, 232
 'hylo-zoism' 14, 117–19
 immanentism 118
 Life and Mind 118
 Naden, Constance and 14, 45, 100, 117–19
 philosophy of mind 118
Lewis, Sarah 34
Light (theosophical journal) 27t
linguistics *see* Welby, Victoria
Link (journal) 27t, 36–7
Logan, Deborah 28–9, 42n.44, 90–1
Lovelace, Ada 3
 analytical engine 3, 28, 99, 101, 103–5, 109, 113
 aristocracy 16–17
 artificial intelligence 3, 14, 28, 98, 101, 105
 Babbage, Charles and 3, 99, 101–2
 Carpenter, William Benjamin and 106–7, 110–11, 113, 131
 computing, visionary anticipation of 3, 101, 103
 death 111
 dualism 14, 98
 education 22–3, 101–2
 imagination 105
 immanentism 110
 letters 102–3, 105
 materialism 14, 98–9, 104n.10, 105–6, 109–10, 131
 mesmerism 98, 107–11, 131, 166
 philosophy of mind 14, 98–111, 131
 publication in journals 27t
 religion 105–6, 109–10
 Romanticism 19
 'thinking machine' 101–2, 104, 113, 131
 translation of Menabrea's essay on the analytical engine 28, 102–3
 unpublished work 3, 102–3, 110
 see also women's filiations/relationships
Lovelace, Ada: works
 Ada: The Enchantress of Numbers (edited by Betty Toole, AEN) 102–3, 105
 Sketch of the Analytical Engine invented by Charles Babbage (trans. and commentary, SAE) 39, 102–4, 107
Lucifer (theosophical journal) 26t, 27t, 95n.59, 125
 Besant, Annie 27t
 Blavatsky, Helena Petrovna 3n.8, 25–7, 27t, 39, 125
Lyell, Charles 41, 82n.38
 Buckley, Arabella and 41, 135–6
 evolution 134–6, 140n.15, 142–3, 149
 Geological Evidences of the Antiquity of Man, The 143

Macmillan, Alexander 138
Macmillan's Magazine 25, 26t, 27t, 38
 anonymity 39
 Buckley, Arabella 148
 Cobbe, Frances Power 31
 Wedgwood, Julia 136–8
Madras Christian College Magazine 52
Maitland, Edward 95n.59
Maitzen, Rohan 173n.16
Mander, W. J. 1n.1, 11
Manichaeanism 152–3, 213
Mansel, Henry 165n.3
Marcet, Jane 41
Martineau, Harriet 9n.18, 15–16, 30–1, 41
 abolitionism 18, 228–9
 as aesthetic moralist 176
 agnosticism 76, 165–7, 167n.8, 180–1, 183n.33
 associationism 69–70
 atheism 2–3, 7–8, 36, 66, 74–6, 79, 97, 167–71, 179, 187–8, 199–200, 205
 Atkinson, Henry George and 2–3, 73–4, 108
 as best-known British female intellectual 2–3, 30
 causation 13–14, 57–8, 66–73, 81
 determinism 2–3, 66, 72–3, 77–8, 97, 170, 177n.25
 determinism, causal 13–14, 66, 68–9, 78
 evolution 134–5
 'exterior point of view' 164, 167–71, 180–1, 191–2
 Hume, critique of 71
 immortality and afterlife 169, 179–80, 183n.33
 induction 13–14, 70, 74–5

Martineau, Harriet (*cont.*)
  as 'journalist' 31–2
  Kant, Immanuel 72, 83
  laws of action/natural laws 72, 78–9, 81, 173–4, 177
  materialism 2–3, 7, 14, 66, 74–5, 77, 79, 97, 99, 131–2
  mesmerism 73–4, 77n.35, 78, 108, 166
  moralist necessarianism (earlier philosophy) 66–73, 79, 81
  morality 34–5, 79
  naturalism 2–3, 13–14, 56–8, 66–81, 97, 171
  omitted in 'public moralists' account 2n.4
  phrenology 29–30, 73–4
  political economy 2–3, 32–3, 71–2
  positivism 2–3, 28, 33–4, 57–8, 66, 79–80, 85–6, 90–1, 166–7, 205–6
  Priestley, Joseph and 66–9, 77–8
  progress in history 15, 196–209, 216, 224–5, 227, 230
  publication in journals 27t, 30–2, 39, 67
  religion and morality 14–15, 34n.33, 36, 164, 167–71, 191–2
  science and religion 91, 97, 141n.16
  scientific method 75, 77
  secularism 164–7, 170, 179, 187–8, 205–7, 210–11
  topics addressed by 2–3, 30, 44
  travels 199–200
  Unitarianism 36, 66–9, 164–5, 180–1, 191–2
  as writer 34, 39
  see also women's filiations/relationships
Martineau, Harriet: *Autobiography* (HMA) 14–15, 28, 32–3, 34n.33, 68–71, 74–5, 77–9, 81, 90, 167, 210
  afterlife and immortality 169, 183n.33
  atheism 167–8, 171, 179, 205
  'exterior point of view' 168–9
  positivism 167
  secularism 167
  travels 199–200
Martineau, Harriet: biographical information 2–3, 16–19
  'Discipulus'/'V' signature 34–5, 39, 67
  education 22–3, 170n.9
  illness 73–4, 74n.27, 81–2, 108–9, 210
  influence by 15–16
  letters by 28–9, 109
  obituary 32–3
Martineau, Harriet: *Eastern Life* (EL) 173–4, 197n.3, 199–200, 210
  ancient Egypt 201–4, 221–2
  Christianity 201–5, 216, 224–5
  Cobbe, Frances Power and 205–7

Greek civilization 201–2, 221–2
  history of Ideas 207
  Islam 204n.16
  Judaism 201–5
  secularism 205, 207, 210–11
  stages of religious and philosophical thought 200–1, 228
Martineau, Harriet: *Illustrations of Political Economy* (IPE) 30, 32–3, 39, 66, 71–2, 175–7
  'Life in the Wild' 200
  ordinary working people 177n.26
  as 'work of Morals' 72n.25
Martineau, Harriet: *The Positive Philosophy of Auguste Comte* (trans. and ed., PP) 2–3, 28, 33–4, 79–80, 85n.43, 89n.53, 168
  evolution 134n.5
  'Law of human progress' 89
Martineau, Harriet: works
  Collected Letters (HMCL) 70–2, 74, 109, 134, 171–2, 176, 187–8, 193, 199–200
  Deerbrook 34
  Devotional Exercises 38–9
  'Essays on the Art of Thinking' (EAT) 67, 70, 72
  'Essays on the Pursuit of Truth' (EPT) 70–1
  'Female Education' 34n.33
  'Female Writers on Practical Divinity' 34n.33, 67, 170
  History of the Thirty Years' Peace, 1816–1846 30
  Letters from Ireland 28–9
  'Letters on Mesmerism' 28–9, 99, 108
  Life in the Sick-Room 33n.30
  Miscellanies 67
  Society in America (SA) 72–3, 228,
  see also Martineau, Harriet: *Eastern Life*; Martineau, Harriet: *Illustrations of Political Economy*; Martineau, Harriet: *The Positive Philosophy of Auguste Comte*; Martineau and Atkinson: *Letters on the Laws of Man's Nature and Development*
Martineau, James 67n.13, 74, 86n.46
Martineau and Atkinson: *Letters on the Laws of Man's Nature and Development* (LLM) 2–3, 9n.18, 28–30, 56–7, 73–81, 97, 169, 187
  atheism 74–6, 199–200
  critique of 74, 99
  Kant, Immanuel 83
  materialism 77, 131–2
  secularism 187
Marx, Eleanor 197n.4
Marx, Karl 196–7
  Capital 197n.4

materialism 117–18, 131–2
  Besant, Annie 100, 127–9, 132
  Blavatsky, Helena Petrovna 100, 125–7, 132
  Carpenter, William Benjamin 107, 109–11
  Cobbe, Frances Power 99, 116–17
  definition 99
  Engledue, William 99–100, 115–18
  Lovelace, Ada 14, 98–9, 104n.10, 105–6, 109–10, 131
  Martineau, Harriet 2–3, 7, 14, 66, 74–5, 77, 79, 97, 99, 131–2
  Naden, Constance 7, 13–14, 98–9, 119–20, 119n.41, 123–5, 127, 131–2
  Tyndall, John 126–7, 131–2
  women philosophers' filiations 99
McRobert, Jennifer 64
meaning theory *see* Welby, Victoria
Meiklejohn, J. M. D. 83
Menabrea, Luigi 28, 102–3
mesmerism 104, 108, 117–18, 166
  Carpenter, William Benjamin 110–11, 113
  Lovelace, Ada 98, 107–11, 131, 166
  Martineau, Harriet 73–4, 77n.35, 78, 108, 166
  'phreno-mesmerism' 73–4, 100, 104
Midgley, Mary 1
Mill, John Stuart 1–2, 11, 30–1, 30n.22, 189
  On Liberty 193–4
  Subjection of Women, The 41
Mind (journal) 25–7, 26t, 27t, 29–30, 42–3
  Welby, Victoria 55, 88
Mivart, St George Jackson 41, 143–4, 146
  Genesis of Species 150n.33
Modern Review (journal) 27t, 47n.49
Monist (journal) 27t, 55, 88–9, 119n.39
  first American specialist philosophy journal 88n.49
Montagu Wynyard, Mrs 73–4
Monthly Repository (journal) 26t, 27t, 67n.14
  Martineau, Harriet 30, 66–7, 70
morality
  anti-moral evolutionism 155–6, 158–9
  atheism and 7–8, 171
  Darwin, Charles: morality and evolution 144–5, 148–9
  duty as basic moral concept 83
  duty/utility distinction 185
  Eliot, George 14–15, 34–5, 174
  Eliot, George: secular morality 166–7, 179–81, 191–2
  evolution and 134, 144–5, 148, 151, 155–6, 160
  as exact science 87–8
  God as ultimate source of our moral obligations 72–3

Martineau, Harriet 34–5, 79
moral action as done from principle and duty 72, 88, 180
naturalism and 171
'public moralists' 2n.4
secular moral evolutionism 155, 158,
  see also Cobbe, Frances Power: moral theory; religion and morality
More, Hannah 19–20, 34
Morley, John 149n.31
Moyar, Dean 11
Müller, Max 52, 197–8, 208–9, 212
  Blavatsky, Helena Petrovna and 221–2
  Chips from a German Workshop 208–9
Murdoch, Iris 1
Murray, John 143–4, 200–1
Myers, Frederick 50–1, 172, 178

Naden, Constance 100n.1
  atheism 5, 118–19, 123
  biographical information 5, 18–19, 53
  'Constance Arden' pseudonym 39, 119
  death 5, 23, 119, 124–5
  dualism 100, 120–2, 131–2
  free will 121–2
  Huxley, Thomas Henry and 100n.2, 121–2
  'hylo-idealism' 5, 14, 98, 118–20, 123–5
  immortality 130
  induction 5, 123
  Lewins, Robert and 14, 45, 100, 117–19
  materialism 7, 13–14, 98–9, 119–20, 119n.41, 123–5, 127, 131–2
  philosophy of mind 98–100, 117–25
  publication in journals 27t
  rationalism/utilitarianism ethical synthesis 5
  religion 122
  religion and morality 36
  as writer 34, 53
  see also women's filiations/relationships
Naden, Constance: works
  'Animal Automatism' 100n.2
  'Brain Theory of Mind and Matter, The' (BT) 119–24
  Complete Poetical Works 39
  Further Reliques (FR) 39, 120, 124–5
  'Hylo-Idealism' (HI) 119, 123–4
  'Hylo-Zoism versus Animism' 120–1
  Induction and Deduction (ID) 39, 120, 122
  'On Mental Physiology and its Place in Philosophy' (MP) 120
  'Philosophical Tracts' 124–5
National Reformer (journal) 27t, 36–7
National Review (journal) 27t

naturalism 56-8, 97, 160-1, 231
  Cobbe, Frances Power 13-14, 56-8, 81-8, 97
  concept of 13-14, 56-7
  empirical science 56-7, 97
  Huxley, Thomas Henry 57-8
  Lewes, George Henry 57-8
  Martineau, Harriet 2-3, 13-14, 56-8, 97, 171
  Martineau's earlier philosophy: moralist necessarianism 66-73, 97
  Martineau's *Letters on the Laws of Man's Nature and Development* 73-81, 97
  morality and 171
  naturalism vs anti-naturalism 56
  science and religion 56, 91, 97
  scientific naturalism 2-3
  Shepherd, Mary 13-14, 56-66, 97
  strands of the cluster concept 57, 64-5, 72-3, 79, 88, 96
  Welby, Victoria 13-14, 56-8, 88-97
  women philosophers' filiations 57-8, 82, 91, 94
  women's contributions to the formulation and development of 79
Nature (journal) 26t
necessarianism 67-8, 176-7
  Martineau's earlier philosophy: moralist necessarianism 66-73, 79, 81
neo-Platonism 217-18
Newnham College (Cambridge) 50-1
New Quarterly Magazine 27t
Nietzsche, Friedrich 35, 155-6, 190n.41
  Cobbe/Nietzsche convergence 192-4
  religion and morality 192-4
Nightingale, Florence 2n.4, 199-200
Nineteenth Century (journal) 26t, 27-8, 38, 89n.54
Norton, Caroline 31n.25

O'Neill, Eileen 5, 8-9, 22n.3
Orientalism 52, 198-9, 209, 223-4, 227
Our Corner (cultural journal) 26t, 27t, 100, 119
  Besant, Annie 25-7, 36-7, 100
Owen, Alex 48-9
Owen, Richard 46

Pall Mall Gazette 27t, 149n.31
panpsychism 13, 132
  Besant, Annie 13, 98, 131
  Blavatsky, Helena Petrovna 13-14, 98, 131-2
  Welby, Victoria 96n.61
pantheism 109-10, 127-30
Paoletti, Cristina 60n.5
Parker, Theodore 33-4
Parkes, Bessie Rayner 27n.17

Pater, Walter 8-9, 30n.22, 181-2
patriarchy 2, 8, 21, 37, 40
  patriarchal constraints on women's intellectual participation 2, 16-17, 20-2, 53, 232
Pattison, E. F. S. (Emilia Dilke) 45-6
Pattison, Mark 45-6
Peirce, Charles 8-9, 28-9, 89n.50, 155
Petrilli, Susan 9n.15, 89nn.50,54
Philosophical Review 88n.49
philosophy
  nineteenth-century forgotten male philosophers 58, 232
  American philosophy 33-4, 88n.49
  empirical science and 57, 64-6, 79, 88
  generalist philosophy 22, 98, 231
  generalist philosophy and print culture 20-2, 29-30, 37, 54, 232
  philosophical debate in print culture 29-32, 37
  professionalization and specialization 22, 42-4, 47, 232
  topics addressed by female philosophers 1, 5n.10, 55, 231
  Western philosophy, women in 1, 55,
  see also history of philosophy; women philosophers (nineteenth-century, Britain)
philosophy of history 15, 209-10
  Eurocentrism 15
  Wedgwood, Julia 197-8, 209-10
  women's contributions to 196-8
philosophy of mind 13-14, 42-3, 98-101, 131-2, 231
  afterlife 98
  Besant, Annie 98, 100, 125-31
  Blavatsky, Helena Petrovna 98, 100, 125-31
  Carpenter, William Benjamin 106-7, 111-14
  Cobbe, Frances Power 7, 10-11, 13, 98, 100, 114-17
  generalist philosophy 29-30, 98
  Huxley, Thomas Henry 121-2
  Lewins, Robert 118
  Lovelace, Ada 14, 98-111, 131
  mysterianism 127n.50
  Naden, Constance 98-100, 117-25
  phrenology 29-30, 73-4
  physiology and 98
  professionalization and specialization 47
  religion and 98-9
  unconscious mind/'mental automatism'/'latent thought' 99
  women philosophers' filiations 99-100, 111, 131
  women philosophers' male interlocutors 100
  see also dualism; materialism; panpsychism

phrenology 29–30, 73–4
  Martineau, Harriet 29–30, 73–4
  'phreno-mesmerism', 73–4, 100, 104
physiology 42–3, 98, 114n.31, 132
  Carpenter, William Benjamin: physiology of mind 106–7, 111–12, 122, 131
  experimental physiology 47
  female physiology 23
Pichanick, Valerie 197n.3
Plato 45–6, 169, 190, 201
political philosophy 5n.10
polytheism 201, 203–8
positivism
  Besant, Annie 4, 158, 229
  Blavatsky, Helena Petrovna 197–8, 217n.30
  Cobbe, Frances Power 197–8, 205–6
  Eliot, George 89n.53, 166–7
  Huxley, Thomas Henry 90–1
  Lewes, George Henry 57–8, 85, 90–1
  Martineau, Harriet 2–3, 28, 33–4, 57–8, 66, 79–80, 85–6, 90–1, 166–7, 205–6
  Welby, Victoria 90–1
Postlethwaite, Diana 9n.18, 75
Priestley, Joseph 11–12, 56–8, 97, 177n.25
  General View of the Arguments for the Unity of God 66–7
  Martineau, Harriet and 66–9, 77–8
  Shepherd, Mary and 68
Prince, Mary: *The History of Mary Prince* 17–18
print culture 21–2, 24–7
  1857 Obscene Publications Act 24–5
  authorship 38–9
  book reviews 28
  diversity of 36–7
  essay/review boundary 28
  fiction writing 24–5, 31–2
  generalist philosophy and 20–2, 29–30, 37, 54, 232
  journal culture 25–8, 30, 36–7, 232
  journalism 31–2
  journals 25–8, 26t, 27t
  magazines 25
  non-fiction writing 24–5
  pamphlets 28
  periodicals 19, 25
  philosophical debate in 29–32, 37
  popular journalism 31–2
  professional critics 28
  religion and 24–5
  specialist academic journals 25–7, 42–4
  translations 28
  women as authors 30–2, 53
  women as editors 25–7, 27t, 30–1, 36–7, 39, 53
Proceedings of the Aristotelian Society (journal) 25–7, 27t

progress in history 15, 196–9
  advancement of course of civilizations 225–7
  Aryan model 202, 208–9, 212, 225
  Blavatsky, Helena Petrovna 15, 196–9, 216–25, 227–8, 230
  British Empire 198–9, 212, 227–30
  Cobbe, Frances Power 15, 196–8, 205–9, 216, 225, 227, 230
  colonialism 198–9, 227–8
  comparison between women's metanarratives 15, 196, 224–30
  directionality: from ancient East to modern West 15, 196, 205, 221–2, 224, 228
  Eurocentrism 15, 198–9, 223–4, 227–8, 230
  Europe's relations with other civilizations 230
  imperialism and race 228–30
  influence on women philosophers 196–8
  'Law of Progress' 15, 30–1
  Martineau, Harriet 15, 196–209, 216, 224–5, 227, 230
  natural selection and 135
  Orientalism 198–9, 209, 223–4, 227
  religion 224–5
  religion-and-morality as measurement for progress 197–8, 217
  sequence of world belief systems 15, 196, 224–5, 226t
  Victorians 15, 31, 135
  Wedgwood, Julia 15, 138–9, 196–8, 209–16, 225–7, 230
  women philosophers' filiations 198
  world-historical progression culminating in modern Europe 15, 196, 198–9, 217, 224, 228, 230
  see also animism; Buddhism; Christianity; Hinduism; Judaism; Zoroastrianism
Protagoras 123n.45, 125–6
Pythagoras 201

Quarterly Review (journal) 25, 26t

Rasmussen, Joel D. S., Judith Wolfe, and Johannes Zachhuber 165–6
Reasoner (journal) 187
Reed, Edward S. 99
Reeve, Henry 80–1, 87
Reichenbach, Karl von 110–11
Reid, Elizabeth Jesser 205n.17
Reid, Thomas 82n.37
religion
  nineteenth-century British intellectual life 12, 162–3
  philosophy of mind and 98–9
  progress in history 224–5

religion (cont.)
  progress in history: sequence of world belief systems 15, 196, 224–5, 226t
  religious dissent 12, 164–5
  see also 'alternative' spiritual currents; science and religion; secularism
religion and morality 7–8, 14–15, 36, 164–7, 191–5, 231
  Besant, Annie 14–15, 36, 164
  Besant–Cobbe debate 187–91
  Christianity 164–5, 173, 191–2, 194–5
  Cobbe, Frances Power 7–8, 14–15, 114, 133, 164, 167, 179–92, 207
  Darwin, Charles 133, 144
  defending morality over religion 20, 36
  Eliot, George 36, 164, 167, 171–9
  evolution 133, 155, 158–9
  Lee, Vernon 36, 164
  Lee–Cobbe debate 167, 181–7, 192
  Martineau, Harriet 14–15, 34n.33, 36, 164, 167–71, 191–2
  Naden, Constance 36
  Nietzsche, Friedrich 192–4
  progress in history, religion-and-morality as measurement for 197–8, 217
  secularism 164–5, 191–2
  women philosophers' filiations 166–7, 191–5
  see also secularism
Remond, Sarah Parker 17–18, 35–6
Rhodes, G. M.: *The Nine Circles of the Hell of the Innocent* 48
Richards, Robert 144n.24
Roberts, Caroline 173n.17
Robinson, Mary 33n.28
Rogers, Annie 23
Romanticism 19, 32–3
  Symphilosophie (collaborative philosophizing), Germany 38n.37
Rose, Jonathan 16–17
Rosicrucianism 217–18
Roy, Ram Mohun 209
Rubery, Matthew 32
Rudboeg, Tim 218

Sanders, Valerie 173n.19
Santucci, James 222–3
Saturday Review (journal) 26t, 27t
Schneewind, Jerome B. 44
Schopenhauer, Arthur 79
science
  exact sciences 84
  morality as exact science 87–8
  natural science 56–7, 110
  physical sciences 84

scientific method 75
Welby, Victoria: science and meaning 88, 91–3, 95–7, 160–1
see also empirical science
science and religion 56, 141
  Buckley, Arabella 149–50, 160
  Martineau, Harriet 91, 97, 141n.16
  naturalism 56, 91, 97
  Wedgwood, Julia 160–2, 216, 224–5
  Welby, Victoria 161–2
Scientific Memoirs (journal) 27t, 102–3
Seacole, Mary 17n.25
secularism 165
  nineteenth-century British intellectual life 12, 165–6
  Besant, Annie 4, 7–8, 14–15, 36–7, 100, 127, 164–7, 187–8, 194, 229
  Besant, Annie: secular moral evolutionism 155, 158
  Eliot, George 165–6, 178–9
  Eliot, George: secular morality 166–7, 179–81, 191–2
  Holyoake, George 7n.12, 76n.33, 165, 187–8
  Lee, Vernon 165–6, 182–3, 185
  Martineau, Harriet 164–7, 170, 179, 187–8, 205–7, 210–11
  National Secular Society 100, 187, 194
  religion and morality 164–5, 191–2
  secular forms of belief 166
  secularism/atheism distinction 7n.12, 187–8
  secular moral evolutionism 155, 158
  secular morality 7–8, 165–7, 185
  Wedgwood, Julia 214
Semple, John 83
Sen, Keshub Chunder 209
'separate spheres' ideology 19–21, 37
  as constraint on women 2, 21–3
  letters and the private sphere 28–9
  privacy of home as space for debate 28–9
  private sphere as home, charity and philanthropy 20
  spiritualism and 48–9
  women and the private sphere 2, 10, 20–1, 34
  women and the public sphere 10, 34–5
  women's moral superiority and the private sphere 34
Seymour, Miranda 9n.17
Shapiro, Lisa 6–7
Shepherd, Mary 15–16, 82, 231–2
  afterlife 65
  anti-naturalism 13–14, 56–66, 97
  associationism 69n.20
  Babbage, Charles and 8–9
  Berkeley, critique of 2, 55

biographical information 2, 16–19
causation 13–14, 42, 56–66, 68, 71, 82
dualism 65–6
Hume, critique of 2, 55, 58, 68, 71, 86
metaphysics 2
ontology 65–6
Priestley, Joseph and 68
publication in journals 27t
publications 2, 42
reason and causation 59–61
reason and like causes 61–2
synchronicity 63–4
theory of knowledge 2
see also women's filiations/relationships
Shepherd, Mary: works
 Essays on the Perception of an External Universe (EPEU) 2, 58, 68
 Essay upon the Relation of Cause and Effect, An (ERCE) 2, 38–9, 58–66, 82
Shohat, Ella and Robert Stam 228
Sidgwick, Eleanor 50–1, 52n.63, 53n.66
Sidgwick, Henry 1–2, 11, 44, 168
Sinnett, Alfred Percy 49
 Esoteric Buddhism 49, 95n.59
Skorupski, John 56
slavery 17–18
 abolitionism 35–6, 228
 Cobbe, Frances Power: abolitionism 18, 228
 Martineau, Harriet: abolitionism 18, 228–9
Smith, Adam 200
Smith, Mary 16–17
socialism 36–7, 45
 Christian socialism 137n.14
 Fabian socialism 4, 80n.36, 154
Somerville, Mary 22–3, 46, 188n.38
Somerville College (Oxford) 22–3, 45–6
Spectator (journal) 27t, 39, 136–7, 144n.23
Spencer, Herbert 11, 23, 30–1, 134–5
 'survival of the fittest' 147n.29
Spicer, Finn 57
Spinoza, Baruch 170
 Eliot's translation of 3, 33–4, 170n.9
spiritualism 48–9, 54n.67, 166
 Blavatsky, Helena Petrovna 48–9, 166
 Buckley, Arabella 166
 critique of 77
 women in 48–9
Spiritualist (theosophical journal) 27t
SPR (Society for Psychical Research) 50–2, 53n.66
Stainthorp, Clare 100n.1
Stedman Jones, Gareth and Gregory Claeys 1n.1
Stein, Edith 1

Stephen, James Fitzjames 189–92
Stern, Robert 56
Stewart, Dugald 82n.37
Stoicism 170, 213
Stott, Anne 20
Stout, George 43–4, 47
Strauss, David Friedrich: Eliot's translation of 3, 33–4, 39, 172–4
Stuart-Glennie, John 210
supernaturalism 56–7, 97, 115–17, 128–9

Taylor Mill, Harriet 5n.10
Tennyson, Alfred 21n.1, 46
Thales of Miletus 201
theism
 Besant, Annie 4, 187, 194
 Cobbe, Frances Power: Theism/theism 36, 82–3, 86–7, 131–2, 164–7, 191–2
 Darwin, Charles 138, 153–4
Theological Review (journal) 27t, 31, 144n.21, 150n.32
Theosophical Society
 Indian headquarters 4, 49–50, 216–17
 investigated by Society for Psychical Research (SPR) 50–2
Theosophist (journal) 26t, 27t
 Blavatsky, Helena Petrovna 25–7, 27t, 125, 216–17
theosophy 45, 49, 166
 anti-vivisectionism 198n.7
 Besant, Annie 4, 14, 94–5, 100, 127–31, 166, 194, 229
 Blavatsky, Helena Petrovna 3–4, 7, 14, 18–19, 36, 49, 130–1, 166, 194–5, 224–5
 Indian nationalism and 18, 224, 227, 229
 pantheism 127–30
 as spiritual and philosophical endeavour 36
 theosophical journals 25–7
 Welby, Victoria 94–5
Thompson, Edith 41–2
Torgersen, Beth 98
transcendentalism 33–4, 57–8, 110
Trollope, Anthony 30n.22
Trompf, Garry 218
Trotter Cockburn, Catharine 1
Turing, Alan 101
Tyndall, John 46–7
 1874 Belfast Address 126–7
 materialism 126–7, 131–2
 mysterianism 127n.50
 objective/subjective explanatory gap 100, 127, 132, 152, 156–7
 'Scientific Materialism' 126–7

Unitarianism 66-8, 109n.24, 170
  Martineau, Harriet 36, 66-9, 164-5, 180-1, 191-2
University of London 22-3
University Magazine 27t, 157n.40
utilitarianism 83, 146, 152-3, 189
  Besant, Annie 4, 188-9
  Darwin, Charles 146, 152-3, 158-9
  duty/utility distinction 185
  Lee, Vernon 4-5, 185
  Naden, Constance 5

Vickery, Amanda 21-2
Visram, Rozina 17n.24
vivisection 46-8, 55
  anti-vivisection 35, 45
  Besant, Annie: anti-vivisectionism 198n.7
  Blavatsky, Helena Petrovna: anti-vivisectionism 198n.7
  Cobbe, Frances Power: anti-vivisectionism 36-7, 46-8, 135n.8, 189, 197n.6
  Lee, Vernon 4-5, 182-3, 186n.34
  Wedgwood, Julia: anti-vivisection 135n.8, 136-7
Vogt, Karl 128

Waithe, Mary Ellen 12, 55
Wallace, Alfred Russel 54n.67, 134, 143-4, 148-9, 151-2, 157n.40
Walters, Margaret 173n.19
Ward, James 47
Ward, Mary Augusta (Mrs Humphry Ward) 2n.4, 8-9, 28-9, 46, 181-2
  Robert Elsmere 34
Watts, Charles 188
Webb, Beatrice 80n.36, 154, 197n.4
Webb, R. K. 9n.18, 30n.22, 74
Wedgwood, Fanny (Julia Wedgwood's mother) 210
Wedgwood, Hensleigh (Julia Wedgwood's father) 50-1, 136-7
Wedgwood, Josiah (Julia Wedgwood's great-grandfather) 136-7
Wedgwood, Julia 15-16, 231
  anonymity and signature 136-8
  anti-vivisection 135n.8, 136-7
  biblical criticism 4
  biographical information 4, 16-17, 19, 136-7
  Christianity 137n.14, 211, 224-5
  conflicting ideas, importance and syntheses of 4, 15, 138-9, 162, 196-7, 209-10
  Darwin, Charles and 8-9, 137-8, 144
  education 23-4
  evolution 4, 14, 133, 135-6, 158-63
  evolution/Christian belief compatibility 14, 138-43
  evolution as moral progression 142
  feminism 4, 212n.25, 214-15
  as forgotten over time 136-7
  Hegel, Georg Wilhelm Friedrich and 138, 196-7, 215-16
  Judaism 4, 136-7, 213
  letters 136-7
  philosophy of history 197-8, 209-10
  progress in history 15, 138-9, 196-8, 209-16, 225-7, 230
  publication in journals 27t, 39, 136-7
  science and religion 160-2, 216, 224-5
  topics addressed by 136-7
  as writer 34, 53, 136-7
  see also women's filiations/relationships
Wedgwood, Julia: *The Moral Ideal* (MI) 15, 136-7, 198, 209-16, 225
  Aryan 'culture' 212
  aspiration 211, 214, 216
  Christianity 213-16
  Egypt 212n.25
  Greece 211-13, 215-16
  India 211-12, 215-16
  Judaism 213, 215n.27
  Persia 211-12, 215-16
  Protestantism 213-14
  Rome 213-16
  secularism 214
  virtue 214
Wedgwood, Julia: works
  'Boundaries of Science, The' (BS) 14, 136, 138-42, 144n.23, 215
  'Ethics and Science' 159-60
  Message of Israel in the Light of Modern Criticism, The 136-7, 215n.27
  'Moral Influence of George Eliot, The' 178-9
  'Natural and the Supernatural, The' 144n.23
  Nineteenth-Century Teachers (NCT) 32-3, 136-7, 159, 197n.6
  see also Wedgwood, Julia: *The Moral Ideal*
Welby, Victoria 231-2
  anti-naturalism 13-14, 56-8, 88-97
  biographical information 4, 16-19
  'Critique of Plain Meaning' 91-2, 94
  education 88
  empiricism 41-2, 92-3, 96-7
  Hegel, Georg Wilhelm Friedrich 94n.58
  Huxley, Thomas Henry and 41-2, 89-91
  idealism 94, 97
  letters as philosophical writing 28-9, 89
  linguistics 4, 91-4, 96

INDEX 273

meaning theory 4, 13–14, 28–9, 88, 91–4, 96
metaphor as essential to language 4, 92–4
panpsychism 96n.61
positivism 90–1
publication in journals 27t, 55, 88–9
science and meaning 88, 91–3, 95–7, 160–1
science and religion 161–2
scientific knowledge 4, 90–1
scriptural interpretation 4
significs 4
theosophy 94–5
time, reality of 89
topics addressed by 89
see also women's filiations/relationships
Welby, Victoria: *Signifying and Understanding*
(SU) 89n.50, 96
'Heliology' 161–2
'Is There a Break in Mental Evolution?' 90
'Law of the Three Stages' 88–90, 95
'Truthfulness in Science and Religion' 90
Welby, Victoria: works
Echoes of Larger Life (ELL) 89n.50, 161–3
Grains of Sense (GS) 89, 92
Links and Clues 38–9, 88–9, 161
'Meaning and Metaphor' (MM) 39, 88, 90
'Sense, Meaning and Interpretation' (SMI) 88, 91–3
Significs and Language 89
What is Meaning? 89
see also Welby, Victoria: *Signifying and Understanding*
Wellek, René 83
Wellesley Index to Victorian Periodicals 38
Wells, Ida B. 17–18
Wesley, John 136–7, 210n.23
Westminster Review (journal) 25, 26t, 27t
anonymity 39
as 'Comtist coterie' 90–1
Eliot, George 3, 25–7, 30–1, 39, 171–2
Martineau, Harriet 30, 39, 57–8, 85–6, 171–2
Wheatley, Vera 9n.18
Whewell, William 42, 57–8, 82, 84–5
Wilde, Oscar 119n.39
Winkworth, Susanna 66–7
Wittgenstein, Ludwig 13
Witz, Anne 43–4
Wollstonecraft, Mary 19–20, 34n.33, 37–8
women
academia 23, 27–8
as authors 30–2, 53
as editors 25–7, 27t, 30–1, 36–7, 39, 53
as educators 33–4, 42
epistemic authority 35, 40, 42, 48–9, 52n.64, 224

exclusion from academia 27–8
intellectual and cultural spaces, exclusion from 23, 28–30, 37, 232
as 'journalists' 31–2
mission of 19–20, 34n.32, 193
moral authority 34–5, 39
moral mission 20, 34–5
moral vocation 34–5
professional life, exclusion from 2, 23
religious and spiritual authority 36, 39
social and political reform 35–6
translations by 33–4
Western philosophy, women in 1, 1n.2, 55
women's omission in history of philosophy 6–7, 11, 49
women's rights 4, 16–17, 19–20, 23, 30, 35
as writers 34, 45–6, 53
see also gender-related issues; women's education
women philosophers (nineteenth-century, Britain) 1–5, 3n.8, 231–2
approach and methodology 6–13
black and ethnic minority women 17–18
evaluation question 12, 55
as forgotten over time 2n.4, 22, 42–6, 54, 136–7
invisibility of 1–2, 5, 8–9, 232
literature and other forms of writing 2
male interlocutors 8–9, 11–12, 89, 100, 232
methodological recommendations 22, 54–5
networks 9–10
philosophical prose works 2
philosophy of history 15, 196–8, 209–10
Romantic era (c.1790–1837) 19
social and historical context of 16–20
topics covered by 1, 5n.10, 55, 231
Victorian era 19
white women 17–18
as 'writers' or 'reformers' 231–2,
see also women's constraints; women's filiations/relationships; women's participation strategies
women philosophers (nineteenth-century, Britain): sources on 9–10
biographical and historical scholarship and autobiographical works 9–10, 232
correspondence 10, 232
forgotten sources 5–6, 22
women's published writings 10
women's constraints 22–32, 54–5, 232
gender constraints 2, 16n.22, 23
morality 20
patriarchal constraints 2, 16–17, 20–2, 53, 232
professionalization of philosophy 42–7, 53–4

women's constraints (*cont.*)
  'separate spheres' ideology 2, 21–3
  signature vs anonymity 40, 42
  women's education 22–4
women's education 6–7, 20, 34–5
  1870 Education Act 16–17
  autodidacticism 16–17, 23–4, 88
  Cobbe, Frances Power 22n.4
  education at home 22–3
  higher education and university 23, 44, 53
  higher education and university: exclusion from 2, 21–3, 44, 54
  languages 23–4
  More, Hannah 20
  pooling knowledge 23–4
  universal schooling 16–17
  women and the private sphere 2, 21–3
women's filiations/relationships 7–13, 15–16, 57–8, 198, 232
  Besant/Blavatsky relations 7, 100
  Besant/Cobbe relations 7–8, 14–15, 100, 166–7, 187–91
  Besant/Martineau relations 187
  Besant/Welby relations 89, 91–2, 94–5
  Blavatsky/Naden relations 7, 100, 132
  Buckley/Wedgwood relations 159–60
  Cobbe/Lee relations 7–8, 166–7, 181–7
  Cobbe/Martineau relations 81–2, 85–6, 179, 183n.33, 198, 205–9
  Cobbe/Wedgwood relations 135–6, 198, 211
  Eliot/Martineau relations 166–7, 171–7
  Eliot/Wedgwood relations 173n.15, 178–9
  on evolution 135–6, 148–53, 158–9
  on evolution: Buckley against Cobbe 148–53, 155
  Lee/Wedgwood relations 182n.31
  Lee/Welby relations 89

Lovelace/Martineau relations 108–9, 111
Martineau/Shepherd relations 70–1
Martineau/Wedgwood relations 136–7, 182n.31, 198, 210–11
Martineau/Welby relations 89–91, 94
  on materialism 99
  on naturalism 57–8, 82, 91, 94
  on philosophy of mind 99–100, 111, 131
  on progress in history 198
  on religion and morality 166–7, 191–5
  on religion and morality: Besant–Cobbe debate 187–91
  on religion and morality: Lee–Cobbe debate 167, 181–7, 192
  Wedgwood/Welby relations 89, 136–7, 160–3, 216n.28
women's participation strategies 32–7, 54, 89
  adverse consequences of 42, 45
  anonymous and pseudonymous publication 37, 42
  popularization 32–3, 42, 231–2
  print culture diversity 36–7
  religious and spiritual authority 36
  social and political reform 35–6
  translating and educating 33–4, 42, 231–2
  women's moral authority 34–5
  'writing' 34
Wood, Allen and Songsuk Susan Hahn 1n.1
Wright, Frances 5n.10

Young, Robert 133

Zoist (journal) 14, 104, 108
  'hylo-idealism' 14, 118–19
  'hylo-zoism' 14
Zoophilist (journal) 26*t*, 27*t*, 36–7
Zoroastrianism 207–8, 211–13, 219n.35, 226*t*